# Advance Praise

"Network slicing is a key enabler for current and future business innovations and new opportunities across a wide range of use cases and industries. This book is very timely and deals with the topic very well by first setting the stage and then going deep across various vectors. This makes it a suitable read across the board from implementers, operators as well as academia. It explains how to harness IPv6 in the Network Slicing realm to provide a scalable solution for current and future needs. I especially enjoyed all the stories spread across the chapters, it brought back memories (sometimes I was in the room when they were in motion)."

**Dhruv Dhody**
*IAB Member, PCE WG Co-chair,*
*and proponent of IETF Network Slicing*

"Network slicing is an important innovation not only in 5G wireless networks but also in IP based transport networks. Its use cases can spread across many different industries and applications. This book provides a systematic view of IP based network slicing. It begins with the background of network slicing, then dives into the architecture, solutions and key technologies of realizing network slices, taking advantage of the enhanced capability of IPv6. It also provides typical use cases about the deployment of IPv6 network slices in real networks."

**James Guichard**
*IETF Routing Area Director*

"Network slicing is a hot topic in standards organizations and operator's community now becoming a reality by some early implementations. It represents an architectural innovation that enables operator's wireless and transport networks to provide advanced services for a variety of industries and customers. The authors of this book are close to both the network slicing standards and the solution development, which makes it a rich and enlightening book with focus on IPv6 network slicing from both theoretical and practical perspectives. I am also glad to see the stories about network slicing standards and development clearly captured in this book."

**Dr. Luis M. Contreras**
*Telefonica, IETF CCAMP WG*
*Co-chair and proponent of IETF Network Slicing*

"In this [book] Li Zhenbin walks the reader through the concepts of network slicing and how the IPv6 network slicing applicability is extensible beyond 5G use cases to general Enhanced VPN (VPN+) use cases. An important topic regarding network slicing is the concept of 'soft' and 'hard' network slicing, and the degree of 'hard' network slicing. The concept of 'soft slicing' relates to traffic and routing isolation which could be provided by the L2 or L3 overlay VPN services, while the concept of 'hard slicing' relates to interference isolation which can be enabled by different underlay resource partitioning technologies. The concept and the degree of hard slicing is very important as it is what makes network slicing come to fruition and viable for network operators as a value added service to both 5G and other general scenarios."

**Gyan Mishra**
*IETF network slicing technology and standards expert*

"As technologies such as 5G, cloud computing, and the Internet of Things (IoT) converge with industry digitalization at an increasing pace, the IPv6 Enhanced (IPE) network innovation system—represented by technologies such as Segment Routing, network programming, network slicing, and IFIT—is developing rapidly. In particular, network slicing, a core technology for improving deterministic experience of mission-critical services, is attracting more and more attention from industry insiders and related research institutes. Committed to innovation and practical application of new networks, Huawei has been focusing on datacom technologies and industry evolution for many years. It has achieved major success in the research of innovative IPE network technologies, product R&D,

and solutions, and has gained significant experience. This book brings together the theoretical ideas, technological innovations, and industry practices of the team led by Zhenbin Li in the network slicing field, and demonstrates the high-quality development prospects of data communication networks with refined expression, in-depth thinking, and unique perspectives. It will bring new inspiration to scientific and technological workers, engineers, teachers, and students engaged in research and development in this field."

**Hui Tian**

*Deputy Secretary-General of China's Expert Committee for Promoting Large-Scale IPv6 Deployment and Director of Convergence Innovation Center, China Academy of Information and Communications Technology (CAICT)*

"Network slicing is an important innovation direction in the network field in recent years. With the large-scale deployment of next-generation network technologies such as 5G, carriers have begun to provide 5G network slicing services for customers, opening up a new model of business to business (2B) services. To implement end-to-end network slicing, the way that IP networks provide slicing services has attracted a great deal of attention. This book has emerged at the right time to systematically explore IPv6 network slicing. Continuous promotion of large-scale IPv6 deployment is one of the important foundations for building a network power. IPv6 network slicing will provide high-quality network services for users and accelerate the development of IPv6 applications from the public Internet to the industrial Internet. In addition, computing networks have become a hot topic and important direction in the industry. IPv6 network slicing provides important technical support for computing-network convergence and accelerates the implementation of computing networks. We hope that this book can promote the large-scale commercial use of IPv6 network slicing and provide a solid technical reference for the industry."

**Xiaodong Duan**

*Director of the Department of Network and IT Technology China Mobile Research Institute*

"In the digital economy era, the accelerated development of network intelligence, business digitalization, data monetization, and AI computing drives the in-depth integration of IT and CT, connection and computing power, and applications and networks. Explosive growth of massive data and billions of ubiquitous access requirements pose unprecedented challenges to network SLAs. As a key enabling technology designed to cope with future digital floods, IPv6 network slicing will play an important role in accelerating the construction of new future-oriented information infrastructure. This technology is also a key enabler for building an end-to-end IPv6 bearer base. *IPv6 Network Slicing* integrates the research results of Huawei and the industry in the field of network slicing technologies and systematically describes slicing-related architecture principles, application practices in the industry, and future technology prospects. Focusing on systematicness, simplicity, and practicability, this book is an extremely valuable reference for researchers and engineering and technical personnel."

**Yunqing Chen**
*Vice President of China Telecom Research Institute*

"IPE has reached a consensus in the industry. During the exploration of computing power networks, China Unicom has gradually formed an IPE-based multiple-pillar architecture, in which network slicing is the most important pillar. Network slicing enables one network to fulfill multiple purposes and helps develop capabilities with more flexible differentiation, higher isolation, and lower latency. This book describes the technical principles, solution deployment, application scenarios, and standards of network slicing. It is an invaluable reference for network research, deployment, and application. The publication of this book will no doubt promote the prosperity of the IPE industry."

**Xiongyan Tang**
*Vice President and Chief Scientist of China Unicom Research Institute*

"Network slicing is a hot technology in the industry. Published at the right time, this book not only describes the technical architecture and implementation details of network slicing, but also recounts the network slicing design experience and stories behind the design, demonstrating the authors' solid technical expertise and profound industry background. With the guidance of this book, China Unicom's commercial deployment of network slicing will be more efficient, smooth, and reliable."

**Libiao Tu**
*Network Line Expert, China Unicom*

"Network slicing is one of the core technologies of IPE. It allows one physical network to be logically divided into multiple network slices, which are logically isolated from each other. This not only helps implement intensive network construction but also meets diversified and differentiated service deployment requirements. Against the current backdrop of digital government construction, the government extranet faces various challenges during its intelligent and intensive construction, such as private network migration, service integration, data security, resource scheduling, and network access perception. The network slicing technology effectively addresses these challenges, and Huawei is a leader in this technology. This book describes the network slicing system architecture, controller, and forwarding plane in detail. It is a valuable book for understanding the network slicing technology and provides reference for future technology evolution of the government extranet."

**Mengran Jin**
*Deputy Director of the Government Extranet Technology Management Department of the State Information Center*

# IPv6 Network Slicing

This book is an essential guide to IPv6 network slicing. It covers both the fundamentals and cutting-edge technologies of IPv6 network slicing and provides insights into future industry developments.

IP network slicing is an architectural innovation that provides multiple dedicated logical networks on a shared physical network. It comprises a complete set of solutions designed to meet the differentiated service requirements of the 5G and cloud era. This book focuses on IP network slicing based on the data plane of IPv6, a second-generation network layer protocol standard designed to address many of the problems encountered with IPv4. The book explores the technical implementation of IPv6 network slicing by introducing its architecture, implementation solutions, resource partitioning technologies, data plane technologies, and control plane technologies. It also explains how to deploy IPv6 network slicing through slice controllers and provides deployment suggestions based on Huawei practices.

It is a must-read for professional engineers involved in network planning, design, and technology support. Researchers and students in information and communication technology and communication system design will also find it useful.

**Zhenbin Li** is the chief protocol expert at Huawei, responsible for IP protocol research and standards promotion at Huawei. He was a member of the Internet Engineering Task Force (IETF) Internet Architecture Board (IAB) from 2019 to 2023. His recent publication with CRC Press includes *SRv6 Network Programming: Ushering in a New Era of IP Networks*.

**Jie Dong** is a Huawei protocol expert in data communication, mainly responsible for technical research and innovation related to 5G/6G transport networks. He is currently the secretary of the IETF Inter-Domain Routing (IDR) Working Group. His recent publication with CRC Press includes *SRv6 Network Programming: Ushering in a New Era of IP Networks*.

**Yawei Zhang** is a Huawei architect of data communication network slicing solutions, responsible for the planning and design of such solutions.

**Xinzong Zeng** is the chief architect of Huawei's IP network controllers, the Network Cloud Engine (NCE), responsible for the planning and design of such controllers.

## Data Communication Series

*Cloud Data Center Network Architectures and Technologies*
Lei Zhang and Le Chen

*Campus Network Architectures and Technologies*
Ningguo Shen, Bin Yu, Mingxiang Huang, and Hailin Xu

*Enterprise Wireless Local Area Network Architectures and Technologies*
Rihai Wu, Xun Yang, Xia Zhou, and Yibo Wang

*Software-Defined Wide Area Network Architectures and Technologies*
Cheng Sheng, Jie Bai, and Qi Sun

*SRv6 Network Programming: Ushering in a New Era of IP Networks*
Zhenbin Li, Zhibo Hu, and Cheng Li

*IPv6 Network Slicing: Offering New Experience for Industries*
Zhenbin Li, Jie Dong, Yawei Zhang, and Xinzong Zeng

For more information on this series, please visit: https://www.routledge.com/
Data-Communication-Series/book-series/DCSHW

# IPv6 Network Slicing
## Offering New Experience for Industries

Zhenbin Li, Jie Dong, Yawei Zhang,
and Xinzong Zeng

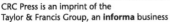

CRC Press is an imprint of the
Taylor & Francis Group, an **informa** business

The cover image is from Huawei's internal gallery and is copyrighted for all purposes.

First edition published 2024
by CRC Press
2385 NW Executive Center Drive, Suite 320, Boca Raton FL 33431

and by CRC Press
4 Park Square, Milton Park, Abingdon, Oxon, OX14 4RN

*CRC Press is an imprint of Taylor & Francis Group, LLC*

© 2024 Zhenbin Li, Jie Dong, Yawei Zhang, and Xinzong Zeng
Translated by Wei Li, Yanqing Zhao, and Zhaodi Zhang

English Version by permission of Posts and Telecom Press Co., Ltd.

ISBN: 978-1-032-69735-2 (hbk)
ISBN: 978-1-032-69985-1 (pbk)
ISBN: 978-1-032-69986-8 (ebk)

DOI: 10.1201/9781032699868

Typeset in Minion
by codeMantra

# Contents

P<small>ART</small> III  **Summary**

# Foreword I

RESERVING RESOURCES IN NETWORKS to support or enable specific services is a well-established practice dating back to circuit switching technologies that were in use even before the Internet was first put together. Connection-oriented resource reservation became a critical component of transport networks built on the time division multiplexing network technologies SDH and SONET and was a fundamental element of ATM. These approaches, known as Traffic Engineering (TE), enabled operators to make service-level guarantees and maximize the use of their network resources through the combination of policies applied to traffic entering the network, steering traffic onto specific paths within the network, and management of the resources available to and consumed by the traffic as it transits the network.

With the invention of Multiprotocol Label Switching (MPLS) at the end of the last century, it became possible to apply these traffic engineering techniques to packet-based networks, and MPLS-TE was born. An MPLS underlay provides tools for network operators to plan their packet networks, optimize the use of their resources, provide new services, and develop new revenue streams.

Traffic engineering techniques enable network virtualization. A virtual network provides the look and feel of a network built from physical resources and can be managed as a real network, but is constructed by dividing or partitioning the physical network resources to be shared by multiple virtual networks. Many network providers deliver virtual networks as services to their customers; Layer 2 and Layer 3 virtual private networks (L2VPN and L3VPN) are the most popular examples. But, increasingly, more complex virtual networks are built and delivered for the customer to operate with their own resources.

The Internet runs on IP, the Internet Protocol. IP is the glue that carries users' data in packets across many interconnected networks based on a host of different technologies. For many years, everyone used IPv4, and everything was fine. However, it gradually became apparent that there would be more end-systems attached to the Internet than there are globally unique addresses in the IPv4 address space, so the IETF worked to develop a new revision of IP, which was called IPv6. With 128-bit addresses, IPv6 had enough resources to address anything and everything. Although IPv6 had a slow start to its adoption, partly due to the ingenious invention of ways to extend the reach of the IPv4 address space, it is now very widely used, with around three-quarters of a billion users connected to the Internet via IPv6 without even being aware of it.

A nice feature of IPv6, beyond its large address space, is its ability to support mobile networking. The 3rd Generation Partnership Project (better known as the 3GPP), the primary standards organization for standardizing protocols for mobile communication, adopted IP as its data encapsulation and recognized transmission of mobile voice and data over the Internet as a fundamental part of the 3GPP architecture.

Mobile communications have evolved from 3G and 4G to the latest 5G standards. Along with improvements in radio communications and the bandwidth connectivity that is supported, 5G has opened up aspirations for what the wireless user will be able to do with the service. Applications as diverse as holographic video conferencing and telesurgery, or self-driving cars and enhanced online gaming, are considered to be on the horizon.

These services place competing demands on the networks that support them. Some services may have a high priority (for example, public protection and disaster relief, or PPDR) with an absolute requirement that no data be lost. Other services may be highly sensitive to both data loss and variations in latency (such as remote surgery), while others may require the lowest possible latency (in cases varying from autonomous vehicles to automated trading to virtual or augmented reality gaming). Furthermore, some services will know a priori that they only need to exchange low levels of traffic, but others may require large, often very large, volumes.

But the Internet was designed as a best-effort delivery mechanism: every effort will be made to deliver data passed to the Internet, but it may be queued, re-routed, buffered, and possibly dropped. This is not ideal for the delivery of these advanced 5G services, and additional mechanisms need to be developed to support them.

A fundamental approach to meeting these requirements is known as Network Slicing. A network slice is a connectivity and resource commitment that models a VPN service with the assurance of meeting a set of specific network performance objectives. An IETF Network Slice is a network slice built using IETF technologies and expressed in terms of connectivity constructs and service objectives.

Network slicing is a form of network virtualization and achieving network slicing with a traffic engineering technology such as MPLS is relatively straightforward. As an example, a set of TE tunnels provisioned with known properties and reserved resources could be considered a network slice. But building network slices on IPv6 is more complicated. It requires a combination of existing and new techniques in the data plane and the control/management plane. Fortunately, most of the building blocks already exist. We can call upon Differentiated Services (DiffServ), IPv6 extension headers, Segment Routing for IPv6 (SRv6), multi-topology IGP, and control plane protocols like BGP-LS and PCE, both of which I helped pioneer in the IETF. The few missing pieces are being actively worked on within the IETF.

All that is needed is a cookbook to help the implementer know how to put all of the pieces together and build a functional network slicing system. This book is exactly that: an explanation of the protocols and encapsulations and an introduction to the network architectures and deployment modes that will enable IPv6 network slicing to support a wide range of applications and use cases.

In many ways, network slicing is not a radical new idea. But its application to IPv6 networks is an innovation that proposes to offer significant opportunities for network operators to distinguish traffic flows and to deliver different treatments for traffic so as to guarantee the varied service levels that current and future use cases and applications will require. This will enable advances in user experience and the development of new technologies, which may open up new revenue streams for service providers.

**Adrian Farrel**
Editor of *A Framework for IETF Network Slices*
Editor of *Overview and Principles of Internet Traffic Engineering*

# Foreword II

IPv6 NETWORK SLICING IS another system-level innovation in the IPv6 technology field. The concept of network slicing, which originates from 5G requirements, has undergone continuous development and extension since it was first proposed. Currently, network slicing can be used not only for mobile services but also for various public fixed network services and enterprise services. With the rapid development of enterprise cloudification and 2B services, network service quality is coming under increasing pressure to meet the higher requirements of services. IPv6 network slicing provides optimization solutions for service isolation and resource isolation, better serving various industries on one network and meeting the service requirements of different industries and users. IPv6 network slicing has a broad application prospect and high industry value.

Since the General Office of the CPC Central Committee and the State Council issued the *Action Plan for Advancing the Extensive Deployment of Internet Protocol Version 6 (IPv6)* in November 2017, China has achieved significant success not only in large-scale IPv6 deployment but also in 5G- and cloud-oriented IPv6 technology innovation. In November 2019, China's Expert Committee for Promoting Large-Scale IPv6 Deployment approved the establishment of the IPv6 Enhanced Technology Innovation Working Group to further stimulate system innovation that is based on IPv6 next-generation Internet technologies. To date, SRv6 has been deployed at more than 100 sites around the world, and SRv6 standards are becoming increasingly mature. Research and standardization of IPv6 technology innovation, such as in network slicing, IFIT, and Application-aware Networking (APN), are also being carried out systematically. IPv6 network slicing has been put into large-scale commercial use at dozens of sites. As another important IPv6 innovation following SRv6, IPv6 network slicing further improves the value of IPv6 and promotes the wide deployment and application of IPv6.

Starting technical research on IPv6 network slicing at an early age, Huawei has realized numerous achievements in technological innovation, product development, and standardization through proactive cooperation with the industry. In addition, Huawei has accumulated rich practical experience in helping carriers and enterprises test, verify, deploy, and apply IPv6 network slicing. On this basis, Huawei's IPE technology innovation team compiled the book *IPv6 Network Slicing*. This book systematically describes the technical system architecture, key technologies, application methods, and practical experience of IPv6 network slicing. Each chapter ends with stories behind IPv6 network slicing design, summarizing the design experience to help readers further understand the background, standardization process, and problem-oriented solution of the IPv6 network slicing technology. This book is of great reference value for network product development personnel, network O&M personnel, and vertical industry application departments, and its publication will surely have a positive impact on the development of the IPv6 industry.

**Hequan Wu**
*Director of China's Expert Committee for*
*Promoting Large-Scale IPv6 Deployment*

# Preface

THE DEVELOPMENT OF 5G gave rise to the emergence of network slicing, which was initially applied to 5G mobile transport networks and then extended to support fixed and enterprise services. Today, it can also be applied to IP metro and backbone networks. Currently, IP network slicing, which plays an important role in supporting the 2B services of carriers, is being widely applied and deployed.

In terms of realizing the IP-based Service-Level Agreement (SLA) guarantee, IP network slicing can be considered a significant leap forward. Initially, IP networks used Quality of Service (QoS) technologies such as DiffServ to guarantee service quality on single devices. Later, Traffic Engineering (TE) technologies such as Multiprotocol Label Switching (MPLS) TE were developed to provide service quality guarantee through TE paths. Now, IP network slicing is introduced to guarantee service quality through network-wide resource isolation. Moreover, compared with establishing physical private networks, deploying IP network slicing helps to significantly reduce costs.

Huawei Data Communication Product Line has been investing in the innovation and standardization of IP network slicing technologies since 2015. Together with industry partners, Huawei has promoted multiple network slicing technologies (e.g., SR SID-based network slicing, slice ID-based network slicing, inter-domain network slicing, and hierarchical network slicing), gradually setting up the architecture and technical system of IP network slicing. In this process, we were deeply aware of how important and urgent it was for us to explain this architecture and technical system in a comprehensive and systematic manner. We therefore wrote this book — built on our years of experience in IP network slicing R&D, standardization, and deployment — with the aim of helping readers gain a far greater understanding of IP network slicing technologies and further promoting technology and industry development.

IPv6 plays a pivotal role in IP network slicing. IP network slicing needs to not only support ordinary topology-based IP forwarding but also identify resources corresponding to network slices to guarantee service quality. To achieve the latter, resource identifiers need to be introduced in the data plane, raising new requirements for data-plane encapsulation extensions. Thanks to the IPv6 extension header mechanism — which was defined during the inception of IPv6 and is also more mature than the MPLS extension mechanism — resource identification information can be carried using IPv6 extension headers. This meets the requirements of IP network slicing for the data plane in a much more effective manner. Focusing on key technologies involved in realizing network slicing based on IPv6, this book is titled *IPv6 Network Slicing*. We believe that network slicing will be a key application of IPv6 and will further promote large-scale deployment and application of IPv6.

## OVERVIEW

This book consists of eleven chapters that are organized into three parts. The first part — Chapter 1 — focuses on the background and benefits of IP network slicing. Part II — Chapters 2 to 9 — describes the various technologies involved in IPv6 network slicing. Part III — Chapters 10 and 11 — wraps up this book by summarizing the development of the IP network slicing industry and exploring its future.

## CHAPTER 1: OVERVIEW OF IP NETWORK SLICING

This chapter starts by discussing the diversified services emerging in the 5G and cloud era. It then analyzes the challenges facing IP networks, introduces the background of IP network slicing, describes its benefits, and reviews the current development of IPv6 network slicing technologies.

## CHAPTER 2: ARCHITECTURE AND TECHNICAL SYSTEM OF IPV6 NETWORK SLICING

This chapter starts by introducing the technical system and architecture of IPv6 network slicing. It then discusses how the scalability of IPv6 network slices impacts IPv6 network slicing technologies and solutions and introduces the key technologies involved in IPv6 network slicing.

## CHAPTER 3: IPV6 NETWORK SLICING SOLUTIONS

This chapter describes the solutions for realizing IPv6 network slicing — the SRv6 SID-based network slicing solution, slice ID-based network slicing solution, hierarchical IPv6 network slicing solution, and mapping solution between IPv6 service slices and resource slices.

## CHAPTER 4: RESOURCE PARTITIONING TECHNOLOGIES FOR IPV6 NETWORK SLICING

This chapter describes the resource partitioning technologies used in IPv6 network slicing, including Flexible Ethernet (FlexE) interface, HQoS-based channelized sub-interface, and Flex-Channel. It also compares these resource partitioning technologies.

## CHAPTER 5: DATA PLANE TECHNOLOGIES FOR IPV6 NETWORK SLICING

This chapter describes the data plane technologies used in IPv6 network slicing and how to carry network slice information based on IPv6 extension headers and SRv6 SIDs.

## CHAPTER 6: CONTROL PLANE TECHNOLOGIES FOR IPV6 NETWORK SLICING

This chapter describes the control plane technologies used in IPv6 network slicing by focusing on related control protocol extensions, including the IGP Multi-Topology (MT), Flexible Algorithm (Flex-Algo), Border Gateway Protocol-Link State (BGP-LS), BGP Shortest Path First (SPF), and Segment Routing (SR) Policy extensions for network slicing, as well as the Flow Specification (FlowSpec) extensions used for traffic steering to network resource slices.

## CHAPTER 7: IPV6 NETWORK SLICE CONTROLLERS

This chapter first introduces the architectures of typical network controllers and IPv6 network slice controllers. It then describes the functions of IPv6 network slice controllers and interfaces for external interaction.

## CHAPTER 8: INTER-DOMAIN IPV6 NETWORK SLICING TECHNOLOGIES

This chapter starts by describing the structure, procedure, and implementation of mapping 5G E2E network slices to IPv6 network slices. It then introduces the technologies involved in inter-domain IPv6 network slicing and SRv6-based inter-domain IPv6 network slicing. Finally, it explains the intent-based routing mechanism, which can be used to steer traffic to IPv6 network slices in different network domains.

## CHAPTER 9: IPV6 NETWORK SLICING DEPLOYMENT

This chapter focuses on the deployment of IPv6 network slicing. It starts by introducing the network slicing solutions designed for smart healthcare, smart government, smart port, smart grid, and smart enterprise scenarios. Next, it describes how to configure resource partitioning in network slicing solutions and how to deploy such solutions based on SRv6 SIDs and slice IDs. Then, it explains how to deploy single-layer slicing, hierarchical slicing, and inter-domain slicing solutions using controllers.

## CHAPTER 10: INDUSTRY DEVELOPMENT AND FUTURE OF IP NETWORK SLICING

This chapter summarizes the industry development of IP network slicing and predicts what the future holds for IP network slicing, including further atomization of IP network slicing services, finer-grained and dynamic network slicing, and deterministic resource guarantee for network slicing.

In "Road of IPv6 Network Slicing", at the end of this book, Zhenbin Li summarizes the development history of IP network slicing technologies and Huawei's participation in innovation and standards promotion. Each chapter also ends with stories behind IPv6 network slicing design, summarizing the design experience of involved technologies and helping readers further understand the design and deepen their understanding of such technologies. Some of the content constitutes the author's opinion and should be used for reference only.

Zhenbin Li and Jie Dong are the editors-in-chief of this book, and Yawei Zhang and Xinzong Zeng are the deputy editors-in-chief. This book — meticulously compiled by Zhenbin Li — is the culmination of extensive efforts by multiple teams from the Huawei Data Communication Product Line. Experts such as Yongpeng Zhao, Xuesong Geng, Bo Wu, Qin Wu, Dong Lv, and Jian Wang provided a great deal of materials to facilitate the compilation.

# Acknowledgments

WHILE PROMOTING THE INNOVATION and standardization of IP network slicing, we have received extensive support and help from both inside and outside Huawei. We would like to take this opportunity to express our heartfelt thanks to Kewen Hu, Lei Wang, Meng Zuo, Zhipeng Zhao, Juye Wu, Shaowei Liu, Yuefeng Qiu, Su Feng, Zhaokun Ding, Yanmiao Wang, Xiao Qian, Jianbing Wang, Jianping Sun, Huizhi Wen, Wenjun Meng, Xiaopan Li, Minwei Jin, Keyi Zhu, Dawei Fan, Rui Gu, Yue Liu, Shucheng Liu, Juhua Xu, Xinjun Chen, Lei Bao, Juan Zheng, Yunhong Huang, Chengxia Yao, Zhaoyang Yan, Shuying Liu, Yi Zeng, Yanhui Lu, Tongxin Sun, Songyan Chen, Cen Ma, Wei Fang, Xun Hu, Zhiyong Li, Xiugang Wei, Lu Li, Zhenqiang Xie, Yunfei Li, Zhengliang Li, Zhewen Wu, Zhaosheng Wu, Weiwei Chen, Junxiang Zhu, Yu Jiang, Qi Wei, Xiaopeng Wang, Fei Chen, Zuopeng Yin, Qin Wang, Chunyue Hu, Yanjie Ge, Ming Yang, Gang Zhao, Xiaoqi Gao, Jialing Li, Peng Zheng, Peng Wu, Guoyi Chen, Bo Wu, Xuesong Geng, Xin Yan, Hong Shen, Wenxia Dong, Guanjun Zhou, Zhijun Jing, Yuanyi Sun, Leyan Wang, Shuhui Wang, Xiaohui Tong, Mingyan Xi, Xiaoling Wang, Yonghua Mao, Lin Ma, Lu Huang, Kaichun Wang, Huaguo Mo, Huihui Tian, Baihui Wang, Guangyao Meng, Qiang Guo, Hongkun Li, Taixu Tian, Yang Xia, Gang Yan, Fenghua Zhao, Pingan Yang, Cheng Sheng, Haibo Wang, Shunwan Zhuang, Qiangzhou Gao, Sheng Fang, Zhenxing Wang, Haifei Zeng, Yongping Zhang, Wenwu Zhang, Chuang Chen, Ka Zhang, Dapeng Chen, Guoqi Xu, Guofeng Qian, Zhong Chen, Li Zhang, Wenqiang Wang, Tongfu Hu, Xiaoling Mei, Changsheng Sun, Mingxing Ma, Chuang Zhang, Chun Liu, and other leaders and colleagues from Huawei. In addition to Hui Tian, Feng Zhao, Yunqing Chen, Huiling Zhao, Jiguang Cao, Junfeng Ma, Chongfeng Xie, Cong Li, Chenhao Ma, Aijun Wang, Yongqing Zhu, Huanan Chen, Guangming Yang, Rui Luo, Yusong Ma,

Xiaodong Duan, Weiqiang Cheng, Zhenqiang Li, Wenying Jiang, Fengwei Qin, Liyan Gong, Zongpeng Du, Xinlin Li, Xiongyan Tang, Chang Cao, Libiao Tu, Ran Pang, Jiandong Zhang, Fuyou Miao, Zhuangzhuang Qin, Mengran Jin, Gang Wu, and other technical experts in China's IP field, we sincerely thank Adrian Farrel, Stewart Bryant, Daniel King, Susan Hares, Stefano Previdi, Loa Andersson, James Guichard, Dhruv Dhody, Linda Dunbar, Donald Eastlake, Kiran Makhijani, Yingzhen Qu, Alvaro Retana, Benoit Claise, Jari Arkko, Lou Berger, Bruno Decraene, Luis M. Contreras, Oscar González de Dios, John Scudder, Deborah Brungard, Nicolai Leymann, Julien Meuric, Jeff Tantsura, Keyur Patel, Satoru Matsushima, Carsten Rossenhovel, Mohamed Boucadair, Takuya Miyasaka, Kenichi Ogaki, Gyan Mishra, Shunsuke Homma, Daniel Voyer, Daniel Bernier, Thomas Graf, Houcine Allahoum, Carlo Richartz, Jaehwan Jin, Jongyoon Shin, Clarence Filsfils, Tarek Saad, Francois Clad, Ketan Talaulikar, Joel Halpern, Vishnu Pavan Beeram, John Drake, Shraddha Hegde, Tony Przygienda, Wim Henderickx, Martin Vigoureux, Reza Rokui, Alexander Vainshtein, Andy Malis, Charlie Perkins, and other IP experts in the industry who helped us with work on IP network slicing. Finally, we would like to express our special thanks to Adrian Farrel and Hequan Wu, both of whom wrote Forewords for this book.

We have written this book with the intention of creating a comprehensive reference that presents the IPv6 network slicing architecture, related technologies, and deployment. While we have made every effort to ensure the accuracy and completeness of this book, IPv6 network slicing is an evolving technology, and errors or omissions may occur. We would therefore be grateful for any feedback about such issues.

**Zhenbin Li**

# Teams

## TECHNICAL REVIEWERS

**Zhibo Hu** is a senior Huawei expert in SR and IGP, responsible for SR and IGP planning and innovation. Currently, he is mainly engaged in the research of SR-MPLS/SRv6 protocols and 5G network slicing technologies. Since 2017, he has been actively engaged in the innovation and standardization work in the IETF and played an important role in the development of standards related to SRv6 reliability, SRv6 YANG, network slicing, and IGP. He is committed to leveraging IP innovations to support network evolution toward 5G and cloudification.

**Jianwu Hao** is the chief architect of carrier IP networks in the Huawei Data Communication Product Line. He joined Huawei in 2004 and has spent a great deal of time engaged in solution planning and design. He has previously led the R&D team of Huawei Data Communication Product Line to plan and design 3G, 4G, and 5G mobile transport solutions, accumulating extensive experience in the planning, design, and verification of data communication product solutions. From 2018 to 2019, he worked in Japan and South Korea, where he promoted the construction and development of 5G transport networks based on Huawei's advanced solutions. Currently, he heads up the design of intelligent cloud-network solutions in an effort to offer leading solutions in the era featuring cloud-network synergy and computing-network convergence.

# Authors

**Zhenbin Li** is the chief protocol expert at Huawei and a member of the Internet Engineering Task Force (IETF) Internet Architecture Board (IAB). He is responsible for IP protocol research and standards promotion at Huawei. He joined Huawei in 2000 and, for more than a decade, was in charge of the architecture, design, and development of Huawei's IP operating system — Versatile Routing Platform (VRP) — and the Multiprotocol Label Switching (MPLS) sub-system, first as an architect and then as a system engineer. From 2015 to 2017, he worked as a Software-Defined Networking (SDN) architect and was responsible for the research, architecture design, and development of network controllers. Since 2009, he has been active in standards innovation in the IETF, continuously promoting the innovation and standardization of numerous protocols, such as SDN southbound protocols, Segment Routing over IPv6 (SRv6), 5G transport, telemetry, and Application-Aware Networking (APN). To date, he has led and participated in more than 100 IETF RFCs/drafts, applied for more than 110 patents, and compiled the technical book *SRv6 Network Programming: Ushering in a New Era of IP Networks* as the editor-in-chief. He was elected as a member of the IETF IAB in 2019 and then reelected in 2021.

**Jie Dong** is a Huawei protocol expert in data communication, mainly responsible for technical research and innovation related to 5G/6G transport networks. Since 2007, he has been engaged in the research and standardization of IP protocols covering multiple fields, including routing, MPLS, VPN, SDN, SR-MPLS/SRv6, and IPv6. He began participating in IETF standards promotion in 2009 and currently works as the secretary of the IETF Inter-Domain Routing (IDR) Working Group. To date, he has published 12 RFCs. In addition, he was involved in the development of the book *SRv6 Network Programming: Ushering in a New Era of IP Networks.*

**Yawei Zhang** is a Huawei architect of data communication network slicing solutions, responsible for the planning and design of such solutions. Since 2006, she has been engaged in data communication product R&D and solution design, which covers 5G mobile transport and intelligent cloud-network solutions. She participates in the design of Huawei's IP network slicing solution and strives to realize innovations in network slicing in an effort to support the development of transport networks.

**Xinzong Zeng** is the chief architect of Huawei's IP network controllers, responsible for the planning and design of such controllers. Since 2005, he has been engaged in the IP and controller fields, working as not only an MPLS and PCE designer and technical owner but also the chief architect of IP network controllers Agile Controller-WAN and iMaster NCE-IP. He has a profound understanding and extensive experience in carrier IP scenarios and solutions, as well as in the evolution and implementation of technologies including MPLS, SRv6, and network slicing.

# Terminology for Network Slicing

INTERNET PROTOCOL (IP) NETWORK slicing originates from 5G network slicing, which involves Radio Access Network (RAN), Transport Network (TN), and Core Network (CN) slices. IP network slicing was initially applied to 5G transport networks (also called IP mobile transport networks) and then extended to IP metro and backbone networks. As such, IP network slices are classified as IP mobile transport network slices, IP metro network slices, or IP backbone network slices, depending on the network domain.

While developing network slicing standards, the IETF defined the term "IETF network slice" to distinguish its network slices from those defined by 3GPP for 5G. Because IP is a core protocol that the IETF is responsible for, IETF network slices are synonymous with IP network slices, which are presented as services to external systems through the northbound IP network slice service interface of a network slice controller. IP network slicing mainly involves the following terms:

- Overlay and underlay slices: IP network slicing is typically realized through two layers of slices — overlay and underlay slices. Overlay slices are provided at the edge of an IP network to achieve service access and isolation, whereas underlay slices are provided within an IP network to achieve network-wide resource isolation and routing control. Overlay slices need to be mapped to corresponding underlay slices.

- Service and resource slices: Because overlay slices are used for service access and isolation while underlay slices are used for resource isolation on the network side, they are also called service and resource slices, respectively.

- VPN+, VPN, and Virtual Transport Network (VTN): VPN+ is a framework defined in the IETF to realize IP network slicing, where IP network slices are deployed as enhanced VPN services. Service slices are realized through various VPN technologies, whereas resource slices are realized based on transport network enhancements achieved through the VTN technology.

- Network Resource Partition (NRP): The IETF uses this term to refer to the implementation of an underlay slice. This term is synonymous with both the terms "resource slice" and "VTN."

- MPLS and IPv6 network slices: Both MPLS and IPv6 can be extended to support IP network slicing. As such, the network slices supported by MPLS and IPv6 are called MPLS and IPv6 network slices, respectively.

To simplify the terminology and facilitate understanding, this book takes the following approaches:

- This book uses the term "5G network slice" only in specific sections; it uses the term "slice" in all other sections to refer to IP network slices.

- For IP network slices, this book uses the term "service slice" only in specific sections; it uses the term "IP network slice" in all other sections to refer to the term "resource slice."

- For resource slices, this book uses the term "MPLS slice" only in specific sections; it uses the term "resource slice" in all other sections to refer to the term "IPv6 network slice."

In addition, to keep terms short where possible, "network slice" and "IP network slice" are called "slice" and "IP slice," respectively.

In different chapters, terms relating to IP network slicing are used as follows:

- In Chapter 1, which provides an overview of IP network slicing, the term "IP network slice" is not specific to IPv6 network slices.

- In Chapter 2, the term "IP network slice" mentioned in the part describing the IP network slicing architecture is not specific to IPv6 network slices. Because this chapter also describes the 5G End-to-End (E2E) network slicing architecture, the terms "RAN slice" and "CN slice" are used to differentiate such slices from IP network slices. And in the sections describing key technologies, IP network slicing technologies refer exclusively to IPv6 network slicing-related technologies and exclude other technologies, such as those used for MPLS network slicing.

- In Chapters 3–9, which focus on the solutions, technologies, and deployment of IPv6 network slicing, the term "IP network slice" always refers to IPv6 network slices. Section 8.1, which introduces the 5G E2E slicing solution, uses both the "5G slice" and "IP slice" terms for differentiation. And Section 3.6, which introduces the solution used to map service slices to resource slices, as well as Sections 9.3 and 9.4, which describe how to deploy such a solution, use both the "service slice" and "resource slice" terms for differentiation.

- In Chapter 10, which summarizes the industry development and future of IP network slicing, the term "IP network slice" is not specific to IPv6 network slices.

# PART I

## Overview

# CHAPTER 1

# Overview of IP Network Slicing

I P NETWORK SLICING IS an architectural innovation of the IP network. Comprising a complete set of solutions, it was proposed to meet the ever-increasing differentiated service requirements in the 5G and cloud era. Since it was proposed, it has been successfully applied in multiple industries in just a few years. This chapter starts by discussing the diversified services emerging in the 5G and cloud era. It then analyzes the challenges facing IP networks, introduces the background of IP network slicing, describes the corresponding benefits, and reviews the current development of IPv6 network slicing technologies.

## 1.1 BACKGROUND OF IP NETWORK SLICING

### 1.1.1 Emerging Diversified Services

As diverse services and new connection modes emerge in the 5G and cloud era, different industries, users, and services are posing a range of new requirements on the network in terms of access density, delay, reliability, and more.

#### 1.1.1.1 5G Services

With 5G comes a wealth of new scenarios and services. They impose more and higher requirements on networks, for example, stricter Service Level Agreement (SLA) guarantee and ultra-low delay. In addition, various types of clouds are gaining popularity, further eroding the boundary between

DOI: 10.1201/9781032699868-2

3

physical and virtual network devices. Consequently, the service access locations are more flexible, and the integration of services and networks is tighter. All this causes changes in the coverage of network connections.

In the 5G era, services of different types and different industries have significantly different characteristics. Services such as mobile communication, environment monitoring, smart home, smart agriculture, and smart metering require huge numbers of device connections and frequent transmission of many small packets. Other services such as live streaming, video uploading, and mobile healthcare require higher transmission rates, whereas Internet of Vehicles (IoV), smart grid, and industrial control services require millisecond-level delay and near-100% reliability. As such, 5G networks must provide capabilities such as massive access, ultra-low delay, and ultra-high reliability to meet the diversified service requirements of users and vertical industries.

Considering the main scenarios and service requirements of mobile Internet and the Internet of Things (IoT), the International Telecommunication Union (ITU) has defined three typical 5G application scenarios,[1] as shown in Figure 1.1.

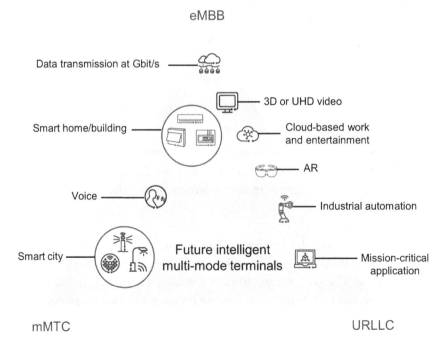

FIGURE 1.1 Typical application scenarios in the 5G era.

- Enhanced Mobile Broadband (eMBB): focuses on bandwidth-intensive services, such as High Definition (HD) video and Augmented Reality (AR).

- Ultra-Reliable Low-Latency Communication (URLLC): focuses on services that are extremely sensitive to delay and reliability, such as industrial automation services.

- Massive Machine-Type Communications (mMTC): focuses on scenarios involving high connection density, such as smart city.

These 5G application scenarios each require completely different network functions and performance levels — requirements that cannot be met using a single network.

### 1.1.1.2 Cloud Services

With the rapid development of the Internet and cloud, a growing number of enterprises are implementing digital transformation, as shown in Figure 1.2.

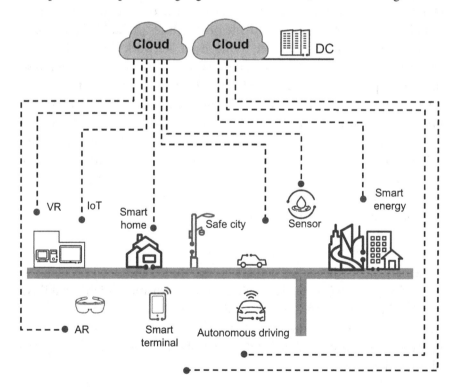

FIGURE 1.2    Industry digital transformation.

Through digital transformation, enterprises hope to achieve asset-light operations (i.e., by gradually cloudifying various internal applications and systems) along with the greater efficiency and agility that come with cloud services. Enterprise cloudification can be completed in three phases: portal website cloudification, followed by office and IT system cloudification, and finally enterprise production system cloudification. Enterprises moving their applications to the cloud gives rise to the reconstruction of private line networks that connect enterprises to clouds, enterprises to enterprises, and clouds to clouds, reshaping carriers' 2B services. Given this, the most critical requirement imposed on enterprise network construction is the ability to provide one-stop cloud-network services. In addition, as migrating enterprise production systems and core services to clouds poses unprecedented requirements on network SLAs, network slicing is needed to meet these requirements.

In the enterprise ICT market, more and more industry players are proposing different solutions to meet customer requirements. Public cloud providers tap into cloud backbone networks to provide one-stop cloud-network services, gradually changing the requirements on traditional site-to-Internet and site-to-site private lines. In addition, vendors involved with Software-Defined Wide Area Network (SD-WAN) provide flexible and cost-effective solutions to meet customers' interconnection requirements. These products and services not only transform how private lines are delivered but also provide flexible connections, fast provisioning, and dynamic adjustment capabilities. Consequently, the market share of carriers' traditional private line services is under significant threat. To maintain competitiveness in the 2B market, carriers must leverage their advantages in the network and provide flexible, agile, and SLA-guaranteed private line services with wide coverage and cloud-network convergence capabilities.

### 1.1.2 SLA Challenges Facing IP Networks

The emergence of diversified new services in the 5G and cloud era requires networks to provide ultra-low delay, security isolation, high reliability, and flexible connections, and to be able to intelligently manage services in a fine-grained way. However, traditional IP networks provide only best-effort forwarding capabilities and fall far short of meeting such service SLA requirements.

### 1.1.2.1 Ultra-Low Delay

An IP network is typically divided into access, aggregation, and backbone layers. From the access to the aggregation layers and then to the backbone layer, the planned bandwidth is converged with a certain ratio. Such bandwidth convergence enables the statistical multiplexing capability provided by IP networks to be fully utilized, significantly reducing the network construction cost by allowing resources to be shared. However, there is a downside: When traffic enters the network through multiple interfaces but leaves through only one, congestion is likely to occur. Although routers use large interface buffers to prevent packet loss caused by congestion, buffering packets leads to a higher queuing delay if congestion occurs.

Figure 1.3 illustrates some of the diversified new 5G services. Different services have different requirements for bandwidth and delay. For example, live video services are bursty and thus prone to instantaneous congestion, meaning they require high bandwidth but are not sensitive to delay. In contrast, services such as telemedicine, VR gaming, and precision manufacturing require ultra-low delays. Given this, data channels that can provide differentiated delays are required.

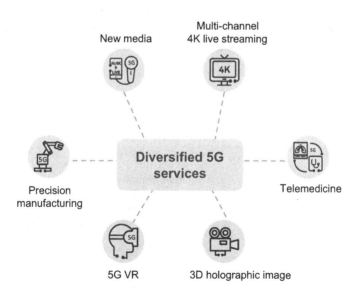

FIGURE 1.3   Diversified new 5G services.

### 1.1.2.2 Security Isolation

Production, manufacturing, and interactive services in vertical industries such as government, finance, and healthcare have specific requirements for service security and stability, as shown in Figure 1.4. To ensure that these critical services are not affected by other services (e.g., enterprise information management and public network services), dedicated private networks are usually used for the purpose of isolation. However, factors such as construction costs, Operations and Maintenance (O&M), and rapid service expansion have given rise to enterprises seeking new ways to carry these critical services while also meeting security isolation requirements. With statistical multiplexing in traditional IP networks, services are likely to preempt each other's resources. As such, only best-effort services can be provided, and there are no security isolation capabilities. In addition, traditional Multi-Service Transfer Platform (MSTP) private lines are being phased out, and some MSTP-based financial and government private line services are gradually being migrated to IP networks. These services also require security isolation and the exclusive use of resources.

### 1.1.2.3 Extremely High Availability

High-value services require IP networks to provide high-availability enterprise private lines. For example, such services in the government, financial, and healthcare sectors usually require an availability of up to 99.99%,

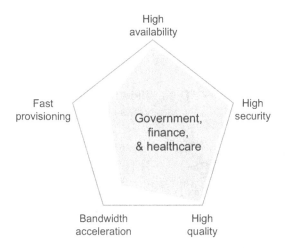

FIGURE 1.4 Key network requirements of some industries.

as shown in Figure 1.4. Meanwhile, 5G services, especially URLLC services, require an availability of 99.999%. Other mission-critical services related to social and human safety, such as remote control and high-voltage power supply, require even higher availability (99.9999%). As such, providing highly reliable private lines on an IP network to carry these services is crucial.

### 1.1.2.4 Flexible Connections

In the 5G and cloud era, the single service type evolves toward diverse types, and the singular traffic pattern evolves toward multi-direction patterns. This results in network connections becoming more flexible, complex, and dynamic, as shown in Figure 1.5. As the 5G core network is cloudified, User Plane Functions (UPFs) are moved closer to users, and Multi-Access Edge Computing (MEC) is widely applied, the connections between base stations, between base stations and Data Centers (DCs) at different network layers, and between these DCs, become increasingly complex and changeable. This requires networks to provide flexible, on-demand connections. In addition, because service scopes and access locations in networks and clouds vary with industries, services, and users, customized network topologies and connections are required.

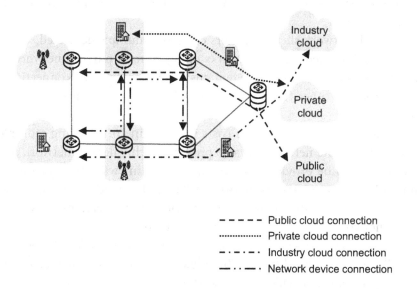

FIGURE 1.5  Complex IP network connections caused by diversified services.

*1.1.2.5 Fine-Grained and Intelligent Service Management*
Vertical industries have varied service types and therefore have different requirements for networks. Providing differentiated, dynamic, and real-time network services has become essential for SLA guarantee. On traditional IP networks, service planning is relatively static, and the collection and monitoring of network utilization statistics is performed at an interval of minutes. As a result, traffic burst characteristics at the microlevel cannot be measured. This approach cannot prevent services from affecting each other (necessary for guaranteeing service SLAs), nor can it meet service requirements on dynamic deployment and flexible adjustment. Evidently, a traditional IP network is inadequate for providing tenant-level, fine-grained, and intelligent service management.

## 1.1.3 Birth of IP Network Slicing

Traditional IP networks use statistical multiplexing to forward data packets in a best-effort manner and can provide flexible network connections at a low cost. However, this approach cannot efficiently provide differentiated and guaranteed SLAs for different services on the networks, nor can it isolate services or network users for independent operations. To meet the differentiated requirements of various services on the same IP network, the industry proposes the concept of IP network slicing.

With IP network slicing, carriers can build multiple dedicated, virtualized, and isolated logical networks on a common physical network to meet the requirements of different customers for network connections, resources, and other functions. Figure 1.6 shows an example of IP network slicing.

Network slicing reduces the costs involved in constructing multiple dedicated private networks. It also provides highly flexible network services that can be provisioned on demand. In this way, network slicing not only improves carriers' network value and monetization capability but also facilitates the digital transformation of various industries.

IP network slices were initially used to function as 5G transport network slices. However, as IP networks can be used to carry not only mobile services but also fixed broadband services and various enterprise private line services, IP network slices can be applied to a wider range of fields.

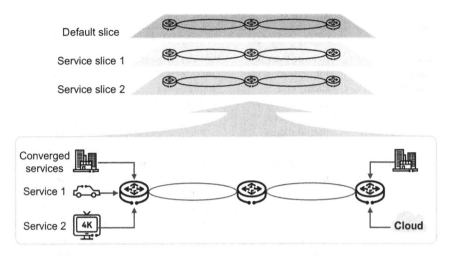

FIGURE 1.6 Network slicing.

## 1.1.4 Applications of IP Network Slicing

Network slicing can be used in numerous scenarios. Table 1.1 describes some typical ones.

IP network slices can be classified based on different dimensions. For example:

- By usage: commercial slices and self-operated slices

- By serving scope: industry slices and tenant slices

- By user type: 2B slices and 2C slices

- By network domain: mobile transport network slices, metro network slices, and backbone network slices

- By network connection model: Point-to-Point (P2P) private line slices, Multipoint-to-Multipoint (MP2MP) slices, and hybrid slices

Figure 1.7 shows the three types of slices classified by network connection model.

- For P2P private line network slices, such as those for governments and enterprises, slicing is implemented according to the specified service access points. Such network slices usually require exclusive

TABLE 1.1    Applications of IP Network Slicing

| Type | Slice Specifications | Business Model | Typical Application |
|---|---|---|---|
| Network slices for vertical industries | No more than 100 for network-wide slicing and potentially up to thousands for partial slicing | Provides network slices for specific industries or industry users. | Smart power distribution network |
| Network slices for carrier self-operated services | Usually no more than 100 for network-wide slicing | Network slices are transparent to end users. Carriers optimize their networks through network slicing. | Isolation of carrier services such as mobile transport, fixed broadband, and enterprise services |
| Network slices for third-party services | Usually no more than 100 for network-wide slicing | Provides network slices for third-party service platforms. | Services that predominantly require experience guarantee, such as cloud gaming, high-definition videos, and online conferencing |
| Dynamic on-demand network slices | Usually no more than 100 for network-wide slicing and potentially up to thousands for on-demand slicing | Provides fast provisioning and guarantee of network slicing for slice users on demand. | Outdoor unplanned 4K/8K UHD/Cloud VR live streaming, remote/mobile emergency medical care, and drone control |
| Private line slices that enable exclusive use of resources | Up to tens of thousands for partial slicing | Sold to customers as premium private line services. | High-value private lines for governments and enterprises (e.g., banks) |

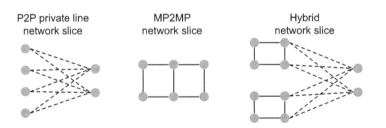

FIGURE 1.7    Slice classification by network connection model.

use of bandwidth. In most cases, a P2P private line network slice requires interconnection only between a limited number of service access points, and the connection relationship between access points is relatively fixed. Thus, a single P2P private line network slice has only a limited number of connections, while the number of P2P private line network slices across a network is relatively large.

- For MP2MP network slices, the physical network can be sliced — either wholly or partially — and nodes in such a network slice are fully meshed. Typical MP2MP network slices include carrier self-operated service slices, industry-specific slices, and VIP customer-specific slices. In most cases, network resources cannot be shared between different MP2MP network slices, but they can be shared between different connections in the same slice. An MP2MP network slice usually requires MP2MP interconnection, resulting in a large number of connections and complex connection relationships.

- A hybrid slice is a combination of the preceding two types and shares both of their characteristics.

## 1.2 BENEFITS OF IP NETWORK SLICING

IP network slicing enables resource and security isolation, a differentiated SLA guarantee, high reliability, and flexible topology customization. Its use fuels the growth of intelligent cloud networks and facilitates the digital transformation of enterprises.

### 1.2.1 Resource and Security Isolation

By deploying IP network slicing, the same network can be used to carry traffic from different industries, services, or users through different slices. These IP network slices can provide different types and degrees of isolation based on service and customer requirements.

In terms of service performance, IP network slicing ensures that service traffic bursts or abnormal traffic in one slice does not affect services in other slices on the same network. This is especially important for vertical industries, such as smart grid, smart healthcare, and smart port, which have strict requirements on delay and jitter and are highly sensitive to impacts from other services. In terms of security, IP network slicing ensures that services (such as financial and government private line services) or users in one slice cannot be accessed by users in other slices.

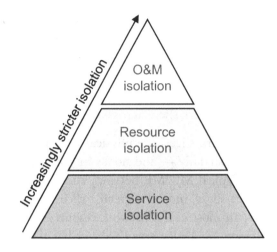

FIGURE 1.8    Levels of isolation provided by IP network slicing.

As shown in Figure 1.8, IP network slicing provides three levels of isolation: service isolation, resource isolation, and O&M isolation.

- Service isolation: Network slices are created for different services carried on the same common network to isolate service access and connections. Note that service isolation cannot guarantee SLAs. One network slice may still affect other slices, even if service isolation is used. As such, this level of isolation is suitable for isolating only some traditional services that do not have strict SLA requirements.

- Resource isolation: Network resources can be exclusively used on a per-slice basis or shared among multiple slices. Resource isolation is paramount for 5G URLLC services, which usually have strict SLA requirements and do not tolerate interference from other services. Two types of resource isolation are available: hard isolation and soft isolation. They differ in the degree to which the resources are isolated. Carriers can mix-and-match their use of hard isolation and soft isolation to determine which network slices use exclusive resources and which share resources. This allows a single physical network to meet differentiated service SLAs.

- O&M isolation: Some tenants require independent O&M on network slices allocated by carriers, similar to using private networks. Network slicing enables O&M isolation through open management plane interfaces.

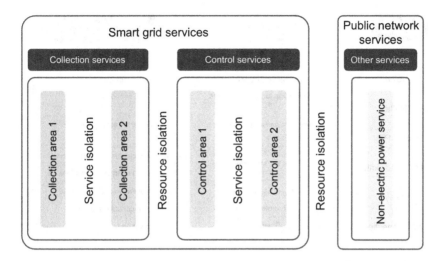

FIGURE 1.9   Isolation between different power grid services.

Take a smart grid scenario as an example. As shown in Figure 1.9, smart grid services are classified as collection or control services. These two types of services have different SLA requirements and therefore require resource isolation. In contrast, services of the same type require only service isolation. Network slicing is ideal for such a scenario, as it provides not only resource and security isolation between smart grid and public network services but also resource isolation between smart grid collection and control services.

## 1.2.2 Differentiated SLA Guarantee

The rapid development of network services, in addition to bringing a sharp increase in network traffic, gives rise to extreme requirements for network performance. Because different industries, services, or users have different SLA requirements on network bandwidth, delay, and jitter, the same network infrastructure needs to meet differentiated SLA requirements in different service scenarios. On a shared network infrastructure, network slicing can meet such requirements.

In particular, IP network slicing enables carriers to provide differentiated services for 2B and 2C scenarios instead of only selling bandwidth. As shown in Figure 1.10, slices are provided to tenants as services. By reinforcing their ability to provide on-demand, customized, and differentiated services, carriers will drive new value growth in the future.

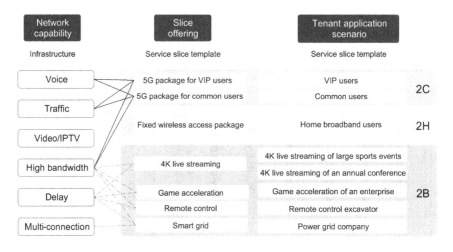

FIGURE 1.10  Slicing as a service.

## 1.2.3  High Reliability

On IPv6 networks, URLLC and other high-value services require high availability and millisecond-level failure recovery. SRv6-based network slicing provides local protection technologies — such as Topology-Independent Loop-Free Alternate(TI-LFA) and midpoint protection — against any failure point on an IPv6 network. These technologies enhance the reliability of IPv6 network slices as they drastically increase the likelihood of recovering from failure. Furthermore, link failure-triggered switching in a slice can be controlled within the slice without affecting other slices, as shown in Figure 1.11.

## 1.2.4  Flexible Topology Customization

Network connections are becoming more flexible, complex, and dynamic thanks to the ongoing development of services in the 5G and cloud era. As shown in Figure 1.12, logical topologies can be defined for network slices to provide on-demand and customized topologies and connections, meeting the differentiated network connection requirements of different industries, services, and users.

After a logical topology is customized for a network slice, services deployed in this slice are confined to the slice's specific topology, and the slice is aware of only its own topology connections — it is oblivious to the

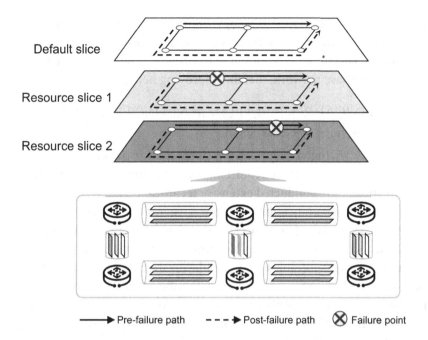

FIGURE 1.11    Link failure-triggered switching in a network slice.

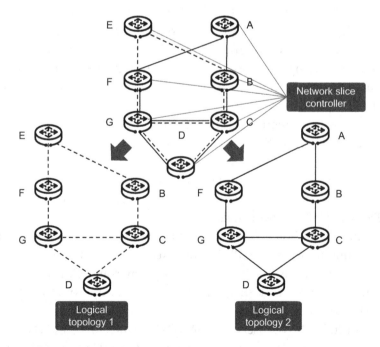

FIGURE 1.12    Flexible topology customization.

base network's full network topology. For network slice users, this simplifies the network information that they need to perceive and maintain. And for carriers, this limits the amount of information network slice users can see about the base network, thereby improving network security.

## 1.3 TECHNICAL RESEARCH ON IP NETWORK SLICING

### 1.3.1 Research on Network Slicing

The network slicing concept was first proposed in wireless networks to meet diversified 5G service requirements. Ever since, different standards organizations have conducted extensive technical research on this important architecture innovation. The 3rd Generation Partnership Project (3GPP) plays a leading role in research related to wireless network slicing. And focusing on IP network slicing, the Internet Engineering Task Force (IETF) is responsible for the standardization of the architecture and protocols for IETF network slicing. A number of other standards organizations have also contributed to the development of network slicing. This section describes the research on network slicing by 3GPP, IETF, and other standards organizations.

*1.3.1.1 3GPP Research on Network Slicing*

In the 3GPP organizational structure, the Project Coordination Group (PCG) is the highest decision-making body responsible for overall coordination, overseeing the 3GPP organizational structure, time frame, and work distribution. Technical work is completed by Technology Standards Groups (TSGs).

The 3GPP is currently divided into three TSGs: TSG Radio Access Network (RAN), TSG Service and System Aspects (SA), and TSG Core Network and Terminal (CT). Each TSG is divided into multiple Working Groups (WGs) that are each responsible for specific tasks. There are currently 16 WGs — 6 in the TSG RAN, 6 in the TSG SA, and 4 in the TSG CT. Figure 1.13 shows the details.

As the main body responsible for standardizing mobile communications networks, 3GPP began research on and formulation of 5G-related standards in 2015. Among the numerous 3GPP WGs, those participating in network slicing research are mainly from the TSG SA and TSG RAN.

They include SA WG1 (services), SA WG2 (architecture), SA WG3 (security), and SA WG5 (telecom management) from the TSG SA, as well as RAN

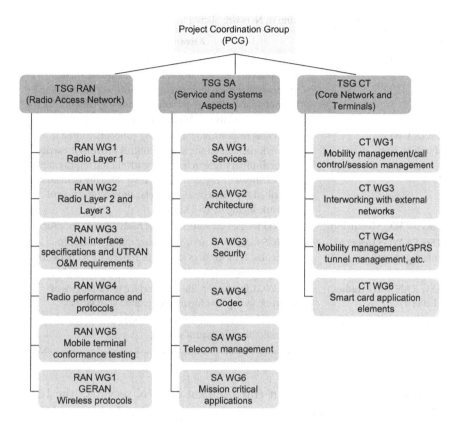

FIGURE 1.13    3GPP organizational structure.

WG1 (radio Layer 1) and RAN WG2 (radio Layers 2 and 3) from the TSG RAN. Table 1.2 lists the major WGs involved in network slicing in 3GPP.

As can be seen from the table, 3GPP defines not only the overall architecture of 5G network slicing but also the network slicing technologies and standards related to 5G core and access networks.

### 1.3.1.2 IETF Research on Network Slicing

In addition to being used as the transport network slice of a 5G End-to-End (E2E) slice, the network slice defined by the IETF can be used in other non-5G scenarios.

The IETF started the research and standardization of network slicing in 2016. Huawei first initiated the discussion on IP network slicing (including network slicing architecture) in the IETF and first proposed the network slicing realization framework — Enhanced VPN (VPN+)[2] — which

TABLE 1.2    Major WGs Involving in Network Slicing in 3GPP

| WG | Research Direction |
|---|---|
| TSG SA WG1 (services) | SA WG1 is responsible for analyzing network slicing requirements and scenarios. In 3GPP Release 14, it proposed network slicing requirements in TR 22.864 and further analyzed the requirements of using network slicing as a basic capability of 5G in TS 22.261. |
| TSG SA WG2 (architecture) | SA WG2 is responsible for defining concepts related to network slicing and the slicing control process. It carried out preliminary research on network slicing requirements and solutions in TR 23.799, and then formally defined and described the concepts, identifiers, and architecture of network slicing in TS 23.501. |
| TSG SA WG3 (security) | SA WG3 focuses on security issues related to network slicing. |
| TSG SA WG5 (telecom management) | SA WG5 focuses on network slicing management. In particular, it formulates standards related to 5G network slicing management. |
| TSG RAN WG1 (radio Layer 1) | RAN WG1 focuses on the air interface technologies of network slicing and formulates related standards. |
| TSG RAN WG2 (radio Layers 2 and 3) | RAN WG2 focuses on the network-side interface technologies of network slicing. |

takes IP network slices as an enhancement of VPN services. The IETF also defined the concepts, terminologies, and general architecture of IETF network slicing. Because IETF network slicing is mainly realized using IP and related technologies, this book also refers to IETF network slicing as IP network slicing. The IETF is now in the process of defining the technical architecture and protocol extensions used for realizing network slicing based on technologies such as VPN, Traffic Engineering (TE), and Segment Routing (SR). Related work includes extending data plane encapsulation protocols and control protocols in order to support network slicing and defining management interface models used for network slicing management and deployment.

With the support of Huawei, other network device vendors, and carriers, the IETF initially focused on key technologies and protocols of the data and control planes in the SR-based network slicing solution. To ensure the scalability of network slicing, the IETF then began to research network slicing scalability technologies. Recently, there have also been proposals in the IETF about the requirements, scenarios, and technical research directions related to inter-domain network slicing, hierarchical network slicing, and the like.

*1.3.1.3 Research on Network Slicing by Other Standards Organizations*
Although 3GPP and IETF perform much of the research and standardization of network slicing, other standards organizations also make contributions. For example:

Broadband Forum (BBF): mainly describes the requirements on transport network slicing management interfaces that are used for interconnection between the transport network and 5G network slice manager. It also
defines the information model of such interfaces.

European Telecommunications Standards Institute (ETSI): assigns its
Industry Specification Group (ISG) on Zero-touch Network & Service
Management (ZSM) to standardize automatic management of the E2E
network slicing lifecycle.

Optical Internetworking Forum (OIF), Institute of Electrical and
Electronics Engineers (IEEE), and International Telecommunication
Union-Telecommunication Standardization Sector (ITU-T): mainly work
on the research and standardization of Layer 2 and lower-layer forwarding
plane technologies related to network slicing. These technologies under-
pin the IETF network slicing realization architecture and enable the isolation of forwarding resources between network slices.

China Communications Standards Association (CCSA): focuses on the
interconnection between 5G E2E network slices and IP network slices, IP
network slicing architecture, realization requirements of network slicing
based on VPN+, and more. Figure 1.14 shows the work of standards organizations in network slicing.

## 1.3.2 Development of IPv6 Network Slicing Technologies

*1.3.2.1 Origin of IPv6 Network Slicing*
IPv6, also referred to as IP Next Generation (IPng),[3] is a second-generation network layer protocol standard[4] — it is an upgraded version of IPv4
designed by the IETF. Given that IPv6 is a core protocol of the IETF, IPv6
network slicing is a major realization of IP network slicing.

IPv4 is the predominant protocol used across the Internet. It developed rapidly in the early stages of the Internet due to its simplicity, ease
of implementation, and good interoperability. However, as the Internet
has continued to evolve, some of the design decisions made in IPv4 have
become problematic. For example, IPv4 has insufficient address space, its
packet headers and options are complex to process, address maintenance
is heavy, and route aggregation is inefficient. Furthermore, it lacks effec
tive solutions for security, Quality of Service (QoS), and mobility.

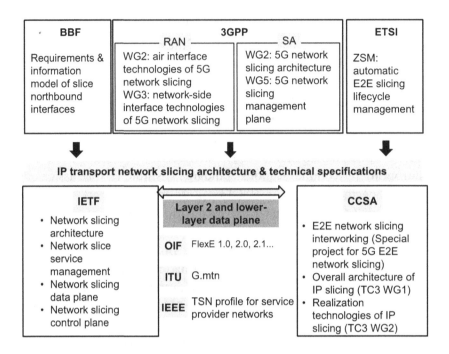

FIGURE 1.14   Complete picture of network slicing standards.

IPv6 was developed to address many of the problems faced with IPv4. However, the deployment and application of IPv6 have yet to gather pace since its development. The root cause of this is that there are solutions such as Classless Inter-Domain Routing (CIDR) and Network Address Translation (NAT) available to alleviate the shortage of IPv4 addresses, plus IPv6 lacks any killer applications. But as new services such as 5G and cloud services gain traction, IPv6 encounters new innovation and development opportunities.

The essence of IP networks is connectivity. 5G changes the attributes of connections, and the cloud changes their scope. The development of 5G services poses higher requirements on network connections; for example, they require stricter SLA guarantees and deterministic latency. Packets therefore need to carry additional information necessary for guiding and assisting packet processing so that they can be forwarded properly — this is made possible by the IPv6 extension. The development of cloud services makes service processing locations more flexible. Some cloud services (such as Telco Cloud) further break down the boundary between physical and virtual network devices, integrating services and transport networks.

All of this changes the scope of network connections. To adapt to these changes, network connections must be native IP-based so that they can take advantage of ubiquitous IP reachability, making the establishment of such connections much faster and more flexible. And although MPLS has been extremely successful throughout the development of IP technology, it requires extra signaling and a network-wide upgrade. It cannot adapt to the development of 5G and cloud. In contrast, IPv6 is natively IP-reachable and easily enables function extensions to encapsulate more types of information through IPv6 extension headers. This is an important reason why IPv6 network slicing is developing so quickly.

### 1.3.2.2 Origin of SRv6 Network Slicing

SR is a source routing paradigm in which segments represent any instruction, regardless of whether it is topology- or service-based. Segments, each of which is identified by a Segment Identifier (SID), can be inserted into packets on the ingress in a desired order to guide packet forwarding.[5] Compared with Resource Reservation Protocol-Traffic Engineering (RSVP-TE), SR is more advantageous in implementing TE. For example, it simplifies the control plane and reduces the number of network states.

SR currently supports MPLS and IPv6 data planes. SR based on the MPLS data plane is called Segment Routing-Multiprotocol Label Switching (SR-MPLS) and uses MPLS labels as its SIDs. SR based on the IPv6 data plane is called SRv6 and uses IPv6 addresses as SIDs.[6]

As shown in Figure 1.15, SRv6 combines the advantages of SR (which allows network programming on the ingress) and IPv6 packet header extensibility, creating new opportunities for IPv6 network slicing innovation.

SR is commonly understood as a mechanism that provides explicit paths with high extensibility. It provides different paths by combining different segments, such as node and link segments, to meet specific service requirements. From this perspective, SR shares the same objective as IP network slicing and can be used as a technology for realizing P2P private line slicing.

From another perspective, SR can also be seen as a technology for creating virtual networks. Node and link segments in SR can be seen as virtual nodes and links, respectively, and they can be combined to easily create a virtual network. In this sense, SR can be used to realize MP2MP network slicing.

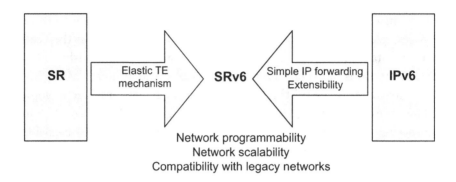

FIGURE 1.15   SR + IPv6 = SRv6.

## 1.4 STORIES BEHIND NETWORK SLICING

### 1.4.1 Understanding IP Network Slicing as a Technical System

Our understanding of IP network slicing has evolved gradually. We initially thought that it was only an important feature of SR and an integral part of 5G slicing.

In the process of innovation, we began to realize that our understanding of network slicing was incomplete. IP network slicing was much more complex than we had originally thought — it could be a standalone system rather than a part of something else. First, there is no need to bind IP network slicing to SR. Especially in the slice ID-based slicing solution, the independent identifier for slice resources introduced in the data plane can also be used with other types of tunnels for the purpose of network slicing. In addition, IP network slicing is closely related to the development of hardware technologies and underpinned by hardware-based resource partitioning technology — such characteristics are not present in the SR feature. Second, while IP network slicing stems from 5G, it can also be used for fixed and enterprise services — as well as for mobile services — due to the diversity of application scenarios and services of IP networks. Furthermore, it can be used for IP metro networks and backbone networks in addition to mobile transport networks. IP network slicing also enhances the original IP private line service by providing a better resource isolation guarantee. We therefore concluded that IP network slicing could stand on its own rather than depend on 5G.

As IP network slicing can be used in many scenarios and involves many technologies (including resource isolation technologies, control plane technologies, and data plane technologies), it has become a relatively independent technical system.

## 1.4.2 Private Line vs. Private Network

IP network slicing provides a relatively simple and efficient method for creating a "private network." Constructing a physical private network is costly and laborious and is usually outside the budget of smaller enterprises. IP network slicing can be used to create dedicated logical networks for enterprises or industries atop a physical network through resource isolation. This reduces network construction costs by a significant margin, making it affordable for smaller enterprises. So IP network slicing may open the floodgates for establishing "private networks," presenting a good opportunity for carriers to capitalize on the likelihood of its wide application.

A problem that comes with the introduction of IP network slicing is how to define traditional IP private line services.

Can the traditional VPN-based private line be referred to as the IP network slice?

Can the VPN-based private line over Multi-Protocol Label Switching Traffic Engineering (MPLS TE) or SR-MPLS TE tunnel be referred to as the IP network slice?

And can the VPN-based private line over an MPLS TE tunnel path that has resources reserved end-to-end through RSVP-TE be referred to as the IP network slice?

If these private lines cannot be called network slices, what about an IP network slicing-based "private network" whose topology consists of only two endpoints? Should it be called a private line or a slice?

Though there are similarities between IP network slicing and private lines in specific scenarios, in order to respect the historical evolution of IP technologies and avoid excessive expansion of the IP network slicing concept, this book defines IP network slicing as follows: A technical solution that uses specific control plane technologies (such as the affinity attribute, IGP multi-topology, or flexible algorithms) to construct topology attributes and uses specific data plane technologies (such as SRv6 SIDs or slice IDs) to indicate resource attributes. According to this definition, a VPN-based private line over an MPLS TE path established using RSVP-TE is not considered a network slice in this book, and a VPN-based private line over an SR TE path is considered a network slice in this book, but only when it meets the preceding two constraints.

## REFERENCES

[1] Husenovic K, Bedi I, Maddens S, et al. Setting the scene for 5G: Opportunities & challenges. International Telecommunication Union, 2018(56).

[2] Dong J, Bryant S, Li Z, et al. A Framework for Enhanced Virtual Private Networks (VPN+) Services [EB/OL]. (2022-9-20)[2022-09-30]. draft-ietf-teas-enhanced-vpn-11.

[3] Bradner S, Mankin A. The Recommendation for the IP Next Generation Protocol [EB/OL]. (1995-01)[2022-09-30]. RFC 1752.

[4] Deering S, Hinden R. Internet Protocol, Version 6 (IPv6) Specification. (2017-07)[2022-09-30]. RFC 8200.

[5] Filsfils C, Previdi S, Ginsberg L, et al. Segment Routing Architecture [EB/OL]. (2018-12-19)[2022-09-30]. RFC 8402.

[6] Filsfils C, Camarillo P, Li Z, et al. Segment Routing over IPv6 (SRv6) Network Programming [EB/OL]. (2021-02)[2022-09-30]. RFC 8986.

# PART II

Technologies

# CHAPTER 2

# Architecture of IPv6 Network Slicing

IPv6 NETWORK SLICING IS a complete technical system that involves key technologies at different network layers and in different areas. This chapter describes the architecture and basic deployment procedure of IPv6 network slicing, the relationship between IPv6 network slices and 5G network slices, and the scalability of IPv6 network slices. It also provides an overview of the key technologies involved in IPv6 network slicing.

Note: To avoid conflicts with live-network addresses, RFC 3849 recommends using IPv6 addresses with the prefix 2001:DB8::/32 as examples in books.[1] However, 2001:DB8::/32 is too long to fit neatly into figures. Therefore, short addresses such as A1::1 and 1::1 are often used in this book. Unless otherwise specified, all IPv6 addresses in this book are examples only.

## 2.1 ARCHITECTURE OF IP NETWORK SLICING

### 2.1.1 Architecture of 5G Network Slicing

Driven by new applications in 5G, the mobile communications field was the first to propose the concept of network slicing. Third Generation Partnership Project (3GPP) TS 283.501 defines a network slice as a logical network that provides specific network capabilities and characteristics. A network slice, which consists of a set of network functions and allocated resources (e.g., compute, storage, and network resources), aims to meet the

DOI: 10.1201/9781032699868-4

differentiated requirements of 5G services on a common mobile communications network. A 5G network slice is an End-to-End (E2E) dedicated logical network that provides specific network capabilities. It consists of network slice subnets in three technical domains: Radio Access Network (RAN), Transport Network (TN), and Core Network (CN). As shown in Figure 2.1, the 5G E2E network slicing management architecture defined by 3GPP is divided into three layers.

- Communication Service Management Function (CSMF): corresponds to the Business Support System (BSS). It is responsible for slice service operations, charging, and the like.

- Network Slice Management Function (NSMF): corresponds to the Operations Support System (OSS). Located below the CSMF, it is responsible for the planning, deployment, and O&M of E2E network slices.

- Network Slice Subnet Management Function (NSSMF): corresponds to the network management and control system of each sub-domain such as RAN, TN, and CN. It is responsible for the management and O&M of each network slice subnet.

Figure 2.1 shows the 5G E2E network slicing management architecture, in which the TN plays an important role as it interconnects NEs on the RAN and CN. Likewise, TN slices interconnect RAN and CN slices. These TN

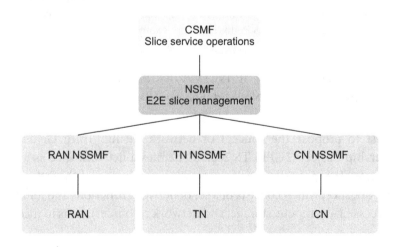

FIGURE 2.1   5G E2E network slicing management architecture.

slices offer performance guarantees, and collaborate with RAN and CN slices to provide differentiated Service Level Agreements (SLAs), security isolation, and other functions for E2E network slice services. Because different 5G E2E network slices may place very different requirements on the topology connections and performance, the TN must be able to provide multiple differentiated TN slices.

3GPP mainly defines the network slicing architecture, procedure, and technical specifications of the RAN and CN, whereas the Internet Engineering Task Force (IETF) formulates the standards and technical specifications of TN slicing. As per the IETF definition, an IETF network slice[2] is a logical network that uses a set of shared or dedicated network resources to connect multiple Service Demarcation Points (SDPs). These resources are used to meet specific Service Level Objectives (SLOs) and Service Level Expectations (SLEs). IPv6 network slicing allows carriers to build multiple dedicated and isolated logical networks on a common physical network, thereby meeting the differentiated requirements of different customers in terms of network connections, resources, and other functions.

## 2.1.2 Layered Architecture of IP Network Slicing

Various Virtual Private Network (VPN) technologies have been widely deployed and verified on IP networks to provide logical isolation between multiple tenants and different services; they are also used to carry 3G and 4G mobile services and numerous enterprise private line services. But as new services and vertical industry services emerge alongside the rise of 5G and the cloud, service requirements are becoming stricter and more diverse. Such requirements vary significantly in terms of bandwidth, delay, reliability, isolation, and security, among others. Due to the emergence of 5G network slicing concepts and related technologies and the inability of traditional VPN technologies to fully meet the requirements of 5G and cloud for network slicing, there is a pressing need for architecture changes, technology optimization, and innovation on IP networks.

IP network slices need to be consistent with 5G network slices in terms of concepts and architecture and coordinate with 5G E2E network slices through the TN NSSMF. In addition, 5G network slices need to map to IP network slices through the network slice interworking identifier. In order to meet the requirements for network slices, IP network slicing builds on the existing VPN and traffic engineering (TE) technologies and introduces various architectural and technological enhancements.

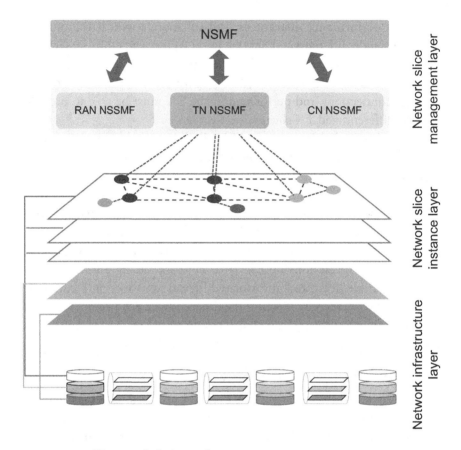

FIGURE 2.2    IP network slicing architecture.

As shown in Figure 2.2, the IP network slicing architecture consists of three layers: the network infrastructure layer, the network slice instance layer, and the network slice management layer. Each layer adopts both existing and new technologies to meet customers' requirements for IP network slicing.

### 2.1.2.1  Network Infrastructure Layer

The network infrastructure layer, composed of physical network devices, serves as the base network on which IP network slice instances are created. To meet requirements on resource isolation and SLA assurance in different network slicing scenarios, this layer needs to be capable of flexibly partitioning and reserving network resources (such as bandwidth, queue, cache, and scheduling resources) on the physical network based on the required granularity for different network slices. Technologies such as Flexible Ethernet (FlexE), channelized sub-interfaces, and Flex-Channel can be used to isolate resources.

### 2.1.2.2 Network Slice Instance Layer

The network slice instance layer provides the functions necessary to form network slices that meet specific service requirements. Specifically, it generates different logical network slice instances on a physical network, provides logical network topologies and connections that are customized on demand, and integrates them with a set of network resources allocated by the network infrastructure layer. The network slice instance layer is composed of an upper service slice sub-layer and a lower resource slice sub-layer. An IP network slice instance can be realized by mapping a service slice to a resource slice that meets the service requirements.

The service slice sub-layer — also referred to as the VPN layer — is used to provide virtual connections between network slice SDPs and logically isolate different network slice services. Various existing and under-development multi-tenant virtual network technologies, such as L2VPN, L3VPN, EVPN, and VXLAN, can be used to provide the functions required by this sub-layer.

The resource slice sub-layer — also referred to as the Virtual Transport Network (VTN) or Network Resource Partition (NRP) layer — is newly introduced to meet the resource isolation and path control requirements of IP network slicing. It provides customized network topologies required for slice service connections, in addition to exclusive or partially shared network resources required to meet SLA requirements for slice services. The resource slice sub-layer consists of the control plane and the data plane.

- The control plane defines and collects logical topologies, resource attributes, and state information for different resource slices so that it can provide the information necessary for network devices and controllers to generate different resource slice views. This plane also provides route and path computation based on resource slice topologies and resource constraints, and in some network slicing scenarios, it maps services of different network slices to corresponding resource slices based on slice service requirements. In order to construct the control plane of the resource slice sub-layer, the best practice is to use a centralized controller together with distributed control protocols. This brings the global planning and optimization capabilities of centralized control as well as advantages such as fast response, high reliability, and flexible expansion offered by distributed protocols.

- In the data plane, the identification information of resource slices is added to service data packets. This information is used to guide the forwarding and processing of packets in different network slices according to constraints such as the topologies and resources of specific network slices. In order to decouple from certain resource partitioning technologies used at the network infrastructure layer, the data plane needs to provide a universal identification mechanism. At present, the identification information of resource slices in the data plane is carried using the SRv6 Segment Identifier (SID) or slice ID.

In terms of the service slice sub-layer, there are various mature and widely used overlay VPN technologies. As such, subsequent chapters focus on the functions of the resource slice sub-layer at the network slice instance layer.

### 2.1.2.3 Network Slice Management Layer

The network slicing management layer mainly provides lifecycle management functions — such as planning, deployment, Operations and Maintenance (O&M), and optimization — for network slices. As the demand for network slices grows in vertical industries, network management will become more complex due to the increasing number of slices. Consequently, the network slice management layer must support dynamic and on-demand provisioning of network slices and be capable of automatically and intelligently managing them.

To realize 5G E2E network slicing, the management layer of IPv6 network slicing also needs to provide management interfaces. These interfaces are necessary for the management layer to exchange information — such as network slice requirements, capabilities, and states — with the 5G NSMF, in addition to achieving negotiation and interconnection with RAN and CN slices.

In summary, the architecture for realizing IPv6 network slicing is made up of the network infrastructure layer with resource partitioning capabilities, the network slice instance layer consisting of the service slice and resource slice sub-layers, and the network slice management layer with management interfaces. Different technologies can be used for corresponding layers in the network slicing architecture to meet different network slicing requirements, thereby forming a complete IPv6 network slicing solution. As technologies develop and new application scenarios for network slicing emerge, the technical architecture of IPv6 network slicing will be continuously enriched.

The IETF is currently standardizing the draft *draft-ietf-teas-enhanced-vpn*,[3] which describes the architecture for realizing IP network slicing and has been accepted as a Working Group (WG) document. In addition to the layered network architecture of IP network slicing, this document describes key technologies that can be selected at each layer, covering existing technologies as well as their extensions, along with a series of technical innovations. VPN+, as its name suggests, provides a series of enhancements to conventional VPN in terms of functionality, deployment mode, and business model. Conventional VPN is mainly used to isolate services of different tenants but falls short in SLA guarantee and open management. To provide differentiated SLA guarantee for different types of services, IP network slicing adopts resource isolation technologies for on-demand integration of logical service connections and underlying network topologies and resources based on the mapping between upper-layer service slices and low-layer resource slices. By leveraging the VPN+ architecture and adopting a combination of technologies at different layers, IP network slicing can be realized to meet diversified requirements.

### 2.1.3 Basic Procedure for Deploying IP Network Slices

Figure 2.3 shows the procedure for deploying IP network slices.

1. Receives network slice service requests

    The IP Network Slice Controller (NSC) receives customer requests through its northbound service management interface to create network slice services. The requests include SDPs, connection relationships, and SLO and SLE requirements (e.g., bandwidth, delay, isolation, and reliability). The NSC creates service slices based on the slice service requirements it receives and determines whether to use existing resource slices or create new ones to carry the network slice services.

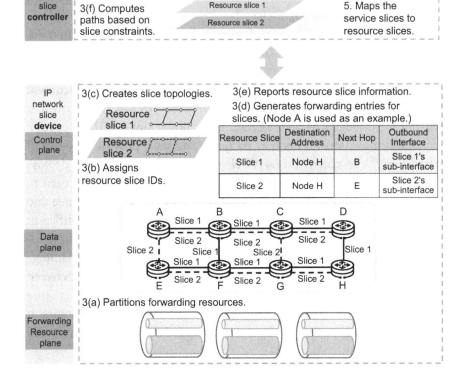

FIGURE 2.3  Basic procedure for deploying IP network slices.

2. Plans network resource slices

Network resource slices can be pre-deployed by a carrier based on a network resource planning policy. Alternatively, they can be created on demand when one or a group of users raise service requirements. Each network resource slice has exclusive or partially shared network resources and needs to be associated with a customized logical network topology.

Based on the topology and available resources of the physical infrastructure network, the NSC determines the logical topology of each network resource slice that meets the carrier's or customer's requirements and determines the network forwarding resources (e.g., bandwidth, queue, and buffer resources) that need to be allocated to each resource slice on each network node and link. When planning and creating a new network resource slice, the IP NSC can take into account the status of existing resource slices in order to achieve globally optimal deployment of network resource slices.

3. Creates network resource slices

Following the planning results, the NSC instructs each network device in the network resource slice to allocate the required network resources. In addition, network devices allocate forwarding resources to each network resource slice by using different resource partitioning and reservation technologies based on the service requirements and capabilities of network devices.

The NSC and network devices also need to allocate data plane identifiers to each network resource slice. The identifiers are used to instruct network devices to process and forward the received data packets using the network resources reserved for each resource slice. The technology used to encapsulate the data plane identifiers of a network resource slice can be selected based on the network slice scenario and the capabilities of network devices.

Network devices in a network resource slice can advertise information — such as the slice's local topology connection, data plane identifier, and allocated forwarding resources — on the network through a control protocol. Such devices can perform route computation based on the logical topology information of the resource slice collected through the control protocol, generate shortest-path routing entries in the resource slice, and deliver the entries to the forwarding table.

Furthermore, these devices report information such as the logical topology, reserved resources, and data plane identifier of each resource slice to the NSC, which can then compute paths and generate explicit forwarding paths that meet specific constraints in each network resource slice.

4. Creates service slices

The NSC creates independent service slices for customers according to the connection and access isolation requirements of network slices. And to provide service slices, the NSC uses appropriate overlay multi-tenant technologies (such as L2VPN, L3VPN, EVPN, and VXLAN, which are selected based on different service types and connection requirements). Because this procedure is similar to that used in deploying conventional VPN services, it is not described in this book.

5. Maps service slices to resource slices

A slice service mapping policy specified by a carrier is used to determine how edge devices of network slices map slice service flows to resource slices. Service packets mapped to a resource slice are processed and forwarded using the forwarding resources reserved for the resource slice, thereby providing differentiated and guaranteed services for different network slice services.

## 2.2 SCALABILITY OF IPV6 NETWORK SLICING

There is no definitive answer to how many network slices an IP network needs to provide. One common view is that in the early stages of 5G, during which mainly eMBB services are developed, only a few network slices — around 10 — are required to provide coarse-grained service isolation on a network. As 5G-related technologies mature, the development of Ultra-Reliable Low-Latency Communication (URLLC) services and the emergence of various vertical services will push the number of network slices needed on an IP network to hundreds or even thousands. As such, the network must be capable of providing more fine-grained and customized network slices. In addition, a network slicing solution must not only meet requirements in terms of slice quantity and scale in the early stages of 5G but also support more and larger network slices as networks evolve.

The scalability of network slices hinges mainly on that of the control and data planes, as described in the following two sections.

### 2.2.1 Control Plane Scalability of Network Slicing

The control plane of IPv6 network slicing covers the service slice sub-layer and the resource slice sub-layer. The control plane of the service slice sub-layer mainly distributes information about service connection relationships and service routes by using control protocols such as Multiprotocol Extensions for Border Gateway Protocol (MP-BGP). Because the scalability of the service slice sub-layer's control plane has already been extensively verified, this section focuses on the control plane scalability of the resource slice sub-layer in IPv6 network slicing.

The control plane of network slicing is mainly responsible for delivering and collecting topology and attribute information for network slices, computing routes for each network slice based on slice attributes and constraints, and delivering the computed routes and paths to forwarding tables. Because the number of system resources consumed for information distribution and route computation on the control plane increases as the number of network slices increases, optimization technologies need to be considered to reduce related overhead. The control plane scalability of network slicing is optimized as follows:

1. Uses a shared control plane session to exchange information about multiple network slices. This is possible when adjacent network devices belong to multiple network slices. This optimization prevents the number of control plane sessions from multiplying as the number of network slices increases, thereby avoiding overhead involved in additional control plane session maintenance and information exchange. Note that when a shared control plane session is used to advertise information about multiple network slices, attribute information for different network slices needs to be distinguished using unique network slice identifiers in control messages.

2. Decouples different attributes of a network slice. This optimization enables the control plane to separately distribute and process different types of attribute information for network slices. A network slice has various types of attributes, some of which are processed separately on the control plane. IETF's draft that analyzes the scalability of network slices — *draft-ietf-teas-nrp-scalability*[4] — proposes two basic attributes of network slices: the topology attribute and the resource attribute.

Figure 2.4 shows two different logical network topologies that are defined on one physical network to meet the connection requirements of different

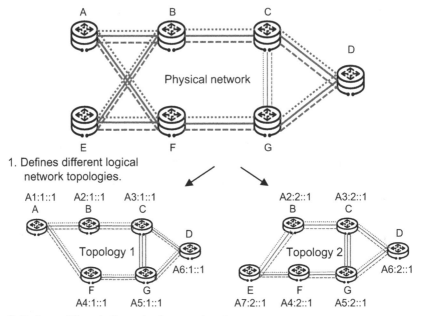

1. Defines different logical network topologies.

2. Defines different slices sharing one topology.

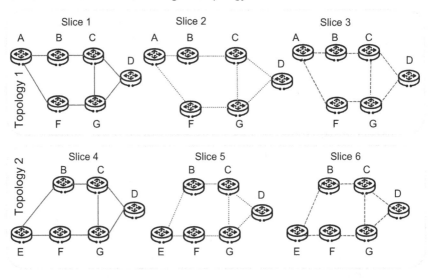

FIGURE 2.4   Network slices sharing one logical topology.

network slices. The resources that need to be allocated to each network slice are determined based on the SLA and isolation requirements of each slice. Because each network slice is a combination of its topology and resource attributes, unique network slices can be formed over the same logical topology by using different resources. The topology and resource attributes of network slices can be decoupled to some extent during information advertisement and computation processing in the control plane. For multiple network slices that share one topology, after the mapping between these network slices and the topology is advertised in the control plane, the topology attribute needs to be advertised only once. This topology attribute can be referenced by multiple network slices sharing the same topology, and the path computation result based on the logical topology can be shared among them.

In Figure 2.4, network slices 1, 2, and 3 share one topology, and 4, 5, and 6 share another. In order to allow all network nodes to obtain the topology information of all six network slices, carriers need to associate slices 1, 2, and 3 with topology 1, and slices 4, 5, and 6 with topology 2, and then enable the network nodes to separately advertise the attributes of these two topologies. This simple approach requires far fewer messages to be exchanged compared with advertising the topology attribute separately for each network slice. It also enables multiple network slices with the same topology to share route computation results based on the logical topology, thereby avoiding overhead caused by performing topology-based path computation separately for each network slice. If a device maintains mapping relationships between network slices and logical topologies, it needs to maintain routing information based on only the logical topologies. The device uses this information to perform a table lookup and determine the outbound interface and next hop for forwarding packets of network slices with the same topology. For example, the metric value of the A-B-C-D link is lower than that of the A-F-G-D link. As such, for slices 1, 2, and 3 that share topology 1, the next hop from node A to the destination (node D) is node B, and the outbound interface is the interface connecting node A to node B. Note that the forwarding resources allocated to different network slices on the same outbound interface are different. Consequently, based on the network slice identifiers carried by the data plane, data packets belonging to different network slices are forwarded and processed on this outbound interface using corresponding resources reserved for each network slice.

Similarly, multiple network slices can share one set of forwarding resources allocated by network nodes. In this case, the shared network resource attribute needs to be advertised only once     as opposed to multiple times — in the control plane, and information about the network slices that use the resources needs to be advertised. For example, if network slices 1 and 4 share the same channelized sub-interface on the link from node B to node C, the channelized sub-interface's resource information needs to be advertised only once in the control plane. At the same time, the control plane needs to indicate that the resource is used by both network slices 1 and 4. The resource information advertised by the control plane for network slices can be used by the NSC and the ingress of a network path to collect and generate complete information about network slices. In this way, the NSC and ingress can perform constrained path computation based on the resource attributes of network slices. Note that when forwarding data packets in different network slices, a network node needs to obtain resources (i.e., sub-interface or sub-channel of the outbound interface) reserved for the corresponding network slice based on network slice identification information carried in packets.

To support the decoupling between the topology and resource attributes of a network slice and enable the flexible combination of these attributes into different network slices, a network node needs to advertise the definition of network slices through a control protocol. This ensures that all network nodes in a network slice have a consistent understanding of the topology and resource attributes associated with the network slice. In addition, topology, resources, and other attributes associated with a network slice can be separately advertised using corresponding protocol mechanisms.

### 2.2.2 Data Plane Scalability of Network Slicing

At the network infrastructure layer, there is a limit to the number of partitions that the network resources can be sliced into. To support more network slices, enhanced resource partitioning capabilities are required on the underlay network. To achieve this, new technologies that support finer-grained partitioning of resources need to be introduced to the underlay network. In addition, the cost-effectiveness of network slicing needs to be considered. This means introducing a certain degree of resource sharing on top of resource isolation. In other words, a combination of soft and hard isolation needs to be used for allocating resources to network slices so as to meet differentiated SLAs and isolation requirements for different services.

The data plane also needs to generate different forwarding entries for different network slices. Consequently, the number of data plane entries increases each time a network slice is added. Take the SRv6 SID-based network slicing data plane as an example. Using unique SRv6 locators and SIDs to differentiate between network slices requires more locator and SID resources, significantly complicating network planning.

One approach to optimizing network slicing's data plane is to transform the forwarding structure from using a single data plane identifier for packet forwarding into one that uses multiple data plane identifiers. This will reduce the number of forwarding entries that need to be maintained across the entire network because some forwarding information is only maintained locally on individual network nodes. For example, a data plane slice identifier, which is independent of the data plane routing and topology identification information, can be introduced for a network slice. When a data packet is forwarded within the network slice, the next hop is first determined by looking up routing and topology identifiers in the packet. The resources used to forward the packet to the next hop are then identified according to the network slice identifier in the packet. From the perspective of how the data plane encapsulates, processes, and forwards packets, introducing multiple identifiers to the data plane requires much higher flexibility and extensibility. The IPv6 extension header mechanism offers a way to meet such requirements effectively.

To sum up, a network can provide a massive number of large-scale network slices that are needed to meet the requirements of the ever-growing network slice services in the 5G and cloud era by adopting the following measures: improve the resource partitioning and isolation capabilities of network devices, combine soft and hard isolation for network slice planning, decouple and optimize the functions on the network slicing control plane, and introduce multi-dimensional forwarding identifiers and entries on the network slice data plane.

## 2.3 KEY TECHNOLOGIES OF IPV6 NETWORK SLICING

Under the IPv6 network slicing architecture described in Section 2.1.2 Layered Architecture of IP Network Slicing, multiple solutions for realizing IPv6 network slicing can be provided by combining a series of key technologies.

Figure 2.5 outlines the key technologies involved in IPv6 network slicing.

IPv6 network slicing technologies are classified as either controller-side or device-side technologies.

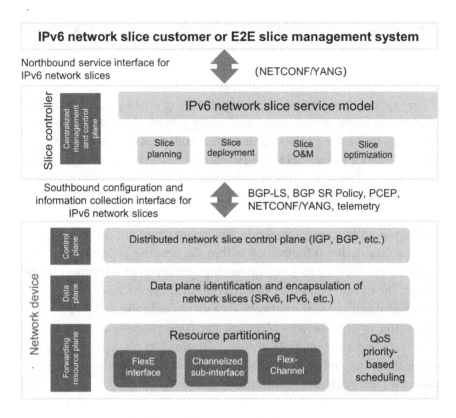

FIGURE 2.5   Key technologies of IPv6 network slicing.

Controller-side technologies mainly include:

- Network slice northbound service model.

- Full lifecycle management of network slices, including planning, deployment, O&M, and optimization of network slices.

- Network slice southbound interfaces and related protocols, including Border Gateway Protocol-Link State (BGP-LS), BGP SR Policy, Path Computation Element Communication Protocol (PCEP), Network Configuration Protocol (NETCONF), Yet Another Next Generation (YANG), and telemetry.

Device-side technologies mainly include:

- Network slice forwarding resource partitioning technologies, including FlexE, channelized sub-interface, and Flex-Channel.

- Network slice data plane identification and encapsulation technologies, including data plane identification based on SRv6 and IPv6.

- Distributed control plane protocols, including Interior Gateway Protocol (IGP) and BGP.

## 2.3.1 Network Resource Partitioning Technologies

Network slice customers expect a private network-like service experience when using network slices — this is a critical requirement. Put differently, customers of one network slice should not be able to perceive those of another network slice, nor should the service experience of each network slice customer be affected by changes or abnormal events of another network slice or non-slice services on the network.

Network slicing can provide different levels and degrees of isolation to meet the requirements of network slice customers. While various VPN technologies can provide access isolation between users of different network slices, network slice resources also need to be isolated if the services of users in different network slices must not affect each other. Based on the degree of resource isolation between network slices, resource isolation is classified as either soft or hard isolation.

Soft isolation means that different network slices share the same set of network resources. This mode inherits the statistical multiplexing feature of IP networks and, based on different classes of service, can provide differentiated services for different network slices. In addition, different service forwarding paths can be generated for different network slices based on differentiated logical topologies and path computation constraints. However, soft isolation cannot provide guaranteed SLAs for network slices.

In contrast to soft isolation, hard isolation allocates exclusive network resources to different network slices on a network. This ensures that services from different network slices are processed and forwarded on the network using dedicated network resources. And because it prevents services in different slices from affecting each other, hard isolation can effectively ensure the SLAs of network slices.

There are a number of ways in which hard isolation of network slice resources can be realized. Furthermore, different resource partitioning mechanisms provide isolation capabilities of varying degrees and granularities. For example, network slice resources can be isolated at the granularities of a physical interface, an independent FlexE interface, and a sub-interface or sub-channel that has reserved resources. And in order to realize hierarchical slicing of IPv6 networks, hierarchical resource partitioning technologies are needed. One way to realize hierarchical resource partitioning is through Flex-Channels nested in FlexE interfaces or channelized sub-interfaces. According to service requirements, different resource partitioning technologies can be selected to provide fine-grained resource allocation for different network slicing scenarios. The following describes how to partition and reserve resources.

### 2.3.1.1 Presentation of Network Slice Resources to Upper-Layer Protocols

Forwarding resources reserved on a physical link for different network slices need to be presented on a network in a certain form. This is necessary for the resources to be separately used by the network's control and data planes for route computation and packet forwarding. There are three ways of presenting the resources reserved for network slices:

- Using Layer 3 sub-interfaces

- Using Layer 2 sub-interfaces

- Using sub-channels with reserved bandwidth of Layer 3 interfaces.

### 2.3.1.2 Using Layer 3 Sub-Interfaces

When forwarding resources reserved on a link for network slices are presented using Layer 3 sub-interfaces, the Layer 3 sub-interface of each network slice is assigned an independent IP address and has Layer 3 protocols enabled. This method facilitates independent management and monitoring of resources reserved for each network slice and the status of each slice, and it allows routes to be computed based on attributes of Layer 3 sub-interfaces. One of the drawbacks of this method, however, is that the number of Layer 3 sub-interfaces and protocol sessions that need to be managed on the network increases as the number of network slices increases. This leads to an increase in the number of flooded protocol messages. In terms of scalability, the management and control planes face major challenges when there are many network slices. Figure 2.6 shows the use of Layer 3 sub-interfaces to present resources reserved for network slices.

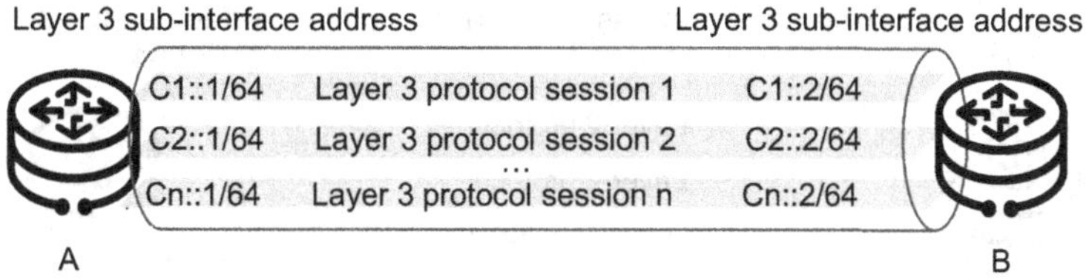

Layer 3 sub-interface address                    Layer 3 sub-interface address

| C1::1/64 | Layer 3 protocol session 1 | C1::2/64 |
| C2::1/64 | Layer 3 protocol session 2 | C2::2/64 |
| Cn::1/64 | Layer 3 protocol session n | Cn::2/64 |

A                                                                           B

FIGURE 2.6   Using Layer 3 sub-interfaces to present resources reserved for net-work slices.

### 2.3.1.3 Using Layer 2 Sub-Interfaces

When forwarding resources reserved for network slices are presented using Layer 2 sub-interfaces, the IP address and protocol session of the Layer 3 main interface are used to exchange the information of network slices with other network nodes. This is because a Layer 2 sub-interface does not have Layer 3 attributes. One of the advantages of this method is that there is no need to assign an additional IP address or establish an additional Layer 3 protocol session for each network slice. Instead, the Layer 2 sub-interface of each slice only needs to run necessary Layer 2 protocols, thereby reducing overhead of the management and control planes caused by an increase in network slices. This, in effect, contributes to an improvement in network scalability. And because Layer 2 sub-interface information is invisible to Layer 3 IP route computation, network nodes in each network slice can use only the attributes of the Layer 3 main interface for path computation. Figure 2.7 shows the use of Layer 2 sub-interfaces to present resources reserved for network slices.

### 2.3.1.4 Using Sub-Channels with Reserved Bandwidth

When the forwarding resources of different network slices are presented using sub-channels with reserved bandwidth, each network slice corresponds to a logical channel that has guaranteed bandwidth under a Layer 3 main interface. In this case, the protocol session of the Layer 3 main interface can be used to advertise resource and status information of each network slice, eliminating the need to create an independent Layer 3 or Layer 2 protocol session for each network slice. Therefore, this method can further reduce the overhead of the management and control planes caused by an increase in network slices. Figure 2.8 shows the use of sub-channels with reserved bandwidth to present resources reserved for net-work slices.

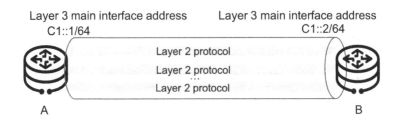

FIGURE 2.7 Using Layer 2 sub-interfaces to present resources reserved for network slices.

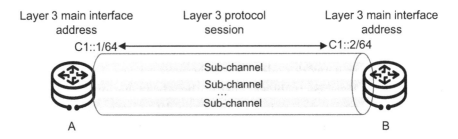

FIGURE 2.8 Using sub-channels with reserved bandwidth to present resources reserved for network slices.

Appropriately planning resources for network slices and using different hard isolation technologies enable flexible selection of exclusive resources or shared resources for different network slices. This meets the differentiated service and SLA assurance requirements of different services over one network.

### 2.3.2 Data Plane Technologies

On a conventional IP network, IP packets are forwarded according to the longest match rule based on the destination address in the packets to determine the outbound interface on the local network device and the next hop for the packets. On an IP/Multi-Protocol Label Switching (MPLS) network, MPLS data packets are forwarded according to a table lookup based on the outermost MPLS label in the packets to determine the outbound interface on the local network device and the next hop for the packets. Conventional IP/MPLS networks typically forward packets based on only a single data plane identifier (one-dimensional forwarding mechanism).

IP network slicing divides an infrastructure IP network into multiple logical networks. In addition to the IP network's destination address-based forwarding, IP network slicing adds a forwarding action to determine network slice resources, transforming the IP network from single-plane to multi-plane. This requires the IP network to establish a forwarding mechanism based on two-dimensional data plane identification and both topology/path identifiers and slice resource identifiers encapsulated into data packets, as shown in Figure 2.9. There are two typical methods to implement two-dimensional data plane identifiers on the IP network.

The first method reuses the existing data plane identifier in an IP packet but adds resource semantics to the identifier. In this way, it can be used as a multi-semantic identifier, as shown in Figure 2.10. For example, resource semantics can be added to a destination address or an SR SID. This method

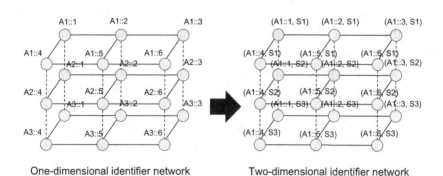

One-dimensional identifier network          Two-dimensional identifier network

FIGURE 2.9 Transformation from one-dimensional identifier-based networks to two-dimensional identifier-based networks.

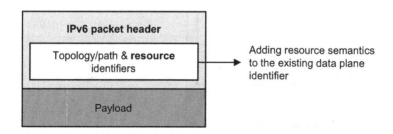

FIGURE 2.10 Two-dimensional data plane identification — multi-semantic identifier.

allows the original data plane identifier to be used to indicate not only a topology or path but also the resources of a network slice.

The second method introduces a new network slice identifier for an IP packet. This identifier is used together with existing information, such as the destination address, to indicate a network slice's different attributes (e.g., the topology, path, and network slice resources used for data packet forwarding), as shown in Figure 2.11. For example, a dedicated slice resource identifier is added to an IPv6 packet header.

The preceding two methods both have advantages and disadvantages.

The first method allows the existing IP packet encapsulation to be reused without needing to modify the packet format. As such, it facilitates network slice deployment on an existing IP network and helps carriers quickly verify solution feasibility and commercially deploy network slices. However, due to the additional semantics required, the main disadvantage of this method is that the number of existing data plane identifiers rapidly increases as the number of network slices increases. In turn, this will cause the number of forwarding entries to increase and bring challenges to network planning and management.

The second method can effectively avoid the main disadvantage of the first method. It improves the data plane scalability of network slices and better supports scenarios where massive numbers of network slices are required. However, the newly added slice resource identifier requires the data packet format to be extended and the forwarding table of a device to be modified accordingly. This method is better suited to scenarios where network slice scalability and massive numbers of network slices are required.

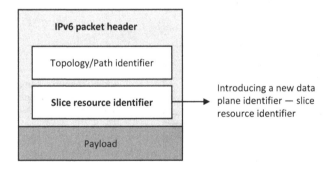

FIGURE 2.11  Two-dimensional data plane identification — a newly added network slice identifier.

### 2.3.3 Control-Plane Technologies

The control plane of IP network slicing includes two types of control protocols: centralized ones running between a centralized NSC and network devices, and distributed ones running between network devices. Such a control plane — referred to as a hybrid control plane — combines the advantages of both centralized and distributed protocols. Specifically, it not only has the global planning and optimization capabilities of centralized control but also delivers the advantages of distributed protocols, such as fast response and high reliability.

As shown in Figure 2.12, the centralized NSC can use BGP and PCEP to collect information about network slice topologies and resources (for global computation and optimization of forwarding paths in network slices) and to deliver network slice-specific paths to network devices. In order to synchronize information about network slice topologies and states across the entire network and to quickly respond to and recover from faults in network slices, the distributed control plane can use a distributed protocol such as Intermediate System to Intermediate System (IS-IS), Open Shortest Path First (OSPF), or BGP to distribute network slice information among network devices.

The control plane of IP network slices consists of the following:

- The control plane of the service slice sub-layer (VPN): mainly used to establish and maintain service node connections and distribute service routing information.

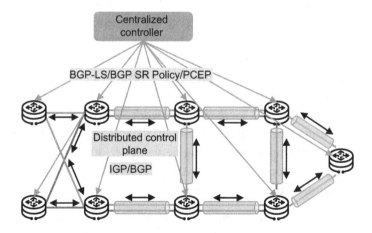

FIGURE 2.12   Centralized NSC and distributed control plane.

- The control plane of the resource slice sub-layer (VTN): mainly used to distribute and collect information, including the topology and resource attributes of resource slices. The NSC, or ingress, computes and establishes TE paths based on topology and resource information, as well as other constraints, of resource slices. Each network device in a resource slice performs distributed route computation based on the topology constraints of the resource slice in order to generate the shortest path (BE) forwarding entries for this slice. The control plane of resource slices needs to extend distributed protocols such as IGP and BGP, and protocols for interworking between the controller and network devices such as BGP-LS, BGP SR Policy, and PCEP.

In addition, the control plane of network slices can be used to map each service slice to the resource slice.

## 2.3.4 Management-Plane Technologies

The network slice management layer mainly provides lifecycle management functions for network slices. This includes functions in the network slice planning, deployment, O&M, and optimization phases. For network slice management, the management plane includes centralized and distributed management planes that collaborate with each other.

- The centralized management plane runs on the NSC and offers a network-wide global perspective. It manages the entire network as a single object in order to complete service and resource slice planning in the network planning phase, slice deployment in the network construction phase, slice operating status monitoring and adjustment in the network maintenance phase, and slice resource optimization in the network optimization phase. The centralized management plane can achieve automatic service provisioning and on-demand network slice deployment on a group of network devices, ensuring correct forwarding of network traffic among devices in each network slice while monitoring and analyzing network performance. In addition, it enables the root cause of a fault in a network slice to be quickly located, analyzed, and rectified.

- The distributed management plane runs on network devices. It takes a single network device as a managed object to provide device configuration, alarm management, customer management, security management, and running and performance status monitoring. This plane is more reliable than the centralized management plane because it runs on the device itself. It allows the device to be logged in to, maintained, and configured, ensuring correct device operation.

To implement the preceding functions, the management plane of network slicing needs to support the following key technologies:

- Network-level transaction management: During slice deployment, multiple network devices function as recipients of configuration data. If the configuration on some devices fails, devices that are successfully configured need to be rolled back to ensure transaction integrity. The network-level transaction framework defines and manages a unified transaction state machine to drive transaction participants to complete operations and ensure data persistence, thereby achieving consistency of configuration status among participants.

- Service consistency assurance: The centralized and distributed management planes are deployed on the controller, and different network nodes and data on these two planes may be inconsistent. The unified service consistency framework must be able to identify data inconsistency and ensure that incremental configuration changes do not affect existing network services, even if the data is inconsistent.

- Efficient slice resource partitioning algorithm: During slice planning and deployment, fixed physical networks need to carry more slice services and enable slice services to meet customer requirements. Efficient slice resource partitioning algorithms can optimize network resource slices to better meet the requirements of slice service customers.

- Large-scale network performance optimization: The centralized slice management plane is oriented to thousands, tens of thousands, or even hundreds of thousands of network devices. Appropriate concurrency control, distributed storage, and time-based scheduling of common processing paths are necessary to meet the performance requirements of large-scale networks.

- Southbound and northbound interface technology: The NSC receives service requests for network slices through an abstract northbound interface. It then converts these requests into a group of parameters for network slices through centralized computation and configures network devices through a southbound interface of the controller to deploy network slices. The NSC needs to define suitable YANG models for southbound and northbound network slice interfaces to ensure the realization of network slice services. In addition, the NSC provides mechanisms such as a model-driven mechanism for network slice management.

- Telemetry technology: The monitoring and maintenance of network slices involve multiple planes (e.g., the data plane, control plane, and management plane) and require the collection of massive amounts of network status data. Because the traditional Simple Network Management Protocol (SNMP) cannot fully meet the performance and data requirements, telemetry technologies need to be introduced. The Network Telemetry Framework (NTF)[5] can provide network performance monitoring within seconds and real-time routing information collection. In addition, technologies such as In-situ Flow Information Telemetry (IFIT) can be used to accurately monitor services on the data plane.

## 2.4 STORIES BEHIND NETWORK SLICING

### 2.4.1 Establishing Network Slicing Terminology

Many debates were held in the IETF about the terminology involved in IP network slicing, affecting the process of its standardization.

In 2016, we defined VPN+ as the framework for realizing IP network slicing based on an analysis of requirements and technologies. The following year, after reaching a consensus with industry experts on how to promote network slicing in the IETF, we submitted a draft of the VPN+ framework to the IETF. This draft was eventually adopted by the IETF's Traffic Engineering Architecture and Signaling (TEAS) WG at the beginning of 2019. There were two reasons why we chose the name VPN+. One was that IP network slicing can be regarded as an enhancement of VPN functions. On top of the service isolation provided by traditional VPNs on the network edge, network slicing also provides resource isolation within the network. The other reason was due to the term "network slicing" being considered closely associated with 5G. However, the technology and architecture we described were universal and could be used in non-5G scenarios. During the IETF's discussions on network slicing terms in 2017, the general opinion was to use relatively neutral technical terms instead of network slicing-specific ones. As such, the name VPN+ was chosen to better align with this consensus.

During network slicing innovation and standards promotion, a question emerged: what exactly does VPN+ add to VPN? In the past, common thinking was that a VPN maps to a virtual underlay network (e.g., resource slice) with guaranteed resources in a network domain. However, no clear term had been defined for this. Because many fields involved in the protocol extensions we were defining for network slicing related to this, we found it difficult to name these fields given that there was no term. It was not until the beginning of 2020, after discussions with Jie Dong, that we decided to use VTN as a general term to name resource slices.

It was not until later that I realized the debate over IP network slicing terms had just begun. As IP network slicing grew in popularity, various terms related to network slicing were generated in our teams. Examples include FlexE-based slicing, soft slicing, hard slicing, affinity attribute-based slicing, Flex-Algo-based slicing, exclusive/premium/express slices, industry slices, and tenant slices.

The various terms caused much conceptual confusion and brought difficulties to the technical discussions. As we had different understandings of network slicing terms and lacked agreement on basic terminology, discussions on technical solutions easily plunged into chaos. We therefore held several rounds of internal discussions to clarify concepts and define terms.

At the same time, chaos also plagued the IETF in terms of network slicing directions. Few cared about network slicing when it first emerged, but later, many wanted to get involved. As the saying goes, care leads to chaos. After heated debates, the most basic terms became uncertain. Given that 3GPP had defined network slicing, what could we call IETF's network slicing? The original suggestion was to inherit a 3GPP-defined TN slice. However, the term "transport" would be controversial because it has too many meanings in the IETF. After a series of debates, a compromise was made to call it "IETF network slicing". On top of that, people in the past generally said that network slicing could meet SLA requirements. But what does the SLA of network slicing actually mean? After another round of discussion, the terms SLO and SLE were finally determined. The IETF's network slicing design team was troubled by naming — an often painful process with which we sympathize — following our internal terminology discussions.

There was another big change in the term VTN. We introduced the concept of VTN in the VPN+ framework draft. Later, because some drafts used other terms for resource slices in the network domain, to reach an agreement on this important term, the IETF TEAS WG started to discuss the term for the resource slice. The parties then compromised to re-reach a consensus on the term NRP. But because multiple drafts related to VTN had already been accepted by related IETF WGs, the terms VTN and NRP both existed. The IETF community originally wanted to use terms unrelated to slicing. However, because the network slicing concept was deeply rooted in people's minds during application and deployment, unrelated terms made it difficult for people to understand and accept this concept. In NRP terminology, the meaning of "partition" is isolation, similar to that of resource slice. To avoid confusion caused by the terms VTN and NRP, this book uses resource slice (which is used together with service slice) as the basic term to introduce technical principles. In contrast, protocol extensions use VTN or NRP based on the terms in the current IETF drafts.

Finally, we determined the basic terms of network slicing as follows: The controller provides network slicing service interfaces in the northbound direction; the realization on the network side is divided into service slices (realized based on VPN technologies) and resource slices (realized based on VTN technologies). Other terms involved in network slicing are defined separately as follows: First, the initial concept of soft slicing is that only VPN-based service isolation is provided, and there is no resource isolation within the network. Hard slicing involves VPN-based service isolation on the edge side and resource isolation on the network side. To better reflect their characteristics, they are redefined as soft isolation and hard isolation. Second, although not defined as technical terms, exclusive/premium/express slices are used by carriers to provide IP network slicing as a commercial service for their customers. Third, FlexE-based slicing and affinity attribute-based slicing, the two most widely used terms internally, emphasize resource isolation and control plane technologies used by IP network slicing, respectively, and are not suitable for defining the overall solution. At the time of writing this book, two basic resource slicing solutions have been determined: SRv6 SID-based slicing and slice ID-based slicing. These two solutions adopt different combinations of resource partitioning and control plane technologies.

As the saying goes, if the name is not correct, the words will not ring true. The development of a technology is often accompanied by the birth of a new term system. However, many factors need to be considered in the process of defining terms — such a task is no easy feat. We gained a deeper understanding of this during the development of IP network slicing technologies. It is also an important goal of this book to determine these terms or at least set up a baseline to avoid potential chaos, even if they cannot be completely determined or may change in the future.

## 2.4.2 Why Is IPv6 Network Slicing Used?

IP network slicing can be realized based on either the IPv6 or MPLS data plane. If network slicing functions are provided based on IPv4, MPLS is required. In this sense, MPLS extends IPv4 functions.

The IPv4 data plane also supports extended functions, which can be implemented through the Options fields. However, because the software and hardware in earlier years delivered only limited forwarding capabilities, introducing extended functions through the Options field will lead to degraded forwarding or even prevent the functions from being implemented. This is why mainstream vendors are not willing to support IPv4 options on their devices. This unwillingness was further compounded with the development of IPv6, especially in 2016, when the IAB issued a statement suggesting that new functions be extended and standardized based on IPv6.

MPLS extends IP functions to some extent by adding a shim layer before the IP packet header. This means that, to implement the extensions of these functions, the entire network needs to be upgraded to use MPLS label-based forwarding to replace IP route forwarding. The implementation of MPLS becomes even more complex in inter-domain scenarios. These are the challenges facing MPLS.

Furthermore, as new network services are developed, MPLS faces more challenges. Such services require the MPLS data plane to carry metadata, but this cannot be achieved using either traditional MPLS labels or label stacks. For example, in the slice ID-based network slicing solution, the data plane needs to carry slice ID information. This requires an extension mechanism to be introduced to the MPLS data plane in order to carry the metadata. At the beginning of 2021, the IETF MPLS WG established a design team to define the MPLS data plane extension mechanism. The design of this mechanism is still in progress. The IPv6 extension header mechanism was defined at the beginning of the IPv6 design and can be easily extended to support new functions. However, this extension mechanism was not considered at the beginning of the MPLS design. Currently, the MPLS design team is considering the extension modes based on in-stack data and post-stack data.[6] Either mode would mean significant changes to the basic MPLS mechanism and many challenges in terms of compatibility and incremental deployment. Whether these modes can be widely recognized and deployed on a large scale is full of uncertainty.

The IPv6 data plane has taken the lead in the new era of 5G and cloud thanks to the following advantages: First, IPv6-based bearing technologies, such as SRv6, can flexibly use IP reachability to establish connections without needing to upgrade the entire network, as is the case with MPLS. Second, the IPv6 extension header mechanism makes it easy for the IPv6 data plane to provide encapsulation for new functions and implement incremental evolution. In other words, an IPv6 node that can support the new functions will parse their encapsulation and forward packets according to these functions, while an IPv6 node that cannot support the new functions will forward packets to other nodes as common IPv6 packets. These advantages are hugely beneficial in IPv6 supporting functions such as network slicing. In addition, IPv6 is relatively mature. This is why this book focuses on IPv6 network slicing.

MPLS network slicing is similar to IPv6 network slicing. The SR-MPLS-based network slicing solution is almost the same as the SRv6 SID-based network slicing solution. But there are some differences between MPLS and IPv6 slice ID-based network slicing solutions. When the IPv6 data plane is adopted, SRv6 SIDs can be used to obtain the next hop and outbound interface to forward packets. In addition, slice IDs carried in the packets can be used to indicate resources for service isolation. Similarly, when the MPLS data plane is used, SR-MPLS labels are used to obtain the next hop and outbound interface to forward packets. However, a new MPLS extension mechanism is required to carry slice IDs to indicate network resources reserved for slices. This book does not describe the data plane or control plane protocol extensions of MPLS used for IP network slicing. For more information on these, you can refer to related IETF drafts.

The development of a particular technology is closely related to its era and application requirements. For example, in the era of limited software and hardware capabilities, MPLS adopted a hardware-friendly design. With its advantages in forwarding performance and extension of functions such as VPN, TE, and FRR, MPLS drives the adoption of IP technologies on telecom networks. Currently, in an era where software and hardware capabilities are vastly improved, IPv6 will be predominant because it can meet the requirements of 5G and cloud services more conveniently based on the simplicity of IP-based connections and more flexible encapsulation and extension.

### 2.4.3 Transformation of the Network Identification System

Identification, forwarding, and control are three elements that make up the network architecture, with each one having a different impact on the architecture.

In the past, MPLS, IPv4, and IPv6 network systems were relatively stable as they had limited changes in identification and forwarding, meaning that network innovation focused on control. Typical examples of such innovation include path optimization based on MPLS TE and Software-Defined Networking (SDN).

The SR technology developed in the SDN era is a paradigm shift in terms of the forwarding mechanism. SR uses the source routing technology to replace the traditional MPLS forwarding technology, causing additional changes in route control — forwarding control becoming stateless rather than stateful.

Furthermore, IP network slicing brings about changes in network identification. Specifically, it introduces not only the location-oriented forwarding identifier but also the resource-oriented forwarding identifier. IP network slicing is a typical example of how changes to network identification affect both forwarding and control.

IP network slicing introduces the network-level resource identifier, which is different from the Differentiated Services Code Point (DSCP) used in traditional IP QoS to guarantee SLAs on specific nodes. IPv6 network slicing — following SRv6 network programming — is also a continuation of Layer 3.5 network innovation. It introduces new encapsulation and identification information through IPv6 extension headers to extend network functions.

It should be noted that, currently, the resource identifier introduced by IP network slicing takes effect in only limited domains. Whether it can take effect on the entire Internet in the future, like the DSCP of DiffServ does, needs to be further verified and observed.

## REFERENCES

[1] Huston G, Lord A, Smith P. IPv6 Address Prefix Reserved for Documentation [EB/OL]. (2004-07)[2022-09-30]. RFC 3849.

[2] Farrel A, Gray E, Drake J, et al. A Framework for IETF Network Slices [EB/OL]. (2022-12-21)[2022-12-30]. draft-ietf-teas-ietf-network-slices-17.

[3] Dong J, Bryant S, Li Z, et al. A Framework for Enhanced Virtual Private Networks (VPN+) Services [EB/OL]. (2022-9-20)[2022-09-30]. draft-ietf-teas-enhanced-vpn-11.

[4] Dong J, Li Z, Gong L, et al. Scalability Considerations for Network Resource Partition[EB/OL]. (2022-10-24)[2022-12-31]. draft-ietf-teas-nrp-scalability-01.

[5] Song H, Qin F, Ciavaglia L, Wang A. Network Telemetry Framework [EB/OL]. (2022-05-27)[2022-09-30]. RFC 9232.

[6] Bocci M, Bryant S, Drake J. Requirements for MPLS Network Action Indicators and MPLS Ancillary Data [EB/OL]. (2022-10-13)[2022-10-30]. draft-ietf-mpls-mna-requirements-04.

# CHAPTER 3

# Solutions for Realizing IPv6 Network Slicing

A COMPLETE IPv6 NETWORK SLICING solution must cover forwarding resource partitioning technologies, data-plane slice identification technologies, control-plane centralized and distributed control protocols, network slicing lifecycle management, and interfaces for interaction with customers' higher-level operation systems. For different network slicing scenarios where the slices, as well as the nodes and links they contain, vary in quantity, it is essential to select appropriate technologies in each plane of a network and then combine them to provide a network slicing solution that meets the requirements of slice services and network scalability. This chapter describes the solutions for realizing IPv6 network slicing — the SRv6 Segment Identifier (SID)-based network slicing solution, slice ID-based network slicing solution, hierarchical IPv6 network slicing solution, and mapping solution between IPv6 service slices and resource slices.

## 3.1 IPV6 NETWORK SLICING SOLUTION OVERVIEW

IPv6 network slicing solutions are mainly classified into the following two types according to the slice identification method adopted in the data plane:

SRv6 SID-based network slicing solution: SRv6 SIDs are used in the data plane to identify forwarding resources (such as interfaces, sub-interfaces, or Flex-Channels) reserved for different network slices.

DOI: 10.1201/9781032699868-5

The control plane defines the topology of each network slice based on the affinity attribute, Multi-Topology (MT), or Flexible Algorithm (Flex-Algo). This solution integrates existing control- and data-plane protocol mechanisms and leverages the forwarding resource partitioning capabilities of devices, making it possible to quickly deploy and apply network slices on existing networks based on service requirements.

Slice ID-based network slicing solution: Global slice IDs are used in the data plane to identify forwarding resources (such as interfaces, sub-interfaces, or Flex-Channels) reserved for different network slices. The control plane defines the topology of each network slice based on MT, or Flex-Algo. By extending data- and control-plane protocols, this solution allows multiple network slices to share one logical topology and resource attributes, thereby improving network slice scalability. It applies to scenarios where a large number of network slices with numerous nodes and links need to be deployed.

## 3.2 SRV6 SID-BASED NETWORK SLICING SOLUTION

The SRv6 SID-based network slicing solution uses the existing control- and data-plane protocol mechanisms to quickly create and adjust network slices based on service requirements, enabling fast slice deployment.

### 3.2.1 Data Plane in the SRv6 SID-Based Network Slicing Solution

SRv6 features flexible programmability, good scalability, and potential for realizing end-to-end converged transport. These features can be applied to network slicing to instantiate network slices and form an SRv6-based network slicing solution.

In the data plane, in addition to indicating network nodes and various network functions, SRv6 SIDs can have their semantics extended to indicate the network slices to which the nodes belong and the resource attributes of these network slices. Such SRv6 SIDs are called resource-aware SIDs. To differentiate packets from different network slices, a unique SRv6 SID needs to be allocated to each network slice. Network devices can determine the network slice to which a data packet belongs based on the SRv6 SID carried in the packet. The network devices can then process and forward the packet based on the attributes of the network slice. Resource-aware SRv6 SIDs can also be used to identify network resources allocated to network slices by network devices and links along the packet forwarding path — this is necessary if the network slices have a resource isolation requirement. This approach

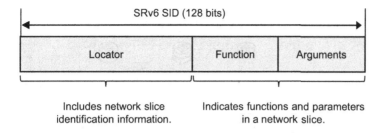

FIGURE 3.1    SRv6 SID structure.

ensures that resources reserved for a given slice are used to process and forward packets in that slice, thereby providing a reliable and deterministic SLA guarantee for services in the slice.

Figure 3.1 shows the structure of an SRv6 SID, which consists of the Locator and Function parts and may also include the optional Arguments part. During data packet forwarding on an SRv6 network, transit nodes do not need to identify or parse the Function part of an SRv6 SID. Instead, they only need to perform a table lookup based on the Locator part and then forward packets.[1] As such, to ensure that packets are processed in the same network slice from end to end, the Locator part of an SRv6 SID needs to include identification information for the network slice. In other words, the SRv6 Locator can be used to identify a network node and the network slice to which the node belongs. The Function and Arguments parts in an SRv6 SID can be used to respectively indicate the functions and parameters defined in a network slice.

Figure 3.2 provides an example of SRv6-based network slices. A carrier's Network Slice Controller (NSC) obtains the topology and resource attributes of a network slice based on network slice service requirements. It also instructs each network node in this topology to allocate the required network resources to the network slice. Network nodes can allocate resources in different ways (e.g., using FlexE interfaces, channelized sub-interfaces, or Flex-Channels).

Each network node needs to allocate a dedicated SRv6 locator — as well as specified network resources — to each network slice to which the node belongs. This locator is used to identify the location of the node in a specified network slice. With extended semantics, SRv6 Locator identifies not only network nodes but also network slices to which the nodes belong. Based on the SRv6 Locator, a forwarding node can determine the network slice to which a packet belongs and can then determine the forwarding

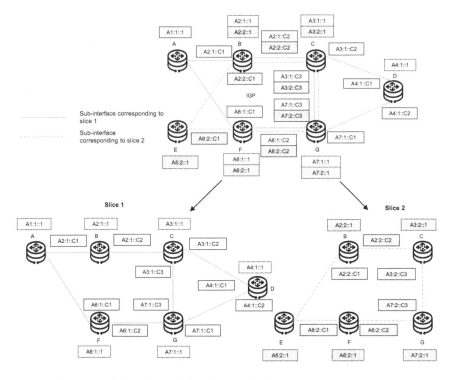

FIGURE 3.2    Example of SRv6-based network slices.

resources it allocates to the network slice. As shown in Figure 3.2, node B belongs to both network slices 1 and 2. Two SRv6 locators, A2:1::/64 and A2:2::/64, need to be allocated to node B, corresponding to slices 1 and 2, respectively.

To indicate various SRv6 functions in a network slice to which a network node belongs, the locator corresponding to the network slice needs to be used as a prefix, and SRv6 SIDs corresponding to these functions in the network slice need to be prefixed with the locator and then allocated. The SRv6 SIDs are used to instruct the involved node to perform packet forwarding corresponding to the SRv6 functions using the resources allocated to the slice. For example, in Figure 3.2, the physical interfaces that connect node B and node C belong to two network slices. As such, for each of these two slices, node B creates different sub-interfaces or sub-channels to partition slice resources. In addition, the SRv6 locators of these network slices are used as prefixes, and different End.X SIDs (A2:1::C2 and A2:2::C2) are allocated to these sub-interfaces or sub-channels with the prefixes. The End.X SIDs, respectively, instruct node B to use sub-interface

1 corresponding to network slice 1, or to use sub-interface 2 corresponding to network slice 2, to forward packets to node C.

By allocating corresponding forwarding resources, SRv6 locators, and SRv6 SIDs to different network slices, a single physical network can provide multiple isolated SRv6-based network slices.

Each network node in a network slice needs to compute and generate forwarding entries destined for other nodes in this slice. If multiple network slices have the same destination node, they need to have separate forwarding entries. In this case, each entry needs to use the locator allocated to the corresponding network slice as the route prefix. The IPv6 prefixes in the forwarding table are matched against the Locator part in the SRv6 SID carried in the Destination Address field of a data packet, thereby determining the next hop and outbound interface of the packet. If the outbound interface allocates exclusive resources to different network slices, the sub-interfaces or sub-channels on the outbound interface for these slices are also determined from the forwarding table.

Figure 3.2 is used as an example. Node A belongs to network slice 1, nodes D and E belong to network slice 2, and nodes B, C, F, and G belong to both network slice 1 and network slice 2. For simplicity, assume that the metric values of all links in the figure are the same. Table 3.1 provides the IPv6 forwarding table of node B.

SRv6 SIDs allocated by each network node to different network slices are stored in the corresponding node's local SID table. Each SID indicates how each node performs the SID-identified function in a specified network slice using the resources allocated to the slice. For example, in Table 3.2, End.X SID A2:2::C2 allocated for node B can be used to instruct node B to forward data packets to node C using sub-interface 2 of the B-C link in

TABLE 3.1    IPv6 Forwarding Table of Node B

| IPv6 Prefix | Next Hop | Outbound Interface/Sub-Interface |
|---|---|---|
| A1:1:: (node A in slice 1) | Node A | B's sub-interface 1 to A |
| A3:1:: (node C in slice 1) | Node C | B's sub-interface 1 to C |
| A3:2:: (node C in slice 2) | Node C | B's sub-interface 2 to C |
| A4:1:: (node D in slice 1) | Node C | B's sub-interface 1 to C |
| A5:2:: (node E in slice 2) | Node E | B's sub-interface 2 to E |
| A6:1:: (node F in slice 1) | Node A | B's sub-interface 1 to A |
| A6:2:: (node F in slice 2) | Node E | B's sub-interface 2 to E |
| A7:1:: (node G in slice 1) | Node C | B's sub-interface 1 to C |
| A7:2:: (node G in slice 2) | Node C | B's sub-interface 2 to C |

TABLE 3.2   Local SID Table of Node B

| SRv6 Local SID | Operation | Forwarding Instruction |
|---|---|---|
| A2:1::C1 | End.X | Use the sub-interface of the B-A link in slice 1 to forward the packet to node A. |
| A2:2::C1 | End.X | Use the sub-interface of the B-E link in slice 2 to forward the packet to node E. |
| A2:1::C2 | End.X | Use sub-interface 1 of the B-C link in slice 1 to forward the packet to node C. |
| A2:2::C2 | End.X | Use sub-interface 2 of the B-C link in slice 2 to forward the packet to node C. |
| A2:1::1 | End | Read the next SID in the SID list and forward the packet as instructed. |
| A2:2::1 | End | Read the next SID in the SID list and forward the packet as instructed. |

network slice 2. The End SID of node B is mainly used by transit network nodes on the forwarding path to perform the longest prefix match against the IPv6 forwarding table. Based on the IPv6 route prefix corresponding to the End SID's locator, a network node can determine the outbound interface from itself to node B. In addition, the network node can determine the forwarding resources reserved on this interface for the network slice that is indicated by the End SID's locator.

In each SRv6-based network slice, the SRv6 forwarding path of a data packet can be either an explicit path computed by a controller (centralized) or a shortest path computed by network nodes (distributed). The explicit path computed by a controller needs to be computed based on the topology and resource attributes of a network slice as well as other path constraints for services. The shortest path in a network slice computed by network nodes also needs to be computed based on the topology and metrics of the network slice. Figure 3.3 shows data packet forwarding using the SRv6 TE explicit path and the SRv6 BE path in a network slice. For a data packet to be forwarded using an SRv6 TE explicit path (A-F-G-D) in the network slice, an Segment Routing Header (SRH) needs to be encapsulated into the packet header. The SRH carries SRv6 End.X SIDs that identify links hop by hop in the slice, explicitly specifying a packet forwarding path and the sub-interface used by each hop. Forwarding data packets using an SRv6 BE path does not require an SRH to be encapsulated into the packet header. Instead, only the End SID of destination node D in the network slice is set in the Destination Address field of the IPv6 header. In this case, each network node along the path looks up the

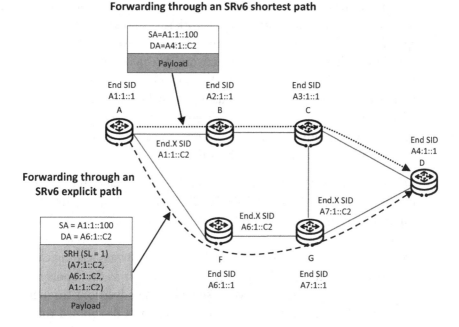

FIGURE 3.3 Data packet forwarding using the SRv6 TE explicit path and the SRv6 BE path.

destination address contained in the IPv6 header in the IPv6 forwarding table. These nodes can then determine their outbound interface and next hop by matching against the End SID's locator. In addition, each node determines the network resources to be used on the outbound interface according to the network slice associated with the locator.

### 3.2.2 Control Plane in the SRv6 SID-Based Network Slicing Solution

The control plane technologies involved in the SRv6 SID-based network slicing solution include the affinity attribute, MT, and Flex-Algo.

- The affinity attribute defines matching rules (i.e., include-any, include-all, and exclude-any) for links' administrative group attributes so as to select a group of links for constrained path computation. The administrative group attribute, in the bit mask form, contains information about link administration. Each bit represents an administrative group and is usually referred to as the color of a link. By setting a specific bit in the administrative group attribute of a link, a network administrator can set the color of the link. The SRv6

SID-based network slicing solution with the affinity attribute needs to specify a unique color for each network slice and set the bit corresponding to the specified color in the administrative group attribute for all links that belong to a given network slice in order to determine the topology of the network slice. This way, a group of links with the specified color can be selected by using the include-all matching rule of the affinity attribute to form a corresponding network slice topology. This group of links can be used for centralized computation of constrained paths in the network slice.

- MT — the Interior Gateway Protocol (IGP) MT routing technology — is defined in RFC 4915[2] and RFC 5120[3] published by the Internet Engineering Task Force (IETF). It is used to define multiple logical network topologies on an IP network and independently generate different routing tables for different logical topologies. By associating each network slice with an IGP topology, attributes such as the topologies and resources of different network slices can be advertised through MT. Then, both centralized path computation and distributed route computation for different network slices can be implemented based on their own attributes.

- Flex-Algo can be used to define a specific distributed route computation method, including the metric, constraint, algorithm, and other information related to route computation.[4] On a given network, all devices that use the same Flex-Algo to compute routes generate the same computation results, preventing routing loops from occurring. In this way, distributed route computation based on specific constraints is implemented. Each network slice is associated with a Flex-Algo, thereby allowing distributed constrained path computation to be implemented in different network slices based on Flex-Algo-defined constraints and path computation rules.

In the SRv6 SID-based network slicing solution, independent interfaces, or sub-interfaces, are created on each network node for different network slices. As described earlier, a network node allocates a unique SRv6 locator to each network slice. The node then uses the locator as a prefix and allocates a unique SRv6 End.X SID with the prefix to each interface or sub-interface of a network slice. This allows each node on the network to determine the corresponding interface or sub-interface for packet forwarding based on the SRv6 SID carried in a packet.

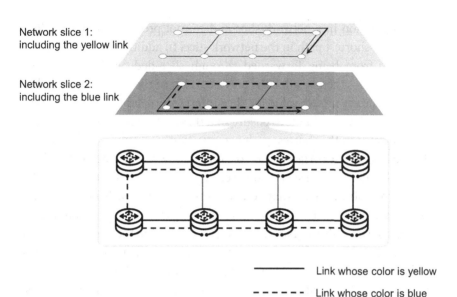

Network slice 1:
including the yellow link

Network slice 2:
including the blue link

——————— Link whose color is yellow

— — — — — Link whose color is blue

FIGURE 3.4   Affinity-based network slicing control plane.

With the affinity attribute-based control plane, as shown in Figure 3.4, a unique color needs to be specified for each network slice. On the interface or sub-interface that reserves resources for each of these network slices, the administrative group attribute — in which the bit corresponding to the specified color is set — needs to be configured. This makes it possible to group links with the same color into the same network slice in the control plane based on the affinity attribute. Each network node floods information about network topology connections, link administrative group attributes, SRv6 SIDs, and other TE attributes on the network through protocols such as IGP and reports the information to the NSC through protocols such as Border Gateway Protocol-Link State (BGP-LS). After collecting such information for the entire network, the NSC can form independent network slice views based on the affinity attribute. It can also compute explicit paths that meet specific constraints in each network slice based on TE attributes such as the bandwidth of the network slice.

Explicit paths computed based on a slice's affinity and other TE attributes by the NSC can be programmed as a SID list consisting of SRv6 SIDs corresponding to the slice's interfaces or sub-interfaces. This list can be used to explicitly indicate a packet forwarding path and forwarding resources reserved for processing slice service packets along the path on the SRv6 network. The affinity-based control plane solution supports only strict explicit path computation in a network slice and cannot provide data forwarding based on the shortest path in the network slice. In addition, to prevent non-slice traffic from being forwarded through slice-dedicated interfaces or sub-interfaces — thereby affecting service traffic in the slice — you need to configure a larger metric value for slice interfaces or sub-interfaces during network deployment. This is to ensure that these interfaces or sub-interfaces are not selected in the shortest path computation.

In the MT- or Flex-Algo-based control plane, a corresponding topology or Flex-Algo needs to be specified for each network slice. Furthermore, the interface or sub-interface that reserves resources for each network slice needs to be associated with the topology or Flex-Algo corresponding to the network slice. This makes it possible to determine the nodes and links included in a network slice in addition to the attribute information of this slice based on MT or Flex-Algo. Using either MT or Flex-Algo, each network node floods information about the topology connections, SRv6 SIDs, and TE attributes of each network slice on the network through protocols such as IGP and reports the information to the NSC through protocols such as BGP-LS. Based on MT and Flex-Algo, the NSC generates an independent network slice view for each network slice. It also computes explicit paths that meet specific constraints based on TE attributes such as the bandwidth of the network slice. When the MT- or Flex-Algo-based control plane is used, network devices are aware of the topology and path computation constraints of a network slice. In this way, these devices can support the distributed computation of the shortest path in the network slice based on the topology and path computation rules of the network slice.

## 3.3 SLICE ID-BASED NETWORK SLICING SOLUTION

In the SRv6 SID-based network slicing solution, when devices reserve resources for network slices, each device needs to plan a different logical topology for each network slice, as well as allocate a different SRv6 locator and different SRv6 SIDs to each network slice. However, the number of topologies, as well as SRv6 locators and SIDs, that need to be planned or allocated surges as the number of network slices increases, complicating network planning and management. Furthermore, network scalability is hampered because the control plane needs to advertise more information and the data plane needs to process more forwarding entries. To address these issues, one topology can be shared among multiple network slices, while dedicated slice IDs can be introduced to data packets to indicate the resources reserved for network slices used for packet forwarding. This not only reduces the number of topologies that need to be maintained on a network but also prevents the number of SRv6 locators and SIDs from multiplying as the number of slices increases. This effectively relieves the scalability pressure on the control and data planes caused by the growing number of network slices.

### 3.3.1 Data Plane in the Slice ID-Based Network Slicing Solution

The slice ID-based network slicing solution introduces the slice ID to data packets as a new identifier for network slices, allowing each network slice to have a resource identifier independent of the topology/path identifier. This solution also allows multiple network slices with the same topology to reuse the same topology/path identifier. For example, on an SRv6 network, when multiple network slices share one topology, they can use the same group of SRv6 locators and SIDs to indicate the next hop or forwarding path to the destination node. This effectively avoids the scalability problem in the SRv6 SID-based network slicing solution.

In the slice ID-based network slicing solution, a globally planned and allocated slice ID is used to identify forwarding resources (such as sub-interfaces or sub-channels) allocated by each network device to a network slice on an interface. This makes it possible to differentiate different sub-interfaces or sub-channels corresponding to different network slices on the same Layer 3 link and interface. A network device uses a two-dimensional forwarding identifier — consisting of a destination address in the IPv6 header and a slice ID — to jointly guide the forwarding of packets belonging to a particular network slice. The destination address is used to determine the topology and path for forwarding the packets, as well as to obtain the Layer 3 outbound interface for forwarding the packets. The slice ID is used to select the corresponding slice's sub-interface or sub-channel to the next-hop network device on the Layer 3 outbound interface.

As shown in Figure 3.5, three network slices are created on an SRv6 network. Network slices 2 and 3 have the same topology, which differs from that of network slice 1. As such, network slice 1 corresponds to a group of SRv6 locators and SIDs, and network slices 2 and 3 share another group of SRv6 locators and SIDs. On a physical interface that belongs to multiple network slices, different slice IDs are used to distinguish between sub-interfaces or sub-channels allocated to different network slices.

In the slice ID-based network slicing solution, two types of forwarding tables need to be generated on network devices.

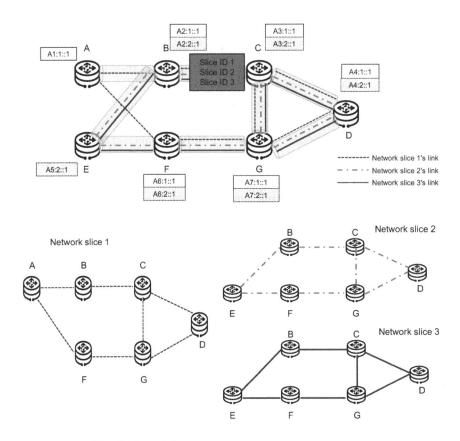

FIGURE 3.5 Slice ID-based data plane.

- Routing table, or SID table, is used to determine the Layer 3 outbound interface based on the SRv6 SID carried in the Destination Address field of a packet.

- Slice resource mapping table of the Layer 3 interface: used to determine the sub-interface or sub-channel of the Layer 3 interface for a slice according to the slice ID in a packet.

After receiving a data packet, a network device searches its routing table or local SID table based on the SRv6 SID in the destination address to obtain the next-hop device and Layer 3 outbound interface. This device then looks up the slice ID in the slice resource mapping table of the Layer 3 interface to determine the sub-interface or sub-channel of the slice.

Finally, the device uses the corresponding sub-interface or sub-channel to forward the service packet.

### 3.3.2 Control Plane in the Slice ID-Based Network Slicing Solution

As the number of network slices increases, so does the pressure on the control plane. To relieve this pressure, different network slices can reuse the same control protocol session, and network slices with the same topology can further reuse route computation results. If some network slices have different topologies, network nodes can define and advertise logical topologies and path computation constraints for network slices using MT or Flex-Algo. These nodes then advertise the mapping between network slices and topologies/Flex-Algos using control protocols such as IGP. Network nodes also need to report the collected topology and Flex-Algo information to the NSC using protocols such as BGP-LS. Each network device can compute routes from itself to other network nodes in a distributed manner based on the collected topology/Flex-Algo information and determine the shortest path in the network slice associated with the topology/Flex-Algo. Based on the collected topology and Flex-Algo information, as well as TE attributes such as network slice resources, the NSC computes explicit paths that meet specific service constraints in the network slice. The NSC then delivers these explicit paths to the headend through SRv6 Policies for forwarding specific services in the network slice.

## 3.4 COMPARISON BETWEEN IPV6 NETWORK SLICING SOLUTIONS

Table 3.3 compares the SRv6 SID-based network slicing solution with the slice ID-based network slicing solution.

Currently, the SRv6 SID-based network slicing solution can be quickly deployed on a network where SRv6 has been deployed. However, this solution has problems such as a small number of slices supported, complex configuration, and high control plane overhead. The slice ID-based network slicing solution solves these problems, but the IPv6 data plane needs to be extended. To meet future service requirements and ensure long-term sustainable development of networks, the slice ID-based network slicing solution is recommended.

TABLE 3.3 Comparison between Network Slicing Solutions

| Item | SRv6 SID-Based Network Slicing Solution | Slice ID-Based Network Slicing Solution |
|---|---|---|
| Slice quantity | About 10 | Thousands |
| Forwarding resource partitioning technologies | FlexE interface, channelized sub-interface, and Flex-Channel | FlexE interface, channelized sub-interface, and Flex-Channel |
| SLA guarantee | Strict | Strict |
| SRv6 locator/SIDs allocated to each slice | Yes | No |
| Configuration complexity | Complex | Simple |
| Slice topology presentation | Default or customized topology | Default or customized topology |
| Control plane overhead | Large | Small |
| Slice deployment mode | Pre-deployment | Pre-deployment or on-demand deployment |
| Whether a controller is required | Recommended | Recommended |
| Application scenario | A small number of network slices are required, and fast deployment is required on legacy networks. | A large number of tenant-level network slices need to be provided. |

## 3.5 HIERARCHICAL IPV6 NETWORK SLICING

In some network scenarios, hierarchical network slicing needs to be deployed. This type of network slicing allows level-2 network slices (sub-slices) to be created in a level-1 network slice (main network slice) by using a resource isolation technology such as Flex-Channel, thereby meeting the more refined network requirements of users. It can provide industry network slices, customer-oriented tenant network slices, and wholesale network slices,[5] among others. This section describes typical application scenarios for hierarchical slicing on IPv6 networks and provides possible technical solutions.

### 3.5.1 Application Scenarios of Hierarchical IPv6 Network Slicing

*3.5.1.1 Providing Tenant-Level Slices in an Industry Network Slice*

A typical deployment scenario for network slicing is to deploy network slices based on different industries, that is, to provide services that meet the requirements of multiple vertical industries on the same physical network. For example, industries such as healthcare, education, manufacturing, and government affairs each require dedicated IP network slices. In an industry-specific network slice, some or all customers in the industry may further need a separate network slice. This is where hierarchical network slicing comes in.

As shown in Figure 3.6, some universities in the education network slice may need independent network slices to connect different branch campuses of the same university. Similarly, in the healthcare network slice, some hospitals may need independent network slices to provide connections and services between different branch hospitals of the same hospital.

### 3.5.1.2 Providing Application-Level Network Slices in a Tenant Network Slice

Another deployment scenario is to provide a dedicated IP network slice as a level-1 network slice for an important customer. In this case, the customer may need to further split the network slice into different sub-slices to provide services for different applications.

As shown in Figure 3.7, the healthcare network slice can be further divided according to different types of medical services, such as remote

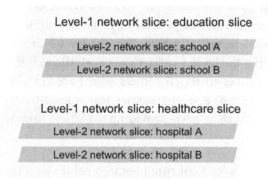

FIGURE 3.6　Hierarchical network slicing scenario 1.

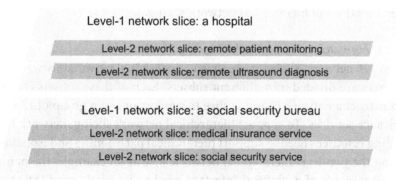

FIGURE 3.7　Hierarchical network slicing scenario 2.

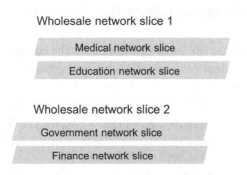

Wholesale network slice 1

Medical network slice

Education network slice

Wholesale network slice 2

Government network slice

Finance network slice

FIGURE 3.8    Hierarchical network slicing scenario 3.

patient monitoring and remote ultrasound diagnosis. Similarly, the government network slice can be further divided into a medical insurance service slice and a social security service slice.

### 3.5.1.3 Providing Network Slice Services in a Wholesale Network Slice

IP network slices can also be provided by a level-1 carrier to a level-2 carrier as a wholesale service. In this case, the level-2 carrier is not only a customer (leasing the level-1 carrier's network slices) but also a provider (providing sub-slices to its customers who have certain SLA requirements). In Figure 3.8, a level-1 carrier leases level-1 network slices to different level-2 carriers, each providing sub-slices oriented to different industries.

### 3.5.2 Technologies for Realizing Hierarchical IPv6 Network Slicing

This section describes forwarding resource partitioning modeling, data-plane resource identifiers, control-plane functions, and management-plane functions of hierarchical network slicing.

### 3.5.2.1 Forwarding Resource Partitioning Modeling

When IP network slicing is realized, underlying network forwarding resources are divided into different subsets. Each of these subsets is used to construct a network resource slice to support one or a group of IP network slice services. To support hierarchical network slicing, network forwarding resources need to support hierarchical partitioning and isolation. Taking the two-level hierarchical network slice as an example, the bandwidth resources of a physical interface need to be partitioned into two levels — this can be accomplished via multiple models.

In the first model, forwarding resources in a level-1 network slice are represented as a group of Layer 3 interfaces or sub-interfaces that have dedicated network resources. For the forwarding resources in a level-2 network slice, they are represented as virtual Layer 2 data channels on Layer 3 interfaces or sub-interfaces. Figure 3.9 shows this model.

In the second model, the resources of a level-1 network slice are represented as Layer 2 virtual sub-interfaces on Layer 3 interfaces. For resources in a level-2 network slice, they are represented as virtual data channels on Layer 2 virtual sub-interfaces. Figure 3.10 shows this model.

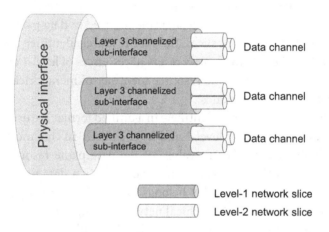

FIGURE 3.9   Model 1 for interfaces to reserve resources for slices.

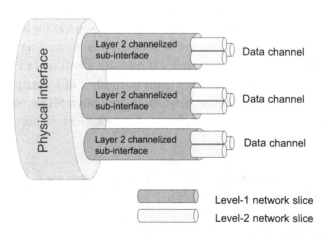

FIGURE 3.10   Model 2 for interfaces to reserve resources for slices.

The amount of information that the control plane protocol needs to distribute differs depending on the model selected. Different slice resource models can be used based on network slice deployment requirements.

### 3.5.2.2 Data-Plane Resource Identifier

Data packets can be steered to an IP network slice based on one or more fields in the packets. They are forwarded using forwarding resources reserved on the network for the slice. On a network edge node, service flows can be classified and mapped to corresponding network slices according to the local policy of the carrier. However, on a network transit node, a set of resources reserved for network slices can be determined using the dedicated slice resource identifier carried in data packets.

For hierarchical network slices, the slice resource identifier used in the data plane must be able to identify reserved resources of level-1 and level-2 network slices. The data plane resource identifier of hierarchical network slices is available in two modes:

First, data plane resource identifiers in a unified format are used to identify resources reserved for level-1 and level-2 slices. In this mode, level-1 and level-2 slices use different values of the data plane resource identifiers. The value of the resource identifier carried in a data packet is used to determine whether the packet belongs to the level-1 or level-2 network slice. For example, when hierarchical network slicing is realized using the slice ID-based network slicing solution, slice IDs with different values can be used to identify the level-1 and level-2 network slices.

Second, a hierarchical data plane identifier is used to identify resources reserved for level-1 and level-2 slices, as shown in Figure 3.11. This identifier is split into two parts: the first part identifies resources for level-1 slices; the second part identifies resources for level-2 slices. According to the data plane technology in use, the hierarchical resource identifier can be carried in consecutive fields or in different fields or headers of a data packet. For example, to realize hierarchical network slicing, SRv6 SIDs and slice IDs can be used to identify level-1 and level-2 network slices, respectively.

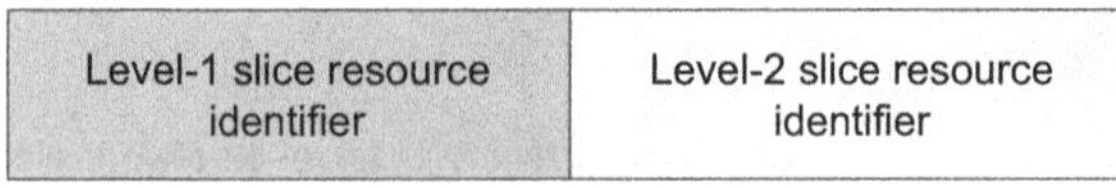

| Level-1 slice resource identifier | Level-2 slice resource identifier |
|---|---|

FIGURE 3.11   Hierarchical data-plane resource identifier.

### 3.5.2.3 Control-Plane Functions

The control plane can advertise resource attributes of network slices and associated data plane identifiers between network nodes and between network nodes and the NSC. For different resource partitioning models, resource information from hierarchical network slicing can be advertised as Layer 3 or Layer 2 network information using control protocols, thereby affecting the scalability of the network control plane to different degrees. In hierarchical network slicing scenarios, as the number of level-1 and level-2 network slices increases, selecting different forwarding resource partitioning models and data-plane identification technologies may have varying impacts on the control plane. For example, if the data plane of hierarchical network slicing uses a unified global resource identifier, its control plane functions in a similar way to that of a single-layer network slice, and information about the mapping between a level-1 network slice and a level-2 network slice can be advertised as required.

### 3.5.2.4 Management-Plane Functions

The hierarchical network slice management and control system needs to provide complete lifecycle management functions for level-1 and level-2 network slices. Level-1 and level-2 slices may be managed as independent resource slice instances, and inheritance and dependency relationships between the level-1 and level-2 slices need to be maintained.

## 3.6 IPV6 NETWORK SLICE MAPPING SOLUTION

On an edge node of a network slice, data packets from a service slice need to be mapped to the corresponding resource slice according to specified rules. In addition, resource slice identification information needs to be encapsulated into packet headers. There are multiple modes in which service slices can be mapped to resource slices, each involving different mapping rules. This book mainly describes the typical service slice mapping modes used on SRv6 networks.

On an SRv6 network, service slices can be mapped to either SRv6 Policies (TE explicit paths) or SRv6 shortest (BE) paths in resource slices, depending on the bearing mode of service slice packets over resource slices.

Figure 3.12 shows how service slice packets are steered to SRv6 Policies for resource slices.

The color extended community attribute plays an important role in the mapping from service slices to resource slices. RFC 9012 defines this

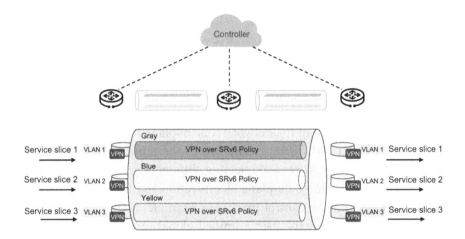

FIGURE 3.12    Service slice packets steered to SRv6 Policies in resource slices.

attribute, which is used for mapping service routes to bearing paths.[6] Each SRv6 Policy is uniquely identified by a combination of <Headend, Color, Endpoint>. The color attribute indicates the intent of an SRv6 Policy. It can be matched against the color attribute of a service route to map this route to the SRv6 Policy. For example, when BGP is used to advertise Virtual Private Network (VPN) service routes, the color extended community attribute can be carried. A simpler method is to directly configure the color attribute in the VPN instance corresponding to the service slice on the headend, indicating that the color attribute applies to all service routes in the VPN instance. The headend of an SRv6 Policy matches the color extended community attribute carried in the VPN service route or the color attribute configured in the VPN instance together with the next hop of the VPN service route against <Color, Endpoint> of the SRv6 Policy. The headend then maps the service route to the SRv6 Policy that meets the service intent. In this way, service packets can be steered to the SRv6 TE explicit path specified by the SRv6 Policy.

When service slices are mapped to SRv6 Policies in resource slices, the NSC uses control protocols such as BGP SRv6 Policy to deliver the SRv6 explicit path computed based on resource slices to the headend of the path. The headend matches the color extended community attribute and next hop carried in the service slice's service route advertised through BGP against the <Color, Endpoint> of the SRv6 Policy in the resource slice. This allows data packets from service slices to be steered to SRv6

Policies in the corresponding resource slices. The headend encapsulates the corresponding slice resource identifier and SRv6 SID list information into data packets based on the SRv6 Policy that the service route matches, instructs data packets to be forwarded along the explicit path indicated by the SRv6 SID list, and guides packet forwarding on each node along the path using the network resources indicated by the slice resource identifier. SRv6 Policies in resource slices are used to constrain data packets of service slices to be forwarded using only the paths and resources reserved in the resource slices. This provides resource isolation between different service slices and provides differentiated paths for different service flows among service slices.

Figure 3.13 shows how service slice packets are steered to SRv6 shortest (BE) paths in resource slices. When service slices are mapped to SRv6 shortest paths in resource slices, the NSC can use mapping policies to associate VPN instances of service slices with resource slices. In this way, data packets in service slices can be steered to SRv6 BE paths in corresponding resource slices. For example, the color attribute representing an intent can be configured for a resource slice, and the color attribute configured in the VPN instance of a service slice or the color extended community attribute carried in a service route advertised by BGP for the service slice can be matched with the color attribute of the resource slice. This allows data packets from service slice corresponding to the VPN instance to be steered to an SRv6 BE path in the corresponding resource slice.

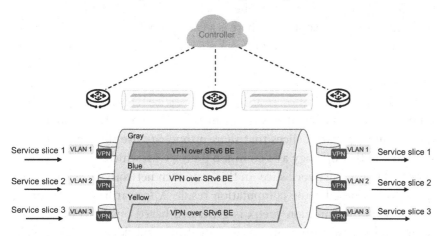

FIGURE 3.13    Service slice packets steered to SRv6 shortest (BE) paths in resource slices.

In addition to the preceding two modes, there is a more flexible method of mapping service slices to resource slices. This method specifies certain fields in a service slice data packet to be matched through the traffic matching policy of the headend for steering packets to the corresponding resource slice. For example, the DSCP field in an IP packet header, the 802.1p field in an Ethernet frame header, the source and destination IP addresses in packet headers, or information about the port through which the network edge node receives data packets can be specified for matching. When this method is adopted, packets can be mapped to an SRv6 Policy in a resource slice according to a matching policy, or SRv6 BE paths can be used to forward packets in a resource slice.

## 3.7 STORIES BEHIND NETWORK SLICING

### 3.7.1 SRv6 SID-Based Shared Topology Network Slicing Solution

This book defines two basic IP network slicing solutions: SRv6 SID-based network slicing and slice ID-based network slicing. The SRv6 SID-based network slicing solution adopts a per-slice, per-topology approach for advertising topology information and computing routes. This approach is constrained by IGP scalability, meaning that only a limited number of network slices can be supported. In contrast, the slice ID-based network slicing solution adopts a shared topology approach for advertising topology information and computing routes. This effectively reduces the IGP load and significantly improves the scalability of IP network slicing.

Besides these two solutions, there is a transitional solution that can also improve the scalability of IP network slicing. This solution is built upon the SRv6 SID-based network slicing solution. Specifically, different network slices advertise different SRv6 SIDs but can share topology information and route computation results, like in the slice ID-based network slice solution. The following takes SRv6 as an example. In the transitional solution, multiple network slices that share a topology use the locator corresponding to the topology as a common prefix, with which a sub-locator is allocated to each network slice. In this way, such network slices can share the topology-based route computation result. A forwarding entry corresponding to the common prefix is generated based on the computation result, and a forwarding entry prefixed with the sub-locator of each network slice is obtained based on the mapping relationship between slices and resources on the outbound interface. During packet forwarding, the traditional longest route match rule of IPv6 is used for table lookup.

Binding SRv6 SIDs to resources reserved on interfaces for slices is essentially the same as binding slice IDs to the resources. The main difference lies in data plane identification. Binding slice IDs rather than SRv6 SIDs to resources brings two advantages. First, slice IDs have a broader application than only in SR. For example, slice IDs can also be used with other types of IP tunnels to isolate resources. Second, in the slice ID-based network slicing solution, a slice ID has global significance and only needs to be locally configured on each network node — it does not need to be advertised using IGP. Even if the transitional solution adopts the shared topology approach, the binding relationships between SRv6 SIDs and network slices still need to be advertised to other network nodes through IGP, and the information is used for route computation. In other words, in the transitional solution, although sharing topology information can reduce route computation overhead, the amount of SRv6 SID information that IGP needs to advertise cannot be reduced. This is one of the main reasons why the SRv6 SID-based network slicing solution still lags behind the slice ID-based network slicing solution in terms of scalability.

The complexity or flexibility of the IP network slicing solution centers on there being multiple options at each layer. For example, resource partitioning and isolation technologies include FlexE, channelized sub-interface, and Flex-Channel; data-plane technologies include SR-MPLS, SRv6, and IPv6; and control-plane technologies include the affinity attribute, Flex-Algo, and MT. In terms of the approaches used to realize network slicing, the per-slice per-topology and shared topology approaches are available. The possibility of interleaving these different technologies and approaches means that there are many solution options. To keep this book relatively concise while also offering technical completeness, it focuses on the SRv6 SID-based per-slice per-topology network slicing solution and the slice ID-based shared topology network slicing solution among such solutions that use the IPv6 data plane. This book does not describe the MPLS-based network slicing solution or the SRv6 SID-based shared topology network slicing solution. For details about these solutions, see related documents.

### 3.7.2 Color/Affinity Attribute/Link Administrative Group

Color — a common term used in network slicing — is a concept that can easily cause confusion. To begin with, the color of a link and that of an SR Policy must be correctly distinguished. The link color indicates that the link belongs to a specific administrative group, whereas the SR Policy color represents an intent (i.e., a specific service requirement such as high bandwidth or low delay).

Terms related to the link color also include the administrative group and the affinity attribute. An administrative group is a link attribute defined in IGP and is used to indicate that a link belongs to an administrative group identified by one or more different colors. The affinity attribute is a tunnel attribute used as a constraint for tunnel path computation. That is, appropriate links can be selected based on affinity attributes as constraints to form a tunnel path. Affinity attribute rules for link selection include Include-Any, Include-All, and Exclude-Any. The term "color" may take on different meanings in different contexts. In some cases, it refers to an administrative group, which is a link attribute; in other cases, color refers to the affinity attribute, which is a tunnel attribute and corresponds to a constraint during path computation. Therefore, the true meaning of the word color needs to be distinguished based on the context.

In the Flex-Algo draft, Flex-Algo uses the term "link administrative groups (colors)" to refer to path computation constraints for selecting appropriate links. Flex-Algo also supports constraint rules such as Include-Any, Include-All, and Exclude. Based on the preceding discrimination of concepts, the affinity attribute should be used instead of the link administrative group (color). When we introduce the use of Flex-Algo as a control plane protocol in network slicing in this book, we still use the term "link administrative group" to comply with the Flex-Algo draft. However, we hope readers can appreciate the difference between the "link administrative group" as a link attribute and the "link administrative group" as a constraint for selecting links in Flex-Algo. We use the term "affinity attribute" in the control plane protocol part of this book where Flex-Algo is not involved and link colors are used as constraints for link selection.

## REFERENCES

[1] Filsfils C, Camarillo P, Leddy J, et al. Segment Routing over IPv6 (SRv6) Network Programming [EB/OL]. (2021–02)[2022–09–30]. RFC 8986.

[2] Psenak P, Mirtorabi S, Roy A, et al. Multi-Topology (MT) Routing in OSPF [EB/OL]. (2007-06)[2022–09–30]. RFC 4915.

[3] Przygienda T, Shen N, Sheth N. M-ISIS: Multi Topology (MT) Routing in Intermediate System to Intermediate Systems (IS-ISs) [EB/OL]. (2008-02) [2022–09–30]. RFC 5120.

[4] Psenak P, Hegde S, Filsfils C, et al. IGP Flexible Algorithm [EB/OL]. (2022-10-17)[2022-10-30]. draft-ietf-lsr-flex-algo-26.

[5] Dong J, Li Z. Considerations about Hierarchical IETF Network Slices [EB/OL]. (2022-09-07)[2022-09-30]. draft-dong-teas-hierarchical-ietf-network-slice-01.

[6] Patel K, Van de Velde G, Sangli S, et al. The BGP Tunnel Encapsulation Attribute [EB/OL]. (2021-03)[2022-09-30]. RFC 9012.

# CHAPTER 4

# Resource Partitioning Technologies for IPv6 Network Slicing

To meet diversified and differentiated service connection and quality requirements while also ensuring that different slice services on the same IPv6 network do not affect each other, IPv6 network slicing requires network devices to have resource partitioning capability. With this capability, network devices can allocate isolated forwarding resources to different network slices. This chapter describes the main technologies used to implement forwarding resource partitioning for IPv6 network slicing, including Flexible Ethernet (FlexE) and Hierarchical Quality of Service (HQoS)-based resource partitioning technologies — channelized sub-interface and Flex-Channel.

## 4.1 FLEXE-BASED RESOURCE PARTITIONING

The 5G era has given rise to increasing demand for higher mobile transport bandwidth. Furthermore, customers expect a unified network to transport various services, such as home broadband, private line access, and mobile transport services. Consequently, telecommunication network interfaces are facing much higher requirements.

Standard Ethernet interfaces, when used as telecommunication network interfaces, lead to the following issues:

DOI: 10.1201/9781032699868-6

- Inability to support more flexible bandwidth granularities: IEEE 802.3 typically needs several years to define a new interface standard, making it impossible to respond to fast-changing service and application requirements. Because formulating an interface standard requires triggering conditions, new standards cannot be created immediately whenever a new bandwidth requirement arises. Furthermore, the rates of Ethernet interfaces are restricted by the IEEE 802.3-defined interface rate ladder (10GE-25GE-40GE-50GE-100GE-200GE-400GE). The combination of these factors means that Ethernet interfaces cannot address the need for more flexible bandwidth granularities in diverse service and application scenarios.

- Rate adaptation required between an interconnected IP device and optical transmission device: If these two types of devices are interconnected, the link rate of the optical transmission device must adapt to the Ethernet rate of the corresponding User-Network Interface (UNI). In terms of interface capabilities, however, IP and optical transmission devices develop at different paces. This may cause the interconnection to fail.

- Inability to support enhanced QoS for multi-service transport: Standard Ethernet interfaces perform scheduling based on QoS packet priorities. As a result, long packets will block the pipe and increase the delay of short packets, meaning that one service may affect other ones.

These issues are solved by FlexE,[1] an interface technology that can be used to partition resources for network slicing on a transport network. As shown in Figure 4.1, based on the standard Ethernet technology defined in IEEE 802.3, FlexE decouples the MAC layer of a FlexE interface from its Physical Layer (PHY) by adding a FlexE shim layer between them. With FlexE, there no longer needs to be a one-to-one mapping between MACs and PHYs.

FlexE interfaces have the following advantages:

- More flexible bandwidth granularities: The rates of FlexE clients can be flexibly configured based on diverse services and application scenarios rather than being limited to those defined in the existing IEEE 802.3 standard.

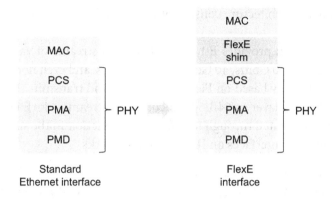

PCS: Physical Coding Sublayer
PMA: Physical Medium Attachment
PMD: Physical Media Dependent

FIGURE 4.1   Structures of standard Ethernet and FlexE interfaces.

- Decoupling from optical transmission device capabilities: The sub-rating function of FlexE enables the Ethernet interface rates of IP devices to be decoupled from the link rates of optical transmission devices. This means that rate adaptation between the two types of devices is no longer necessary, allowing the existing optical transmission network to be maximally utilized to support Ethernet interfaces with new standard bandwidths.

- Supporting Service-Level Agreement (SLA) guarantee for multiservice transport: FlexE interfaces provide isolation of channelized hardware resources at the PHY to guarantee SLAs and bandwidth for services.

### 4.1.1  General Architecture of FlexE

FlexE adopts the client/group architecture, as shown in Figure 4.2. In this architecture, multiple Ethernet PHYs are bonded to form a FlexE group, and multiple FlexE clients can be mapped to one or more PHYs in the group for packet transmission. Owing to the reuse of IEEE 802.3-defined Ethernet technology, the FlexE architecture can provide enhanced functions based on existing Ethernet MACs and PHYs.

The general architecture consists of three parts:

- FlexE client: provides Ethernet MAC data streams of various rates (including 10 Gbit/s, 40 Gbit/s, $N$ x 25 Gbit/s, and even non-standard rates) flexibly based on FlexE technology and transmits them to the FlexE shim layer as 64B/66B encoded bit streams. FlexE clients can be implemented through interfaces and function in the same way as traditional interfaces on IP/Ethernet networks.

- FlexE shim: a logical layer inserted between the MAC and PCS sublayers of the standard Ethernet architecture. It implements core FlexE functions through calendar slot distribution.

- FlexE group: a set of Ethernet physical interfaces (PHYs) defined in IEEE 802.3. It divides the bandwidths of multiple PHYs based on the 5 Gbit/s timeslot granularity.

In Figure 4.2, multiple Ethernet PHYs are bonded into a FlexE group to carry one or more FlexE client data streams that are distributed and mapped by the FlexE shim.

To describe how the FlexE shim — the core function of FlexE interfaces — is implemented, the following uses a FlexE group that consists of 100GE PHYs as an example.

As shown in Figure 4.3, the FlexE shim divides each 100GE PHY in a FlexE group into 20 timeslots for data transmission, with each timeslot

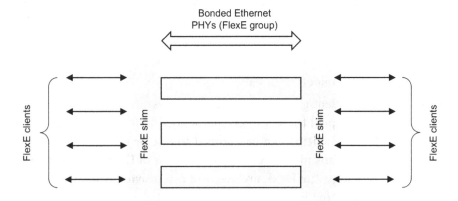

FIGURE 4.2   General architecture of FlexE.

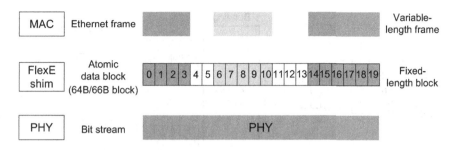

FIGURE 4.3   FlexE shim mechanism.

providing a bandwidth of 5 Gbit/s. This means that a FlexE client can be flexibly assigned bandwidth in integer multiples of 5 Gbit/s. The Ethernet frames of FlexE clients are partitioned into 64B/66B blocks, which are then mapped and distributed to timeslots of a FlexE group through the FlexE shim, thereby achieving strict isolation between the blocks.

### 4.1.2  FlexE Functions

FlexE provides three main functions: bonding, channelization, and subrating. The mappings between FlexE clients and groups allow FlexE clients to flexibly provide bandwidth to upper-layer applications without being constrained to the rates supported by Ethernet PHYs.

Based on these functions, FlexE can implement on-demand interface bandwidth allocation and hard isolation. It can be used on IP networks to provide ultra-high bandwidth interfaces, network slicing, interconnection with optical transmission devices, and more.

#### 4.1.2.1  Bonding

As shown in Figure 4.4, multiple PHYs are bonded through the FlexE shim to achieve a higher interface rate. For example, two 100GE PHYs can be bonded to provide a MAC rate of 200 Gbit/s.

#### 4.1.2.2  Channelization

As shown in Figure 4.5, channelization allows multiple low-rate MAC data streams to share one or more PHYs. Specifically, data from different FlexE clients is transmitted in different timeslots for one or multiple PHYs. For example, one 100GE PHY is divided into twenty 5 Gbit/s timeslots, which are combined based on service requirements to carry four MAC data streams (35 Gbit/s, 25 Gbit/s, 20 Gbit/s, and 20 Gbit/s),

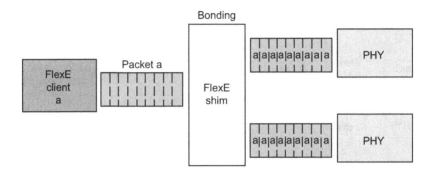

FIGURE 4.4    Bonding.

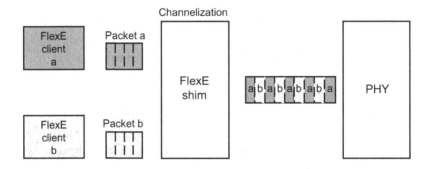

FIGURE 4.5    Channelization.

or a FlexE group consisting of three 100GE PHYs is divided into sixty 5 Gbit/s timeslots to carry three MAC data streams (150 Gbit/s, 125 Gbit/s, and 25 Gbit/s).

### 4.1.2.3 Sub-Rating

As shown in Figure 4.6, sub-rating allows MAC data streams with a single low rate to share one or more PHYs. Specifically, some timeslots of the PHYs are allocated to FlexE clients, and specially defined error control blocks are not used to carry services, lowering the interface rate. For example, a 100GE PHY carries only 50 Gbit/s MAC data streams. To some extent, sub-rating can be considered a subset of channelization.

To sum up, in the FlexE-based client/group architecture, multiple FlexE clients can be mapped to a FlexE group consisting of PHYs for data transmission, implementing bonding, channelization, and sub-rating functions.

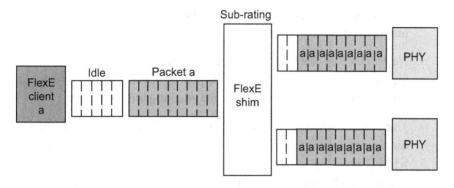

FIGURE 4.6　Sub-rating.

### 4.1.3　FlexE for IPv6 Network Slicing

After the FlexE shim layer is introduced, the resources of a physical interface can be divided into several sub-channels (called FlexE interfaces) based on timeslots. This enables flexible use and refined management of interface resources. A FlexE interface is equivalent to a physical interface, with its bandwidth resources strictly isolated from those of other FlexE interfaces. FlexE interfaces can provide an ultra-low delay and have extremely little delay interference with each other. This means they can be used to carry Ultra-Reliable Low-Latency Communication (URLLC) services — such as differential protection services for power grids — that have high requirements on delay SLAs.

Using FlexE technology to provide resource partitioning for network slicing has the following advantages:

- Partitioned FlexE interfaces can provide guaranteed bandwidth and a stable delay. And they can hard-isolate resources between network slices so that services in different network slices do not affect each other.

- Through Time Division Multiplexing (TDM), one standard FlexE 5 Gbit/s timeslot can be further divided into multiple sub-timeslots. The minimum resource partitioning granularity is 1 Gbit/s, meeting the requirements of 5G vertical industries for planning network slices with $N \times 1$ Gbit/s bandwidth.

- Combined with other resource partitioning technologies, such as channelized sub-interface or Flex-Channel, the FlexE interface technology supports hierarchical network slicing to meet requirements for more complex service isolation.

- Network slices can be deployed in minutes for fast service provisioning. Network slice resources can be pre-deployed through a network slice controller or deployed on demand along with services.

- The bandwidth of a network slice can be dynamically adjusted by increasing or decreasing the corresponding FlexE interface bandwidth, avoiding unnecessary hardware costs — such as those involved in board replacement — while also ensuring smooth service scaling.

## 4.2 QOS FUNDAMENTALS

### 4.2.1 QoS Overview

Quality of Service (QoS) refers to an assembly of techniques for providing various network services with the required quality. While it does not increase the network bandwidth, it does improve the utilization of network resources and allows different types of traffic to compete for such resources based on their priorities. This allows important data applications such as voice and video to be processed preferentially on the network.

The quality of service can be characterized by the following parameters:

- Bandwidth: refers to the maximum number of data bits transmitted between two ends within a specified period or the average rate at which specific data flows are transmitted between two network nodes.

- Delay: refers to the period of time between when a source device sends a packet and when a destination device receives the packet. Take voice transmission as an example. Here, delay refers to the period from when words are spoken to when they are heard. A long delay during voice transmission may distort or even interrupt conversations.

- Jitter: refers to the difference in delays of packets in the same flow. Some services, especially real-time services such as voice and video, are highly sensitive to jitter, which may interrupt them. Jitter may also affect the proper functioning of network protocols. For example, extreme jitter may cause specific protocols whose packets are expected to be transmitted at a fixed interval to flap.

- Packet loss rate: refers to the percentage of packets lost during packet transmission. Slight packet loss does not affect services severely. For example, users cannot perceive the loss of a bit or a packet in voice transmission. However, heavy packet loss over a period of time affects the service experience. Therefore, QoS focuses more on the packet loss rate.

### 4.2.1.1 QoS Service Models

Network applications require successful E2E communication. Because traffic may traverse multiple devices on one or more networks before reaching the destination host, the capability to provide an E2E QoS is required. This capability is provided through service models based on specific requirements.

QoS service models include Best-Effort (BE), Integrated Service (IntServ),[2] and Differentiated Service (DiffServ).[3]

4.2.1.1.1 BE Model   This is the default service model on the Internet and the simplest of the three. It applies to services that do not have high requirements on delay or jitter, such as File Transfer Protocol (FTP) and email. In this model, without any notification to the network, an application can send any number of packets at any time. The network then makes best efforts to send the packets but does not provide any assurance for delay, jitter, or other performance indicators.

4.2.1.1.2 IntServ Model   In the IntServ model, an application uses a signaling protocol to notify a network node of its traffic parameters and apply for a specific level of QoS before sending packets, as shown in Figure 4.7. Within the range specified by the traffic parameters, the network node attempts to reserve resources for the application. If the network node cannot meet the requirement, it returns a failure message. Otherwise, it sends an acknowledgment message, indicating that the application can start to send packets. The packets sent by the application must be within the range specified by the traffic parameters. To satisfy the performance requirements of the application, the network node maintains a state for each data flow and performs QoS behaviors based on this state.

The IntServ model uses the Resource Reservation Protocol (RSVP) as the signaling protocol. RSVP is a control protocol running above the IP

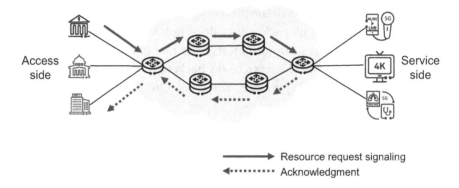

Resource request signaling
Acknowledgment

FIGURE 4.7    IntServ model.

layer. It is used to transmit resource reservation information between net-work nodes and reserve resources.

During the establishment of E2E connections through RSVP, network nodes along the path must maintain state information (called soft state) for each data flow. A soft state is a temporary state that is periodically refreshed by RSVP. Through the soft state, each network node can deter-mine whether sufficient resources can be reserved. A path can be estab-lished only when all network nodes provide sufficient resources for RSVP requests of the same data flow.

Because the IntServ model uses RSVP to request and reserve resources across the entire network, all network nodes must support RSVP. Each network node must also periodically exchange state information with its neighbor, consuming many resources. More importantly, all network nodes need to maintain state information for each data flow. As there are thousands of data flows on the backbone network, the IntServ model is not widely used due to the inherent scalability problems of RSVP.

4.2.1.1.3 DiffServ Model    The DiffServ model classifies traffic on a net-work into multiple classes and provides differentiated processing for each class, meeting the requirements of different services for performance indi-cators such as packet loss rate and delay.

As shown in Figure 4.8, a DiffServ domain consists of multiple network nodes. The ingress node can flexibly classify packets based on multiple conditions (such as the source address, destination address, and protocol type), marking different classes of packets with appropriate DSCP values.

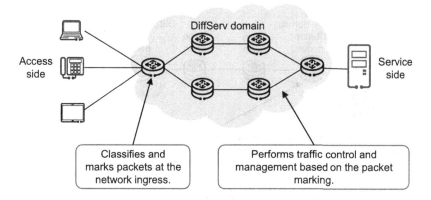

FIGURE 4.8   DiffServ model.

Other nodes in the DiffServ domain only need to identify these markings and perform corresponding traffic control and management.

Unlike the IntServ model, the DiffServ model does not require a signaling protocol. In the DiffServ model, an application does not need to apply for resources from a network node before sending packets. Instead, the application notifies the network node of its QoS requirements by setting QoS parameters in the packet header. Furthermore, the network node provides services based on the QoS parameters specified for each data flow, controls and forwards traffic in a differentiated manner, and provides an E2E QoS, meaning it does not need to maintain a state for each data flow.

The DiffServ model fully leverages the flexibility and scalability of IP networks and transforms the complex QoS requirements into Per-Hop Behaviors (PHBs) using the Traffic Class field in packets, greatly reducing the use of signaling. Therefore, the DiffServ model not only meets the scalability requirements of carrier networks, but also is easy to deploy.

## 4.2.2  DiffServ QoS

### 4.2.2.1  Fundamentals of the DiffServ Model

4.2.2.1.1  DiffServ Domain   A Differentiated Services (DiffServ) domain is the basic unit for implementing the DiffServ model. It consists of a group of connected DiffServ nodes that use the same service policy and implement a consistent PHB, and it typically comprises one or more networks belonging to the same administrative department. For example, a DiffServ domain can be an Internet Service Provider (ISP) network or an intranet of an enterprise. As shown in Figure 4.9, one or more DiffServ domains may exist in a DiffServ model.

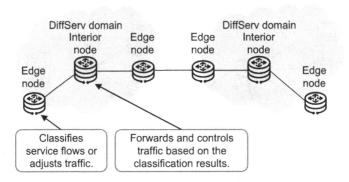

FIGURE 4.9    Basic composition of the DiffServ model.

A DiffServ node is classified as either a DiffServ interior node or a DiffServ edge node. A DiffServ edge node is connected to another DiffServ domain or a DiffServ-incapable domain, classifying or conditioning service traffic entering this DiffServ domain. A DiffServ interior node is used for connecting DiffServ edge nodes and other interior nodes in the same DiffServ domain and performs traffic classification and control.

4.2.2.1.2 QoS Priority Fields    The DiffServ model provides differentiated service quality based on the QoS information recorded in some fields of the packet header.

As shown in Figure 4.10, an IPv4 packet is identified using the first six bits (DSCP) of the Type of Service (ToS) field in the IPv4 header. IPv4 packets can be classified into a maximum of 64 types. The TC field in the IPv6 header is eight bits long, and its first six bits (DSCP) are used to identify the service type of a packet. The TC field has the same function as the ToS field in an IPv4 packet.

4.2.2.1.3 PHB    Another important concept in the DiffServ model is PHB,[3] which reflects the Class of Service during packet forwarding. PHBs describe the externally visible forwarding behaviors adopted by a DiffServ node for packets with the same DSCP value. PHBs can be defined by DSCP values or some visible service characteristics, such as the delay, jitter, or packet loss rate. PHBs define only some externally visible forwarding behaviors but do not specify the implementation mechanism.

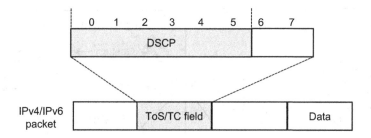

FIGURE 4.10   ToS/TC field in an IPv4/IPv6 packet.

The IETF defines four standard PHBs: Class Selector (CS), Expedited Forwarding (EF), Assured Forwarding (AF), and BE. BE is the default PHB. For details about the DSCP value and meaning corresponding to each PHB, see related standards.

### 4.2.2.2 Basic Components of the DiffServ Model

The DiffServ model consists of four components:

- Traffic classification and marking: Data packets are placed into different classes (traffic classification) and marked with different priorities (traffic marking) to implement differentiated services. Traffic classification does not modify the original data packets, but traffic marking does.

- Traffic policing and shaping: The traffic rate is limited to the specified bandwidth. Traffic policing drops excess traffic when the traffic rate exceeds the limit, whereas traffic shaping buffers excess traffic.

- Congestion avoidance: The usage of network resources is monitored. If congestion worsens, packets are dropped to relieve network congestion.

- Congestion management: If congestion occurs, packets are buffered in queues and forwarded in the sequence determined by a scheduling algorithm.

Among the preceding four components, the traffic classification and marking component is the prerequisite and basis for implementing differentiated services. The other three components control network traffic and allocated resources from different aspects to provide differentiated services. The four components typically work in the sequence shown in Figure 4.11.

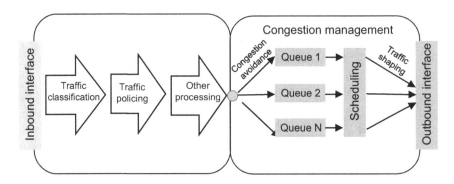

FIGURE 4.11   Workflow of the DiffServ model's components.

A network node processes a packet on both the inbound and outbound interfaces. On the inbound interface, the node classifies or marks the packet and limits the traffic rate through traffic policing. On the outbound interface, the node uses congestion avoidance to monitor the usage of network resources in real time. If congestion occurs, it uses congestion management to schedule network resources and uses traffic shaping to buffer excess traffic before the packet leaves. This reduces the impact of traffic bursts on downstream nodes.

On the basis of BE forwarding on an IP network, DiffServ QoS implements differentiated scheduling for services with different priorities and provides differentiated services with coarse granularity. This meets the requirements of traditional services on the IP network. However, because DiffServ QoS cannot differentiate different users or services with the same priority, reserve resources for them, or prevent them from impacting each other, it is typically not considered a resource partitioning technology for network slicing.

### 4.2.2.3 Basic QoS Scheduling Model

As shown in Figure 4.12, the scheduling model consists of a scheduler and scheduled objects.

The scheduler schedules multiple queues and utilizes a specific scheduling algorithm to determine the sequence in which packets are sent among the queues. Scheduling algorithms include Strict Priority (SP), Deficit Round Robin (DRR), Weighted Round Robin (WRR), Weighted Deficit Round Robin (WDRR), and Weighted Fair Queuing (WFQ).

The scheduler has only one action — selecting a queue. When the scheduler selects a queue, it preferentially sends the packets in the queue.

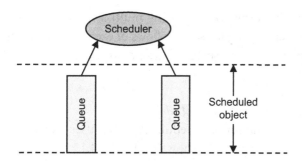

FIGURE 4.12    Basic QoS scheduling model.

Scheduled objects are also called queues. Packets enter different queues according to certain mappings. Queues are assigned the following attributes:

1. Priority or weight

2. Peak Information Rate (PIR)

3. Tail drop and Weighted Random Early Detection (WRED)

A queue involves the following actions:

1. Entering a queue: The system determines whether to drop a received packet based on the drop policy. If the packet is not dropped, it enters the tail of the queue.

2. Leaving a queue: After a queue is selected by the scheduler, the packets in the front of the queue are shaped and then sent out of the queue.

### 4.2.3  HQoS

HQoS uses a multi-level queue scheduling mechanism to guarantee the bandwidth of multiple services for multiple users in the DiffServ model.

Unlike HQoS, DiffServ QoS uses one-level scheduling. Traffic scheduling based on a port can only enable the port to differentiate service priorities instead of users. As long as the traffic of the same priority uses the same port queue, the traffic of different users competes for the same queue resource. This makes it impossible to distinguish the single service flow of a single user on the port. By using multi-level scheduling, HQoS performs queue scheduling for service flows of each user, differentiating traffic of different users and services and providing independent bandwidth management.

### 4.2.3.1 Hierarchical Scheduling Model

To implement hierarchical scheduling, HQoS uses a tree-shaped hierarchical scheduling model. As shown in Figure 4.13, the model consists of the following three types of nodes:

- Leaf node: is located at the bottom layer and identifies a queue.

- Branch/Transit node: is located at the middle layer and functions as both a scheduler and a scheduled object.

- Root node: is located at the top layer and identifies the top-level scheduler.

A scheduler can schedule multiple queues or other schedulers. It can be considered a parent node, with the scheduled queues and schedulers being considered its child nodes. The parent node is the traffic aggregation point of multiple child nodes.

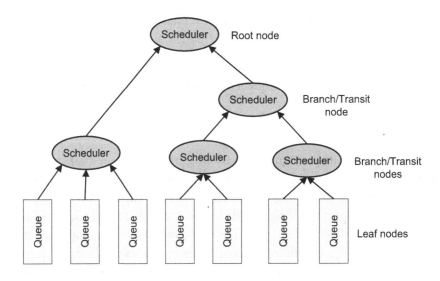

FIGURE 4.13  Hierarchical scheduling model.

Classification rules and control parameters can be specified for each node to classify and control traffic. Such rules based on different requirements (e.g., user or service requirements) can be configured for nodes at different layers, and different control actions can be performed for traffic on different nodes. This achieves multi-layer, multi-user, and multi-service traffic management.

### 4.2.3.2 HQoS Hierarchies

HQoS adopts flexible hierarchies to implement more flexible scheduling, as shown in Figure 4.14. It can maintain only one layer of transit nodes to implement three-layer (root/transit/leaf) scheduling or use multiple layers of transit nodes to implement multi-layer scheduling. It can also combine two or more scheduling models hierarchically by mapping packets output from one scheduling model to leaf nodes in another scheduling model.

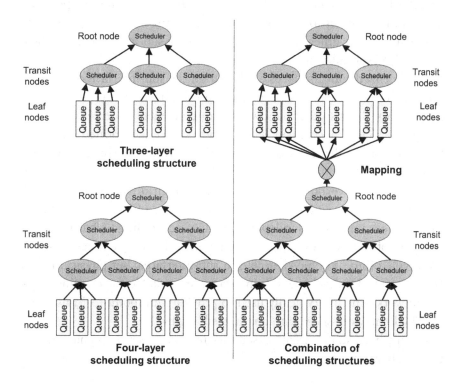

FIGURE 4.14 Flexible HQoS hierarchies.

## 4.3 HQOS-BASED RESOURCE PARTITIONING TECHNOLOGIES

HQoS scheduling is a single-node behavior, meaning that it is performed only on an access node and not on any other nodes on the network. Consequently, in order to implement resource assurance and traffic scheduling for each network slice consistently across the entire network, slice-specific resource reservation and queue scheduling need to be deployed on each node. This ensures that the network provides E2E-guaranteed performance for network slicing services.

### 4.3.1 Channelized Sub-Interface

A channelized sub-interface is created by dividing an Ethernet physical interface into sub-interfaces and enabling channelization on them. With physical interfaces now supporting higher and higher bandwidths, a single physical interface usually carries traffic from multiple service types or multiple users. In this case, HQoS can be used to divide a high-rate physical Ethernet interface into sub-interfaces and allocate independent bandwidth resources to each one, thereby isolating different types of services carried over different sub-interfaces. These sub-interfaces are called channelized sub-interfaces.

Channelized sub-interfaces are based on the sub-interface configuration model. Independent channelized sub-interfaces can be configured for network slices so that bandwidth can be flexibly allocated by leveraging the HQoS mechanism. Each network slice is allocated exclusive bandwidth and a dedicated scheduling tree to reserve resources for slice services.

Different service flows are forwarded through different channelized sub-interfaces with dot1q (VLAN) encapsulation, and each channelized sub-interface implements independent HQoS scheduling to isolate different types of services. As shown in Figure 4.15, physical interfaces 1 and 2 are divided into multiple channelized sub-interfaces, but physical interface 3 is not. Channelized sub-interfaces are suitable for creating logical networks and are typically used to provide Multipoint-to-Multipoint (MP2MP) network slices with guaranteed bandwidth.

Channelized sub-interface-based slice resource reservation has the following characteristics:

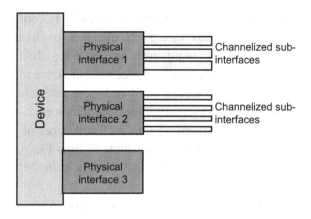

FIGURE 4.15    Channelized sub-interfaces.

- Strict resource isolation: Based on the sub-interface configuration model, slice resources are reserved to prevent slice services from preempting the resources of other network slices when traffic bursts occur.

- Fine bandwidth granularity: Channelized sub-interfaces can be used together with physical interfaces or FlexE interfaces to divide a high-rate interface into multiple lower-rate sub-interfaces, providing resource slices with more flexible bandwidth.

If we compare a physical interface to a multi-lane road, we can view a channelized sub-interface as an independent "lane" on that road. Each of these "lanes" is assigned to each network slice on a network device. Service traffic in a "lane" cannot preempt another "lane" during transmission. This ensures strict isolation of services in different slices and effectively prevents resource preemption between slices when traffic bursts occur.

### 4.3.2 Flex-Channel

In some network slicing applications where additional overheads of interface configuration and management need to be avoided, Flex-Channel technology can be used to flexibly partition network resources.

A Flex-Channel is a data channel to which independent queue and bandwidth resources are allocated based on the HQoS mechanism. These bandwidth resources are strictly isolated between each Flex-Channel. An independent sub-channel with reserved bandwidth is configured for a network slice on a physical interface, FlexE interface, or channelized sub-interface in order to allocate bandwidth flexibly. Flex-Channels provide flexible and fine-grained interface resource reservation and enable each network slice to exclusively occupy the bandwidth and scheduling tree, thereby providing resource reservation for network slices.

Flex-Channels can be configured on FlexE interfaces or channelized sub-interfaces. Figure 4.16 shows an example of how Flex-Channels are created on channelized sub-interfaces to further provide fine-grained resource isolation and assurance.

Unlike channelized sub-interfaces, Flex-Channels have no sub-interface configuration model. They are therefore easier to configure and better suited to scenarios where network slices are created on demand. Flex-Channels can be created on physical interfaces to reserve resources for level-1 slices. And they can also be created on FlexE interfaces or channelized sub-interfaces to reserve resources for level-2 slices, providing finer-grained slice resource assurance.

## 4.4 COMPARISON AMONG RESOURCE PARTITIONING TECHNOLOGIES

The preceding sections discussed the functions and characteristics of three resource partitioning technologies—FlexE, channelized sub-interface, and Flex-Channel — in the forwarding plane. This section compares

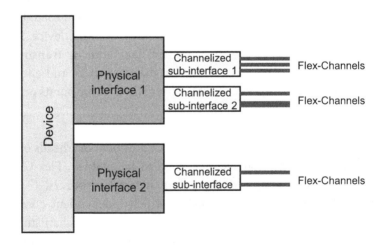

FIGURE 4.16   Flex-Channels created on channelized sub-interfaces.

the characteristics and application scenarios of these three technologies in terms of isolation, delay assurance, and more, with Table 4.1 providing a brief summary of the comparison.

Different resource partitioning technologies can be used together, as shown in Figure 4.17. Carriers typically use FlexE interfaces or channelized sub-interfaces to reserve coarse-grained slice resources for specific industries or service types. Flex-Channels are then created to reserve fine-grained slice resources for different enterprise users.

Network slices with hierarchical scheduling can achieve flexible and refined resource management. For example, on a mobile transport network with 50 Gbit/s bandwidth in the access ring and 100 Gbit/s bandwidth in the aggregation ring, a network slice can be created for a vertical industry, and FlexE interfaces can be used in the access ring to reserve 1 Gbit/s and in the aggregation ring to reserve 2 Gbit/s. This achieves hard isolation of services and meets the requirements of the vertical industry on isolation and ultra-low delay. After entering the aggregation ring from multiple

TABLE 4.1  Comparison among Three Resource Partitioning Technologies in the Forwarding Plane

| Item | FlexE | Channelized Sub-Interface | Flex-Channel |
|---|---|---|---|
| Isolation | Exclusive use of Traffic Manager (TM) resources; interface resource isolation | TM resource reservation; interface resource sharing | TM resource reservation; interface resource sharing |
| Delay assurance | Single-hop delay increase by a maximum of 10 μs when congestion occurs on other FlexE interfaces | Single-hop delay increase by a maximum of 100 μs when congestion occurs on other channelized sub-interfaces | Single-hop delay increase by a maximum of 100 μs when congestion occurs on other Flex-Channels |
| Minimum granularity of resource partitioning | 1 Gbit/s | 2 Mbit/s | 1 Mbit/s |
| Application scenario | Industrial network slice | Industrial network slice and enterprise MP2MP network slice (pre-deployed) | Enterprise P2P network slice and enterprise MP2MP network slice (on-demand slicing) |

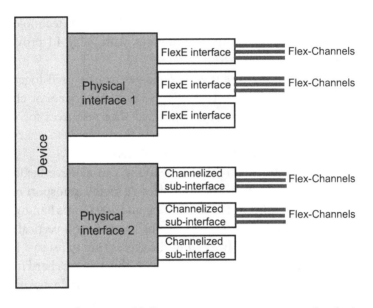

FIGURE 4.17 Combination of different resource partitioning technologies.

access rings, different services in the slice can share the reserved 2 Gbit/s bandwidth. Different service types or users of the vertical industry can continue to use the Flex-Channel technology in the FlexE interface of the slice to perform refined resource reservation and scheduling. This maximizes statistical multiplexing of resources while meeting requirements on slice isolation and the SLA guarantee. In scenarios where network slices require an interface bandwidth granularity of less than 1 Gbit/s, channelized sub-interfaces, or Flex-Channels, are used to divide the bandwidth resources of the network slices. Flex-Channels are then created on channelized sub-interfaces to achieve more refined resource reservation and scheduling.

## 4.5 STORIES BEHIND NETWORK SLICING

### 4.5.1 Development Phases of SLA Guarantee Technologies

SLAs — contracts between carriers and customers — indicate the QoS customers can receive. QoS has always been an important topic for IP networks, and which is why IP network technologies have undergone many years of development to refine the way in which SLA guarantee is provided. These technologies can be classified into three phases: "per-point," "per-line," and "per-plane."

Early IP networks adopted the IntServ model.[2] However, in practice, it is revealed that the model has poor scalability and therefore cannot be applied on a large scale. To address these issues, the DiffServ model[3] is designed to provide differentiated QoS for aggregated flows by configuring QoS priority queues on a "point" (single device). Because this technology is both simple and scalable, it has become a popular choice and found widespread use.

To meet the QoS requirement of services, Multi-Protocol Label Switching Traffic Engineering (MPLS TE) emerged through the development of MPLS technologies. In MPLS TE, paths that meet multiple constraints and provide guaranteed service quality are established in a network, and service flows are steered into these paths at the ingress node. MPLS TE provides QoS through "lines" (E2E MPLS TE paths).

And now, network slicing technologies have enabled IP networks to meet the QoS requirements of different services through network-wide resource reservation and isolation. In other words, IP networks can now provide QoS through "planes" (network slices).

Although these SLA guarantee technologies emerged during different development phases, they are not intended to replace each other. They vary in complexity, require different network resources, and can be selected to adapt to specific application scenarios. They can also be combined to better meet QoS requirements. For example, Segment Routing (SR) TE paths can be used to further meet the specific requirements of certain services in a network slice.

## 4.5.2 Hard Connection and Soft Connection

As network technologies develop, there has been ongoing competition between the use of hard connection and soft connection. An example of hard connection is the switching technology used by the early telecommunication networks, such as telephone and TDM systems. The IP technology developed for the Internet, adopting BE forwarding during initial development, belongs to soft connection. With the wide application of IP technology in different fields, especially after its adoption in telecommunication networks, various technologies that provide hard connection at different levels based on IP have been introduced to meet the requirements of different services. There is the notion that the development of technology is following a spiral trend, while some people assert that it is turning back the hands of time. For example, FlexE technology used for network slicing is considered by some to simply be a rehash of traditional TDM technology.

The development of technologies is closely related to the application requirements and software and hardware capabilities during different periods of time. As such, the development of a given technology may rise or fall, or different technologies with the same technical principles may appear during different periods of time. Artificial intelligence, or deep learning, developing rapidly alongside computing power breakthroughs is a typical example of the former, whereas for the latter, an example is hard connection technologies.

Legacy telecommunication network technologies, such as Asynchronous Transfer Mode (ATM), provide different QoS assurance technologies for different services. However, IP is developed from the bottom up, and its success lies in solving the problem of massive connections — a killer application in the early stages of the Internet. At that time, well-designed ATM failed to make significant progress because the software and hardware capabilities were unable to meet technical requirements and the deployment costs were high. But as software and hardware technologies developed, many of the technical ideas in ATM were retained and gradually integrated into IP. This is also closely related to the requirements of IP multi-service transport. IP is now used to uniformly carry different types of services that have different QoS requirements, thanks to its wide application. These services also have different requirements for network technologies, which makes it inevitable that hard connection will obtain new applications.

### 4.5.3 Catch-Up Lessons on IP

In 2019, I was privileged to attend a speech about China's Internet development at a symposium commemorating the 50th anniversary of the birth of the Internet and the 25th anniversary of China's access to the Internet. He believes that the biggest success of IP is to solve the problem of massive connections, while no other technology can carry massive connections like IP can. In theory, as more connections are added to a network, the more likely it is to crash. He also presented that there are two reasons why IP does not crash. One is that the capabilities of forwarding chips are being continuously enhanced, ensuring that the enormous volume of traffic generated from massive connections can be effectively forwarded.

The other is that the capabilities of computing chips are also being continuously enhanced, ensuring the computing and control capabilities of massive connections.

Professor Qian's speech had a profound impact on me. I had been working on the IP-based Versatile Routing Platform (VRP) and routers for years but had not given the essence of IP much thought. Professor Qian's summary on IP technologies enlightened me. Over the past many years, we have simplified the establishment of connections by relying on dividends from high bandwidth. With the further increase in bandwidth, we can enhance IP attributes and establish more intelligent connections. This is a new benefit resulting from bandwidth. The reason why we can make a series of innovations — such as SRv6, network slicing, Deterministic Networking (DetNet), and In-situ Flow Information Telemetry (IFIT) — is due to the oversupply of hardware and forwarding capabilities. Without such an oversupply, these innovations would be impossible.

The forwarding capability delivered by hardware three decades ago was limited. This meant that Multi-Protocol Label Switching (MPLS) could only be adopted to extend IP functionality and ensure forwarding performance by using hardware-friendly designs such as fixed-length, fixed-domain, and semantic-free label forwarding. Now, thanks to bandwidth oversupply and powerful hardware programmability, we can adopt variable-length IPv6 extension headers to extend IP functionality — an innovation I refer to as "Catch-up Lessons on IP." Compared with many classic telecommunication network technologies, early IP features are too simple. Although we admit that IP can effectively carry massive connections, we also complain that it is difficult to use, and even basic QoS assurance and Operations, Administration, and Maintenance (OAM) have problems. For example, while load balancing is widely used on IP networks to improve bandwidth utilization, it causes out-of-band OAM packets to travel along different paths from service packets. Consequently, the results of connectivity checks and performance measurements are inconsistent with those of actual service packets. On-path telemetry technology can solve this problem. On-path OAM is a traditional technology applied to non-IP networks, and on-path telemetry has been applied to IP networks up to this day. It can only be implemented when the hardware capabilities are much stronger than the guaranteed forwarding performance of massive connections.

Bandwidth oversupply is also the basis of network slicing, which we can compare to dividing a road into lanes. There is no need to divide a narrow road, but as the road is widened, it is gradually divided into two lanes, three lanes, and more. Relying on drivers' judgment to travel along a narrow road with no lanes is not a major problem initially. But as the road becomes wider and wider, drivers may gradually lose their judgment and even veer from side to side. This results in vehicles crossing the paths of others, leading to potential accidents. I have such experience that I once almost lost my sense of direction on U.S. Route 101 from San Francisco International Airport to Silicon Valley because the road was too wide. On the premise of massive bandwidth, IP network slicing can keep forwarding in good order and avoid mutual interference.

In terms of the process involved in IP innovation, I compare it to a "pauper" (basic capability) becoming a "parvenu" (widely accepted) and then a "noble" (refined behaviors). At the beginning, limited bandwidth supports BE forwarding for massive connections. As bandwidth increases, important features such as Virtual Private Network (VPN), TE, and Fast Reroute (FRR) are supported, but their implementation is still complex. Innovative technologies in IPv6 Enhanced enable IP to have more abundant attributes and become more refined and intelligent. Of course, this process may also cause all kinds of adaptability issues. This is similar to a situation in which a poor person has to spend a lot of time adapting to all kinds of new conventions after suddenly becoming noble. In any case, the trend and direction toward IP multi-service transport and refined network services remain unchanged, and IP itself can provide flexible choices for services.

## REFERENCES

[1] Optical Internetworking Forum. Flex Ethernet Implementation Agreement [EB/OL]. (2016-03)[2022-09-30].

[2] Braden R, Clark D, Shenker S. Integrated Services in the Internet Architecture: an Overview [EB/OL]. (1994-06)[2022-09-30]. RFC 1633.

[3] Blake S, Black D, Carlson M et al. An Architecture for Differentiated Services [EB/OL]. (1998-12)[2022-09-30]. RFC 2475.

[4] Babiarz J, Chan K, Baker F. Configuration Guidelines for DiffServ Service Classes [EB/OL]. (2006-08)[2022-09-30]. RFC 4594.

# CHAPTER 5

# Data Plane Technologies for IPv6 Network Slicing

I N IPv6 NETWORK SLICING, the data plane requires service packets to carry network slice identifiers, instructing devices to process and forward the service packets of different network slices according to the topology, resource, and other constraints defined for these slices. Currently, such identifiers can be carried using IPv6 extension headers or Segment Routing over IPv6 (SRv6) Segment Identifiers (SIDs). This chapter provides an overview of IPv6 and SRv6 technologies and describes how to use IPv6 extension headers and SRv6 SIDs to carry network slice identifiers.

## 5.1 IPV6 DATA PLANE

### 5.1.1 IPv6 Address

#### 5.1.1.1 IPv6 Address Format

An IPv6 address is 128 bits long. It is typically expressed as eight groups of four hexadecimal digits, with each group separated by a colon (:). This is the preferred format for an IPv6 address. An example IPv6 address is FC0 0:0000:130F:0000:0000:09C0:876A:130B.

DOI: 10.1201/9781032699868-7

For convenience, IPv6 addresses can be expressed in a compressed format. For the preceding example[1]:

- Leading zeros in each group can be omitted to form FC00:0:130F:0:0:9C0:876A:130B.

- Two or more consecutive all-0 groups can be replaced with a double colon (::) to form FC00:0:130F::9C0:876A:130B.

- An IPv6 address can contain only one double colon (::). Multiple double colons lead to ambiguity, making it difficult to identify the number of 0s represented by each double colon when restoring a 128-bit address from a compressed one.

### 5.1.1.2 IPv6 Address Structure
An IPv6 address consists of the following two parts:

- Network prefix: equivalent to the network ID of an IPv4 address. This prefix is variable in length and expressed in bits.

- Interface ID: equivalent to the host ID of an IPv4 address. This ID is 128 bits minus the length of the network prefix.

For an IPv6 unicast address, if the first three bits are not 000, the interface ID must contain 64 bits. In other cases, there is no such limitation.

An interface ID can be generated using three methods: manual configuration, software-based automatic generation, and IEEE EUI-64-compliant automatic generation. The last of the three is most widely used.

IEEE EUI-64 defines the process of converting an interface MAC address into an IPv6 interface ID. Figure 5.1 shows a 48-bit MAC address, of which the first 24 bits (represented using the letter "c" in this figure) indicate a company/organization identifier and the last 24 bits (represented using the letter "m") indicate an extension identifier. If the seventh most significant bit is 0, the Media Access Control (MAC) address is locally unique.

The conversion starts by converting the hexadecimal "FFFE" into a binary value and then inserting this value between the company/organization identifier and extension identifier in the MAC address. Next, the seventh most significant bit is changed from 0 to 1.

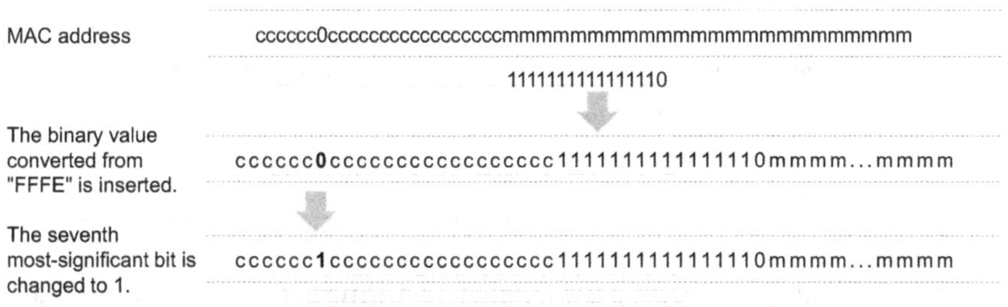

| MAC address | cccccc0ccccccccccccccccmmmmmmmmmmmmmmmmmmmmmmmmm |
|---|---|
| | 1111111111111110 |
| The binary value converted from "FFFE" is inserted. | cccccc0cccccccccccccccccc1111111111111110mmmm...mmmm |
| The seventh most-significant bit is changed to 1. | cccccc1cccccccccccccccccc1111111111111110mmmm...mmmm |

FIGURE 5.1   IEEE EUI-64-compliant conversion.

For example, if the MAC address is 000E-0C82-C4D4, the post-conversion interface ID is 020E:0CFF:FE82:C4D4.

Finally, we obtain a 64-bit (48 + 16 = 64) interface ID. A 64-bit network prefix is then added to form a globally unique IPv6 address.

Converting MAC addresses into IPv6 interface IDs makes configuration easier, especially when Stateless Address Autoconfiguration (SLAAC) is adopted, as only an IPv6 prefix needs to be obtained to form an IPv6 address together with the interface ID. Nevertheless, the biggest disadvantage of this method is that anyone can deduce IPv6 addresses based on MAC addresses, causing security risks.

### 5.1.1.3 IPv6 Address Classification

Unlike IPv4, there are no broadcast addresses in IPv6. Instead, IPv6 addresses are typically classified as unicast, multicast, or anycast addresses.

The following focuses on IPv6 unicast addresses. As the other two types of addresses are irrelevant to the contents of this book, they are not described here.

An IPv6 unicast address identifies an interface. Because each interface belongs to a node, the IPv6 unicast address of any interface on a node can identify the node itself. Packets sent to an IPv6 unicast address are received by the interface identified by that address.

IPv6 defines multiple types of unicast addresses, including unspecified, loopback, global unicast, link-local, and unique local addresses.

TABLE 5.1    Mapping between IPv6 Address Segments and
Unicast Address Types

| Address Type | IPv6 Address Segment |
| --- | --- |
| Global Unicast Address (GUA) | 2000::/3 |
| Link-Local Address (LLA) | FE80::/10 |
| Unique Local Address (ULA) | FC00::/7 |

Table 5.1 lists the mapping between IPv6 address segments and unicast address types.[2]

The IPv6 unspecified address is 0:0:0:0:0:0:0:0/128 or ::/128. It indicates the absence of an IP address on an interface or a node and can be used as the source IP address of some packets. For example, it can be used for Neighbor Solicitation messages — defined by the IPv6 Neighbor Discovery (ND) protocol — involved in duplicate address detection. Routers do not forward packets whose source IP address is an unspecified address.

The IPv6 loopback address is 0:0:0:0:0:0:0:1/128 or ::1/128. Similar to the IPv4 loopback address 127.0.0.1, the IPv6 loopback address is mainly used by a node to send a packet to itself for testing and troubleshooting purposes. It is typically used as the address of a virtual interface, such as a loopback interface. Packets destined for an address other than the originator must not use the loopback address as the source or destination IP address.

An IPv6 GUA has a global unicast prefix and is similar to an IPv4 public address. Such addresses support route prefix aggregation, minimizing the number of global routing entries.

LLAs are used only for communication between nodes on a local link and have a limited application scope in IPv6. An LLA uses a link-local prefix of FE80::/10 (10 most-significant bits: 1111111010 in binary) and adds an interface ID as its 64 least-significant bits.

During the process of starting IPv6 on a node, an LLA that consists of a fixed prefix and an interface ID in EUI-64 format is automatically allocated to each of the interfaces on the node. This mechanism enables two IPv6 nodes on a link to communicate without requiring any additional configuration. As such, IPv6 LLAs are widely used for purposes such as ND and SLAAC[3]

Routers do not forward any IPv6 packets with link-local source or destination addresses to other links.

ULAs, which also have a limited application scope, are used as a better addressing scheme to replace Site-Local Addresses (SLAs). Although SLAs are now obsolete due to many problems,[4] the following briefly describes them to help you understand ULAs.

Similar to private addresses in IPv4, SLAs are address segments used within a single domain. An SLA is an IPv6 address segment with the prefix FEC0::/10. It is routable only within a single site and does not need to be requested from an address allocation organization. Each site independently manages address segment division and address allocation.

SLAs have similar problems as IPv4 private addresses. For example, address conflicts may occur when inter-domain networks need to be connected or networks in multiple domains need to be converged into the same domain. This typically requires replanning and reallocating network segments and addresses in multiple domains, complicating network evolution, increasing workloads, and, in some cases, even interrupting network traffic.

Likewise, ULAs are similar to IPv4 private addresses. They can be used by any organization that does not apply for a GUA segment from an address allocation organization. A ULA is routable only within its local network. Figure 5.2 shows the ULA format.

Table 5.2 describes the involved fields.

The ULA block with the prefix FC00::/7 is allocated separately from the IPv6 address space and supports only intra-domain routability. The prefix used for a single domain is Prefix + L + Global ID. The pseudo-randomness of a global ID ensures that there are no address conflicts between domains that use ULAs.

Each ULA is a globally unique unicast address. The only difference between a ULA and a GUA is that the route prefix of the former is not advertised to the Internet. Consequently, even if route leakage occurs, the original traffic on the Internet and the public network traffic in other domains are not adversely affected. In addition to functioning as private

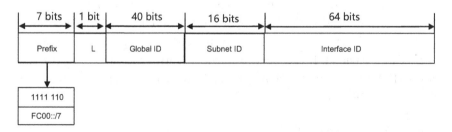

FIGURE 5.2   ULA format.

TABLE 5.2   Fields in a ULA

| Field | Description |
| --- | --- |
| Prefix | Address prefix. The value is fixed at FC00::/7. |
| L | L flag. The value 1 indicates that the address is valid within a local network. The value 0 is reserved for future use. |
| Global ID | Globally unique identifier, which is generated in pseudo-random mode. |
| Subnet ID | Subnet identifier, which is used for subnetting. |
| Interface ID | Interface identifier. |

addresses for intra-domain traffic management, ULAs resolve the major problems associated with SLAs.

Specifically, a ULA has the following characteristics:

- Uses a pseudo-randomly allocated prefix that is highly likely to be unique globally.

- Allows private connections to be established between networks without encountering address conflicts.

- Uses a unified prefix of FC00::/7, facilitating route filtering on edge devices.

- Does not conflict with any other addresses if route leaking occurs, ensuring that Internet traffic is not adversely affected.

- Functions as a GUA for upper-layer applications.

- Is independent of the GUA address spaces of Internet Service Providers (ISPs).

### 5.1.2 IPv6 Header

An IPv6 packet consists of three parts: a basic IPv6 header, one or more IPv6 extension headers, and an upper-layer Protocol Data Unit (PDU).

An upper-layer PDU is typically composed of an upper-layer protocol header and payload. It can be an Internet Control Message Protocol version 6 (ICMPv6), Transmission Control Protocol (TCP), or User Datagram Protocol (UDP) packet.

#### 5.1.2.1 Basic IPv6 Header

A basic IPv6 header has a fixed length of 40 bytes with eight fields. Each IPv6 data packet must contain a basic header, which provides basic packet forwarding information for all devices on the forwarding path to parse. Figure 5.3 shows the format of a basic IPv6 header.

Table 5.3 describes the fields in a basic IPv6 header.

The IPv6 packet format is designed to simplify the basic header. In most cases, a device only needs to process the basic header to forward IP traffic. Unlike the IPv4 header, the IPv6 header does not carry the fields related to fragmentation, checksum, and options. Instead, it carries the Flow Label field, making IPv6 header processing easier and more efficient. In addition, IPv6 utilizes extension headers to support various options without

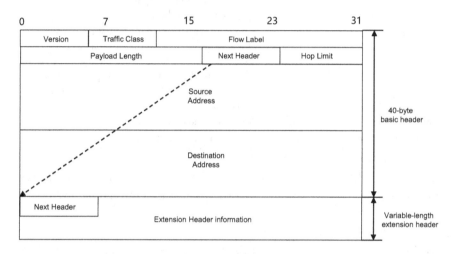

FIGURE 5.3   Format of a basic IPv6 header.

TABLE 5.3   Fields in a Basic IPv6 Header

| Field | Length | Description |
| --- | --- | --- |
| Version | 4 bits | Internet Protocol version number, which is set to 6 in IPv6 scenarios. |
| Traffic Class | 8 bits | Class or priority of an IPv6 packet. This field is similar to the Type of Service (TOS) field in an IPv4 packet and mainly used in Quality of Service (QoS) control. |
| Flow Label | 20 bits | Field added in IPv6 to identify packets that belong to the same data flow. A flow label, source address, and destination address uniquely identify a data flow, enabling transit devices to differentiate data flows more effectively. |

*(Continued)*

TABLE 5.3 (*Continued*)   Fields in a Basic IPv6 Header

| Field | Length | Description |
|---|---|---|
| Payload Length | 16 bits | Length of the payload, which consists of the extension header and upper-layer PDU that immediately follow the basic IPv6 header. If the payload length exceeds the maximum value of 65,535 bytes, this field is set to 0, and the Jumbo Payload option in the Hop-by-Hop Options header is used to express the actual payload length. |
| Next Header | 8 bits | Type of the first extension header (if any) immediately following the IPv6 header, or the protocol type in the upper-layer PDU. |
| Hop Limit | 8 bits | Similar to the TTL field in IPv4, this field defines the maximum number of hops that an IPv6 packet can pass through. The value is decremented by 1 each time the packet passes through a device. If the value reaches 0, the packet is discarded. |
| Source Address | 128 bits | Address of the packet sender. |
| Destination Address | 128 bits | Address of the packet receiver. |

requiring modification of the existing packet format. This not only ensures that packet headers are simple but also achieves exceptional flexibility.

### 5.1.2.2 IPv6 Extension Header

An IPv4 header contains the optional Options field, which involves such options as Security, Timestamp, and Record route. These options extend the IPv4 header length from 20 to 60 bytes. Because processing IPv4 packets with these options requires many resources, such options are rarely used in practice.

Instead of placing options in the basic header, IPv6 places them in extension headers between the basic header and upper-layer PDU. An IPv6 packet may or may not carry extension headers. The sender of a packet adds one or more extension headers to the packet only when it requires a device or the destination node to perform special processing. Thanks to its variable-length extension headers, which are not limited to 40 bytes, IPv6 has better extensibility than IPv4. To improve Options header processing efficiency and transport protocol performance, IPv6 requires that the extension header length be an integer multiple of 8 bytes.

When multiple extension headers are used, the Next Header field of each extension header indicates the type of the next extension header that follows, thereby forming a header chain. As illustrated by Figure 5.4, the Next Header field in the basic IPv6 header indicates the type of the first extension header, the Next Header field in the first extension header indicates the type of the next extension header, and so on. The Next Header field in the final extension header indicates the upper-layer protocol type.

Table 5.4 describes the fields in an IPv6 extension header.

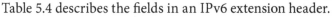
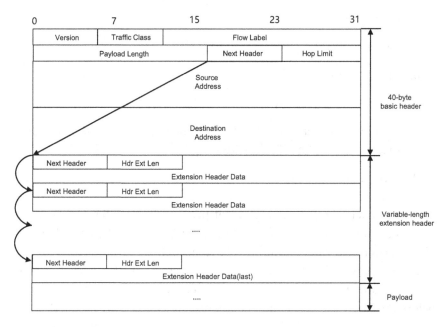

FIGURE 5.4  Format of an IPv6 extension header.

TABLE 5.4  Fields in an IPv6 Extension Header

| Field | Length | Description |
| --- | --- | --- |
| Next Header | 8 bits | Type of the next extension header (if any) or the upper-layer protocol. This field is similar to the Next Header field in the basic header. |
| Extension Header Len | 8 bits | Length of an extension header in 8-byte units, excluding the first 8 bytes. (The minimum extension header length is 8 bytes, in which case this field is set to 0.) |
| Extension Header Data | Variable | Data of an extension header, containing a series of options and the padding field. |

*5.1.2.3 Order of IPv6 Extension Headers*

When an IPv6 packet contains two or more extension headers, the headers must appear in the following order[5]:

1. IPv6 header

2. Hop-by-Hop Options header

3. Destination Options header

4. Routing header

5. Fragment header

6. Authentication header

7. Encapsulating Security Payload header

8. Destination Options header (for options to be processed by the destination node of the IPv6 packet)

9. Upper-Layer header

During packet forwarding, instead of processing all extension headers, routers examine and process only certain extension headers based on the Next Header field value in the basic IPv6 header.

Each extension header can occur only once in an IPv6 packet, except for the Destination Options header, which may occur at most twice (once before the Routing header and once before the Upper-Layer header).

The following briefly describes the Hop-by-Hop Options header, Destination Options header, and Routing header, which are all related to the content of this book.

*5.1.2.4 Hop-by-Hop Options Header*

The Hop-by-Hop Options header is used to carry information that needs to be processed by each router on a forwarding path. It is identified by a Next Header value of 0. Figure 5.5 shows the Hop-by-Hop Options header format.

The Hop-by-Hop Options header includes a series of options used to carry different types of information. Figure 5.6 shows the format of the Type Length Value (TLV)-encoded Options area.

Table 5.5 describes the fields in the Options area.

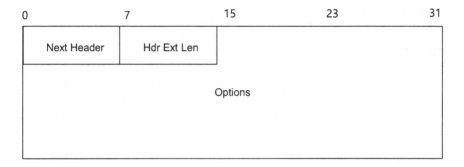

FIGURE 5.5   Hop-by-Hop options header format.

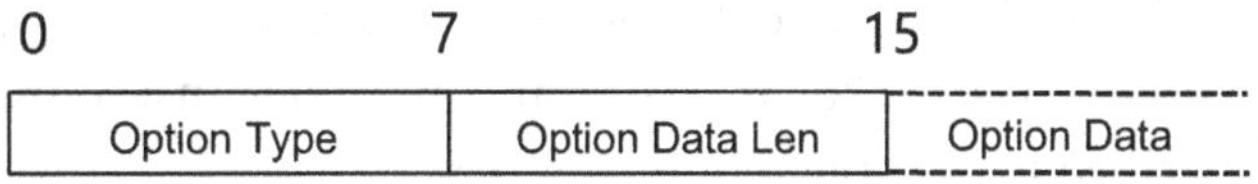

FIGURE 5.6   Format of the options area.

TABLE 5.5   Fields in the Options Area

| Field | Length | Description |
| --- | --- | --- |
| Option Type | 8 bits | Type of the current option. The data format in the Option Data field varies according to the option type. The requirements for using the Option Type field are as follows:<br><br>1. The first and second most-significant bits specify the action that must be taken if the involved node does not support the processing of the current option. Available values and their meanings are as follows:<br><br>• 00: ignores this option and continues processing the next option.<br><br>• 01: discards the packet.<br><br>• 10: discards the packet and sends an ICMP Parameter Problem message to the source address.<br><br>• 11: discards the packet and, only if the IPv6 destination address of the packet is not a multicast address, sends an ICMP Parameter Problem message to the source address.<br><br>2. The third most-significant bit indicates whether the option can be modified during packet forwarding. The values 1 and 0 indicate that the option can and cannot be modified, respectively.<br>3. The remaining five bits are reserved for future use.<br><br>Together, these eight bits are used to identify the type of an option. |

*(Continued)*

TABLE 5.5 (*Continued*)  Fields in the Options Area

| Field | Length | Description |
|---|---|---|
| Option Data Len | 8 bits | Length of the Option Data field of the current option, in bytes. |
| Option Data | Variable | Data of the current option. The length of the Hop-by-Hop Options header must be an integer multiple of 8 bytes. If the data length is not a multiple of 8 bytes, padding options can be used[5] |

### 5.1.2.5 Destination Options Header

The Destination Options header is used to carry information that the packet's destination node needs to process. This node can be either the final destination of the packet or an intermediate node in a source routing scheme (described in Section 5.1.2.6).

The Destination Options header is identified by a Next Header value of 60. The format and requirements for this header are similar to those for the Hop-by-Hop Options header.

### 5.1.2.6 Routing Header

The Routing header is used to list one or more intermediate nodes that a packet must traverse on the way to its destination. This header is used to implement various source routing schemes. The packet originator or a network node inserts the Routing header into a packet, and the subsequent node reads node information from the header and forwards the packet to the specified next hop. This process repeats until the packet reaches its destination. Based on the Routing header, the packet travels along a specified forwarding path instead of using the default shortest path.

The Routing header is identified by a Next Header value of 43. Figure 5.7 shows the Routing header format.

Table 5.6 describes the main fields in the Routing header.

If a router does not support the source routing scheme specified by the Routing Type field, it processes the packet in one of the following ways:

- If the SL value is 0, the router ignores the Routing header and proceeds to process the next header in the packet.

- If the SL value is not 0, the router discards the packet and sends an ICMP Parameter Problem message to the source address.

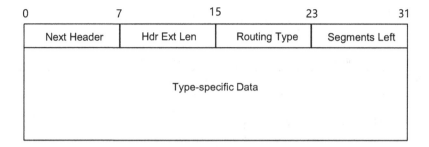

FIGURE 5.7   Routing header format.

TABLE 5.6   Main Fields in the Routing Header

| Field | Length | Description |
|---|---|---|
| Routing Type | 8 bits | Source routing scheme corresponding to the Routing header and data format in the routing data area. |
| Segments Left (SL) | 8 bits | Number of remaining route segments. Specifically, it is the number of explicitly listed intermediate nodes still to be traversed before the packet reaches the final destination. |
| Type-specific Data | Variable | Routing data of a specific Routing header type. The data format is defined in the corresponding source routing scheme. |

### 5.1.3  Carrying Network Slice Information in IPv6 Extension Headers

#### *5.1.3.1 New Option in IPv6 Extension Headers*

The Virtual Transport Network (VTN)[6] option is newly added to enable IPv6 extension headers to carry resource information about network slices. Figure 5.8 shows the format of the VTN option.

Table 5.7 describes the fields in the VTN option.

The length of VTN Resource ID is set to 32 bits to remain consistent with that of the 5G network slice identifier, Single Network Slice Selection Assistance Information (S-NSSAI), defined in 3GPP TS 23.501.[7] This helps implement flexible mapping and interconnection between 5G network slices and IP network slices. The 5G network slice identifier S-NSSAI consists of an 8-bit Slice/Service Type (SST) field and an optional 24-bit Slice Differentiator (SD) field. Figure 5.9 shows the S-NSSAI format.

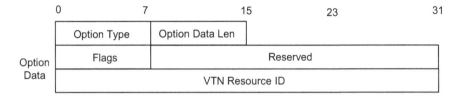

FIGURE 5.8   Format of the VTN option.

TABLE 5.7   Fields in the VTN Option

| Field | Length | Description |
|---|---|---|
| Option Type | 8 bits | VTN option type allocated by the Internet Assigned Numbers Authority (IANA). It is expressed in the BBCTTTTT format, with the three most-significant bits set as follows:<br><br>• The first two bits (BB) are set to 00 to indicate that, if a node does not recognize this option, it will skip this option and proceed to process other fields in the packet header.<br><br>• The third bit (C) is set to 0 to indicate that this option will not be modified during forwarding. |
| Option Data Len | 8 bits | Option data length of the VTN option, in bytes. The value is fixed at 8 bytes. |
| Flags | 8 bits | Flags of the VTN option. The most-significant bit S indicates Strict Match. If the S flag is set, the packet needs to be forwarded through a strictly matched slice resource interface or sub-channel. |
| Reserved | 24 bits | Reserved for future extension. |
| VTN Resource ID | 32 bits | VTN resource identifier (also called network resource slice identifier), which uniquely identifies a set of resources reserved for a network slice. |

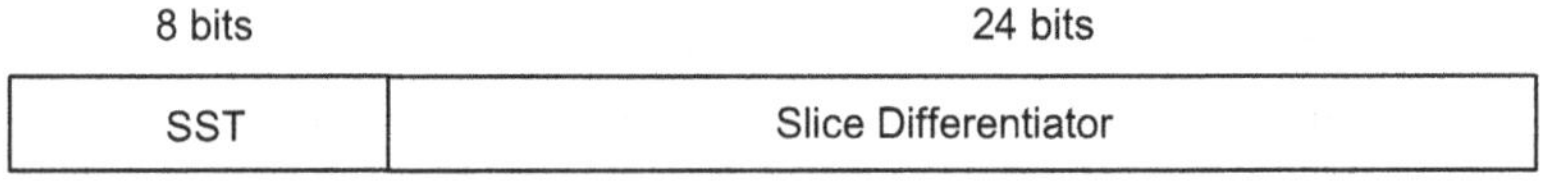

| 8 bits | 24 bits |
|---|---|
| SST | Slice Differentiator |

FIGURE 5.9   S-NSSAI format.

### 5.1.3.2 IPv6 VTN Option Processing

To achieve packet forwarding based on network slice-specific resource constraints, the IPv6 VTN option needs to be parsed and processed by each node on the forwarding path. This requires the VTN option to be carried in the IPv6 Hop-by-Hop Options header. In this case, all network nodes along the path should be able to parse and process the IPv6 Hop-by-Hop Options header in the forwarding plane.

5.1.3.2.1 VTN Option Insertion    After receiving a data packet, the ingress of an IPv6 network steers the packet to a network slice according to a specified traffic classification or mapping policy. In this case, an outer IPv6 header with the Hop-by-Hop Options header carrying the VTN option needs to be added to the data packet, with the VTN Resource ID field in the VTN option set to the resource ID of the network slice.

5.1.3.2.2 VTN Option-Based Packet Forwarding    After receiving a data packet with the VTN option, each IPv6 network node that supports VTN option parsing and processing in the forwarding plane needs to determine the forwarding resources (e.g., node and interface resources) to be allocated to the specified network slice based on the VTN Resource ID in the VTN option. The packet forwarding behavior is determined by both the destination address and the VTN Resource ID. Specifically, the destination address is used to determine the next hop and Layer 3 outbound interface for packet forwarding, whereas the VTN Resource ID is used to determine the set of forwarding resources (e.g., FlexE physical interfaces, channelized sub-interfaces, or Flex-Channels) to be allocated by the outbound interface to the network slice. This ensures that the dedicated resources reserved for this slice are used for packet processing and forwarding. The Traffic Class field in the IPv6 header can be used to provide differentiated service processing for packets with different priorities in the same network slice.

If a device does not have any forwarding resource matching the VTN Resource ID in the packet, it determines the forwarding behavior based on the value of the S (Strict Match) flag.

- If the S flag is set to 1, the packet must be forwarded using resources that strictly match the VTN Resource ID. If such resources are not found, the packet is discarded.

- If the S flag is set to 0, the packet can be forwarded using specified resources (e.g., resources of the default slice) if matching resources are not found.

Network nodes that do not support the IPv6 Hop-by-Hop Options header should ignore it and forward the packet based on only the destination address. If some network nodes support the Hop-by-Hop Options header instead of the VTN option, they should ignore the VTN option and continue to process other options in the Hop-by-Hop Options header.

When the packet reaches the egress of the IPv6 network, the egress needs to remove the outer IPv6 header containing the VTN option and forward the packet to the destination node.

## 5.2 SRV6 DATA PLANE

### 5.2.1 SRv6 Overview

SRv6 provides a basic mechanism and architecture for implementing Segment Routing (SR) based on IPv6 and enables flexible Network Programming (NP).[8] When talking about SRv6, people typically focus more on the SRv6-based network programmability and architecture.

The NP concept stems from computer programming, through which we can convert our intent into a series of instructions that computers can understand and execute to meet our requirements. Similarly, if a network could convert service intent into a series of device-executable forwarding instructions, NP could be achieved, meeting the custom requirements of services. Figure 5.10 compares how computer programming and NP are implemented.

Based on the NP concept, SRv6 is introduced to convert network functions into instructions and encapsulate these instructions into 128-bit IPv6 addresses. Service requirements for an SRv6 network can be converted into an ordered list of instructions, which are then executed by

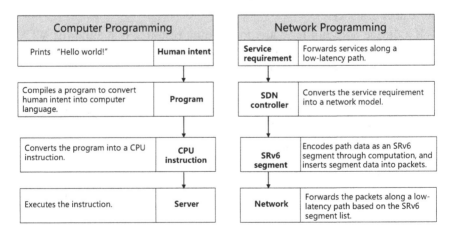

FIGURE 5.10 Computer programming and NP.

network devices along a service forwarding path. This makes it possible to achieve flexible orchestration and on-demand customization of services.

## 5.2.2 Network Instructions: SRv6 Segments

For computer programming, a computer instruction typically consists of an opcode and an operand. The former determines the operation to be performed; the latter determines the operation data and/or memory address to be used. Similarly, network instructions — called SRv6 segments — need to be defined for achieving SRv6 NP. SRv6 segments are identified using 128-bit Segment Identifiers (SIDs),[9] each of which typically consists of three fields: Locator, Function, and Arguments.

The three fields are described as follows:

1. The Locator field identifies a network node that needs to execute the instructions contained in received packets. Locators indicate the locations of network nodes and have two important attributes: routability and aggregatability. Given the routability attribute of locators, after a node advertises a locator-specific IPv6 route prefix to other nodes through IGP, those nodes can generate routing entries corresponding to the locator. They can then forward the packet whose destination IPv6 address matches the locator to the node that advertises this locator. In addition, the route corresponding to a locator can be aggregated, meaning that the locators of multiple nodes can be advertised using an aggregated route. The routability and aggregatability attributes help address problems such as high network complexity and oversized networks.

   Because the locator length is variable, SRv6 SIDs can be used on networks of all sizes.

2. The Function field, like an opcode in a computer instruction, specifies the forwarding behavior to be performed. Similar to the way in which computer instructions are executed, functions are used to express different forwarding behaviors, such as packet forwarding to a specified link and table lookup for packet forwarding. Such behaviors are represented using SIDs defined based on these functions, thereby implementing SRv6 NP.

3. The Arguments (Args) field is optional and defines parameters for instruction execution. The parameters may contain flow, service, and any other related information.

Much like computer programming, which uses a limited instruction set to implement various computing functions, SRv6 also requires an instruction set to be defined for routing and forwarding purposes.

Numerous types of SRv6 SIDs lay the foundation for network programmability, with an ordered list of SIDs capable of representing any end-to-end (E2E) service connection requirement. Leveraging SRv6, the source node encapsulates an ordered list of SRv6 SIDs into packets to instruct specified nodes to execute instructions, thereby achieving network programmability. As SRv6 application scenarios continue to expand, SRv6 instruction sets will evolve to meet future requirements.

### 5.2.3 Network Nodes: SRv6 Nodes

An SRv6 network involves various node roles, mainly including SRv6 source nodes, transit nodes, and SRv6 segment endpoint nodes (endpoint nodes for short).[10] The roles that nodes play on an SRv6 network are related to the tasks that the nodes perform in SRv6 packet forwarding. Each node may play one or more roles — for example, it can be the source node on one SRv6 path and a transit or endpoint node on another SRv6 path.

#### 5.2.3.1 SRv6 Source Node

The SRv6 source node encapsulates a packet with the SRv6 header, using an SRv6 SID as the destination address of the packet. Depending on the number of required SIDs and the adopted policy, the SRv6 packet may or may not carry a Segment Routing Header (SRH). An SRv6 source node can be either an SRv6-capable host where IPv6 packets originate or an edge device in an SRv6 domain.

#### 5.2.3.2 Transit Node

A transit node does not participate in SRv6 processing on the SRv6 packet forwarding path. Instead of processing the DA of a packet as an SRv6 SID or processing the SRH, a transit node only needs to perform ordinary IPv6 forwarding. After receiving an SRv6 packet, the node parses the IPv6 DA field in the packet. If the value of this field is neither a local SRv6 SID nor a local interface address, the node considers the SRv6 packet as an ordinary IPv6 packet. As such, it searches the IPv6 routing table according to the longest match rule and then processes and forwards the packet accordingly.

A transit node can be either an ordinary IPv6 node or an SRv6-capable one.

### 5.2.3.3 Endpoint Node

An endpoint node is one that receives an SRv6 packet in which the IPv6 DA is a local SRv6 SID or interface address. Endpoint nodes process both the SRv6 SID in the IPv6 DA field and the SRH in the received packet.

Figure 5.11 shows the node roles involved in SRv6 packet forwarding.

## 5.2.4 Network Program: SRv6 Extension Header

### 5.2.4.1 SRv6 Extension Header Design

Based on the original IPv6 Routing header, SRv6 defines a new type of extension header called SRH,[10] which carries segment lists and other related information to explicitly specify an SRv6 path.

Figure 5.12 shows the SRH format.

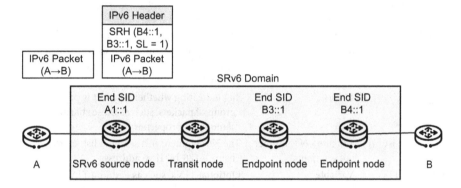

FIGURE 5.11    SRv6 node roles.

| Version | Traffic Class | FlowLabel | | |
|---|---|---|---|---|
| Payload Length | | Next Header = 43 | Hop Limit | IPv6 header |
| Source Address | | | | |
| Destination Address | | | | |
| Next Header | Hdr Ext Len | Routing Type = 4 | Segments Left | |
| Last Entry | Flags | Tag | | |
| Segment List [0] (128-bit IPv6 address) | | | | SRH |
| ... | | | | |
| Segment List [n] (128-bit IPv6 address) | | | | |
| Optional TLV objects (variable) | | | | |
| IPv6 Payload | | | | |

FIGURE 5.12    SRH format.

TABLE 5.8    Fields in an SRH

| Field | Length | Description |
|---|---|---|
| Next Header | 8 bits | Type of the header immediately following the SRH. Common header types are as follows:<br><br>• 4: IPv4 encapsulation<br><br>• 41: IPv6 encapsulation<br><br>• 58: ICMPv6<br><br>• 59: no Next Header for IPv6 |
| Hdr Ext Len | 8 bits | Length of the SRH, excluding the first 8 bytes (fixed length). |
| Routing Type | 8 bits | Type of the extension routing header. SRHs have a routing type value of 4. |
| Segments Left | 8 bits | Number of remaining segments. It is called SL for short. |
| Last Entry | 8 bits | Index of the last element in a segment list. |
| Flags | 8 bits | Flags reserved for special processing, such as Operations, Administration, and Maintenance (OAM). |
| Tag | 16 bits | Tag indicating whether a packet is part of a group of packets, such as those sharing the same set of properties. |
| Segment List [$n$] | 128 bits $\times N$ (Number of segments) | The Nth segment in a segment list, expressed using a 128-bit IPv6 address. |
| Optional TLV | Variable | Optional TLVs, such as Padding TLVs and Hash-based Message Authentication Code (HMAC) TLVs. |

Table 5.8 describes the fields in an SRH.

The SRH stores an ordered SID list for implementing NP. The segments represented by Segment List [0] through Segment List [$n$] are similar to the instructions of a computer program, and Segment List [$n$] indicates the first instruction that needs to be executed. Like the Program Counter (PC) of a computer program, the SL field points to the instruction that is being executed and can be initially set to $n$. Each time an instruction is executed, the SL value is decremented by 1 to point to the next instruction to be executed. As such, the SRv6 forwarding process can be easily simulated using a computer program.

Figure 5.13 shows an abstract of the SRH format to facilitate understanding of the SRv6 data forwarding process.

In Figure 5.13a, angle brackets <> are used to list SIDs in the reverse order in which instructions are executed, for example, <Segment List [0],

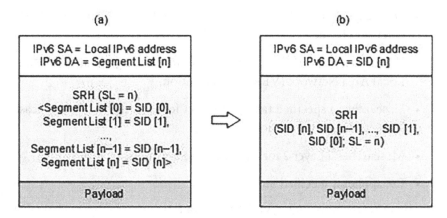

FIGURE 5.13   Abstract SRH.

Segment List [1],..., Segment List [*n*–1], Segment List [*n*]>. To facilitate understanding, parentheses () are used to list SIDs in the order in which instructions are executed, for example, (Segment List [*n*], Segment List [*n*–1],..., Segment List [1], Segment List [0]). For brevity, such representation can be further simplified, as shown in Figure 5.13b.

### 5.2.4.2 SRv6 Instruction Set: Endpoint Node Behaviors

The IETF draft "Segment Routing over IPv6 (SRv6) Network Programming[8]" defines multiple behaviors, which are also called instructions. Each SID is bound to an instruction to specify the action to be taken by a node during SID processing. An SRH can encapsulate an ordered list of SIDs, providing packet-related services such as forwarding, encapsulation, and decapsulation.

SRv6 instructions are named based on their atomic functions. The corresponding naming rules are as follows:

- End: terminates the current instruction and starts executing the next instruction. The corresponding forwarding behavior is to decrement the SL field value by 1 and copy the SID pointed to by the SL field to the DA field in the IPv6 header.

- X: forwards packets through one or a group of Layer 3 outbound interfaces.

- T: searches the routing table and forwards packets.

- D: decapsulates packets by removing the IPv6 header and related extension headers.

- V: searches a specified table for packet forwarding based on Virtual Local Area Network (VLAN) information.

- U: searches a specified table for packet forwarding based on unicast MAC address information.

- M: searches a Layer 2 forwarding table for multicast forwarding.

- B6: applies a specified SRv6 Policy.

- BM: applies a specified SR-MPLS Policy.

Table 5.9 describes the functions of common SRv6 instructions, each of which integrates one or more of the atomic functions listed above.

5.2.4.2.1 End SID    End is the most basic SRv6 instruction. A SID bound to the End instruction is called an End SID, which identifies a node. An End SID instructs a node to forward a packet to the node that advertises the SID. After receiving the packet, the node performs the operations defined by the SID for packet processing.

The End instruction includes the following operations:

1. Decreases the SL value by 1.

2. Obtains the next SID from the SRH based on the SL value.

TABLE 5.9    Functions of Common SRv6 Instructions

| Instruction | Function | Application |
| --- | --- | --- |
| End | Copies the next SID to the IPv6 DA field and searches the routing table for packet forwarding. | Used for packet forwarding through a specified node. An End SID is similar to an SR-MPLS node SID. |
| End.X | Forwards a packet through a specified outbound interface. | Used for packet forwarding through a specified outbound interface. An End.X SID is similar to an SR-MPLS adjacency SID. |
| End.T | Searches a specified IPv6 routing table and then forwards a packet accordingly. | Used in scenarios where multiple routing tables exist. |

3. Updates the DA field in the IPv6 header to the next SID obtained.

4. Searches the routing table and forwards the packet accordingly.

Other parameters, such as Hop Limit, are processed according to the ordinary IPv6 forwarding process.

5.2.4.2.2 End.X SID  The "Endpoint with L3 cross-connect" behavior ("End.X" for short) supports packet forwarding to a Layer 3 adjacency over a specified link in such scenarios as Topology Independent Loop Free Alternate (TI-LFA) and strict explicit path-based Traffic Engineering (TE).

End.X is developed based on the End instruction and can be disassembled into End + X, where X indicates cross-connect (meaning that a device needs to directly forward the associated packet to a specified Layer 3 adjacency without searching the routing table). As such, each End.X SID needs to be bound to one or a group of Layer 3 adjacencies.

The End.X instruction includes the following operations:

1. Decreases the SL value by 1.

2. Obtains the next SID from the SRH based on the SL value.

3. Updates the DA field in the IPv6 header to the next SID.

4. Forwards the IPv6 packet to the Layer 3 adjacency bound to the End.X SID.

5.2.4.2.3 End.T SID  The "Endpoint with specific IPv6 table lookup" behavior ("End.T" for short) supports IPv6 routing table lookup for packet forwarding in common IPv6 routing and VPN scenarios.

End.T SIDs are also developed based on End SIDs. End.T can be disassembled into End + T, where T indicates table lookup for packet forwarding. As such, each End.T SID needs to be bound to an IPv6 routing table.

The End.T instruction includes the following operations:

1. Decreases the SL value by 1.

2. Obtains the next SID from the SRH based on the SL value.

3. Updates the DA field in the IPv6 header to the next SID.

4. Searches the specified routing table and forwards the IPv6 packet accordingly.

## 5.2.5 Network Program Execution: SRv6 Packet Forwarding

*5.2.5.1 Local SID Table*

Each SRv6 node maintains a Local SID Table containing all SRv6 SIDs generated on the node. This table provides the following functions:

- Stores locally generated SIDs, such as End.X SIDs.

- Specifies instructions bound to the SIDs.

- Stores instruction-related forwarding information, such as VPN instance, outbound interface, and next hop information.

*5.2.5.2 Packet Forwarding Process*

In this section, we use an example to describe the SRv6 packet forwarding process.

In Figure 5.14, host H1 needs to send a packet to host H2, and first sends the packet to node A for processing. Note that only nodes A, B, D, and F support SRv6, whereas nodes C and E do not.

NP is implemented on the SRv6 source node A for sending the packet to node F over B–C and D–E links and then to host H2 from node F. The specifics of how the packet is processed when being forwarded from node A to node F are as follows:

Step 1: Processing on SRv6 source node A

As shown in Figure 5.15, node A encapsulates SRv6 path information into the SRH of the packet and specifies End.X SIDs for the B–C and D–E links. Additionally, node A needs to encapsulate the End.DT4 SID A6::100, which is advertised by node F and corresponds to an IPv4 VPN instance of node F. Note that the SIDs are

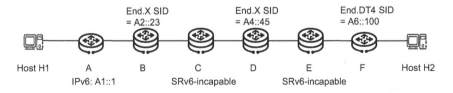

FIGURE 5.14   SRv6 packet forwarding process.

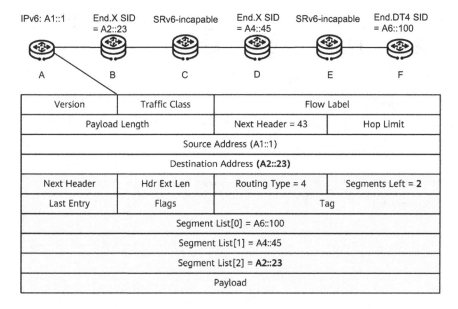

FIGURE 5.15   Processing on SRv6 source node A.

encapsulated in reverse order, and because there are three SIDs, the
SL value in the encapsulated packet is 2. The SL field points to the
segment list to be processed, which is Segment List.[2] Given this,
node A copies the SID A2::23 to the DA field in the IPv6 header,
searches the IPv6 routing table according to the longest-match
rule, and then forwards the packet to node B accordingly.

Step 2: Processing on endpoint node B

As shown in Figure 5.16, after receiving the IPv6 packet, node
B searches the Local SID Table based on the DA A2::23 in the IPv6
header and finds a matching End.X SID. According to the instruction defined by the End.X SID, node B decrements the SL value by
1, updates the DA field in the IPv6 header to the SID indicated by
the SL field, and then sends the packet over the link bound to the
End.X SID.

Step 3: Processing on transit node C

Node C is a transit node and can therefore process only IPv6
headers, not SRHs. As such, node C processes the received
packet in the same way that it does for a common IPv6 packet.

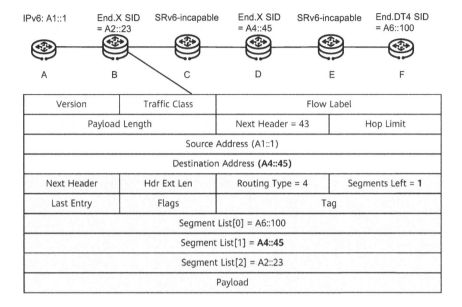

FIGURE 5.16    Processing on endpoint node B.

Specifically, node C searches the IPv6 routing table according to the longest-match rule and then forwards the packet to node D, represented by the current DA.

Step 4: Processing on endpoint node D

As shown in Figure 5.17, after receiving the IPv6 packet, node D searches the Local SID Table based on the DA A4::45 in the IPv6 header and finds a matching End.X SID. According to the instruction defined by the End.X SID, node D decrements the SL value by 1, updates the DA field in the IPv6 header to the SID indicated by the SL field, and then sends the packet over the link bound to the End.X SID. In this case, because the SL value is 0, node D removes the SRH as instructed by the PSP flavor, changing the packet to a common IPv6 one.

Step 5: Processing on transit node E

As shown in Figure 5.18, node E is also a transit node. As such, it processes the received packet in the same way that node C does and then forwards the packet to node F, represented by the current DA.

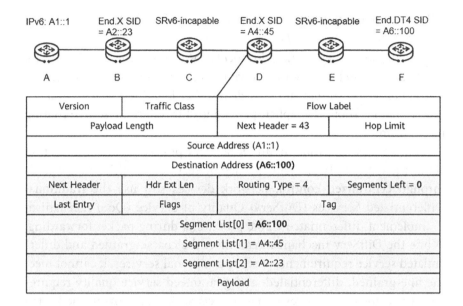

FIGURE 5.17   Processing on endpoint node D.

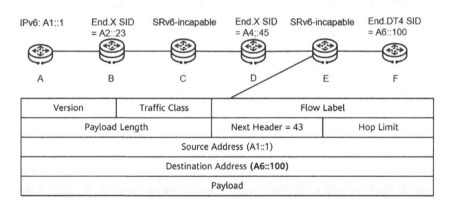

FIGURE 5.18   Processing on transit node E.

Step 6: Processing on endpoint node F

After receiving the packet, node F searches the Local SID Table based on the DA A6::100 in the IPv6 header and finds a matching End.DT4 SID. According to the instruction defined by the End.DT4 SID, node F decapsulates the packet by removing the IPv6 header, searches the IPv4 routing table of the VPN instance bound to the End.DT4 SID, and finally sends the inner IPv4 packet to host H2.

## 5.2.6 Carrying Network Slice Information in SRv6 SIDs

### 5.2.6.1 Resource-Aware SID

Unlike Resource Reservation Protocol-Traffic Engineering (RSVP-TE), SR lacks the functionality to reserve network resources for a specific or a group of services/users and provide resource identifiers in data packets, even though it supports explicit-path control through the source routing mechanism.

Although the controller of an SR network possesses state information about the entire network and can deploy services on different SR paths through centralized control, network devices still use the traditional Differentiated Services (DiffServ) Quality of Service (QoS) mechanism to implement differentiated traffic processing during packet forwarding. While the DiffServ mechanism can meet the coarse-grained and differentiated service requirements of some traditional services, it cannot meet the fine-grained, differentiated, and guaranteed service quality requirements of some new services/users. To meet such requirements, dedicated network resources need to be reserved, thereby achieving resource isolation between different services/users and ensuring service quality.

To enable an SRv6 network to reserve network resources for specific services/users, resource-aware SIDs[11] are introduced to the SR mechanism and can be implemented based on either the SR-MPLS or SRv6 data plane. Instead of requiring new SID types, resource attributes are added to existing SR SIDs (such as SRv6 End SIDs and End.X SIDs), and control plane protocols are used to advertise the mapping between SIDs and resources. In addition to representing a specific network processing function, an SRv6 resource-aware SID specifies the network resources used to implement this function. Typical network resources include link bandwidth, buffer, and queue resources. A specific segment — for example, a node or link segment — can be allocated with multiple resource-aware SIDs, each of which represents the network resource allocated to a specific user or service on this segment. In some cases, a group of reserved network resources can be associated with multiple resource-aware SIDs to flexibly implement exclusive or shared use of these resources.

An SR path with reserved resources can be established based on a group of resource-aware SIDs, thereby bearing private line services that require dedicated network resources. More importantly, resource-aware SIDs can also be used to establish SR-based network slices with specific resource and topology attributes.

### 5.2.6.2 Network Slice Based on Resource-Aware SIDs

A network slice has both resource and topology attributes. On an SRv6 network that supports network slicing, it is necessary to allocate independent resource-aware SRv6 locators/SIDs to different network slices and to establish the mapping between each SRv6 locator/SID and the topology attribute of the associated network slice. Specifically, an SRv6 node needs to allocate an independent resource-aware locator to each network slice that the node involves. Each resource-aware locator is associated with not only the topology or Flexible Algorithm (Flex-Algo) corresponding to the associated network slice but also the forwarding resource allocated to the associated network slice by each node that participates in the network topology or Flex-Algo. When forwarding a data packet that uses the specified resource-aware locator as the prefix of the destination IPv6 address, each network node can obtain the outbound interface and next hop information based on the topology or Flex-Algo corresponding to the resource-aware locator and determine the set of forwarding resources allocated by the outbound interface to the network slice associated with the resource-aware locator. Such forwarding resources include FlexE interfaces, channelized sub-interfaces, and Flex-Channels. This enables the packet to be forwarded using the resources of the outbound interface corresponding to the network slice.

Using the resource-aware SRv6 locator associated with a network slice as a prefix, a node can allocate a group of resource-aware SRv6 SIDs to the network slice in order to represent the logical nodes, logical links, and SRv6 functions in the slice as well as the network resources required to execute the corresponding SRv6 functions in the slice. In the example shown in Figure 5.19, different channelized sub-interfaces are allocated to the three network resource slices on the same physical link. In this case, a network node connected to the link needs to allocate a resource-aware End.X SID to each channelized sub-interface, and the resource-aware End.X SID of each network slice uses the SRv6 locator allocated by the node to the corresponding network slice as a prefix.

| A1:1::C1/64 | Layer 2 protocol | A2:1::C1 |
| A1:2::C1/64 | Layer 2 protocol | A2:2::C1 |
| A1:3::C1/64 | Layer 2 protocol | A2:3::C1 |

A                                                                                                B

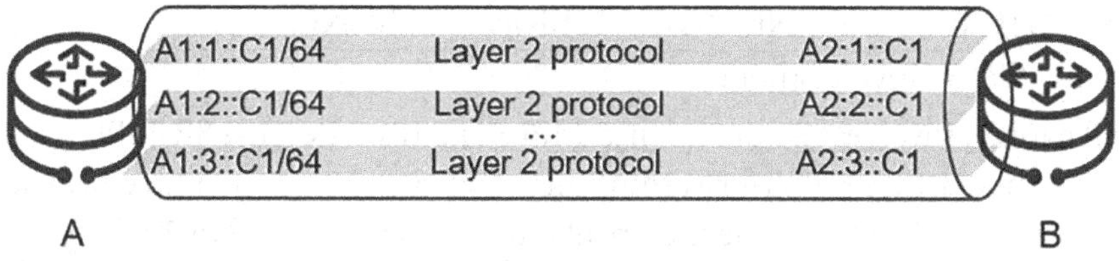

FIGURE 5.19  Example network slices based on resource-aware SIDs.

An SRv6 SID list generated based on a group of resource-aware SIDs instructs network nodes to process data packets using the network resources indicated by the resource-aware SIDs and to forward the packets over a specified SRv6 explicit path.

During packet forwarding, a resource-aware End.X SID is used by the node that allocates this SID to determine the corresponding outbound interface and the forwarding resources to be used for packet forwarding on the outbound interface. In addition, the resource-aware locator of a specific node is used by other SRv6 nodes to determine not only the next hop on the forwarding path destined for the node specified by the locator but also the network resources reserved for packet forwarding on each network node along the forwarding path.

Network slices based on resource-aware SIDs require each network node to allocate independent SRv6 locators/SIDs to the different network slices involved. As the number of network slices required on a network increases, more SRv6 resource-aware locators and SIDs need to be allocated. Consequently, the number of states that need to be maintained on the network also increases. Because the resource reservation mode based on resource-aware SIDs does not require per-path state maintenance and allows multiple paths in the same network slice to share the same resource-aware SID, it offers greater extensibility than RSVP-TE, which implements resource reservation on a per-path basis.

In addition to resource attributes, a network slice has topology attributes. As such, the mapping between resource-aware SRv6 locators/SIDs and the topology attributes of network slices needs to be established and maintained in the control plane. Each resource-aware SRv6 SID-based network slice can correspond to an independent network topology or Flex-Algo. In this case, topology, or Flex-Algo IDs can be used in the control plane to distinguish different network slices, and the resource-aware locator and SID of each network slice can be advertised based on each topology or <Topology, Algorithm> tuple through a control protocol.

## 5.3 STORIES BEHIND NETWORKING SLICING

### 5.3.1 SRv6 Development

SR natively involves two data planes: MPLS and IPv6. Because SR-MPLS can reuse the existing MPLS forwarding mechanism and is easy to implement, it was initially the focus of development after SR was proposed in 2013.

SRv6 NP was proposed a few years later, in 2017, enabling SR to be implemented based on the IPv6 forwarding plane. By adopting the SRv6 segment structure *Locator:Func:Arg*, in which the Locator field offers routability and the Func field acts like an MPLS label, SRv6 integrates the advantages of IP and MPLS forwarding. Working as a Layer 2.5 technology, MPLS is implemented based on IP but adds a shim layer before IP layer encapsulation. This means that the data planes of all IP devices have to be upgraded to support MPLS. In contrast, SRv6 works as a Layer 3.5 technology and adds MPLS-like functions above the IP layer. This makes SRv6 compatible with IPv6 forwarding. As a result, SRv6 can be incrementally deployed based on the IPv6 data plane without requiring a network-wide upgrade. And based on existing IPv6 reachability, SRv6 can be directly deployed across Ass, making it simple to deploy inter-AS E2E VPN services — unlike MPLS, which requires complex inter-AS LSP and VPN technologies. More importantly, the development of 5G, cloud, and other services brings new opportunities for IPv6 innovation, speeding up SRv6 development and achieving large-scale SRv6 deployment. Some carriers and enterprises even skip SR-MPLS and directly deploy SRv6 on their networks. Because MPLS/SR-MPLS on live networks is primarily based on IPv4, whereas SRv6 is based on IPv6, IPv6/SRv6 can be incrementally deployed on an IPv4/MPLS network, forming two independent planes (the IPv4/SR-MPLS plane and the IPv6/SRv6 plane) on the same network. While the incompatibility between IPv6 and IPv4 has been a major factor in slowing down IPv6 deployment, it now enables IPv4 and IPv6 planes to be isolated from each other, facilitating independent deployment of IPv6.

## 5.3.2 Origin of IPv6 Enhanced

The development of 5G and cloud services has given rise to the emergence of more IPv6 innovations. For example, IPv6-based innovative features such as network slicing, In-situ Flow Information Telemetry (IFIT), Deterministic Networking (DetNet), BIER IPv6 Encapsulation (BIERv6), and Application-aware IPv6 Networking (APN6) have emerged in addition to SRv6. These features use the IPv6 Hop-by-Hop Options header and Destination Options header as well as the Routing header, unlike SRv6, which primarily uses only the latter.

There are notable differences between these current IPv6 innovations and previous ones:

1. Previous IPv6 innovations were carried out by focusing on IPv6 address space, including upgrading the network infrastructure to support IPv6, IPv4/IPv6 address translation mechanisms, and so on. In contrast, current IPv6 innovations are carried out by enabling the IPv6 extension header to support new services.

2. Previous IPv6 innovations were benchmarked against IPv4 and offered only a limited number of new applications compared with IPv4. Moreover, some involved features, such as IPv4/IPv6 address translation, consume more network resources. In contrast, current IPv6 innovations are targeted at new 5G and cloud applications, which cannot be supported by IPv4.

3. Previous IPv6 innovations aimed to achieve Internet-oriented E2E interconnection across different networks. The current IPv6 innovations instead tend to be first deployed and applied within limited domains (e.g., IP transport networks).

IPv6 extension headers were standardized very early, but they have been seldom used in the past 20-plus years. During that time, the use of IPv6 extension headers — which featured variable-length encapsulation — would severely affect the forwarding performance due to the limited hardware capabilities. This explains why the development and application of IPv6 extension headers were restricted in those years. In recent years, a new round of IPv6 innovations has taken place by fully utilizing the IPv6 extension mechanism and introducing new encapsulations in the forwarding plane to support new services. Significant improvements in both network software and hardware capabilities have made it possible to develop and apply IPv6 extension headers, achieving flexible NP based on the IPv6 data plane.

The new round of IPv6 innovations is named IPv6 Enhanced to better reflect the differences from previous IPv6 innovations. In an effort to promote these IPv6 innovations, China's Expert Committee for Promoting Large-Scale IPv6 Deployment approved the establishment of the IPv6+ Technology Innovation Working Group at the end of 2019. And at the beginning of 2021, the European Telecommunications Standards Institute (ETSI) established the Industry Specification Group (ISG) IPv6 Enhanced Innovation (IPE) with similar goals in mind. To date, over 100 members and organizations have participated in the ISG.

In the SRv6 and IPv6 Enhanced innovation process, China has delivered a strong performance. It has produced many technological innovations, contributed significantly to the development of international standards in such organizations as the IETF, and taken the lead in large-scale deployment and application of IPv6 Enhanced innovations. These achievements are closely related to the rapid development of 5G and cloud services and the construction of IPv6 infrastructure in China. In keeping with China's plans at the end of 2017 to deploy IPv6 at scale, Huawei began promoting IPv6 Enhanced innovations represented by SRv6, achieving large-scale deployment of not only IPv6 but also IPv6 Enhanced innovations. These IPv6 Enhanced innovations provide strong support for 5G and cloud development. The invaluable experience gained from IPv6 Enhanced innovation and large-scale deployment is currently being shared and applied globally.

Technological innovations take time to develop and mature. Moreover, users' urgency for new service requirements, software and hardware capabilities, and the maturity of industry chains vary with time. As such, to facilitate innovation and achieve orderly industry development, the process of IPv6 Enhanced innovation can be divided into the following three phases:

- IPv6 Enhanced 1.0: focuses on basic SRv6 features such as VPN, TE, and FRR. Because the three features are critical for the success of MPLS, SRv6 must inherit and optimize them.

- IPv6 Enhanced 2.0: focuses on new network applications oriented toward 5G and the cloud. These applications include VPN+ (used to realize network slicing), IFIT, DetNet, Service Function Chaining (SFC), Software Defined Wide Area Network (SD-WAN), and BIERv6. New IPv6 extension header encapsulations and protocol extensions need to be introduced to support them.

- IPv6 Enhanced 3.0: focuses on APN6, which enables a network to be aware of applications. As the cloud and network become more converged, more information needs to be exchanged between them. IPv6 is the most practicable medium for achieving this. APN6 is developed based on IPv6, facilitating the convergence between applications and networks and also bringing significant changes to the network architecture.

Network slicing is not only an important feature of IPv6 Enhanced 2.0 but also a major IPv6 innovation following SRv6. It will further promote IPv6 deployment.

### 5.3.3 Bandwidth Admission Control and Resource Reservation

To support the bandwidth guarantee, SR was initially designed only to deduct the bandwidth required by services from the available link bandwidth during controller-based path computation. If the link bandwidth is insufficient, path computation fails. However, this method — more precisely called Bandwidth Admission Control (BAC) — falls short of what is required. Because the bandwidth required by services is not reserved on the network devices through which an SR path passes, it is challenging to ensure that associated services always obtain the expected guaranteed bandwidth. This is not a major issue on lightly loaded networks. But once congestion occurs, service quality deteriorates because multiple services compete for limited resources, which are not isolated. This issue becomes inevitable given the lack of accurate information about all service traffic on the controller and the burst of IP traffic. As such, there is a gap between the network situation and BAC-based path computation by the controller. In this case, bandwidth resource reservation needs to be provided for SR paths on a network so that services with guaranteed bandwidth can be offered.

To achieve resource reservation in SR, resource-aware SIDs are introduced. These SIDs can indicate not only segments (e.g., node, link, and path segments) but also resources reserved for the segments. In this way, SR paths using resource-aware segments can obtain guaranteed resources, making it possible to better meet the Service-Level Agreement (SLA) requirements of services. In terms of resource-aware segments, the following points are of particular importance:

1. Resource-aware segments are not independently defined as a certain type of segment. All SR segments with resource attributes are called resource-aware segments.

2. Point-to-point private line slices — in addition to multipoint-to-multipoint slices — can use resource-aware segments, thereby improving the quality of private lines through resource isolation.

3. Although RSVP-TE can be used to establish MPLS TE paths with reserved resources, it requires each device on a path to maintain the

resource reservation state of each path, posing scalability challenges. When resource-aware segments are used for network slices or private lines, devices do not need to maintain this state for each path. As such, a given reserved resource can be easily shared by multiple SR paths, achieving greater scalability.

# REFERENCES

[1] Kawamura S, Kawashima M. A Recommendation for IPv6 Address Text Representation [EB/OL]. (2020-01-21)[2022-09-30]. RFC 5952.
[2] IANA. Internet Protocol Version 6 Address Space [EB/OL]. (2019-09-13) [2022-09-30].
[3] Thomson S, Narten T, Jinmei T. IPv6 Stateless Address Autoconfiguration [EB/OL]. (2015-10-14)[2022-09-30]. RFC 4862.
[4] Huitema C, Carpenter B. Deprecating Site Local Addresses [EB/OL]. (2013-03-02)[2022-09-30]. RFC 3879.
[5] Deering S, Hinden R. Internet Protocol, Version 6 (IPv6) Specification [EB/OL]. (2020-02-04)[2022-09-30]. RFC 8200.
[6] Dong J, Li Z, Xie C et al. Carrying Virtual Transport Network (VTN) Identifier in IPv6 Extension Header for Enhanced VPN [EB/OL]. (2022-10-24)[2022-10-30]. draft-ietf-6man-enhanced-vpn-vtn-id-02.
[7] 3 GPP. System Architecture for the 5G System (5GS) [EB/OL]. (2022-03-23) [2022-09-30]. 3GPP TS 23.501.
[8] Filsfils C, Camarillo P, Leddy J, et al. Segment Routing over IPv6 (SRv6) Network Programming [EB/OL]. (2021-2)[2022-09-30]. RFC 8986.
[9] Filsfils C, Previdi S, Ginsberg L, et al. Segment Routing Architecture. (2018-12-19)[2022-09-30]. RFC 8402.
[10] Filsfils C, Dukes D, Previdi S, et al. IPv6 Segment Routing Header (SRH) [EB/OL]. (2020-03-14)[2022-09-30]. RFC 8754.
[11] Dong J, Bryant S, Miyasaka T, et al. Introducing Resource Awareness to SR Segments [EB/OL]. (2022-10-11)[2022-10-30]. draft-ietf-spring-resource-aware-segments-06.

# CHAPTER 6

# Control Plane Technologies for IPv6 Network Slicing

I N ADDITION TO REQUIRING resource partitioning in the forwarding plane and introducing slice identifiers in the data plane, IPv6 network slicing requires control plane technologies. This chapter describes these technologies by focusing on related control protocol extensions, including the IGP Multi-Topology (MT), Flexible Algorithm (Flex-Algo), Border Gateway Protocol-Link State (BGP-LS), BGP Shortest Path First (SPF), and Segment Routing (SR) Policy extensions for network slicing, as well as the Flow Specification (FlowSpec) extensions used for traffic steering to network resource slices.

## 6.1 IGP EXTENSIONS FOR NETWORK SLICING

Network slicing requires control protocols such as IGP to be used to advertise information about the topology and resource attributes of network slices. Based on these attributes, network slice controllers or network devices can perform path computation. In the control plane, the affinity attribute mechanism enables network slice controllers or path ingresses to compute Traffic Engineering (TE) explicit paths within a specified network slice. In addition to this IGP control plane mechanism, two technologies

DOI: 10.1201/9781032699868-8

are related to network slicing: MT and Flex-Algo. These two technologies enable network nodes to compute the shortest path based on the independent topology or Flex-Algo constraints of a slice without being entirely dependent on a controller, thereby better meeting the flexible connection requirements of services in the slice. This section describes the fundamentals of the two technologies, highlighting their characteristics, differences, and similarities. It also explains how these technologies are extended and applied to network slicing.

### 6.1.1 MT and Flex-Algo

#### 6.1.1.1 Background of MT

On a traditional IP network, the same basic network topology is used to compute routes for all services, which share a unique routing table. This leads to the following problems in network deployment:

- Uneven link bandwidth usage: Because only one network topology is used, the forwarding plane has only one unicast forwarding table. This means that all traffic to the same destination passes through the same next hop and is forwarded over the same path. In cases where multiple end-to-end (E2E) services (such as voice and data services) share the same physical link, some links may be congested while others are idle, making poor use of bandwidth resources.

- Packet loss in IPv4/IPv6 dual-stack scenarios: Routers that support IPv4/IPv6 dual-stack may not know that other routers and links do not support IPv6. As a result, these routers may forward IPv6 packets to the IPv6-incapable nodes according to the path computation results, leading to the discarding of such packets. Similarly, IPv4 packets destined for routers and links that do not support IPv4 will be discarded in dual-stack scenarios.

- Heavy dependency of multicast routing on unicast routing: The Reverse Path Forwarding (RPF) check of multicast depends on unicast routing tables. If multicast routing uses the default unicast routing table for RPF check, the following three issues arise:

  a. The changes in unicast routes affect the establishment of a Multicast Distribution Tree (MDT), whose stability depends on the convergence of the unicast routes.

b. Because multicast routing is constrained by unicast routing, it is difficult to plan an MDT that differs from the unicast forwarding path.

c. If a unicast routing table contains a unidirectional tunnel that spans multiple hops, multicast forwarding entries cannot be created on transit nodes along the tunnel path, adversely affecting multicast service forwarding.

IGP MT — proposed in Internet Engineering Task Force (IETF)-released IGP standards such as RFC 4915[1] and RFC 5120[2] — is used to define multiple different logical network topologies on a single IP network and to independently generate different routing tables based on these topologies. Unless otherwise specified, MT in this book refers to IGP MT. Typically, MT is used to separately define logical topologies for IPv4 and IPv6 address families, thereby avoiding the packet loss caused by inconsistent IPv4/IPv6 dual stack support on different nodes in a single topology. It also enables logical topologies to be separately defined for unicast and multicast, so that separate routing tables can be generated for them. This helps avoid the issues mentioned earlier.

To distinguish the prefixes and link attributes of different topologies, IGP is extended for MT by adding MT ID information to basic IGP messages. Different logical topologies can be defined according to the protocols supported by links or nodes or according to service types, and the nodes in these topologies can independently run SPF for route computation. This approach isolates the topologies and routing tables of different services on the same network, thereby improving network utilization.

### 6.1.1.2 Background of Flex-Algo

In distributed route computation through traditional IGP, nodes can rely only on link metric values to compute the shortest path to each destination through the SPF algorithm. Consequently, the differentiated requirements of users cannot be met due to the following limitations:

- Path computation can be performed based on only the default link metric value, meaning that there is only one type of metric value for path computation. However, because users may have diverse requirements for path computation, it is necessary to consider different types of link attributes and metrics — such as delay — for path computation.

- When there are requirements for path computation based on constraints (e.g., some links need to be excluded), traditional distributed route computation is no longer sufficient.

These limitations mean that network operators cannot specify path computation parameters or compute optimal paths according to different requirements. To better meet the requirements of specific users or services, network devices need to use customizable path computation rules when performing distributed route computation. The Flex-Algo technology allows network operators to define different algorithm IDs, each representing a group of parameters related to path computation, including the metric type, route computation algorithm, and constraints. On a network (physical or logical) where all devices use the same Flex-Algo for path computation, these devices will generate the same computation results, and no routing loops will occur. Because such algorithms are defined by network operators instead of standard organizations, they are called Flex-Algos.

### 6.1.1.3 Comparison between MT and Flex-Algo

Although both MT and Flex-Algo adopt similar approaches to provide logical topology definitions for network slicing and support independent route computation in a logical topology, they differ in design concepts and specific functions.

MT is designed to define and manage each logical topology as an independent logical network. This makes it possible to customize and differentiate the attributes of each logical node and logical link in each logical topology. For example, different attributes — such as the metric and administrative group (also referred to as color) — can be defined for the same physical link shared between different logical topologies. The total bandwidth of this physical link can also be divided into multiple bandwidth resources, enabling users to configure an independent bandwidth attribute for the logical links in each logical topology. The node and link attribute information about each logical topology is advertised through the MT-specific Type Length Value (TLV) extensions of IGP.

In MT, the default network topology is usually numbered 0. Although it typically includes all nodes and links throughout the physical network, some of them can belong to only specific network topologies instead of the default one. As such, in MT, the attributes of non-default topologies are independent of those of the default topology. Connections and attributes can be separately defined for each logical topology, and route entries can also be separately computed and generated.

As a control plane technology, MT can be directly applied to the IPv4 or IPv6 data plane and can also be extended to support the SR-MPLS or SRv6 data plane. If SR-MPLS is used, a network node needs to allocate a unique Prefix-SID to each topology to which the node belongs in order to identify itself in different topologies. It also needs to allocate a unique Adj-SID for each topology to which a link belongs in order to identify the link in different topologies. If SRv6 is used, the network node allocates a unique SRv6 locator and a unique End.X SID to identify the node and the link, respectively, in each topology. Prefix-SIDs or locators allocated to different topologies are used to generate routes to the destination node of the corresponding topology in the forwarding table of a device.

Table 6.1 lists the basic characteristics of MT.

On top of the network topology and attribute information, Flex-Algo introduces a path computation algorithm, metric type, and constraint information to ensure that network nodes involved in the same Flex-Algo

TABLE 6.1  Basic Characteristics of MT

| Basic Characteristic | Description |
| --- | --- |
| Design objective | To define independent logical networks. |
| Maximum number of logical topologies supported | IS-IS: 4096; OSPFv2: 128; OSPFv3: 256 (The corresponding draft has not been officially released as an RFC.) |
| Basic attributes of logical topologies | Node, link, and route prefix attributes. |
| Customizable attributes of logical topologies | Attributes such as the link metric, link-specific TE attributes (such as link administrative group), and prefix attributes. |
| Neighbor session establishment | A neighbor session supports multiple logical topologies. |
| Information advertisement | Node and link information about each logical topology is advertised using independent TLVs. |
| Route computation | Independent route computation is performed for each logical topology. |
| Packet forwarding | Class of service, IP address, and SR SID information in the data packet header is used to differentiate topologies. |

can obtain the same constrained path through distributed route computation. Each Flex-Algo needs to be applied to a network topology and uses the information about this topology. In addition to supporting route computation based on the default network topology, Flex-Algo can be combined with MT to apply to logical network topologies.

To ensure that all nodes on a network have a consistent understanding of the same Flex-Algo and that the path computed based on the Flex-Algo is loop-free, Flex-Algo Definition (FAD) information needs to be propagated throughout the network. The Flex-Algo mechanism defines only the path computation algorithm, metric type, and constraints and does not require different attribute values to be customized for Flex-Algos on the same node or link. For example, it does not require different TE metric values or bandwidth attributes to be configured for different Flex-Algos on a link. In practice, network devices can be configured with a group of TE attributes dedicated to the Flex-Algo application and advertise this group without distinguishing the TE attributes of different Flex-Algos or advertising different TE attributes for each Flex-Algo. The color and metric type specified in a FAD are the TE attributes (including the color and metric attributes) of the Flex-Algo application.

As a control plane technology used for path computation, Flex-Algo can use SR-MPLS or SRv6 as the data plane. If SR-MPLS is used, a network node needs to allocate a unique Prefix-SID to each supported Flex-Algo in order to identify itself in each Flex-Algo, thereby generating SR forwarding entries corresponding to these Flex-Algos. If SRv6 is used, a network node needs to allocate a unique SRv6 locator to each supported Flex-Algo in order to identify itself in each Flex-Algo, thereby generating routing entries corresponding to these Flex-Algos. Prefix-SIDs or locators corresponding to different Flex-Algos are used to generate Flex-Algo-based routes to the destination node in the forwarding table of a device. A network node can also allocate different Adj-SIDs or SRv6 End.X SIDs to different Flex-Algos in order to generate an SR explicit path corresponding to the specific Flex-Algo and a Topology Independent Loop Free Alternate (TI-LFA) path that meets the constraints of this Flex-Algo.

Table 6.2 lists the basic characteristics of Flex-Algo.

Both MT and Flex-Algo can be used to define constraints on network topologies and independently compute routes based on a customized

TABLE 6.2    Basic Characteristics of Flex-Algo

| Basic Characteristic | Description |
| --- | --- |
| Design objective | To achieve distributed computation of constrained paths. |
| Maximum number of Flex-Algos supported | 128. |
| FAD content | Includes the metric type, route computation algorithm type, and constraints. |
| Neighbor session establishment | Devices are unaware of Flex-Algo during the process of neighbor session establishment. |
| Information advertisement | The information that can be advertised includes the definition of each Flex-Algo, the Flex-Algo in which a node participates, and the data plane identifiers (e.g., SR SID and SRv6 locator) allocated to nodes and links for corresponding different Flex-Algos. |
| Route computation | Independent route computation is performed for each Flex-Algo. |
| Packet forwarding | The destination address and SR SID information in the data packet header are used to differentiate Flex-Algos. |

topology. MT enables you to further customize the node and link attributes in each logical topology, allowing you to define completely independent and differentiated logical topologies on a single physical network. In contrast, Flex-Algo introduces a path computation algorithm, metric type, and constraint information for route computation based on the attributes of the physical topology or logical topologies, allowing Flex-Algos to be differentiated by referencing different attributes of the associated network topology. To summarize, MT facilitates the customization of logical topologies and attributes, whereas Flex-Algo enables path computation based on existing topology attributes and constraints. As such, Flex-Algo requires less information to be advertised through control protocols. In scenarios where independent attributes do not need to be customized for each logical topology, Flex-Algo can be used as a lightweight alternative to MT technology.

## 6.1.2 MT Extensions for SRv6 SID-Based Network Slicing

This section describes the fundamentals of MT and how it is extended and used for the SRv6 SID-based IP network slicing solution.

### 6.1.2.1 Fundamentals

OSPF MT is similar to IS-IS MT, except for the difference in the extension method of protocol packets and the format of extension fields. As such, this book uses the IS-IS MT extension as an example to explain how MT is implemented. IS-IS MT defines a new TLV to carry the MT ID so that the link state information[2] of different topologies can be identified. After MT is enabled, the Hello packet or Link State PDU (LSP) sent by a router through an interface contains one or more MT TLVs to indicate each topology to which the interface belongs. If the Hello packet or LSP received from a neighbor does not contain any matching MT TLV, the neighbor is considered to belong only to the default IPv4 topology. On a point-to-point link, if two neighbors do not share an identical MT ID, they cannot establish an adjacency with each other. However, on a broadcast link, an adjacency can still be established between neighbors even if they do not share the same MT ID.

Figure 6.1 shows the format of the MT TLV.

Table 6.3 describes the involved fields.

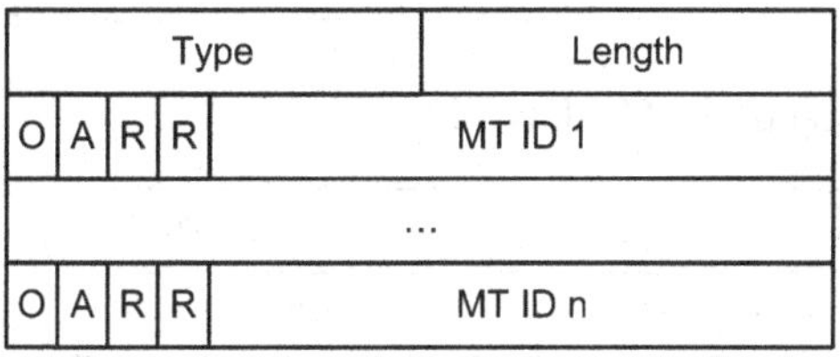

FIGURE 6.1   Format of the MT TLV.

TABLE 6.3   Fields in the MT TLV

| Field | Length | Description |
|---|---|---|
| Type | 8 bits | TLV type. The value is 229. |
| Length | 8 bits | Total length of the TLV (excluding the Type and Length fields), in bytes. The value is twice the number of MT IDs. |
| O | 1 bit | Bit O is the overload bit of an MT. When a device is overloaded in the corresponding MT, this bit is set to 1. (It is valid only in LSP fragment 0 for MTs with non-0 IDs. Otherwise, it should be set to 0 before transmission and ignored upon receipt.) |
| A | 1 bit | Bit A is the Attach bit of an MT. When a device is connected to a Level-2 network in the corresponding MT, this bit is set to 1. (It is valid only in LSP fragment 0 for MTs with non-0 IDs. Otherwise, it should be set to 0 before transmission and ignored upon receipt.) |
| R | 1 bit | Bit R is reserved. It should be set to 0 before transmission and ignored upon receipt. |
| MT ID | 12 bits | MT ID to be advertised. |

After establishing an IS-IS neighbor relationship with a neighboring device, a network device uses the MT Intermediate Systems TLV (MT-ISN TLV, with the type number of 222) in LSPs to advertise the neighbor relationship and link attribute information about a specific topology. The network device also uses the MT IP Reachability TLV (type number: 235) or MT IPv6 Reachability TLV (type number: 237) in LSPs to advertise route prefix information about the topology. Figures 6.2 and 6.3 show the formats of the MT-ISN TLV and MT IPv6 Reachability TLV, respectively.

Tables 6.4 and 6.5 describe the fields in the MT-ISN TLV and MT IPv6 Reachability TLV, respectively.

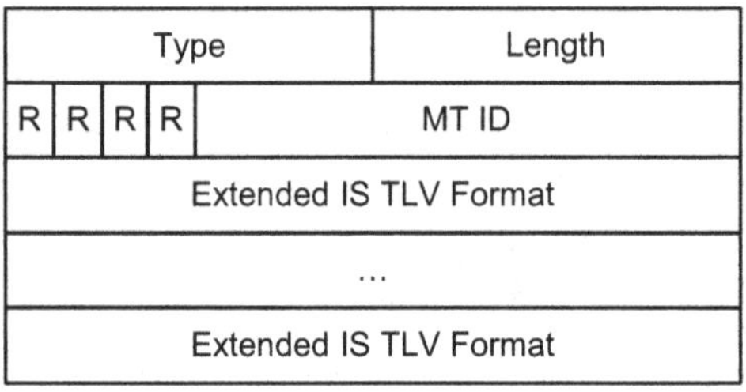

FIGURE 6.2    Format of the MT-ISN TLV.

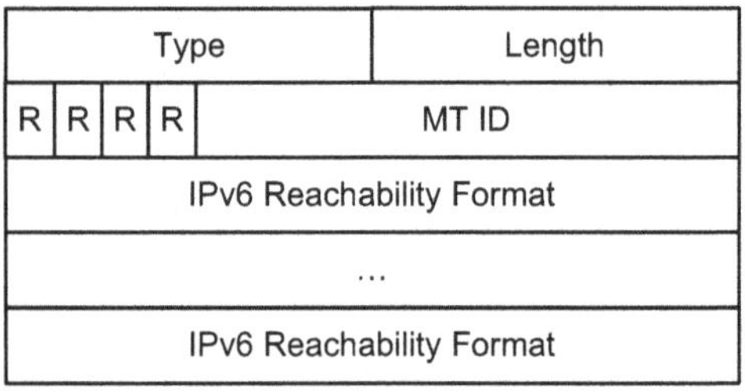

FIGURE 6.3    Format of the MT IPv6 reachability TLV.

TABLE 6.4    Fields in the MT-ISN TLV

| Field | Length | Description |
|---|---|---|
| Type | 8 bits | TLV type. The value is 222. |
| Length | 8 bits | Total length of the TLV (excluding the Type and Length fields), in bytes. |
| R | 1 bit | Bit R is reserved. It should be set to 0 before transmission and ignored upon receipt. |
| MT ID | 12 bits | MT ID to be advertised. If it is set to 0, the TLV must be ignored. |
| Extended IS TLV Format | Variable | It is in the same format as the IS-IS Extended IS Reachability TLV (type number: 22).[3] If no sub-TLVs are used, the Extended IS TLV can contain information about up to 23 neighbors of the same MT. |

TABLE 6.5   Fields in the MT IPv6 Reachability TLV

| Field | Length | Description |
|---|---|---|
| Type | 8 bits | TLV type. The value is 237. |
| Length | 8 bits | Total length of the TLV (excluding the Type and Length fields), in bytes. |
| R | 1 bit | Bit R is reserved. It should be set to 0 before transmission and ignored upon receipt. |
| MT ID | 12 bits | MT ID to be advertised. If it is set to 0, the TLV must be ignored. |
| IPv6 Reachability Format | Variable | It is in the same format as the IPv6 Reachability TLV (type number: 236) described in RFC 5308[4] |

The following describes how to use IS-IS MT to implement dual-stack separation and unicast and multicast topology separation.

6.1.2.1.1  Dual-Stack Separation    On the network shown in Figure 6.4, nodes A, C, and D support the IPv4/IPv6 dual stack, whereas node B supports only IPv4 and is therefore unable to forward IPv6 packets. Without IS-IS MT, all four nodes perform SPF calculations based on only the hybrid topology. In this case, the shortest (least-cost) path from node A to node D is A→B→D. Because node B does not support IPv6, IPv6 packets cannot be forwarded to node D through node B.

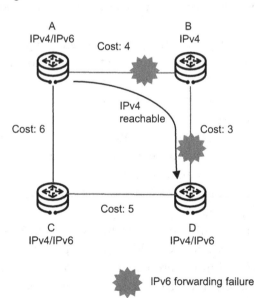

FIGURE 6.4   Hybrid topology with both IPv4 and IPv6.

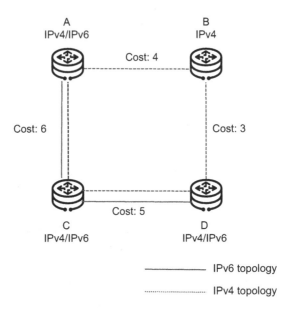

FIGURE 6.5    IPv4 and IPv6 topology separation.

If IS-IS MT is deployed to establish an independent IPv6 topology (as shown in Figure 6.5), node A chooses only IPv6-capable links for IPv6 packet forwarding. In this case, the shortest IPv6 path from node A to node D is A→C→D, through which IPv6 packets can be correctly forwarded.

6.1.2.1.2 Unicast and Multicast Topology Separation    Figure 6.6 shows an example for the networking of unicast and multicast topology separation using IS-IS MT.

On the network shown in Figure 6.6, all routers are connected through IS-IS, and a multi-hop TE tunnel from node E to node A is deployed. Because the outbound interface of the IS-IS-computed optimal route from node E to node A is a TE tunnel interface rather than a physical interface, the transit node C on the tunnel path cannot correctly create multicast forwarding entries in multicast scenarios. This leads to a failure to forward multicast service packets.

IS-IS MT addresses this issue by establishing the unicast topology for non-multicast services and the multicast topology for multicast services. After MT is deployed in the preceding scenario, the multicast topology excludes TE tunnels. This enables the MDT to be established hop by hop, allowing multicast service packets to be properly forwarded without being affected by TE tunnels.

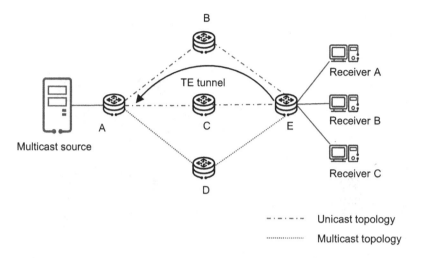

FIGURE 6.6    Unicast and multicast topology separation.

### 6.1.2.2 Combination of MT and SR

In the data plane, MT needs to use some fields in data packets to distinguish the packets of different logical topologies. This is necessary for achieving table lookup and packet forwarding based on the routing information of the corresponding topology. In traditional IP forwarding, the Differentiated Services Code Point (DSCP) field or IP address field in the IP packet header can be used to distinguish the packets of different topologies.

Once SR is introduced, MT can use SR SIDs as data plane identifiers to distinguish packets of different topologies. IGP extensions for SR can employ a combination of MT and SR. With IS-IS extensions for SRv6, different SRv6 locators and End SIDs can be advertised based on different topologies and SRv6 End.X SIDs belonging to different topologies can be advertised using the MT-ISN TLV and  MT IS Neighbor Attribute TLV. This enables a network device to compute and generate a routing entry for the SRv6 locator allocated to a specific topology and to generate local SRv6 SID entries corresponding to the topology. Based on the SRv6 locator or SRv6 SID in the destination address field of the packet header, the device searches the IPv6 forwarding table for the corresponding entry and forwards the packet accordingly. Similarly, in addition to SRv6 End and End.X SIDs, other types of SRv6 SIDs (such as SRv6 VPN SIDs) are associated with specific topologies through SRv6 locators.

Figure 6.7 shows an SRv6 network with two IGP topologies: MT-1 and MT-2. Each network node needs to allocate a unique SRv6 locator to each

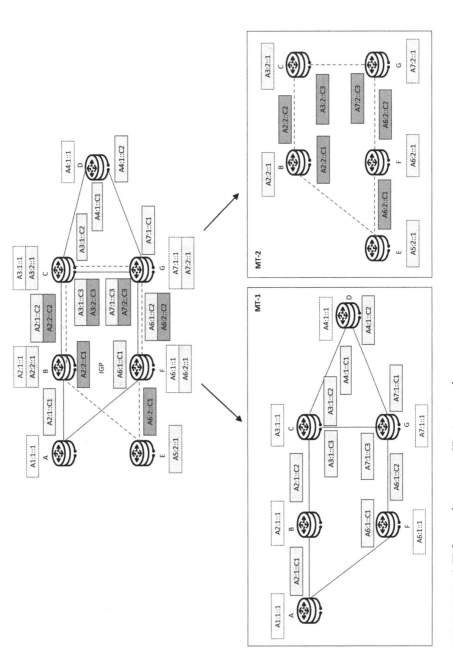

FIGURE 6.7  MT forwarding on an SRv6 network.

topology in which it participates. This locator is used as a prefix to allocate End and End.X SIDs in the topology. The following takes node B as an example and assumes that it allocates SRv6 locators A2:1::/64 and A2:2::/64 to MT-1 and MT-2, respectively. In each of the topologies, node B uses the locator of the topology as a prefix to generate End and End.X SIDs corresponding to the topology. For example, for the link between itself and node C, node B allocates End.X SIDs A2:1::C2 and A2:2::C2 to MT-1 and MT-2, respectively. In this case, all the network nodes compute routes based on each topology in which they participate and then generate routing entries for the SRv6 locators allocated to this topology. The End.X SID of each topology indicates the link over which packets are forwarded in the topology. If an interface belongs to multiple topologies, different End.X SIDs can be allocated so that each End.X SID identifies the topology to which the interface belongs.

The SRv6 Locator TLV[5] is used to advertise SRv6 locators and their associated End SIDs. It carries MT ID information to describe the mapping between locators and topologies. Figure 6.8 shows the format of this TLV. Table 6.6 describes the involved fields.

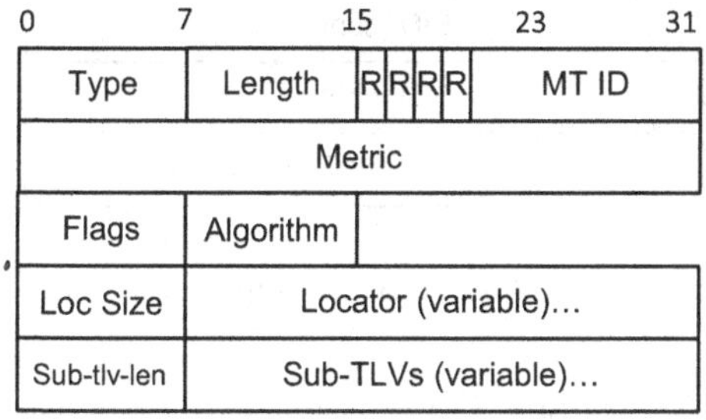

FIGURE 6.8   Format of the SRv6 Locator TLV.

TABLE 6.6   Fields in the SRv6 Locator TLV

| Field | Length | Description |
| --- | --- | --- |
| Type | 1 byte | TLV type. The value is 27. |
| Length | 1 byte | Total length of the TLV (excluding the Type and Length fields), in bytes. |
| MT ID | 12 bits | Multi-topology ID. The value 0 indicates the default topology. |
| Metric | 4 bytes | Metric value. |

*(Continued)*

TABLE 6.6 (*Continued*)   Fields in the SRv6 Locator TLV

| Field | Length | Description |
|-------|--------|-------------|
| Flags | 1 byte | Flags. Currently, only the D bit is available. When a SID is leaked from Level-2 to Level-1, the D bit must be set. SIDs with the D bit set must not be leaked from Level-1 to Level-2. This is to prevent routing loops. |
| Algorithm | 1 byte | Algorithm identifier. |
| Loc Size | 1 byte | Locator length, which indicates the number of bits in the SRv6 locator. |
| Locator | Variable | SRv6 locator to be advertised. |
| Sub-TLV-len | 1 byte | Sub-TLV length. |
| Sub-TLVs | Variable | Included sub-TLVs, such as the SRv6 End SID Sub-TLV. |

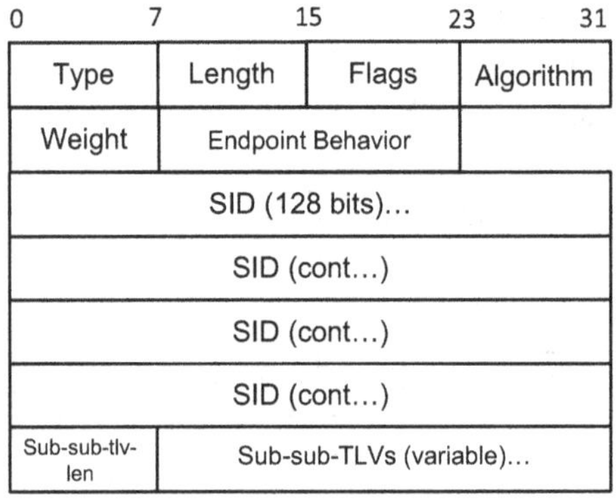

FIGURE 6.9   Format of the SRv6 End.X SID sub-TLV.

The SRv6 End.X SID Sub-TLV[5] is used to advertise the SRv6 End.X SID associated with a P2P adjacency. It can carry an SRv6 End.X SID belonging to a specific topology and is advertised as a sub-TLV of the Extended IS TLV in the MT-ISN TLV (shown in Figure 6.2) that describes the multi-topology neighbor relationship. Figure 6.9 shows the format of this sub-TLV.

Table 6.7 describes the involved fields.

The SRv6 LAN End.X SID Sub-TLV[5] is used to advertise the SRv6 End.X SID associated with a LAN adjacency. It can carry an SRv6 End.X SID belonging to a specific topology and is advertised as a sub-TLV of the Extended IS TLV in the MT-ISN TLV (shown in Figure 6.2) that describes the multi-topology neighbor relationship. Figure 6.10 shows the format of this sub-TLV.

TABLE 6.7    Fields in the SRv6 End.X SID Sub-TLV

| Field | Length | Description |
|-------|--------|-------------|
| Type | 1 byte | Sub-TLV type. The value is 43. |
| Length | 1 byte | Total length of the sub-TLV (excluding the Type and Length fields), in bytes. |
| Flags | 1 byte | Flags. Currently, the B-Flag (backup flag), S-Flag (set flag), and P-Flag (persistent flag) have been defined. Other flag bits should be set to 0 before transmission and ignored upon receipt. |
| Algorithm | 1 byte | Algorithm identifier. |
| Weight | 1 byte | Weight of the End.X SID for the purpose of load balancing. |
| Endpoint Behavior | 2 bytes | SRv6 endpoint behavior. |
| SID | 16 bytes | SRv6 SID to be advertised. |
| Sub-sub-tlv-len | 1 byte | Sub-sub-TLV length. |
| Sub-sub-TLVs (variable) | Variable | Included sub-sub-TLVs. |

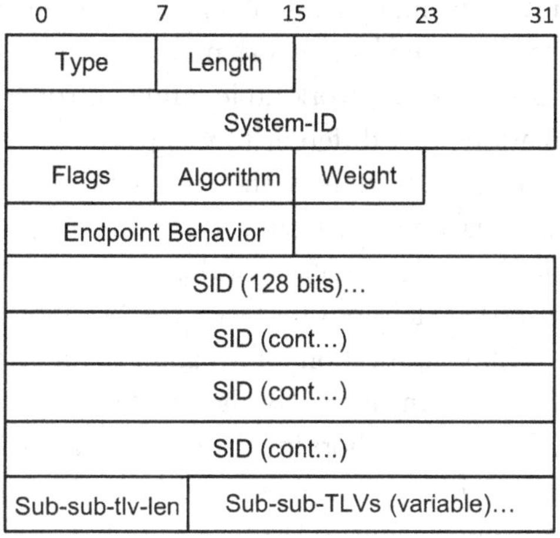

FIGURE 6.10    Format of the SRv6 LAN End.X SID sub-TLV.

TABLE 6.8    System-ID Field in the SRv6 LAN End.X SID Sub-TLV

| Field | Length | Description |
|-------|--------|-------------|
| System-ID | 6 bytes | IS-IS system ID. |

Compared with the SRv6 End.X SID Sub-TLV, the SRv6 LAN End.X SID Sub-TLV has an additional System-ID field, which is described in Table 6.8.

### 6.1.2.3 MT Application in SRv6 SID-Based Network Slicing

In the SRv6 SID-based network slicing solution, each network slice corresponds to an independent logical network topology. This means that a network slice can be identified by a unique MT ID in the control plane without the need to introduce a new control plane identifier. Because IGP extensions for SRv6 support MT, it is possible to advertise independent SRv6 locator, SR End SID, and End.X SID information for each topology. This enables network nodes to compute and generate independent SRv6 routing entries for different SRv6 network slices based on the SRv6 locators and SIDs associated with different topologies.

In addition to defining and advertising connection relationship information of nodes and links in different logical topologies, MT supports the function of defining and advertising the attributes of network nodes and links in different topologies. Although this function is not widely applied in traditional MT scenarios, it can be used in network slicing scenarios to advertise bandwidth information and other TE attributes (e.g., link metric and color attribute) allocated by network nodes and links to different network slices. In this way, the network nodes and controller can obtain network slice information with different topology connections, bandwidth information, and other TE attributes, thereby supporting independent TE path computation in each network slice based on constraints such as the bandwidth, metric, and color attribute of the slice.

For example, in IS-IS extensions for SRv6, the MT-ISN TLV can be used to advertise the neighbor connection information about each topology. Sub-TLVs in the MT-ISN TLV can be used to advertise SRv6 End.X SIDs that indicate Layer 3 adjacencies to neighbors in the topology, bandwidth information about the connection with each neighbor, and other TE attributes (e.g., link metric and color attribute). Figure 6.11 shows the advertisement through the MT-ISN TLV and its sub-TLVs. In the forwarding plane of a network device,

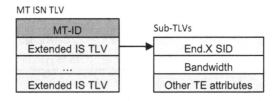

FIGURE 6.11 Advertisement of each topology's SRv6 SIDs and TE attributes through the MT-ISN TLV and its sub-TLVs.

resource reservation interfaces, sub-interfaces, or sub-channels created for different network slices can be associated with the Layer 3 connections in the topology corresponding to a specified network slice. This makes it possible to advertise the attributes of the resource reservation interfaces, sub-interfaces, or sub-channels in these network slices through MT.

Figure 6.12 shows an example for advertising the SR SIDs and TE attributes of each logical topology through IS-IS MT. In this example, two network slices with different topologies need to be established on a physical network, with independent forwarding resources allocated to each network slice. Using FlexE interfaces, channelized sub-interfaces, or Flex-Channels on physical interfaces, network devices can allocate the required bandwidth resources to each network slice. On the network, different logical topologies (MT-1 and MT-2) are defined for each network slice. In each topology, the TE extension of IS-IS MT is used to advertise connections and TE attributes, such as the bandwidth allocated to links.

In the SRv6 SID-based network slicing solution, because each network slice corresponds to an independent logical topology, the number of logical topologies supported by the control plane determines how many network slices can be provided. The MT ID length defined by IS-IS is 12 bits, indicating that MT supports a maximum of 4096 network slices. In real-world applications, however, factors such as the network scale and the

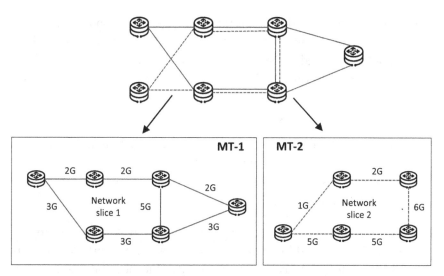

FIGURE 6.12 Advertisement of each logical topology's SR SIDs and TE attributes through IS-IS MT.

control-plane processing capability of network devices limit the number of logical topologies that can be deployed to typically less than 100.

### 6.1.3 Flex-Algo Extensions for SRv6 SID-Based Network Slicing

In distributed route computation through traditional IGP, a node runs SPF to compute the shortest path to the destination based on only the link metric value, failing to meet the differentiated requirements of network operators on algorithm customization.

To better meet the requirements of specific users or services, network devices need to use customizable path computation rules when performing distributed route computation. This is why the Flex-Algo technology was introduced. It allows carriers to define a path computation rule identifier to represent a group of parameters (e.g., the metric type, route computation algorithm, and constraints) related to path computation. A Flex-Algo is mainly defined using the following elements:

- Flex-Algo ID: ID of a Flex-Algo. The value ranges from 128 to 255. (Values 0 to 127 are reserved for standard algorithms.)

- Metric-type: link metric type used for path computation. Currently, the IGP metric, TE default metric, and link delay metric types have been defined.

- Calc-type: type of the algorithm used for route computation. SPF is the most commonly used algorithm. RFC 8402[6] defines two standard algorithm types identified using 0 and 1. The value 0 indicates the SPF algorithm based on the IGP link metric, and the value 1 indicates the strict-SPF algorithm based on the IGP link metric. New algorithm types can be defined later.

- Constraints: path computation constraints, such as the link color and Shared Risk Link Group (SRLG). They are used to determine whether links in a network topology can be included in the Flex-Algo path computation.

Based on the link metric type, path computation algorithm, and topology constraints defined by the specified Flex-Algo, network devices can generate consistent path computation results that meet specific requirements, flexibly supporting traffic engineering through distributed route computation.

### 6.1.3.1 FAD Advertisement

To ensure that the forwarding paths computed through an IGP Flex-Algo are consistent and loop-free, the devices in the same IGP area need to have a consistent understanding of the Flex-Algo. In this case, IGP is used by the devices to advertise FADs and locally supported Flex-Algos. If different FADs are advertised for the same Flex-Algo through IGP, all devices in the IGP area must select the same FAD.

IS-IS advertises a FAD through the IS-IS FAD Sub-TLV,[7] which is carried using the IS-IS Router Capability TLV (type number: 242) and advertised to neighbors. Figure 6.13 shows the format of the IS-IS FAD Sub-TLV. Table 6.9 describes the involved fields.

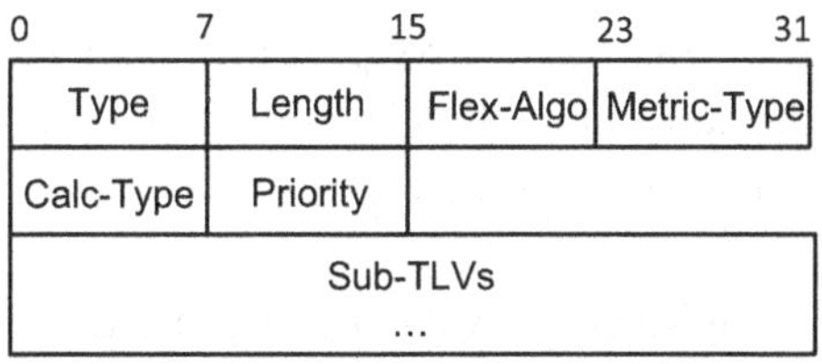

FIGURE 6.13    Format of the IS-IS FAD sub-TLV.

TABLE 6.9    Fields in the IS-IS FAD Sub-TLV

| Field | Length | Description |
|---|---|---|
| Type | 1 byte | Sub-TLV type. The value is 26. |
| Length | 1 byte | Total length of the sub-TLV (excluding the Type and Length fields), in bytes. |
| Flex-Algo | 1 byte | Flex-Algo ID, which is an integer ranging from 128 to 255. |
| Metric-Type | 1 byte | Type of the metric used for path computation. The values and types of supported metrics are as follows:<br><br>• 0: IGP metric<br><br>• 1: minimum unidirectional link delay<br><br>• 2: TE default metric |
| Calc-Type | 1 byte | Calculation type. The value ranges from 0 to 127. If the calculation type is SPF, the value of this field is 0. |
| Priority | 1 byte | FAD priority. A larger value indicates a higher priority. |
| Sub-TLVs | Variable | Optional sub-TLVs, which can be used to define constraints. |

A Flex-Algo is defined by users and typically represented by the 3-tuple <Metric-Type, Calc-Type, Constraints>. Metric-Type and Calc-Type have been described in Table 6.9. Constraints are mainly based on link administrative groups (also referred to as link colors), or SRLGs. Those based on link administrative groups are classified as follows:

- Exclude Administrative Group: A link is excluded from path computation if the associated link administrative group contains any specified administrative group.

- Include-Any Administrative Group: A link is included in path computation if the associated link administrative group contains any specified administrative group.

- Include-All Administrative Group: A link is included in path computation if the associated link administrative group contains all specified administrative groups.

Flex-Algo defines the following SRLG-based constraint:

- Exclude SRLG Sub-TLV: A link is excluded from path computation if it belongs to a specified SRLG.

The preceding constraints are described using the Sub-TLV field in the FAD Sub-TLV.[7] The Exclude Admin Group Sub-TLV, Include-Any Admin Group Sub-TLV, and Include-All Admin Group Sub-TLV share the same format, which is shown in Figure 6.14.

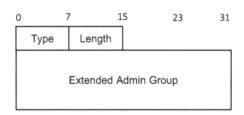

FIGURE 6.14 Format of the exclude/include-any/include-all admin group sub-TLV.

TABLE 6.10 Fields in the Exclude/Include-Any/Include-All Admin Group Sub-TLV

| Field | Length | Description |
|-------|--------|-------------|
| Type | 1 byte | Sub-TLV type. |
| | | • Type=1: Exclude Admin Group |
| | | • Type=2: Include-Any Admin Group |
| | | • Type=3: Include-All Admin Group |
| Length | 1 byte | Total length of the sub-TLV (excluding the Type and Length fields), in bytes. |
| Extended Admin Group | Variable | Field that is used to describe an Admin Group-based constraint according to the value of Type. |

Table 6.10 describes the involved fields.

In the same IGP area, Flex-Algos with the same ID but different meanings may be defined for different devices. If FADs are different, the devices select a FAD according to the following rules:

- The FAD with the highest priority is preferentially selected.

- If the priorities of the FADs advertised by devices through IS-IS are the same, the FAD advertised by the device with the largest system ID is selected.

### 6.1.3.2 Flex-Algo Information Advertisement

Network devices can use different algorithms (e.g., SPF and its variants) to compute the paths to other devices or to specified prefixes. On an SR network, network devices use the IS-IS Router Capability TLV (type number: 242) to carry the newly defined SR-Algorithm Sub-TLV in order to advertise supported algorithms. The SR-Algorithm Sub-TLV can be propagated only within the same IS-IS level; that is, it must not be propagated across IS-IS levels. Figure 6.15 shows the format of the SR-Algorithm Sub-TLV.

Table 6.11 describes the involved fields.

### 6.1.3.3 Advertisement of Flex-Algo Link Attribute Information

A FAD specifies the metric type, path computation algorithm, and link color- or SRLG-based topology constraints used for path computation through the specified Flex-Algo. Based on TE metric types defined in RFC 5305[3] and RFC 8570,[8] various link attributes required by Flex-Algo need

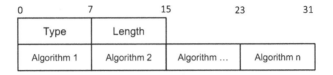

FIGURE 6.15   Format of the SR-algorithm sub-TLV.

TABLE 6.11   Fields in the SR-Algorithm Sub-TLV

| Field | Length | Description |
|-------|--------|-------------|
| Type | 1 byte | Sub-TLV type. The value is 19. |
| Length | 1 byte | Total length of the sub-TLV (excluding the Type and Length fields), in bytes. |
| Algorithm | 1 byte | Node-supported algorithm type, which can be a standard or flexible algorithm. Because a node may support multiple algorithm types, this sub-TLV can have multiple Algorithm fields. |

TABLE 6.12   Typical Link TE Attributes Used by Flex-Algo

| Sub-TLV Type Number | Name | Description |
|---------------------|------|-------------|
| 3 | Administrative group (color) | 32-bit bit mask, with each bit corresponding to one administrative group. |
| 14 | Extended Administrative Group | Bit mask whose length is an integer multiple of 32 bits, with each bit corresponding to one administrative group. |
| 18 | Traffic Engineering Default Metric | Default metric of traffic engineering. The value is a 24-bit unsigned integer assigned by a network administrator. |
| 34 | Min Unidirectional Link Delay | 24-bit field indicating the minimum link delay (in microseconds) measured at a certain interval. |
| 138 | Shared Risk Link Group | 32-bit SRLG identifier. |

to be advertised by network devices. Table 6.12 lists the typical link TE attributes used by Flex-Algo.

To distinguish the link attributes used by Flex-Algo from those already used on the network, RFC 8919[9] and RFC 8920[10] define specific mechanisms that enable the link attributes used by Flex-Algo to be advertised as Application-Specific Link Attributes (ASLAs).

### 6.1.3.4 Advertisement of Flex-Algo-Associated SRv6 SID Information

Since its inception, Flex-Algo has been used in combination with SR technology. In SRv6 scenarios, a network device needs to allocate a unique SRv6 locator to each involved Flex-Algo and associate the SRv6 SID that uses the locator as a prefix with the Flex-Algo. The device also needs to advertise the Flex-Algos, SRv6 locators, and mapping between the Flex-Algos and SRv6 SIDs through IGP, allowing other devices on the network to calculate and generate SRv6 routing entries corresponding to different Flex-Algos based on the path computation rules defined by the Flex-Algos.

For example, in IS-IS scenarios, the mapping between Flex-Algos and SRv6 locators/SIDs can be advertised through the following TLV and sub-TLVs:

- SRv6 Locator TLV: carries the Algorithm field to describe the mapping between locators and algorithms. For details about the format of this TLV, see Figure 6.8 in the previous section.

- SRv6 End.X SID Sub-TLV: carries the Algorithm field to describe the mapping between End.X SIDs and algorithms. For details about the format of this sub-TLV, see Figure 6.9 in the previous section.

- SRv6 LAN End.X SID Sub-TLV: carries the Algorithm field to describe the mapping between End.X SIDs and algorithms. For details about the format of this sub-TLV, see Figure 6.10 in the previous section.

Similarly, in addition to SRv6 End and End.X SIDs, other types of SRv6 SIDs (such as SRv6 VPN SIDs) are associated with specific algorithms through SRv6 locators.

On top of the combination of MT and SR, Flex-Algo further introduces the mapping between SRv6 locators and algorithms, as well as between SIDs and algorithms. In this way, each SRv6 locator and the SIDs associated with this locator can correspond to a <topology, algorithm> pair. Through different Flex-Algos, differentiated path computation constraints and rules can be further defined based on specific topologies.

### 6.1.3.5 SRv6 Flex-Algo Application Examples

This subsection uses Figure 6.16 as an example to describe how SRv6 Flex-Algos are implemented. Assume that two Flex-Algos (Flex-Algos 128 and 129, defined in Table 6.13) are used on the network.

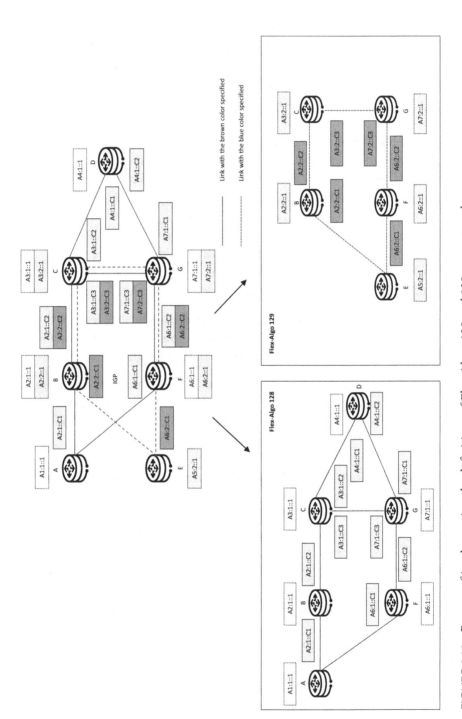

FIGURE 6.16   Process of implementing the definitions of Flex-Algos 128 and 129 on a network.

TABLE 6.13   Definitions of Flex-Algos 128 and 129

| Flex-Algo ID | Metric Type | Calculation Type | Topology Constraint |
| --- | --- | --- | --- |
| Flex-Algo 128 | 0: IGP metric | 0: SPF | Brown links are included. |
| Flex-Algo 129 | 2: TE default metric | 0: SPF | Blue links are included. |

The definitions of Flex-Algos 128 and 129 can be advertised by one or more nodes on the network through the FAD Sub-TLV. In this way, all nodes in the entire IGP area can obtain the same definitions. Each node uses the IS-IS SR-Algorithm Sub-TLV to advertise the Flex-Algo in which it participates.

- Nodes A and D advertise that they participate only in Flex-Algo 128.

- Node E advertises that it participates only in Flex-Algo 129.

- Nodes B, C, F, and G advertise that they participate in both Flex-Algos 128 and 129.

Each network node needs to allocate a unique SRv6 locator to each Flex-Algo in which it participates. This locator is used as a prefix to allocate End and End.X SIDs in the Flex-Algo. The following takes node B as an example and assumes that it allocates SRv6 locators A2:1::/64 and A2:2::/64 to Flex-Algos 128 and 129, respectively. Using the locator corresponding to Flex-Algo 128 as a prefix, node B generates End and End.X SIDs corresponding to the Flex-Algo. For example, for the link between itself and node C, node B allocates End.X SIDs A2:1::C2 and A2:2::C2 to Flex-Algos 128 and 129, respectively.

Network nodes perform route computation based on the rules defined by each Flex-Algo. They also generate routing entries for the SRv6 locator prefix associated with the Flex-Algo. The End and End.X SIDs associated with a Flex-Algo are used to generate SRv6 explicit paths associated with the Flex-Algo or generate local protection paths for the locator prefixes associated with the Flex-Algo. To summarize, Flex-Algo-associated SRv6 SIDs are mainly used to compute routes based on Flex-Algo path computation rules and generate forwarding entries corresponding to the Flex-Algo.

### 6.1.3.6 Flex-Algo Application and Extension in SRv6 SID-Based Network Slicing

Based on Flex-Algo, different topology constraints can be defined for path computation on a physical or logical network. Devices can then perform constraint-based distributed route computation using the metric type and route computation algorithm specified by the Flex-Algo. In the SRv6 SID-based network slicing solution, each network slice can correspond to a Flex-Algo. This means that a network slice can be identified by a unique Flex-Algo ID in the control plane without the need to introduce a new control plane identifier. Because IGP extensions for SRv6 support Flex-Algo, it is possible to advertise independent SRv6 locator, SR End SID, and End.X SID information for each Flex-Algo. A group of SRv6 locators and SIDs associated with a Flex-Algo can be used to identify nodes and various SRv6 functions in an SRv6 network slice corresponding to the Flex-Algo. This enables network nodes to compute and generate independent SRv6 locator routing entries as well as local SRv6 SID entries for different SRv6 network slices based on the SRv6 locators and SIDs associated with Flex-Algos.

However, different resources and TE attributes cannot be defined for network nodes and links based on different Flex-Algos. This is because each Flex-Algo is limited to defining the combination of only the metric type, path computation algorithm, and constraints. In order to implement the binding between Flex-Algos and network slices by leveraging forwarding-plane resource partitioning, Flex-Algos and their related SRv6 SIDs need to be associated with the resource reservation interfaces, sub-interfaces, or sub-channels corresponding to network resource slices. The constrained topology of the Flex-Algo and the forwarding resources of the network slice can be effectively integrated by configuring the color attribute and Flex-Algo-associated SRv6 End.X SID on the resource interface or sub-interface corresponding to the desired network slice and specifying that the constraints of the corresponding FAD contain only the configured color attribute.

### 6.1.3.7 Network Slicing Based on Flex-Algos and Layer 3 Sub-Interfaces

A relatively direct method of implementing network slicing based on Flex-Algos is to consider resources reserved by physical interfaces for network slices as Layer 3 sub-interfaces and configure link administrative group attributes (i.e., color attributes) on the sub-interfaces. The Flex-Algo corresponding to a specified network slice can then be configured to include the color attribute so that the Flex-Algo-constrained topology covers the resource sub-interface of the network slice. Figure 6.17 shows an example for implementing network slicing based on Flex-Algos and Layer 3 sub-interfaces. In this example, three network slices corresponding to different Flex-Algos are deployed on the network. On the physical interfaces between network nodes, different Layer 3 sub-interfaces with IP addresses assigned are allocated to the three network slices. In addition, a different color attribute is configured for each of the network slices.

As described in Table 6.14, in the FAD corresponding to each network slice, the topology constraint includes the color attribute specified for the slice.

Although this network slicing method does not require additional IGP extensions, it does require creating Layer 3 sub-interfaces for each network slice, configuring independent IP addresses, and establishing IGP sessions for the sub-interfaces. This brings a great deal of overhead and performance pressure to the control plane as the number of network slices increases.

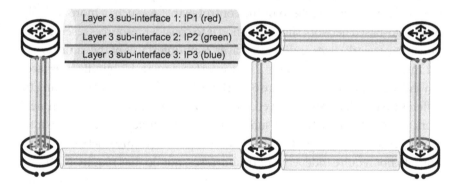

FIGURE 6.17　Network slicing based on Flex-Algos and Layer 3 sub-interfaces.

TABLE 6.14　FAD Corresponding to Each Network Slice

| Network Slice | Flex-Algo ID | Path Computation Algorithm | Metric Type | Topology Constraint |
|---|---|---|---|---|
| Network slice 1 | 128 | SPF algorithm | 0: IGP metric | Only red links are included. |
| Network slice 2 | 129 | SPF algorithm | 2: TE default metric | Only green links are included. |
| Network slice 3 | 130 | SPF algorithm | 1: minimum unidirectional link delay | Only blue links are included. |

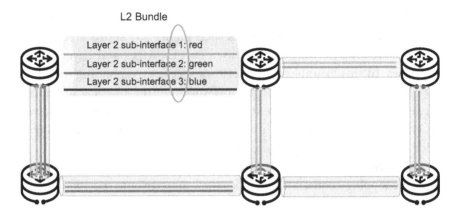

FIGURE 6.18    Network slicing based on Flex-Algos and Layer 2 sub-interfaces.

### *6.1.3.8 Network Slicing Based on Flex-Algos and Layer 2 Sub-Interfaces*

In contrast to the method of network slice resource representation based on Layer 3 sub-interfaces, the method based on Layer 2 sub-interfaces can reduce the protocol overhead of the control plane. As such, a more scalable Flex-Algo-based network slicing method is to consider resources reserved for different network slices as different Layer 2 sub-interfaces of the same physical interface and add the Layer 2 sub-interfaces to an L2 bundle interface. On the network shown in Figure 6.18, three network slices corresponding to different Flex-Algos are deployed. On the physical interfaces between network nodes, different Layer 2 sub-interfaces with independent bandwidth attributes and SRv6 End.X SIDs are allocated to the three network slices. They do not require independent IP addresses, nor do they require IGP to be separately enabled for them. To achieve color-based association between the resource interfaces of the network slices and Flex-Algos, network operators need to configure the link administrative group attribute (i.e., color attribute) for both the Layer 2 sub-interfaces and L2 bundle. Specifically, network operators need to configure this attribute for the Layer 2 sub-interface corresponding to each network slice and configure the color attribute of the L2 bundle to include the color attributes of all these sub-interfaces.

As described in Table 6.15, in the FAD corresponding to each network slice, the associated topology constraint includes the color attributes of the Layer 2 sub-interfaces corresponding to the network slice.

The attribute information (e.g., bandwidth and End.X SID) about Layer 2 sub-interfaces of an L2 bundle interface can be advertised on a network

TABLE 6.15    FAD Corresponding to Each Network Slice

| Network Slice | Flex-Algo ID | Path Computation Algorithm | Metric Type | Topology Constraint |
|---|---|---|---|---|
| Network slice 1 | 128 | SPF algorithm | 0: IGP metric | Only red links are included. |
| Network slice 2 | 129 | SPF algorithm | 2: TE default metric | Only green links are included. |
| Network slice 3 | 130 | SPF algorithm | 1: minimum unidirectional link delay | Only blue links are included. |

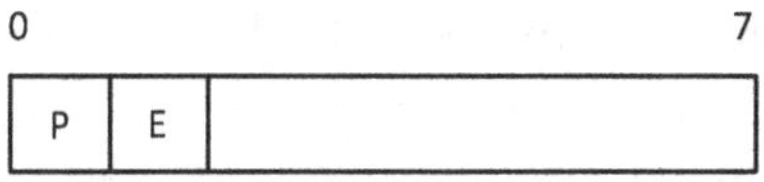

FIGURE 6.19    Flag field in the L2 bundle TLV.

through the IGP L2 bundle mechanism.[11] This mechanism is used to advertise information about Layer 2 member links of a bundle interface. These member links can be used for traffic load balancing on the bundle interface. Alternatively, the member link used for traffic forwarding can be specified based on the End.X SID of this link.

In network slicing scenarios, to prevent traffic from being load-balanced among the Layer 2 sub-interfaces of different network slices and allow the service packets of different network slices to be forwarded through only the corresponding sub-interfaces, the IGP L2 bundle mechanism needs to be extended. This is achieved by defining an E (Exclusive) flag in the Flag field of the L2 Bundle TLV to indicate whether the L2 bundle supports load balancing. Figure 6.19 shows the Flag field in the L2 Bundle TLV.

If the E flag is set to 0, load balancing can be performed among the Layer 2 member links in the L2 bundle. However, if the E flag is set to 1, these links are exclusively used by network slices and therefore cannot be used for load balancing. This meets the requirement for resource isolation between different network slices.

## 6.1.4 IGP Extensions for Slice ID-Based Network Slicing

Network slices can be mapped to different logical topologies or Flex-Algos in order to reuse MT IDs or Flex-Algo IDs as the control plane identifiers of these network slices. This makes it easy to realize SRv6 SID-based network slicing through the existing control plane mechanism. However, in scenarios that require many network slices (e.g., hundreds or even thousands), using a unique topology or Flex-Algo for each network slice greatly increases the overhead of the control plane, adversely affecting device performance and stability. As such, the control plane needs to be further optimized to reduce the overhead caused by the increase in network slices.

A network slice has both topology and resource attributes. If there are only a few network slices, the topology and resource attributes can be coupled by mapping each network slice to an independent logical topology and associating this logical topology with the resource attribute of the network slice. However, if there are many network slices, the topology and resource attributes need to be decoupled so that they can be flexibly combined for different slices. Specifically, network slices that share the same topology can reuse the information advertisement and route computation results in the same logical topology in the control plane, eliminating the overhead generated by separately advertising topology information and computing routes for each network slice. This means that many network slices can be supported by deploying only a few logical topologies. Decoupling the topology and resource attributes of network slices in the control plane drives the decoupling of slice topology identifiers from resource identifiers in the data plane, spurring the development of the slice ID-based network slicing solution. This section further describes the IGP control protocol extensions used for implementing this solution.

There is no one-to-one mapping between network slices and logical topologies in the slice ID-based network slicing solution. As such, each network slice needs to be associated with a logical topology, but different slices can be associated with the same logical topology. To represent the association between network slices and logical topologies accurately as well as enable network devices to have a consistent understanding of the association, network slice identifiers need to be introduced to control protocols, and the association needs to be advertised on a network through IGP. The MT or Flex-Algo technology can be used to advertise the logical topology information about network slices. In addition, IGP extensions need to be used to advertise the resources allocated by nodes and links to each network slice and the related TE attributes. Unlike the SRv6 SID-based network slicing solution, the slice ID-based network slicing solution does not need to advertise (through IGP) the SRv6 resource-aware SIDs allocated by each node and link to different network slices, thanks to the introduction of global network slice IDs in the data plane.

### 6.1.4.1 Advertisement of Network Slice Definitions

Network slice definitions can be advertised through IGP. The following takes IS-IS as an example. The association between the network slice and topology, as well as between the network slice and algorithm, can be advertised through the NRP Definition (NRPD) TLV. Figure 6.20 shows the format of this TLV.

Table 6.16 describes the involved fields.

Generally, networks can support only MT or Flex-Algo. If only MT is enabled, a network slice can be associated with a logical topology. In this case, the MT ID field in the NRPD TLV is set to the MT ID of the topology, and the Algorithm field is set to 0. If only Flex-Algo is enabled, a network slice can be associated with a Flex-Algo. In this case, the MT ID field in the NRPD TLV is set to 0, and the Algorithm field is set to the ID of the Flex-Algo. For networks that support both MT and Flex-Algo,

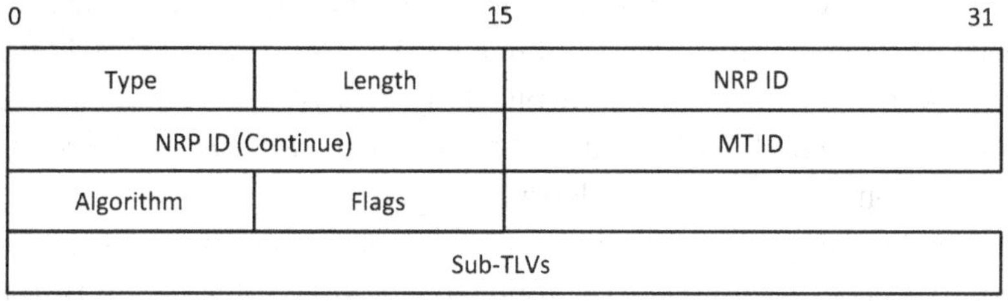

| 0 | 15 | 31 |
|---|---|---|
| Type | Length | NRP ID |
| NRP ID (Continue) | | MT ID |
| Algorithm | Flags | |
| Sub-TLVs | | |

FIGURE 6.20   Format of the NRPD TLV.

TABLE 6.16   Fields in the NRPD TLV

| Field | Length | Description |
|---|---|---|
| Type | 1 byte | TLV type to be allocated by the Internet Assigned Numbers Authority (IANA). |
| Length | 1 byte | Total length of the TLV (excluding the Type and Length fields), in bytes. |
| NRP ID | 4 bytes | Globally unique NRP ID. |
| MT ID | 2 bytes | MT ID to be advertised, with the first four bits reserved and the last 12 bits indicating the topology ID. |
| Algorithm | 1 byte | 8-bit algorithm identifier, which can identify a standard path computation algorithm or Flex-Algo. |
| Flags | 1 byte | 8-bit field for flags. Currently, all flags are reserved for future extension. |
| Sub-TLVs | Variable | Optional sub-TLVs, which can be used to carry other NRP attributes. |

enabling both allows a network slice to be associated with either the combination of a topology and an algorithm (including the combination of MT and a standard path computation algorithm) or the combination of MT and Flex-Algo.

### 6.1.4.2 Advertisement of Network Slice Topology Attributes

In the slice ID-based network slicing solution, a network slice definition includes a reference to an MT ID and algorithm ID. As such, the topology attributes of a network slice can be advertised through the MT or Flex-Algo mechanism. In IS-IS, MT uses the MT ISN TLV (type number: 222) to advertise the connection between each node and its neighbor in each topology, as well as to advertise link attribute information. It also uses the MT IPv6 IP Reach TLV (type number: 237) to advertise the IPv6 address prefix information in different topologies. In contrast, Flex-Algo uses the SR Algorithm Sub-TLV advertised by network nodes to determine the specific nodes participating in a Flex-Algo. In addition, it matches the link-specific color constraint advertised in a FAD against the color attribute of each link to determine the link involved in a Flex-Algo. MT and Flex-Algo can be used in combination with SR to advertise SR SIDs and SRv6 locators based on each <topology, algorithm> pair.

If multiple network slices are associated with the same MT or Flex-Algo, IGP needs to advertise the topology attribute information through the MT or Flex-Algo only once, and the information can be shared by these network slices. This avoids the control protocol overhead caused by separately advertising topology attribute information for each network slice. Such network slices can also share the result of route computation performed based on the MT or Flex-Algo, further reducing the overhead of separately performing route computation for each network slice. With the decoupling of the topology and resource attributes of network slices, multiple network slices are allowed to use the same topology or Flex-Algo, significantly improving the control plane scalability of network slices.

### 6.1.4.3 Advertisement of Network Slice Resource Attributes

Bandwidth resources reserved by a physical link for different network slices can be represented using Layer 3 sub-interfaces, Layer 2 sub-interfaces, or sub-channels with reserved bandwidth. Depending on the representation mode, the IGP extension mechanism used for advertising the resource attributes of network slices differs.

6.1.4.3.1 Mode 1: Using Layer 3 Sub-Interfaces    Using Layer 3 sub-interfaces to represent the reserved resources of different network slices requires IGP to be enabled on each Layer 3 sub-interface. Once IGP is enabled, IGP TE extensions can be used to advertise the TE attributes of the Layer 3 sub-interfaces. For example, the Maximum Link Bandwidth Sub-TLV of IS-IS TE[7] can be used to advertise the bandwidth attributes of the Layer 3 sub-interfaces. Because this mode requires that independent Layer 3 sub-interfaces be created for each network slice, an IP address be configured for each of the sub-interfaces, and IGP be enabled, different network slices cannot share the same topology or protocol session. As such, this mode is not recommended for the slice ID-based network slicing solution.

6.1.4.3.2 Mode 2: Using Layer 2 Sub-Interfaces    Using Layer 2 sub-interfaces to represent the reserved resources of different network slices requires that the IGP L2 bundle mechanism[11] be used to advertise the attributes (e.g., bandwidth attribute) of Layer 2 member interfaces on a Layer 3 interface. In slice ID-based network slicing scenarios, the L2 bundle mechanism needs to be extended to prevent load balancing among a Layer 3 interface's Layer 2 sub-interfaces that belong to different network slices.

To identify the network slice associated with each Layer 2 sub-interface, the NRP-IDs Sub-TLV is defined in the L2 Bundle Attribute Descriptors TLV. Figure 6.21 shows the format of this sub-TLV.

Table 6.17 describes the involved fields.

The NRP IDs Sub-TLV can carry one or more NRP IDs to describe the association between a Layer 2 sub-interface and one or more network slices. If a Layer 2 sub-interface is associated with multiple network

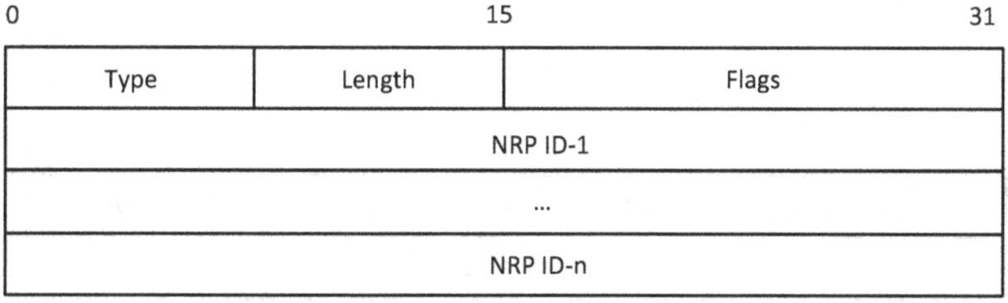

FIGURE 6.21    Format of the NRP-IDs sub-TLV.

TABLE 6.17    Fields in the NRP-IDs Sub-TLV

| Field | Length | Description |
|---|---|---|
| Type | 1 byte | Sub-TLV type to be allocated by the IANA. |
| Length | 1 byte | Total length of the sub-TLV (excluding the Type and Length fields), in bytes. |
| Flags | 2 bytes | Flags. Currently, all flags are reserved for future extension. |
| NRP ID | Integer multiple of 4 bytes | Globally unique NRP ID with a length of 4 bytes. One or more NRP IDs can be carried. |

slices, these network slices can share the bandwidth and other TE attributes of this Layer 2 sub-interface.

6.1.4.3.3 Mode 3: Using Sub-Channels with Reserved Bandwidth    Using sub-channels with reserved bandwidth to represent the resources reserved by interfaces for different network slices eliminates the need to create independent Layer 3 or Layer 2 sub-interfaces for each network slice. Similar to the advertisement of custom TE attributes for different logical topologies in MT, this mode uses the NRP-specific TE Attribute Sub-TLV to advertise TE attributes (e.g., bandwidth resources allocated by a link to multiple network slices) when a Layer 3 interface belongs to these different network slices. Figure 6.22 shows the format of this sub-TLV.

Table 6.18 describes the involved fields.

The NRP-specific TE Attribute Sub-TLV can carry the NRP Bandwidth Sub-sub-TLV, which is used to advertise the bandwidth reserved by a link for the associated NRP. Figure 6.23 shows the format of this sub-sub-TLV.

Table 6.19 describes the involved fields.

If needed, the NRP-specific TE Attribute Sub-TLV can also carry other types of sub-sub-TLVs, which are not detailed in this book.

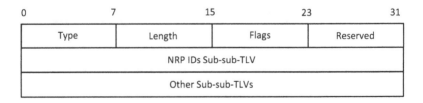

FIGURE 6.22    Format of the NRP-specific TE attribute sub-TLV.

TABLE 6.18    Fields in the NRP-Specific TE Attribute Sub-TLV

| Field | Length | Description |
|---|---|---|
| Type | 1 byte | Sub-TLV type to be allocated by the IANA. |
| Length | 1 byte | Total length of the sub-TLV (excluding the Type and Length fields), in bytes. |
| Flags | 1 byte | Flags. Currently, all flags are reserved for future extension. |
| Reserved | 1 byte | Reserved for future extension. |
| NRP IDs Sub-sub-TLV | Variable | Used to carry one or more globally unique NRP IDs, each with a length of 4 bytes. |
| Other Sub-sub-TLVs | Variable | Used to carry the link TE attribute corresponding to an NRP ID. |

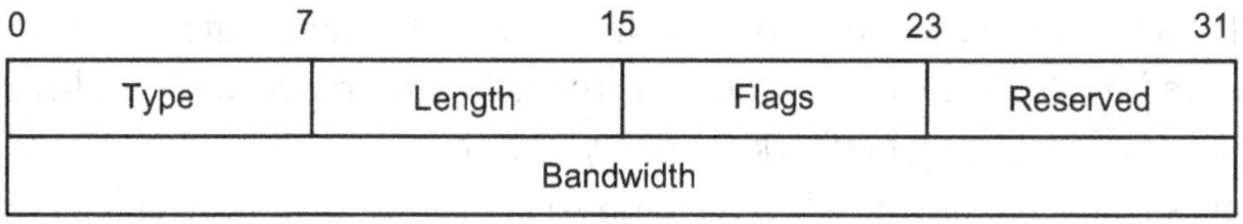

| 0 | | 7 | | 15 | | 23 | | 31 |
|---|---|---|---|---|---|---|---|---|
| Type | | Length | | Flags | | Reserved | | |
| Bandwidth | | | | | | | | |

FIGURE 6.23    Format of the NRP bandwidth sub-sub-TLV.

TABLE 6.19    Fields in the NRP Bandwidth Sub-Sub-TLV

| Field | Length | Description |
|---|---|---|
| Type | 1 byte | Sub-sub-TLV type to be allocated by the IANA. |
| Length | 1 byte | Total length of the sub-sub-TLV (excluding the Type and Length fields), in bytes. |
| Flags | 1 byte | Flags. Currently, all flags are reserved for future extension. |
| Reserved | 1 byte | Reserved for future extension. |
| Bandwidth | 4 bytes | Reserved bandwidth allocated to a specified NRP ID, encoded in IEEE 32-bit floating point format. |

### 6.1.4.4 Advertisement of Data-Plane Network Slice Identifiers

To steer a data packet into a specified network slice and forward it using the resources allocated to this slice, a network device needs to add network slice identification information to the packet and maintain the mapping between the data-plane network slice identification information and forwarding resources.

When a dedicated network slice ID is introduced to the data plane to instruct packet forwarding using the resource of the corresponding network slice, the data-plane network slice ID can be the same as the control-plane network slice ID. Because the mapping between network slice IDs and either sub-interfaces or sub-channels with reserved bandwidth is carried in advertised slice resource attributes, the data-plane network slice ID does not need to be additionally advertised using a protocol. This avoids the control protocol overhead caused by advertising the SRv6 resource-aware SIDs of each network slice for each network node or link in the SRv6 SID-based network slicing solution. As a result, the scalability of the network slice control plane is further improved.

## 6.2 BGP-LS EXTENSIONS FOR NETWORK SLICING

### 6.2.1 BGP-LS Fundamentals

BGP-LS is mainly used to report the link state and TE attribute information collected by devices to a network controller.[12] Compared with traditional methods of reporting network topology and status information using protocols such as IGP, using BGP-LS to do so is simpler and more efficient.

Figure 6.24 shows the typical application scenario and architecture of BGP-LS. Only one routing device in each IGP area needs to run BGP-LS and directly establish a BGP-LS peer relationship with Consumer, which functions as a controller. Alternatively, routing devices can establish BGP-LS peer relationships with a centralized BGP speaker, which establishes a BGP-LS peer relationship with Consumer. With this alternative approach, the BGP route reflection mechanism can be adopted so that Consumer needs to establish only one BGP-LS connection to collect network-wide topology information, thereby simplifying network O&M and deployment.

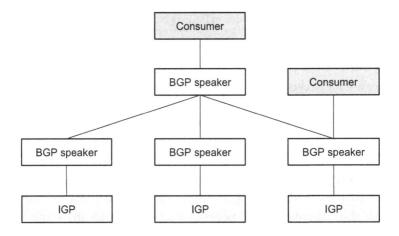

FIGURE 6.24 Typical application scenario and architecture of BGP-LS.

On the basis of BGP, BGP-LS introduces a new address family (with sub-address families) and new Network Layer Reachability Information (NLRI) types to carry information about links, nodes, and IPv4/IPv6 prefixes. The new NLRIs, called Link-State NLRIs, are as follows:

- Node NLRI

- Link NLRI

- IPv4 Topology Prefix NLRI

- IPv6 Topology Prefix NLRI

In addition to defining the preceding Link-State NLRIs, BGP-LS defines corresponding attributes to carry parameters and attributes related to links, nodes, and IPv4/IPv6 prefixes. These BGP-LS attributes, carried in the TLV format with Link-State NLRIs in BGP-LS messages, include the following types:

- Node attribute

- Link attribute

- Prefix attribute

BGP-LS also provides SR-specific protocol extensions to report information about SR network link states and SR SID information of each node and link to the network controller. Take SRv6 as an example: *draft-ietf-idr-bgpls-srv6-ext*[13] defines BGP-LS extensions for SRv6, extending BGP-LS to report SRv6 locator information, various types of SRv6 SIDs, and related attributes.

BGP-LS can collect and report intra-AS topology and state information, inter-AS link connection information, and inter-AS link SR SID information. This information enables the network controller to construct a network topology that spans multiple IGP areas or multiple ASs and implement inter-AS TE path computation through SR. For details about how inter-AS connection information and SR SIDs are collected based on BGP-LS, see IETF RFC 9086[14] and *draft-ietf-idr-bgpls-srv6-ext*.[13]

In a network slicing scenario, BGP-LS can also be used to report information such as intra-AS and inter-AS topologies and links, as well as

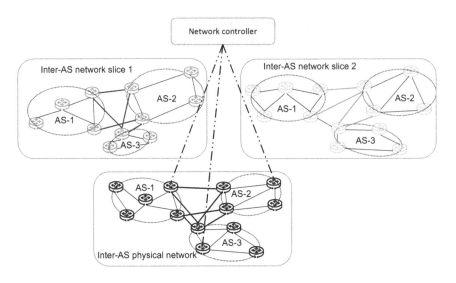

FIGURE 6.25  Collecting network slice information based on BGP-LS.

resource attributes of each network slice, to the controller. In Figure 6.25, the network controller connects to network devices in three ASs through BGP-LS to obtain intra-AS and inter-AS topologies and links, as well as resource attributes of different inter-AS network slices.

## 6.2.2 BGP-LS MT Extensions for SRv6 SID-Based Network Slicing

In SRv6 SID-based network slicing, each network slice corresponds to an independent logical topology. For each network slice, a Multi-Topology Identifier (MT-ID) is used as a control plane identifier. This means that BGP-LS extensions for MT can be used to report intra-AS and inter-AS topology and resource attribute information of network slices to the network controller without requiring new BGP-LS extensions.

### 6.2.2.1 Reporting Topology Information of Network Resource Slices

The reported topology information of network slices includes intra-AS topology information and inter-AS topology and connection information.

The MT-ID TLV defined in RFC 7752[12] can be carried in BGP-LS Link NLRIs as a part of link descriptors, advertised in IPv4/IPv6 Topology Prefix NLRIs as a part of prefix descriptors, or placed in BGP-LS attributes and advertised with the Node NLRI, identifying the logical topology to which the link, IPv4/IPv6 address prefix, and node belongs, respectively. The Link NLRI and IPv4/IPv6 Topology Prefix NLRI can each carry only one MT-ID,

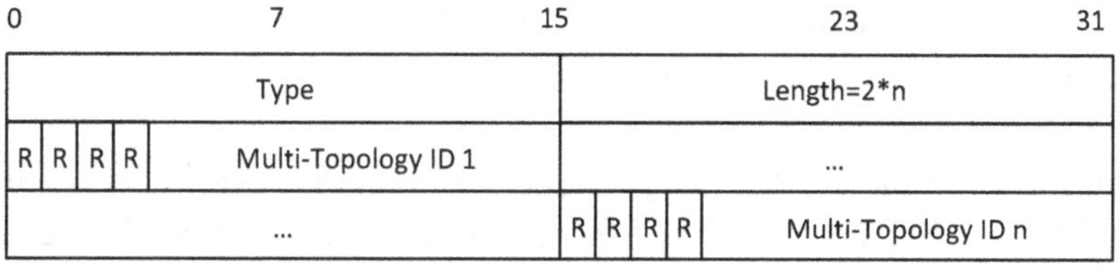

| 0 | 7 | 15 | 23 | 31 |
|---|---|---|---|---|

| Type | Length=2*n |
|---|---|
| R R R R    Multi-Topology ID 1 | ... |
| ...    | R R R R    Multi-Topology ID n |

FIGURE 6.26    Format of the BGP-LS MT-ID TLV.

TABLE 6.20    Fields in the MT-ID TLV

| Field | Length | Description |
|---|---|---|
| Type | 2 bytes | TLV type. The value is 263. |
| Length | 2 bytes | Total length of the TLV (excluding the Type and Length fields), in bytes. The value is twice the number of MT-IDs. |
| R | 4 bits | Each R is a reserved bit. It should be set to 0 before transmission and ignored upon receipt. |
| Multi-Topology ID | 12 bits | Advertised MT-ID. If the MT-ID is obtained from IS-IS, the length is 12 bits. If the MT-ID is obtained from OSPF, the first five bits must be set to 0. |

whereas a Node NLRI can carry a group of MT-IDs. Figure 6.26 shows the format of the BGP-LS MT-ID TLV.

Table 6.20 describes the involved fields.

On an SR network, in addition to MT node, link, and address prefix routes, BGP-LS needs to report SR SID information corresponding to different logical topologies. In this way, SR-based virtual networks corresponding to different logical topologies can be generated on the controller. RFC 9085[15] defines BGP-LS extensions for SR-MPLS, and *draft-ietf-idr-bgpls-srv6-ext*[13] defines BGP-LS extensions for SRv6.

In the case of inter-AS network slices, BGP-LS can advertise both intra-AS logical topology information and inter-AS link connection information to the controller. BGP-LS Egress Peer Engineering (EPE) uses BGP-LS Link NLRIs to advertise inter-AS connection information and defines the following types of BGP peering segments for inter-AS connections:

- Peer node segment (PeerNode SID): indicates that data packets are sent to a specified BGP peer.

- Peer adjacency segment (PeerAdj SID): indicates that data packets are sent to a specified BGP peer through a specified interface.

- Peer set segment (PeerSet SID): indicates that load balancing is performed between a group of BGP peers.

Using MT to define the logical topology of an inter-AS network slice requires that only one MT-ID be planned for involved ASs and inter-AS links and used as the identifier of the control plane of this slice. When BGP-LS is used to advertise inter-AS logical topology connections of an inter-AS network slice, inter-AS Link NLRIs need to carry the MT-ID TLV, which indicates the logical topology to which the inter-AS links belong. RFC 9086[14] and *draft-ietf-idr-bgpls-srv6-ext*[13] define specific BGP-LS extensions for EPE.

### 6.2.2.2 Reporting of Network Slice Resource Attributes

IGP MT supports the advertisement of TE attribute information such as bandwidth resources allocated by network nodes and links for each network slice. Similarly, when advertising link state information of each topology, BGP-LS extensions for MT may also use the BGP-LS attribute corresponding to the Link NLRI to advertise TE attribute information, such as link bandwidth resources of different logical topologies. This makes it possible to report resource attributes of different network slices. TE attribute information, such as link bandwidth resources, in each logical topology corresponds to the resources reserved by the underlying physical network on the corresponding link for the network slice. RFC 7752[12] defines the protocol extensions of BGP-LS for link TE attributes. BGP-LS EPE can use the BGP-LS attribute corresponding to the inter-AS Link NLRI to report the attribute information of resources allocated for network slices on inter-AS links.

## 6.2.3 BGP-LS Flex-Algo Extensions for SRv6 SID-Based Network Slicing

In SRv6 SID-based network slicing, each network slice can correspond to an independent Flex-Algo, meaning that a Flex-Algo ID can be used as the identifier of a network slice's control plane. This requires a minimal amount of extension, in addition to BGP-LS extensions for Flex-Algo and for SR, to enable the reporting of a network slice's intra-AS and inter-AS topology and resource attribute information to the network controller through BGP-LS.

### 6.2.3.1 BGP-LS Extensions for Flex-Algo

Network devices can perform distributed constraint path computation based on the path computation rules in the Flexible Algorithm Definition

(FAD). While the controller can also perform centralized explicit path computation for SR Policies based on Flex-Algo, network devices need to report — to the controller through BGP-LS — information such as the FAD, Flex-Algos that network nodes participate in, and SR SIDs corresponding to Flex-Algos. To implement these functions, BGP-LS is extended as follows:

### 6.2.3.2 FAD TLV

The FAD TLV is carried in the BGP-LS attribute corresponding to the Node NLRI. Figure 6.27 shows the format of this TLV.

The meaning of each field in the FAD TLV of BGP-LS is consistent with that of the same field in the FAD Sub-TLV of the IGP Flex-Algo described in the IGP extensions for Flex-Algo in SRv6 SID network slicing.

### 6.2.3.3 SR-Algorithm TLV

The SR-Algorithm TLV is carried in the BGP-LS attribute corresponding to the Node NLRI and is used to advertise the set of algorithm IDs supported by a node. Figure 6.28 shows the format of this TLV.

The meaning of each field in the SR-Algorithm TLV of BGP-LS is consistent with that of the same field in the SR-Algorithm Sub-TLV of IGP described in the IGP extensions for Flex-Algo in SRv6 SID network slicing.

| 0 | 7 | 15 | 23 | 31 |
|---|---|---|---|---|
| Type | | Length | | |
| Length | Metric-Type | Calc-Type | Priority | |
| Sub-TLVs ... | | | | |

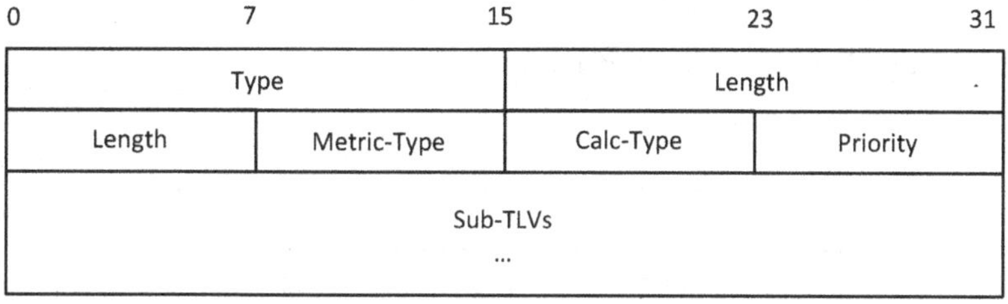

FIGURE 6.27  Format of the FAD TLV.

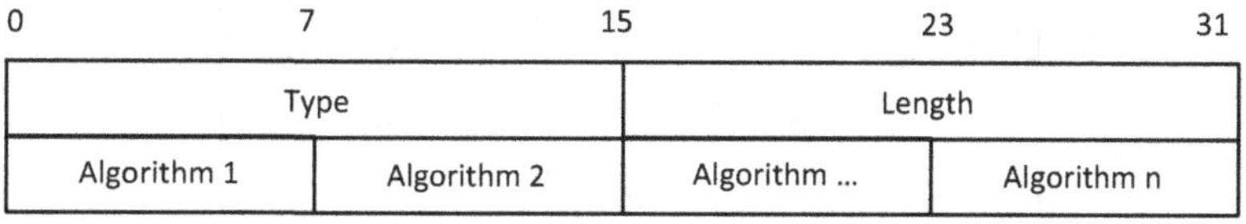

| 0 | 7 | 15 | 23 | 31 |
|---|---|---|---|---|
| Type | | Length | | |
| Algorithm 1 | Algorithm 2 | Algorithm ... | Algorithm n | |

FIGURE 6.28  Format of the SR-algorithm TLV.

### 6.2.3.4 Mapping between SRv6 Locators/SIDs and Flex-Algos

When reporting SRv6 locator and SRv6 SID information through BGP-LS, BGP messages need to carry an algorithm ID, which indicates the mapping between SRv6 locators/SIDs and Flex-Algos.

The SRv6 Locator TLV is carried in the BGP-LS attribute corresponding to the IPv6 Topology Prefix NLRI and used to advertise attribute information related to the SRv6 locator carried in the Topology Prefix NLRI. Figure 6.29 shows the format of this TLV.

The meaning of each field in this TLV of BGP-LS is consistent with that of the same field in the SRv6 locator TLV of IS-IS described in the IGP extensions for MT in SRv6 SID network slicing.

The SRv6 End.X SID TLV and SRv6 LAN End.X SID TLV are carried in the BGP-LS attribute corresponding to the Link NLRI and used to advertise the End.X SID and attribute information associated with the Link NLRI. Figure 6.30 shows the format of the SRv6 End.X SID TLV.

| 0 | 7 | 15 | 23 | 31 |
|---|---|---|---|---|
| Type | | | Length | |
| Flags | Algorithm | | Reserved | |
| Metric | | | | |
| Sub-TLVs (variable) ... | | | | |

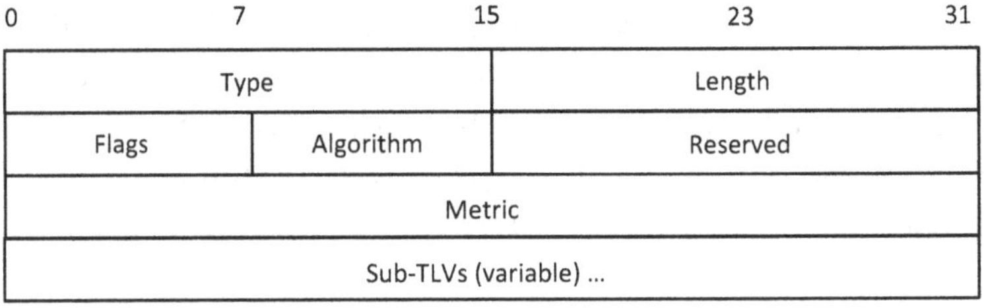

FIGURE 6.29   Format of the SRv6 locator TLV.

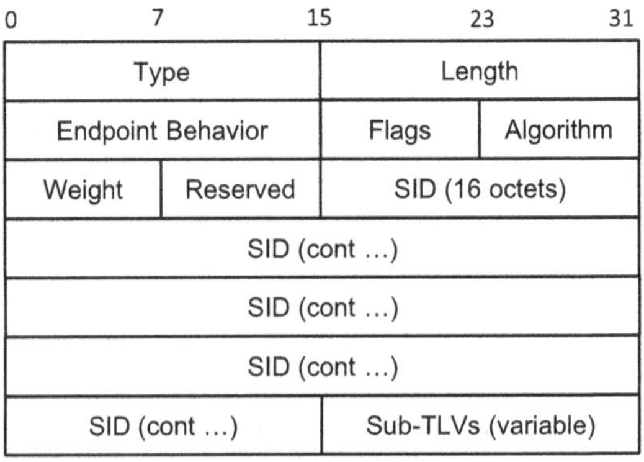

| 0 | 7 | 15 | 23 | 31 |
|---|---|---|---|---|
| Type | | Length | | |
| Endpoint Behavior | | Flags | Algorithm | |
| Weight | Reserved | SID (16 octets) | | |
| SID (cont ...) | | | | |
| SID (cont ...) | | | | |
| SID (cont ...) | | | | |
| SID (cont ...) | | Sub-TLVs (variable) | | |

FIGURE 6.30   Format of the SRv6 End.X SID TLV.

The meaning of each field in this TLV of BGP-LS is consistent with that of the same field in the SRv6 End.X SID Sub-TLV of IS-IS described in the IGP extensions for MT in SRv6 SID network slicing.

Figure 6.31 shows the format of the SRv6 LAN End.X SID TLV.

The meaning of each field in the SRv6 LAN End.X SID TLV of BGP-LS is consistent with that of the same field in the SRv6 LAN End.X SID Sub-TLV of IS-IS described in the IGP extensions for MT in SRv6 SID network slicing.

Other types of SRv6 SIDs other than SRv6 End.X SIDs are advertised using a newly defined type of BGP-LS NLRI — SRv6 SID NLRI. Figure 6.32 shows the format of this NLRI.

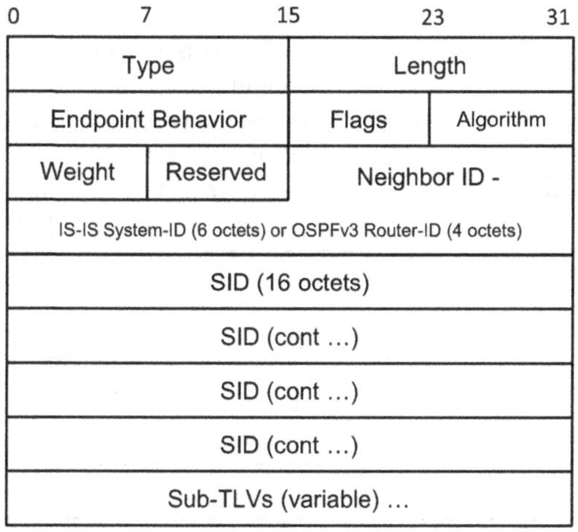

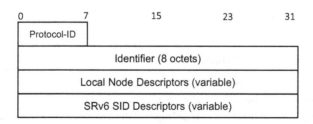

FIGURE 6.31    SRv6  LAN End.X SID TLV.

FIGURE 6.32    SRv6 SID NLRI.

Table 6.21 describes the involved fields.

Figure 6.33 shows the format of the SRv6 SID Information TLV. Table 6.22 describes the involved fields.

The BGP-LS attribute corresponding to the SRv6 SID NLRI can be used to advertise the SRv6 SID type and the corresponding Flex-Algo through the SRv6 Endpoint Behavior TLV. Figure 6.34 shows the format of this TLV. Table 6.23 describes the involved fields.

TABLE 6.21   Fields in the SRv6 SID NLRI

| Field | Length | Description |
| --- | --- | --- |
| Protocol ID | 1 byte | ID of the protocol that provides SRv6 SID information for BGP-LS, for example, IS-IS level-1 (1), IS-IS level-2 (2), and OSPFv2 (3). |
| Identifier | 8 bytes | Identifier defined in RFC 7752.[12] The identifier is used to distinguish different routing spaces (instances). |
| Local Node Descriptors | Variable | Description of the local node. The format is defined in RFC 7752[12] and RFC 9086[14] |
| SRv6 SID Descriptors | Variable | One SRv6 SID Information TLV is mandatory, and the MT-ID TLV is optional. |

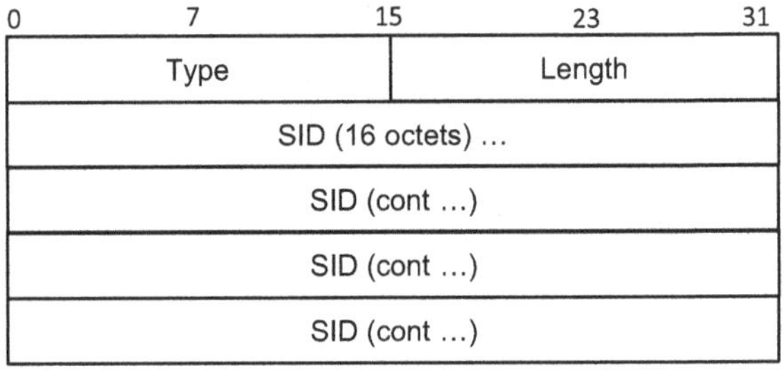

FIGURE 6.33   Format of the SRv6 SID information TLV.

TABLE 6.22   Fields in the SRv6 SID Information TLV

| Field | Length | Description |
| --- | --- | --- |
| Type | 2 bytes | TLV type. The value is 518. |
| Length | 2 bytes | Total length of the TLV (excluding the Type and Length fields), in bytes. The value is 16. |
| SID | 16 bytes | 128-bit SRv6 SID. |

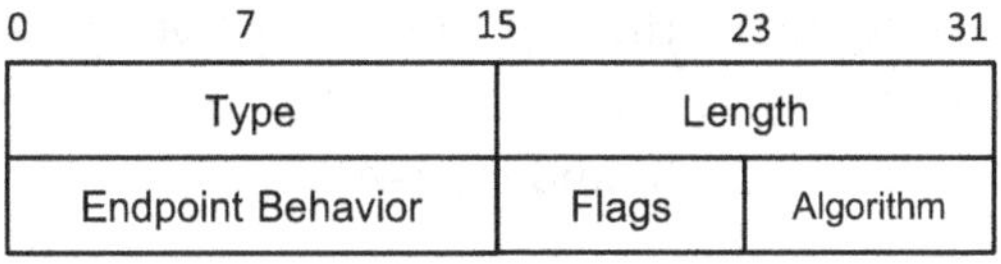

| 0 | 7 | 15 | 23 | 31 |
|---|---|---|---|---|

| Type | | Length | |
|------|--|--------|--|
| Endpoint Behavior | | Flags | Algorithm |

FIGURE 6.34   Format of the SRv6 endpoint behavior TLV.

TABLE 6.23   Fields in the SRv6 Endpoint Behavior TLV

| Field | Length | Description |
|-------|--------|-------------|
| Type | 2 bytes | TLV type. The value is 1250. |
| Length | 2 bytes | Total length of the TLV (excluding the Type and Length fields), in bytes. The value is 4. |
| Endpoint Behavior | 2 bytes | SRv6 Endpoint Behavior type defined in RFC 8986. |
| Flags | 1 byte | Flags, which have not been defined and are reserved for future extension. |
| Algorithm | 1 byte | ID of the algorithm associated with an SRv6 SID. |

## 6.2.3.5 Network Slice Topology Information Reporting based on BGP-LS Flex-Algo

The reported topology information of network slices includes intra-AS topology information and inter-AS topology and connection information.

The FAD information collected by the controller through BGP-LS can be used to determine the topology constraints, metric type, and algorithm type used for Flex-Algo path computation on a specific network topology. Using this FAD information, along with the SRv6 locator and SID information corresponding to each Flex-Algo reported through BGP-LS extensions for SR, the controller can compute and generate SR explicit paths corresponding to different Flex-Algos. An IETF draft (*draft-ietf-idr-bgpls-srv6-ext*[13]) defines BGP-LS extensions for SRv6.

BGP-LS can advertise logical topology information of each IGP area or AS to the controller. In addition, BGP-LS extensions for EPE can be used to advertise inter-AS connection information and SR SID information of inter-AS links to the controller. In this case, the BGP-LS attribute corresponding to the BGP-LS inter-AS Link NLRI needs to carry the color information specified in the FAD. This is necessary in order to associate inter-AS links with Flex-Algos and determine the inter-AS network slice topology. BGP-LS can also advertise the metric type in the corresponding FAD and the metric value for inter-AS links. RFC 9085[15] and *draft-ietf-idr-bgpls-srv6-ext*[13] define BGP-LS EPE extensions for SR-MPLS and BGP-LS EPE extensions for SRv6, respectively.

Using Flex-Algo to define the logical topology of an inter-AS network slice requires that attributes such as Flex-Algo and link color be consistently planned for involved ASs and inter-AS links.

### 6.2.3.6 Network Slice Resource Attribute Reporting based on BGP-LS Flex-Algo

Because each Flex-Algo defines only path computation rules, an auxiliary mechanism is required to associate the Flex-Algo with the resources and TE attributes of the corresponding network slice. IGP extensions for L2 bundles define the mechanism for advertising the attributes of multiple Layer 2 member links that are bundled into a Layer 3 IP link. BGP-LS is extended to report information about L2 bundle member links. To report to the controller information about resources allocated by an IP link for different network slices, the L2 bundle mechanism of BGP-LS needs to be extended. In this case, a new Link Attribute Flags TLV is introduced and a new flag bit "E" is defined so that the L2 bundle can advertise the bandwidth, SR SID, and other TE attributes of multiple Layer 2 member links allocated by a Layer 3 IP link for different network resource slices. In this manner, the groups of SRv6 locators and SIDs associated with each Flex-Algo indicate not only the logical topology and path corresponding to the Flex-Algo but also the Layer 2 member interface resources of a network slice associated with the Flex-Algo. That is, the SRv6 locators and SIDs become resource-aware.

The L2 Bundle Member Attributes TLV defined in the BGP-LS extensions for SR can be used to advertise the information of Layer 2 member links associated with a Layer 3 link.[15] The Layer 3 link is described by the BGP-LS Link NLRI, and the L2 Bundle Member Attributes TLV is carried in the BGP-LS attribute associated with the Link NLRI. Multiple L2 Bundle Member Attributes TLVs can be associated with one Link NLRI. Figure 6.35 shows the format of this TLV.

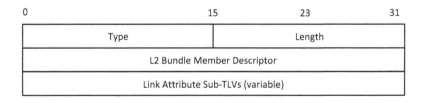

FIGURE 6.35   Format of the L2 bundle member attributes TLV.

TABLE 6.24    Fields in the L2 Bundle Member Attributes TLV

| Field | Length | Description |
|---|---|---|
| Type | 2 bytes | TLV type. The value is 1172. |
| Length | 2 bytes | Total length of the TLV (excluding the Type and Length fields), in bytes. |
| L2 Bundle Member Descriptor | 4 bytes | Local link ID. The field is defined in RFC 4202[16] |
| Link Attribute Sub-TLVs | Variable | Link attribute information of Layer 2 member links. The information is advertised through sub-TLVs. The format is the same as that defined in RFC 7752[12] and *draft-ietf-idr-bgpls-srv6-ext*[13] |

Table 6.24 describes the involved fields.

The L2 Bundle Member Attributes TLV can be used to advertise information such as the bandwidth of Layer 2 member links allocated by Layer 3 links for different network slices, link administrative group (color) information, and SRv6 End.X SID information. The color of each Layer 2 member link is the same as that included in the FAD corresponding to the network slice. This ensures that resources such as bandwidth of the Layer 2 member links can be associated with the Flex-Algo based on the color. The colors of the Layer 3 link corresponding to Layer 2 member links must be the union of the colors of all Layer 2 member links to ensure that Layer 3 logical topologies corresponding to the Flex-Algos contain the Layer 3 link.

To indicate that a Layer 3 link or Layer 2 member link can be used only to carry service traffic of a network slice, a new Link Attribute Flags TLV is added for BGP-LS route attributes. This TLV can be carried in the BGP-LS attribute corresponding to the Link NLRI, or it can be carried in the L2 Bundle Member Attributes TLV as a sub-TLV. Figure 6.36 shows the format of the Link Attribute Flags TLV.

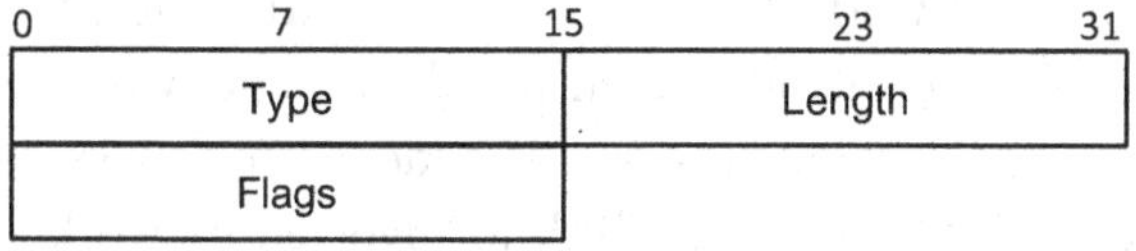

FIGURE 6.36    Format of the link attribute flags TLV.

TABLE 6.25   Fields in the Link Attribute Flags TLV

| Field | Length | Description |
|---|---|---|
| Type | 2 bytes | TLV type, which will be allocated by the IANA. |
| Length | 2 bytes | Total length of the TLV (excluding the Type and Length fields), in bytes. The value is 2. |
| Flags | 2 bytes | Link attribute flags. The meaning of the first two bits in this field complies with RFC 5029.[17] The third bit is a newly defined flag "Link excluded from load balancing." If the value of this bit is 1, the link is used only to carry traffic of a corresponding network slice (not for load balancing). |

Table 6.25 describes the involved fields.

By advertising attributes related to member links of a Layer 3 link through the L2 Bundle Member Attributes TLV and configuring the color attribute corresponding to the Flex-Algo for the member links, it is possible to associate Layer 2 member links with the Flex-Algo. BGP-LS extensions for Flex-Algo and for L2 bundle enable the reserved link bandwidth and other TE attributes of network slices to be reported.

### 6.2.4 BGP-LS Extensions for Slice ID-Based Network Slicing

In the slice ID-based network slicing solution, BGP-LS also needs to be extended so that information about network slices can be collected and reported to a network slice controller.

Because each network slice is associated with one logical topology and multiple network slices can be associated with the same logical topology, there is no one-to-one mapping between a network slice and a logical topology/algorithm. Therefore, network slice identification is required in the control plane, and the mapping between the network slice and the topology/algorithm needs to be reported to the network slice controller through BGP-LS. In addition, BGP-LS needs to be extended to advertise information about resources allocated by nodes and links on the network for each involved network slice and related TE attributes. Because global network slice IDs are introduced in the data plane, when the data and control planes use the same network slice identifier, SRv6 resource-aware SIDs allocated by each node and link to involved network slices do not need to be advertised through BGP-LS (conversely, this is required in the SRv6 SID-based network slicing solution).

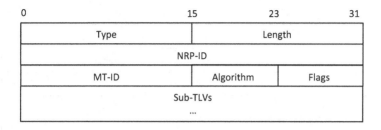

| 0 | | 15 | 23 | 31 |
|---|---|---|---|---|

| Type | | Length | |
|---|---|---|---|
| NRP-ID | | | |
| MT-ID | | Algorithm | Flags |
| Sub-TLVs<br>... | | | |

FIGURE 6.37    Format of the NRPD TLV.

### 6.2.4.1 Reporting of Network Slice Definition Information

The Network Resource Partition Definition (NRPD) TLV is defined in BGP-LS to advertise the mapping between network slices and logical topologies/algorithms. The NRPD TLV is carried in the BGP-LS attribute corresponding to the BGP-LS Node NLRI. Figure 6.37 shows the format of this TLV.

The meaning of each field in the NRPD TLV of BGP-LS is consistent with that of the same field in the NRPD TLV of IGP described in the IGP extensions for slice ID-based network slicing.

The use of MT and Flex-Algo in BGP-LS is the same as that in IGP. MT and Flex-Algo can be used separately or together on a network.

### 6.2.4.2 Reporting of Network Slice Topology Attributes

Because the network slice definition includes reference to an MT ID and an algorithm ID, intra-AS network slice topology attributes can be reported through BGP-LS extensions for MT or Flex-Algo. The mechanisms used to report these attributes are described in the previous two sections. If multiple network slices reference the same MT or Flex-Algo, generating the logical topology for these network slices only requires BGP-LS to report the MT or Flex-Algo information once. This avoids overhead on the control plane caused by independently advertising topology information for each network slice.

In an inter-AS network slice scenario, BGP-LS is used to advertise intra-AS logical topology information to the controller, and BGP-LS extensions for EPE are used to advertise inter-AS link connection information corresponding to the network slice to the controller. To indicate one or more network slices to which an inter-AS link belongs, the NRP IDs TLV is defined. This TLV is carried in the BGP-LS attribute corresponding to

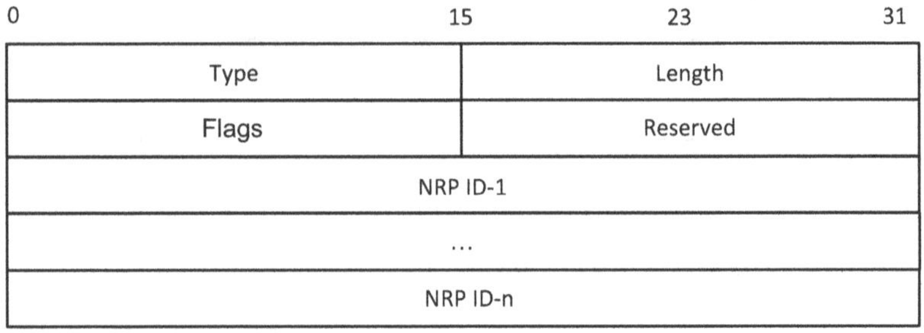

| 0 | 15 | 23 | 31 |
|---|---|---|---|
| Type | | Length | |
| Flags | | Reserved | |
| NRP ID-1 | | | |
| ... | | | |
| NRP ID-n | | | |

FIGURE 6.38  Format of the NRP IDs TLV.

a Link NLRI when inter-AS link connection information is advertised. Figure 6.38 shows the format of this TLV.

The meaning of each field in the NRP IDs TLV of BGP-LS is consistent with that of the same field in the NRP IDs TLV of IGP described in the IGP extensions for slice ID-based network slicing.

### 6.2.4.3 Reporting of Network Slice Resource Attributes

Similar to the mechanism in IGP extensions of the slice ID-based network slicing solution, the way in which resource attributes are reported and BGP is extended varies depending on the network resource reservation mode (through Layer 3 sub-interfaces, Layer 2 sub-interfaces, or sub-channels with reserved bandwidth).

When Layer 3 sub-interfaces are used to reserve network slice resources, an IP address and IGP need to be configured for each of these Layer 3 sub-interfaces. BGP-LS link attribute TLVs can be used by network nodes to advertise the TE attributes (such as bandwidth) of Layer 3 sub-interfaces corresponding to each network slice. Because this mode requires that an independent Layer 3 sub-interface be created for each network slice, an IP address be configured for each of the sub-interfaces, and IGP be enabled, different network slices cannot share the same topology or protocol session. As such, this mode is not recommended for the slice ID-based network slicing solution.

When Layer 2 sub-interfaces are used to reserve network slice resources, the L2 Bundle Member Attributes TLV defined in the BGP-LS extensions for SR (RFC 9085[15]) needs to be used to advertise TE attribute information such as the bandwidth of Layer 2 member sub-interfaces allocated to different network slices by Layer 3 interfaces. Similar to IGP extensions, when applied to a slice ID-based network slicing scenario, the L2 Bundle Member Attributes TLV needs to be extended so that the NRP IDs TLV is used to indicate one or more network slices associated with each Layer 2 member interface.

To indicate that each Layer 2 member sub-interface can be used only to carry service traffic in one network slice, a new Link Attribute Flags TLV is added for BGP-LS route attributes, and a flag bit E is defined. Bit E is used to exclude a Layer 2 member sub-interface from the load balancing group consisting of bundled links. The format of the Link Attribute Flags TLV has been described in the previous section (see Figure 6.36 for details). This TLV can be carried in the BGP-LS attribute corresponding to the Link NLRI, or it can be carried in the L2 Bundle Member Attributes TLV as a sub-TLV.

When sub-channels with reserved bandwidth are used to reserve resources on interfaces for different network slices, resource attributes are reported through a similar mechanism to that used in IGP extensions. If a Layer 3 link belongs to multiple network slices, the attributes carrying the NRP-specific TE Attribute TLV need to be carried. In BGP-LS extensions, the BGP-LS attribute corresponding to the Link NLRI carries the newly defined NRP-specific TE Attribute TLV to advertise the bandwidth allocated by the corresponding link for different network slices and other TE attributes. Figure 6.39 shows the format of the NRP-specific TE Attribute TLV.

The meaning of each field in the NRP-specific TE Attribute TLV of BGP-LS is consistent with that of the same field in the NRP-specific TE Attribute Sub-TLV described in the IGP extensions for slice ID-based network slicing.

### 6.2.4.4 Advertisement of Data-Plane Network Slice Identifiers

To steer a data packet into a specified network slice and forward it using the resources allocated to this slice, a network device needs to add the network slice identifier to the packet and maintain the mapping between the data-plane network slice identifier and forwarding resources.

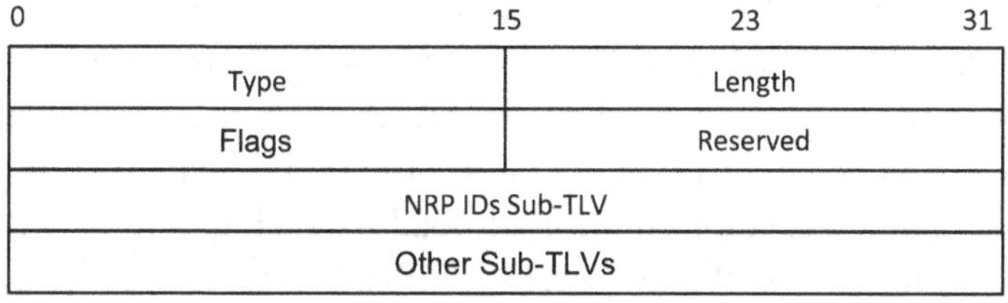

| 0 | 15 | 23 | 31 |
|---|---|---|---|
| Type | | Length | |
| Flags | | Reserved | |
| NRP IDs Sub-TLV | | | |
| Other Sub-TLVs | | | |

FIGURE 6.39   NRP-specific TE attribute TLV.

When a dedicated network slice ID is introduced to the data plane to instruct packet forwarding using the resource of the corresponding network slice, the data-plane network slice ID can be the same as the control-plane network slice ID. Because the mapping between control-plane network slice IDs and either sub-interfaces or sub-channels with reserved bandwidth is reported when the slice resource attributes are reported, the data-plane network slice ID does not need to be additionally advertised using a protocol. This network slice ID advertisement mechanism is similar to that used in the IGP. This avoids the control protocol overhead caused by reporting the SRv6 resource-aware SIDs of each network slice for each network node or link in the SRv6 SID-based network slicing solution. As a result, the scalability of the network slice control plane is further improved.

## 6.3 BGP SPF EXTENSIONS FOR NETWORK SLICING

### 6.3.1 BGP SPF Fundamentals

Being able to collect complete network topology information, link-state-based IGP has advantages in route calculation and convergence speed. However, IGP's dynamic flooding mechanism limits the scale of the networks to which IGP applies. Compared with IGP, BGP has major advantages in transmission reliability, scalability, and support for routing policies. Currently, Massively Scalable Data Center (MSDC) networks tend to use the BGP-based Layer 3 routing technology described in RFC 7938[18] for underlay connections, thereby achieving high network scalability and flexible routing policies. To combine the advantages of IGP and BGP, the industry proposes BGP Shortest Path First (SPF), a new protocol mechanism that applies to large-scale networks with dense network connections.

In the BGP framework, BGP SPF defines the BGP-LS-SPF sub-address family to advertise and synchronize link state information on the network and calculate routes based on the link state information. BGP SPF messages reuse the NLRIs of the BGP-LS address family, BGP-LS route attributes, and related TLVs. In addition, some TLVs dedicated to BGP SPF are defined in BGP-LS attributes. On this basis, BGP SPF uses the SPF-based shortest path calculation mechanism rather than the traditional BGP route selection mechanism. BGP SPF has the same capabilities as IGP in terms of route calculation, multi-path load balancing, and Fast Reroute (FRR). In addition, BGP SPF inherits BGP's advantages in reliable transmission, message sequence preservation, and high scalability. BGP SPF messages can be longer than IGP packets, meaning they can carry more information and advertise more attributes of nodes and links. For details about the BGP SPF mechanism, see *draft-ietf-lsvr-bgp-spf*.[19]

### 6.3.2 BGP SPF-Based Network Slicing

Network slicing further expands the network scale and brings scalability challenges to the control plane of network devices. BGP SPF can be used as an option on the control plane to implement large-scale network slices.

To implement network slicing based on BGP SPF, the existing BGP SPF protocol needs to support MT and Flex-Algo. This is mainly implemented by introducing BGP-LS extensions for MT and Flex-Algo to the BGP-LS-SPF sub-address family. In addition, BGP-LS's protocol extensions designed to support the slice ID-based network slicing solution can be used by BGP SPF. This reduces the overhead of advertising network slice information and calculating routes in the control plane. It also further improves protocol scalability. For details about BGP SPF extensions designed to support network resource slicing, see *draft-dong-lsvr-bgp-spf-nrp*.[20]

The methods and protocol extensions used by BGP SPF are similar to those used by IGP, regardless of whether the SRv6 SID-based or slice ID-based network slicing solution is adopted. However, BGP SPF has higher scalability than IGP and has apparent advantages over IGP in advertising massive network slice information. Therefore, BGP SPF is more suitable for scenarios where massive numbers of network slices are required.

## 6.4 SR POLICY EXTENSIONS FOR NETWORK SLICING

SR Policy, a tunneling technology developed based on SR, can be used to customize SR forwarding paths for services with specific requirements.

Each SR Policy uses the following 3-tuple as key elements:

- Headend: SR Policy headend, which is responsible for steering traffic into the specified SR Policy.

- Color: an attribute used to identify different SR Policies with specified headends and endpoints. It can be associated with a series of service intents (e.g., low latency and high bandwidth), meaning that it can be considered a service requirement template ID. Because there is no unified coding rule, color values need to be allocated by network administrators. The color attribute provides a mechanism used to associate service routes and SR Policies.

- Endpoint: destination address of an SR Policy.

The forwarding path of an SR Policy is computed based on the specified headend, color attribute, and endpoint. Because the headend value of each SR Policy identifies the headend itself, the SR Policy delivered to a specific headend can be uniquely identified using <Color, Endpoint>. In this case, the headend can match the <Color, Endpoint> information about SR Policies against the <Color extended community attribute, Next hop> information of service routes. This makes it possible for the headend to steer traffic to the forwarding path of the matching SR Policy.

Figure 6.40 shows the data structure of an SR Policy, which supports multiple candidate paths working in active/backup mode. Only one of these paths can be active at any given time and used for packet forwarding — the others remain in the backup state. A candidate path can contain multiple Segment Identifier (SID) lists. Each SID list carries the weight attribute and represents an E2E explicit path from the headend to the endpoint, instructing network devices to forward packets over the specified path. Based on the weight attribute, you can control the load-balancing ratio of traffic between different SID lists, thereby implementing Equal-Cost Multiple Path (ECMP) or Unequal-Cost Multiple Path (UCMP).

Multiple methods are available for creating an SR Policy on the headend and delivering the candidate paths of the SR Policy. For example, this

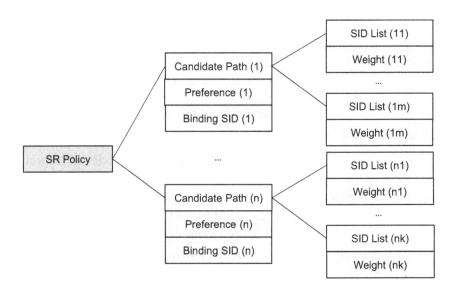

FIGURE 6.40   SR Policy data structure.

can be achieved by using the BGP SR Policy or Path Computation Element Communication Protocol (PCEP) extension or by performing manual configuration.

On a network with multiple network slices, to implement differentiated processing and isolation of data packets from different users or applications while guaranteeing the quality of services, the headend needs to specify the network slice to which the packets will be steered in addition to steering the packets to a specified forwarding path. Depending on the solution used to implement network slicing, an SR Policy can be associated with a specific network slice through the following two methods:

- Method 1: If the SRv6 SID-based network slicing solution is used, resource-aware SIDs corresponding to a network slice can be directly used to form an explicit path for the SR Policy.

- Method 2: If the slice ID-based network slicing solution is used, the data-plane network slice ID associated with candidate paths needs to be specified in SR Policy provisioning.

The following subsections describe SR Policy-related BGP and PCEP extensions, which are used for provisioning SR Policies associated with network slices and for requesting and computing TE paths based on network slice constraints, respectively.

### 6.4.1 BGP SR Policy Extensions for Network Slicing

In BGP, the BGP SR Policy Subsequent Address Family Identifier (SAFI)[21] is defined to provide a mechanism for using BGP to deliver candidate path information for SR Policies between a controller and network device. In the route update messages of the BGP SR Policy SAFI, the <Color, Endpoint> keys of an SR Policy are carried in the NLRI, whereas the candidate path information of the SR Policy is carried by extending the BGP Tunnel Encaps Attribute defined in RFC 9012.[22] The format of a route update message for the BGP SR Policy SAFI is as follows:

```
SR Policy SAFI NLRI: <Distinguisher, Policy-Color,
Endpoint>
Attributes:
Tunnel Encaps Attribute (23)
    Tunnel Type: SR Policy
    Binding SID
```

```
Preference
Priority
Policy Name
Explicit NULL Label Policy (ENLP)
Segment List
    Weight
    Segment
    Segment
    . . .
```

To indicate the network slice corresponding to an SR Policy's candidate path, the route update messages of the BGP SR Policy SAFI need to be extended. This is achieved by adding the NRP Sub-TLV to the Tunnel Encaps Attribute in order to carry information such as the NRP ID. The format of an extended route update message for the BGP SR Policy SAFI is as follows:

```
SR Policy SAFI NLRI: <Distinguisher, Policy-Color,
Endpoint>
Attributes:
Tunnel Encaps Attribute (23)
    Tunnel Type: SR Policy
    Binding SID
    Preference
    Priority
    Policy Name
    Explicit NULL Label Policy (ENLP)
    NRP
    Segment List
        Weight
        Segment
        Segment
        . . .
```

Figure 6.41 shows the format of the NRP Sub-TLV.

Table 6.26 describes the involved fields.

BGP SR Policy extensions for network slicing allow different candidate paths in the same SR Policy to be associated with different network slices. Nevertheless, to ensure consistent mapping between service and resource slices in common network slicing scenarios, it is recommended that all candidate paths in the same SR Policy be associated with the same network slice.

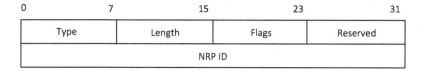

FIGURE 6.41   Format of the NRP sub-TLV.

TABLE 6.26   Fields in the NRP Sub-TLV

| Field | Length | Description |
|---|---|---|
| Type | 1 byte | Sub-TLV type. The value is 123. |
| Length | 1 byte | Total length of the sub-TLV (excluding the Type and Length fields), in bytes. The value is 6. |
| Flags | 1 byte | Flags. Currently, no flag is defined. |
| Reserved | 1 byte | Reserved for future extension. |
| NRP ID | 4 bytes | Globally unique network slice ID. 0 and 0xFFFFFFFF are reserved values. |

## 6.4.2  PCEP Extensions for Network Slicing

PCEP enables path computation request and response messages to be exchanged between a Path Computation Client (PCC) and Path Computation Element (PCE), thereby achieving controller-based computation and delivery of constrained TE paths. As defined in RFC 5440,[23] PCEP was originally used for exchanging TE path computation requests and responses in MPLS and Generalized MPLS (GMPLS) scenarios. As SDN technologies developed, PCEP was extended for network controllers to collect, compute, and deliver stateful TE paths. The main standards involved are RFC 8231[24] and RFC 8281.[25]

Table 6.27 lists the main types of PCEP messages and their corresponding functions.

A PCEP message consists of a common header and various objects, each of which can be further divided into different sub-objects. Table 6.28 lists typical PCEP objects.

With the emergence of SR, PCEP is extended to support SR-MPLS- and SRv6-based TE path computation and delivery as well as SR Policy candidate path delivery. Table 6.29 lists the main standards and drafts involved in PCEP extensions.

To extend PCEP to support network slicing, a constraint for network slice-based path computation needs to be added to the PCReq message, and the PCRep message can indicate the network slice corresponding to the

TABLE 6.27  Main Types of PCEP Messages

| Message Type | Function |
|---|---|
| Open | Establishes a PCEP session. |
| Keepalive | Maintains the PCEP session state and responds to an Open message. |
| PCNtf (Notification) | Advertises a specific event between a PCC and a PCE. |
| PCErr (Path Computation Error) | Advertises fault information between a PCC and a PCE. |
| PCReq (Path Computation Request) | Carries the path computation request sent by a PCC to a PCE. |
| PCRep (Path Computation Reply) | Carries the path computation result sent by a PCE to a PCC. |
| PCRpt (Path Computation LSP State Report) | Carries the path state information reported by a PCC to a PCE. |
| PCUpd (Path Computation LSP Update Request) | Carries the path update request sent by a PCE to a PCC. |
| PCInitiate (LSP Initiate Request) | Carries the TE path creation request sent by a PCE to a PCC. |

TABLE 6.28  Typical PCEP Objects

| Object Type | Function |
|---|---|
| Open Object | Carries PCEP session parameters for capability negotiation. This object is mandatory in Open messages but optional in PCErr messages. |
| RP (Request Parameters) Object | Carries various attributes and parameters of a path computation request. This object is mandatory in PCReq and PCRep messages but optional in PCNtf and PCErr messages. |
| ERO (Explicit Route Object) | Carries specified TE path information. This object can be carried in PCRep, PCRpt, and PCUpd messages. |
| RRO (Reported Route Object) | Carries actual TE path information. This object is optional in PCReq and PCRpt messages. |
| LSPA (LSP Attributes) Object | Carries TE path attributes, which are used by a PCE for path computation. This object is optional in PCReq and PCRep messages. |
| SRP (Stateful PCE Request Parameters) Object | Carries information such as SRP-ID-number in order to associate the path update request sent by a PCE with the path state report information sent by a PCC in stateful PCE scenarios. This object is mandatory in PCUpd messages but optional in PCRpt and PCErr messages. |
| LSP Object | Carries the identifier of an LSP, the operation to be performed on the LSP, and relevant state information. This object is mandatory in PCRpt and PCUpd messages but optional in PCReq and PCRep messages. |

TABLE 6.29    Main Standards and Drafts Involved in PCEP Extension

| Standard/Draft | Description |
|---|---|
| RFC 8664[26] | PCEP extension used to support SR-MPLS-based TE path computation and delivery |
| draft-ietf-pce-segment-routing-ipv6[27] | PCEP extension used to support SRv6-based TE path computation and delivery |
| draft-ietf-pce-segment-routing-policy-cp[28] | PCEP extension used to support the delivery of SR Policies' candidate paths |
| draft-ietf-pce-multipath[29] | PCEP extension used to support carrying multiple paths that meet specific path computation constraints |

to-be-created TE path. In stateful PCE scenarios, the PCUpd and PCRpt messages can indicate the network slice corresponding to the involved TE path. Furthermore, when a PCInitiate message is used for TE path creation in stateful PCE scenarios, the message can also indicate the network slice corresponding to the to-be-created TE path. Currently, PCEP extensions used to support network slicing mainly include the NRP TLV and NRP-CAPABILITY TLV.

NRP TLV: This TLV is defined in the LSPA object of PCEP to use the NRP ID as a TE path attribute. Figure 6.42 shows the format of this TLV. Table 6.30 describes the involved fields.

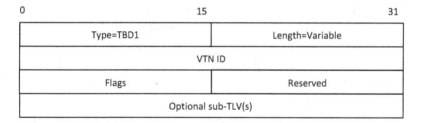

FIGURE 6.42    Format of the NRP TLV.

TABLE 6.30    Fields in the NRP TLV

| Field | Length | Description |
|---|---|---|
| Type | 2 bytes | TLV type to be allocated by the IANA. |
| Length | 2 bytes | Total length of the TLV (excluding the Type and Length fields), in bytes. |
| NRP ID | 4 bytes | Globally unique NRP ID. |
| Flags | 2 bytes | Flags. Currently, no flag is defined. |
| Reserved | 2 bytes | Reserved for future extension. |
| Optional sub-TLV(s) | 4 bytes | Optional sub-TLVs, which can be used to carry additional network slice attributes. |

The NRP TLV is a general extension of PCEP and can be used for computing and delivering TE paths, such as SR-based ones. This extension applies to both SRv6 SID-based and slice ID-based network slicing solutions.

In a PCReq message, the NRP TLV can be carried in the LSPA object as one of the path computation constraints to require a PCE to compute a path based on the attributes (e.g., topology and resource attributes) of a specified network slice. In addition, the NRP TLV can be carried in a PCRep message to indicate the network slice corresponding to the to-be-created TE path. In stateful PCE scenarios, the PCUpd and PCRpt messages can use the NRP TLV to indicate the network slice corresponding to the involved TE path. Furthermore, when a PCInitiate message is used for TE path creation in stateful PCE scenarios, the message can also carry the NRP TLV to indicate the network slice corresponding to the to-be-created TE path.

NRP-CAPABILITY TLV: This TLV is carried in the Open object of an Open message that is sent during PCEP session establishment. It defines a new PCEP capability called NRP-CAPABILITY, which is used by the PCE and PCC to negotiate whether NRP-specific constraint-based path computation and slice ID-based data packet encapsulation are supported during PCEP session establishment. Figure 6.43 shows the format of this TLV.

Table 6.31 describes the involved fields.

The NRP-CAPABILITY TLV in Open messages enables the PCC and PCE to negotiate whether network slice attributes can be used as path computation constraints and whether network slice information corresponding to the target TE path can be carried through PCEP messages in TE path delivery, update, and reporting.

In the SRv6 SID-based network slicing solution, both the PCE and PCC need to set the D flag in the NRP-CAPABILITY TLV to 0. In this case, when PCEP is used to deliver, update, and report TE paths, involved PCE messages need to carry path information formed by SRv6 resource-aware SIDs of the corresponding network slice.

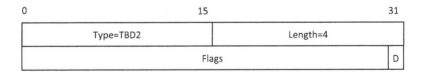

FIGURE 6.43   Format of the NRP-CAPABILITY TLV.

TABLE 6.31    Fields in the NRP-CAPABILITY TLV

| Field | Length | Description |
|-------|--------|-------------|
| Type | 2 bytes | TLV type to be allocated by the IANA. |
| Length | 2 bytes | Total length of the TLV (excluding the Type and Length fields), in bytes. The value is 4. |
| Flags | 4 bytes | Flags. The least-significant bit of the field is the D (Data Plane NRP ID CAPABILITY) flag, which indicates whether data-plane NRP ID encapsulation is supported. If the D flag in an Open message is set to 1 by a PCC, the PCC supports the slice ID-based network slicing solution, and NRP IDs can be encapsulated in data packets. However, if it is set to 1 by a PCE, the PCE supports the slice ID-based network slicing solution, and when the PCE provides TE path information to a PCC, the NRP ID carried in PCE control messages needs to be encapsulated in data packets. |

In the slice ID-based network slicing solution, both the PCE and PCC need to set the D flag in the NRP-CAPABILITY TLV to 1. In this case, when PCEP is used to deliver, update, and report TE paths, involved PCE messages need to carry the path information formed by SRv6 SIDs and the data plane slice identifier indicated by the NRP TLV.

## 6.5 FLOWSPEC EXTENSIONS FOR TRAFFIC STEERING TO NETWORK SLICES

The FlowSpec mechanism is used to deliver flow matching rules and flow forwarding actions between network devices or between a network controller and a network device. It enables network devices to apply a series of matching rules to data packets and implement a specified forwarding action on packets successfully matched. The main elements involved in FlowSpec are as follows:

- Flow matching rule: for example, matching with the source IP address, destination IP address, IP protocol number, transmission protocol port number, DSCP, or specific flags in packets

- Flow forwarding action: for example, packet discarding, rate limiting, priority modification, traffic steering to a specified node or tunnel, and redirection to a specified VPN instance

BGP FlowSpec is implemented based on a new BGP-extended address family. RFC 8955[30] defines basic BGP FlowSpec, and RFC 8956[31] defines BGP FlowSpec extensions for IPv6. Currently, BGP FlowSpec version 2 (*draft-ietf-idr-flowspec-v2*)[32] is being developed in the IETF to further improve protocol scalability. In addition, RFC 9168[33] defines PCEP extensions for FlowSpec, allowing it to steer data packets that match specific flow matching rules to a specified explicit path.

FlowSpec can be used to advertise the flow matching rule and flow forwarding action used to steer the traffic of service slices to resource slices. The FlowSpec-based traffic steering scheme, implemented by matching specific fields in the data packets of service slices against flow matching rules configured on the ingress, steers matching packets to the corresponding resource slice according to the specified flow forwarding action. This scheme supports the following two modes:

- Mode 1: Packets that comply with a specified flow matching rule are steered to the shortest path (referred to as the NRP BE path) in the corresponding resource slice for forwarding.

- Mode 2: Packets that comply with a specified flow matching rule are steered to the TE explicit path (referred to as the NRP TE path) in the corresponding resource slice for forwarding.

BGP FlowSpec flexibly supports the preceding two traffic steering modes. Conversely, because its forwarding behavior is to steer matched traffic to the specified TE path, PCEP FlowSpec supports only the second mode. This section focuses on the protocol extensions for network slice-specific traffic steering based on BGP FlowSpec.

In the SRv6 SID-based network slicing solution, the FlowSpec flow matching rules defined in IETF RFC 8955[30] and RFC 8956[31] can be used to match service slice traffic. The flow matching action defined in the IETF draft *draft-ietf-idr-flowspec-redirect-ip*[34] can be used to implement traffic steering mode 1. Specifically, in a network resource slice, the "Redirect to IPv6" extended community attribute carries the SRv6 resource-aware SID of the egress, instructing network nodes to forward packets over the shortest path. The IETF draft *draft-ietf-idr-ts-flowspec-srv6-policy*[35] defines a mechanism for steering matched traffic to an SRv6 Policy, allowing traffic steering mode 2 to be implemented. In this case, the SRv6 Policy needs to use the resource-aware SIDs associated with the desired resource slice to form an SRv6 explicit path, thereby instructing network nodes to forward packets over this specified path in the resource slice.

In the slice ID-based network slicing solution, defined FlowSpec flow matching rules can be used to match service slice traffic. For traffic steering mode 1, a new flow forwarding action needs to be defined, and resource slice identifiers need to be encapsulated for matched service slice packets to steer traffic from a service slice to a resource slice. For traffic steering mode 2, the traffic steering mechanism described in the IETF draft *draft-ietf-idr-ts-flowspec-srv6-policy*[35] can be used to steer the packets of a service slice to the SRv6 Policy associated with a resource slice. In this case, the ingress needs to encapsulate not only the SID list of the SRv6 Policy but also the corresponding slice ID into the packets.

In slice ID-based cross-domain network slicing scenarios, the service slice packets received by the ingresses in some network domains may carry slice IDs, based on which the ingresses can steer these packets to specified resource slices in their own domains. The slice ID carried in each received packet may be an inter-domain slice ID of an E2E network slice or a slice ID in the previous network domain of an E2E network slice. The ingress of a network domain needs to map packets to the corresponding resource slice in this domain based on the locally maintained mapping between the inter-domain slice ID (or the slice ID in the previous network domain) and intra-domain slice ID, and then encapsulate the intra-domain slice ID into the packets. This requires a new slice ID-based flow matching rule to be defined.

### 6.5.1 NRP ID-Based Flow Matching Rule

A new flow matching rule called NRP ID Component is defined for BGP FlowSpec. It uses the TLV format and complies with the definition in *draft-ietf-idr-flowspec-v2*. Figure 6.44 shows the format of the value part in this rule. Table 6.32 describes the involved fields.

| g | Flags | Reserved |
|---|---|---|
| NRP ID | | |

FIGURE 6.44   Format of the value part in the NRP ID component.

TABLE 6.32   Fields in the Value Part of the NRP ID Component

| Field | Length | Description |
|---|---|---|
| Flags | 1 byte | Flags. Currently, the first bit is defined as the Global (g) bit. The value 1 indicates that the NRP ID is globally unique, and the value 0 indicates that the NRP ID is unique in the local domain. Other flag bits should be set to 0 before transmission and ignored upon receipt. |
| Reserved | 1 byte | Reserved for future extension. |
| NRP ID | 4 bytes | NRP identifier. |

## 6.5.2 NRP ID-Based Flow Forwarding Action

To achieve FlowSpec-based traffic steering to network slices that are implemented using the slice ID-based network slicing solution, a new flow forwarding action needs to be defined for encapsulating network slice IDs. As such, the BGP extended community attribute called Encapsulate-NRP-ID is introduced to indicate the flow forwarding action of encapsulating the specified NRP ID (i.e., network slice ID). Figure 6.45 shows the format of the extended community attribute.

Table 6.33 describes the involved fields.

To steer packets in a service slice to the shortest path in a slice ID-based resource slice, the Encapsulate-NRP-ID extended community attribute is carried in BGP FlowSpec messages. This attribute indicates that corresponding slice IDs need to be encapsulated into matched data packets. If the destination node of a data packet needs to be modified, the flow forwarding action needs to carry the "Redirect to IPv6" extended community attribute. To steer packets in a service slice to the TE path in a slice ID-based resource slice, the color and "Redirect to IPv6" extended community attributes are carried in BGP FlowSpec messages. These attributes help steer data packets matching the specified flow matching rule to the SRv6 Policy associated with a specific resource slice. In slice ID-based inter-domain network slicing scenarios, if a service slice packet received by the ingress of a network domain carries no inter-domain slice ID, the ingress needs to change the slice ID in the packet to its intra-domain slice ID.

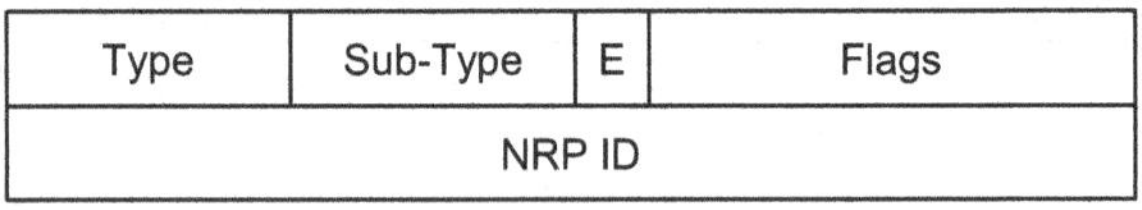

| Type | Sub-Type | E | Flags |
|------|----------|---|-------|
| NRP ID | | | |

FIGURE 6.45    Format of the Encapsulate-NRP-ID extended community attribute.

TABLE 6.33    Fields in the Encapsulate-NRP-ID Extended Community Attribute

| Field | Length | Description |
|-------|--------|-------------|
| Type | 1 byte | Type value to be allocated by the IANA. |
| Sub-Type | 1 byte | Sub-type value to be allocated by the IANA. |
| Flags | 2 bytes | Flags. The first bit is defined as the Encapsulate (E) bit. If this bit is set to 1, a new NRP ID needs to be encapsulated for the packet. If this bit is set to 0, the original NRP ID in the packet needs to be modified. |
| NRP ID | 4 bytes | NRP identifier. |

## 6.6 STORIES BEHIND NETWORKING SLICING

### 6.6.1 From MT to Flex-Algo

Although IGP MT standards[1,2] were officially released for OSPF in 2007 and for IS-IS in 2008, IGP MT has not yet seen widespread uptake. A major application of IGP MT is multicast MT routing, which is used to prevent the multicast Reverse Path Forwarding (RPF) check failure that occurs when the interface of a unidirectional MPLS TE tunnel participates in route computation.

As mentioned in the IGP MT standards, different topologies can be used to provide different QoS levels for services. However, IGP MT-based QoS routing failed to make any significant progress for two reasons: 1. There was no strong driving force from applications at the time when these standards were released. 2. There was no appropriate identifier in the data plane to carry the topology ID. Even though DSCP can be used to identify MTs, it conflicts with the DSCP function used for DiffServ QoS, which causes the compatibility issue.

Later, Label Distribution Protocol (LDP) MT[36] was developed to identify MTs through MPLS labels in the data plane. To achieve MT identification, it was possible to use a single label to identify the <MT, Address prefix> combination or use two labels to respectively represent the MT and the address prefix in the corresponding topology. Because the latter approach is difficult to implement and can be supported only after upgrading the MPLS forwarding plane, the former is adopted in LDP MT. In this way, only LDP in the control plane needs to be extended, while the forwarding plane can directly use the existing MPLS forwarding mechanism without requiring any extension or upgrade. Unlike IPv4 and MPLS, IPv6 can be more conveniently extended to support MT by carrying a topology ID in the IPv6 extension header.[37] From the extensions used to identify IGP MT in the data plane, we can see that MPLS was developed to extend IP functions to some extent. However, due to the limited hardware capabilities at the time when MPLS was proposed, a hardware-friendly implementation mechanism needed to be adopted. But with significant improvements in hardware (especially programmable chipset) capabilities, it has been possible to unleash the extensibility of IPv6 and implement extensions of the data plane in a simpler and more direct way.

LDP MT could have had better development prospects. To achieve 100% network coverage for IP FRR, Maximum Redundancy Tree (MRT) FRR[38] was designed to protect the primary path in the default topology through backup paths in different topologies (red and blue topologies). It needed to be combined with LDP MT in order to identify MTs. However, the emergence of SR interrupted the development of LDP MT. Consequently, IGP replaced LDP, and TI-LFA was used to achieve 100% network coverage for IP FRR.

As 5G and network slicing develop, services have different requirements for coverage scopes and customized topologies, meaning that IP network slicing needs to support different logical topologies. Although IGP MT is presented with another good opportunity for development, the emerging Flex-Algo technology is gaining the upper hand due to its lightweight design and support for path computation in different topologies. Because most device vendors consider adopting Flex-Algo as the control plane technology for use in network slicing, IGP MT is unlikely to become the mainstream control plane technology for network slicing.

In fact, Flex-Algo is not designed to replace MT. Rather, it is derived from MT and can be applied to different MTs. When defining logical topologies for network slicing, we typically need to apply different Flex-Algos only to the default topology, not to any non-default one. In general, only one level of customization is needed for the logical topology of a network slice. Such a topology can be defined by using Flex-Algo based on the default topology or by combining different MTs with a fixed algorithm. This results in a competition between MT and Flex-Algo.

The fate of the IGP MT technology is really bumpy. Flex-Algo's simplicity makes it more attractive than MT. Nevertheless, Flex-Algo cannot provide some functions that MT offers but are relatively less important at present. The development history of IGP MT proves that the rise and fall of a technology depends on not only the technology itself but also factors such as application scenarios and opportunities. In addition, the choices made by industry leaders play a vital role in the development of technologies. Some technologies are simply born at the wrong time, which is a pity. Despite this, the ideas behind such technologies may be retained and will be developed if appropriate opportunities arise. Mastering the original essence will always be helpful for the development of new technologies.

### 6.6.2 Logical Topology and SR-Based Logical Topology

In network slicing, logical topologies can be generated based on IGP MT and Flex-Algo, both of which need to be combined with SR. IGP MT was proposed before SR; Flex-Algo was initially bound to SR, and then IP Flex-Algo[39] was introduced. This means that IGP MT and Flex-Algo can be decoupled from SR. To explain why IGP MT and Flex-Algo must be combined with SR in network slicing, let's use IGP MT as an example. The implementation of IGP Flex-Algo is similar to that of IGP MT.

Before the emergence of network slicing and SR, IGP MT could be implemented using either of the following methods:

- Method 1: Bind a node to different MTs based on different IP addresses. For example, bind the same node to MT-1 based on IP address A1 and to MT-2 based on IP address A2. In this case, although the node is bound to multiple topologies, the same routing table can be used thanks to the use of different addresses, ensuring that packets forwarded in different topologies only need to carry different destination addresses. This method is simple but consumes more IP addresses and requires a large amount of information to be propagated through IGP.

- Method 2: Bind a node to MTs based on the same IP address. For example, bind the same node to MT-1 and MT-2 based on the same IP address A. In this case, <MT-1, A> and <MT-2, A> need to be used to identify the mapping between this address and different MTs. Because different MTs use the same IP address, multiple routing tables are required for isolation. This means that different MTs correspond to different forwarding tables in the forwarding plane. In addition to the destination address, additional topology identification information needs to be carried in packets forwarded in different topologies so that different routing tables can be identified. This implementation is similar to that in MPLS VPN, which requires identifiers to be used to distinguish different VPN instances that may use the same IP address. In MPLS VPN, VPN labels are typically used to identify the forwarding tables of different VPN instances.

In this chapter, IGP MT or Flex-Algo functions as a control plane protocol for network slicing using method 1, which determines that different SRv6 locators need to be configured when IGP MT or Flex-Algo is applied to different network slices. One challenge of method 2 is that routing instance identifiers need to be introduced in the forwarding plane. A possible way was recommended to distinguish the routing instances of different IGP MTs based on DSCP values. However, given that DSCP for DiffServ had been widely applied and there were compatibility issues, using DSCP for MT was not adopted. In

Chapter 10, which discusses the technical prospects of network slicing, we present the method of introducing dedicated topology IDs in the data plane.

In network slicing, IGP MT or IGP Flex-Algo can only achieve route-based forwarding in different logical topologies. To better ensure SLA, the following two important features need to be supported:

- Resource isolation: This feature requires network slicing to use new identifiers to identify resources. In the slice ID-based network slicing solution, slice IDs can be used as identifiers. However, in the SR SID-based network slicing solution, only SR SIDs can be used to identify resources used for slice isolation.

- Explicit path: The nodes and links that a path traverses need to be specified. These nodes and links need to be identified using SR SIDs.

Because ordinary IP route-based forwarding does not support the preceding two features, IGP MT or Flex-Algo must be combined with SR in order to meet network slicing requirements.

In terms of implementing network slicing, SRv6 has advantages over SR-MPLS. Specifically, SR-MPLS can be used only after the entire network is upgraded based on MT routes and label forwarding entries are generated for these routes. In contrast, SRv6 is compatible with IPv6 forwarding and can forward packets based on the IPv6 forwarding table. This gives SRv6 the following advantages:

- When SRv6 is used to support network slicing, MT routing tables can be directly used for forwarding without the need to distribute labels and generate label forwarding entries. This simplifies service deployment and O&M.

- SRv6 for network slicing supports incremental evolution, meaning that nodes on the network can be upgraded on demand to support features (e.g., resource isolation and explicit paths) required by network slicing. In this case, packets can traverse nodes that do not support network slicing through common IPv6 routes.

SRv6 is simpler and more flexible than MPLS in implementing network slicing. If inter-domain network slicing is considered, using MPLS is more complex, and SRv6 can be used to further simplify the deployment.

### 6.6.3 BGP SPF

Large-scale data centers pose challenges to the scalability of traditional IGP, leading to the inability to support large-scale Layer 3 networks required by data centers. To improve the IGP's scalability, the following three technical directions came up in the IETF:

- Optimize IGP and introduce new algorithms to reduce the number of IGP messages to be propagated. This work is being carried out by the existing Link-State Routing (LSR) Working Group.

- Define the Routing in Fat Trees (RIFT) protocol,[40] a new IGP that adapts to the data center network architecture. The RIFT Working Group has been established to promote this work.

- Replace IGP with BGP. This involves extensions of BGP and is being carried out by the Inter-Domain Routing (IDR) Working Group and the Link-State Vector Routing (LSVR) Working Group.

For the third direction, we are accustomed to using BGP as an overlay protocol for VPN. As a result, we somewhat ignore the fact that BGP, functioning as a routing protocol, can also be used on the underlay network. Some enterprises with large data centers put forward the idea of using BGP as an underlay routing protocol to support large-scale data center networks.[18] Although this solution was a little unexpected, it was reasonable. However, when BGP is directly used as the underlay protocol, the following issues exist:

- Due to the lack of link state and topology information, relying exclusively on distance-vector routes causes problems such as slow route convergence.

- In contrast to IGP, BGP involves complex configuration, which makes O&M difficult.

To resolve the first issue, the BGP SPF scheme was proposed in the IETF, introducing the link-state route mechanism to BGP so that BGP can leverage the advantages of IGP. And to resolve the second issue, the BGP Autoconf Design Team was set up to define methods and protocol extensions for simplifying BGP configuration.

Network slicing also causes IGP scalability issues, which occur when the number of logical networks increases through network slicing but the scale of the associated physical network remains unchanged. This differs from IGP scalability issues that occur when the scale of the physical network increases due to the spine-leaf network architecture of a data center being continuously expanded. In the slice ID-based network slicing solution, the decoupling of slices and topologies greatly improves IGP scalability and reduces the control plane pressure. This is true when there are a large number of slices but only a limited number of topologies corresponding to the slices. If there are many topologies after slices are enabled to share the topology, IGP still needs to propagate a large amount of topology information. This also leads to scalability challenges. If such scenarios exist with the large-scale deployment of network slicing, BGP SPF can be introduced to improve scalability.

## REFERENCES

[1] Psenak P, Mirtorabi S, Roy A, et al. Multi-Topology (MT) Routing in OSPF [EB/OL]. (2007-06)[2022-09-30]. RFC 4915.

[2] Przygienda T, Shen N, Sheth N. M-ISIS: Multi Topology (MT) Routing in Intermediate System to Intermediate Systems (IS-ISs) [EB/OL]. (2008-02) [2022-09-30]. RFC 5120.

[3] Li T, Redback Networks Inc., Smit H. IS-IS Extensions for Traffic Engineering [EB/OL]. (2008-10)[2022-09-30]. RFC 5305.

[4] Hopps C. Routing IPv6 with IS-IS [EB/OL]. (2008-10)[2022-09-30]. RFC 5308.

[5] Psenak P, Filsfils C, Cisco Systems, et al. IS-IS Extension to Support Segment Routing over IPv6 Dataplane [EB/OL]. (2022-11-21)[2022-11-30]. draft-ietf-lsr-isis-srv6-extensions-19.

[6] Filsfils C, Previdi S, Ginsberg L, et al. Segment Routing Architecture [EB/OL]. (2018-07)[2022-09-30]. RFC 8402.

[7] Psenak P, Hegde S, Filsfils C, et al. IGP Flexible Algorithm [EB/OL]. (2022-10-17)[2022-10-30]. draft-ietf-lsr-flex-algo-26.

[8] Ginsberg L, Cisco Systems, Previdi S. IS-IS Traffic Engineering (TE) Metric Extensions [EB/OL]. (2019-03)[2022-09-30]. RFC 8570.

[9] Ginsberg L, Psenak P, Cisco Systems. IS-IS Application-Specific Link Attributes [EB/OL]. (2020-10)[2022-09-30]. RFC 8919.

[10] Psenak P, Ginsberg L, Henderickx W, et al. OSPF Application-Specific Link Attributes [EB/OL]. (2020-10)[2022-09-30]. RFC 8920.

[11] Ginsberg L, Cisco Systems, Bashandy A. Advertising Layer 2 Bundle Member Link Attributes in IS-IS [EB/OL]. (2019-12)[2022-09-30]. RFC 8668.

[12] Gredler H, Individual Contributor, Medved J, et al. North-Bound Distribution of Link-State and Traffic Engineering (TE) Information Using BGP [EB/OL]. (2016-03)[2022-09-30]. RFC 7752.

[13] Dawra G, LinkedIn, Filsfils C, et al. BGP Link State Extensions for SRv6 [EB/OL]. (2022-12-0-15)[2022-12-30]. draft-ietf-idr-bgpls-srv6-ext-12.

[14] Previdi S, Talaulikar K, Filsfils C. Border Gateway Protocol – Link State (BGP-LS) Extensions for Segment Routing BGP Egress Peer Engineering [EB/OL]. (2021-08)[2022-09-30]. RFC 9086.

[15] Previdi S, Huawei Technologies, Talaulikar K, et al. Border Gateway Protocol - Link State (BGP-LS) Extensions for Segment Routing [EB/OL]. (2021-08) [2022-09-30]. RFC 9085.

[16] Kompella K, Rekhter Y, Juniper Networks. Routing Extensions in Support of Generalized Multi-Protocol Label Switching (GMPLS) [EB/OL]. (2005-10) [2022-09-30]. RFC 4202.

[17] Vasseur JP, Previdi S, Cisco Systems. Definition of an IS-IS Link Attribute Sub-TLV [EB/OL]. (2007-09)[2022-09-30]. RFC 5029.

[18] Lapukhov P, Facebook, Premji A, et al. Use of BGP for Routing in Large-Scale Data Centers [EB/OL]. (2016-08)[2022-09-30]. RFC 7938.

[19] Patel K, Lindem A, Zandi S, et al. BGP Link-State Shortest Path First (SPF) Routing [EB/OL]. (2022-02)[2022-09-30]. draft-ietf-lsvr-bgp-spf-16.

[20] Dong J, Li Z, Wang H. BGP SPF for Network Resource Partitions [EB/OL]. (2022-10-16)[2022-10-30]. draft-dong-lsvr-bgp-spf-nrp-01.

[21] Previdi S, Filsfils C, Tataulikar K, et al. Advertising Segment Routing Policies in BGP [EB/OL]. (2022-07-27)[2022-09-30]. draft-ietf-idr-segment-routing-te-policy-20.

[22] Patel K, Van de Velde G, Sanli S. The BGP Tunnel Encapsulation Attribute [EB/OL]. (2021-04)[2022-09-30]. RFC 9012.

[23] Vasseur JP, Cisco Systems, Le Roux JL, et al. Path Computation Element (PCE) Communication Protocol (PCEP) [EB/OL]. (2009-03)[2022-09-30]. RFC 5440.

[24] Crabbe E, Oracle, Minei I, et al. Path Computation Element Communication Protocol (PCEP) Extensions for Stateful PCE [EB/OL]. (2017-09)[2022-09-30]. RFC 8231.

[25] Crabbe E, Individual Contributor, Minei I, et al. Path Computation Element Communication Protocol (PCEP) Extensions for PCE-Initiated LSP Setup in a Stateful PCE Model [EB/OL]. (2017-12)[2022-09-30]. RFC 8281.

[26] Sivabalan S, Filsfils C, Tantsura J, et al. Path Computation Element Communication Protocol (PCEP) Extensions for Segment Routing [EB/OL]. (2019-12)[2022-09-30]. RFC 8664.

[27] Li C, Negi M, Sivabalan S, et al. PCEP Extensions for Segment Routing leveraging the IPv6 data plane [EB/OL]. (2022-10-23)[2022-10-30]. draft-ietf-pce-segment-routing-ipv6-15.

[28] Koldychev M, Sivabalan S, Barth C, et al. PCEP extension to support Segment Routing Policy Candidate Paths [EB/OL]. (2020-06-24)[2022-09-30]. draft-ietf-pce-segment-routing-policy-cp-06.

[29] Koldychev M, Cisco System, Sivabalan S, et al. PCEP Extensions for Signaling Multipath Information [EB/OL]. (2022-11-14)[2022-09-30]. draft-ietf-pce-multipath-07.

[30] Loibl C, Next layer Telekom GmbH, Hares S, et al. Dissemination of Flow Specification Rules [EB/OL]. (2020-12)[2022-09-30]. RFC 8955.

[31] Loibl C, Next layer Telekom GmbH, Raszuk R, et al. Dissemination of Flow Specification Rules for IPv6 [EB/OL]. (2020-12)[2022-09-30]. RFC 8956.

[32] Hares S, Eastlake D, Yadlapalli C, et al. BGP Flow Specification Version 2 [EB/OL]. (2022-10-21)[2022-10-30]. draft-ietf-idr-flowspec-v2-01.

[33] Dhody D, Huawei Technologies, Farrel A, et al. Path Computation Element Communication Protocol (PCEP) Extension for Flow Specification [EB/OL]. (2022-01)[2022-09-30]. RFC 9168.

[34] Uttaro J, Haas J, Texier M, et al. BGP Flow-Spec Redirect to IP Action [EB/OL]. (2015-08-09)[2022-09-30]. draft-ietf-idr-flowspec-redirect-ip-02.

[35] Jiang W, Liu Y, Chen S, et al. Traffic Steering using BGP Flowspec with SRv6 Policy [EB/OL]. [2022-09-24](2022-09-30). draft-ietf-idr-flowspec-ts-srv6-policy-07.

[36] Zhao Q, Raza K, Fang L, et al. LDP Extensions for Multi-Topology [EB/OL]. (2014-07)[2022-09-30]. RFC 7307.

[37] Li Z, Hu Z, Dong J. Topology Identifier in IPv6 Extension Header [EB/OL]. (2022-09-21)[2022-09-30]. draft-li-6man-topology-id-00.

[38] Enyedi G, Csaszar A, Atlas A, et al. An Algorithm for Computing IP/LDP Fast Reroute Using Maximally Redundant Trees (MRT-FRR) [EB/OL]. (2016-06)[2022-09-30]. RFC 7811.

[39] Britto W, Hegde S, Kaneriya P, et al. IGP Flexible Algorithms (Flex-Algorithm) In IP Networks [EB/OL]. (2022-12-19)[2022-12-30]. draft-ietf-lsr-ip-flexalgo-08.

[40] Przygienda A, Sharma A, Thubert P, et al. RIFT: Routing in Fat Trees [EB/OL]. (2022-09-12)[2022-09-30]. draft-ietf-rift-rift-16.

# CHAPTER 7

# IPv6 Network Slice Controllers

A N IPv6 NETWORK SLICE controller provides a complete picture of the network. It possesses network information such as the topology, device configuration, and states of a network, serving as a hugely beneficial component in a network slicing solution. This chapter describes the key technologies and fundamentals of IPv6 network slice controllers, covering their architecture, key functions, and external interfaces.

## 7.1 ARCHITECTURE OF AN IPV6 NETWORK SLICE CONTROLLER

### 7.1.1 Architecture of a Typical Network Controller

The Network Management System (NMS) is one of the first systems designed for network Operations and Maintenance (O&M). It provides Fault, Configuration, Accounting, Performance, and Security (FCAPS) management functions.

While the NMS made network O&M easier, greater controllability of networks was achieved with the introduction of network control systems — brought about by the emergence of Software-Defined Networking (SDN) that uses OpenFlow to control the forwarding behaviors of network devices. Later, protocols such as Path Computation Element

DOI: 10.1201/9781032699868-9

Communication Protocol (PCEP) and Border Gateway Protocol (BGP) were also introduced for the network control system to indirectly control forwarding behaviors by affecting the behaviors in the control plane. However, network control systems can only control devices but cannot provide comprehensive network management and services, thereby failing to meet the complex multi-service transport requirements of IP networks. This is why a new integrated management and control system has attracted significant attention and has gradually become the mainstream of network O&M in recent years.

This book defines the integrated management and control system — a key function of which is network slicing — as the network controller. In the following sections, we first introduce the network controller to help you better understand the working mechanism of a network slice controller.

### 7.1.1.1 Challenges and Opportunities Facing Network Controllers

As new services and requirements continue to emerge in the 5G and cloud era, the IP transport network — an indispensable bridge that connects various Internet services — inevitably faces an onslaught of new challenges.

- The capacity of the IP transport network needs to be frequently expanded to cope with the ever-increasing volume of traffic. The rapid development of applications such as 4K and virtual reality gives rise to a burgeoning volume of video traffic that consumes much of the available bandwidth. This poses challenges to the capacity, power consumption, and scalability of core routers on the backbone network.

- The network structure and O&M are complex. The same network uses various network technologies (e.g., VPN, routing, tunneling, and QoS), multiple network layers (including the transport, access, aggregation, and backbone layers), and multiple network topology types (e.g., ring, star, and mesh), complicating services and the network structure while prolonging service deployment. As a result, the Total Cost of Operation (TCO) increases continuously.

- The specific Service-Level Agreement (SLA) requirements of new services are increasing. 5G technologies have given rise to new services that cannot employ the best-effort forwarding provided by a traditional IP transport network because their SLA requirements are more specific and exacting. These services need the same IP transport network to meet different SLA requirements of various types of services, such as low delay, high bandwidth, and high reliability.

- Services are changing and difficult to plan. Service cloudification has become a trend, and cloud data centers are the new rendezvous nodes for traffic. And because of the uncertainty involved in cloud services, it is difficult to predict traffic, monitor congestion, and adjust services.

It is no longer possible to address the preceding challenges with the traditional network operations mode, in which routing protocols are used to control data forwarding on network devices and an NMS is used to manage and maintain the network. As such, SDN-based big data, Artificial Intelligence (AI), and network-level control capabilities are needed to help carriers effectively reduce operating expense while also meeting the requirements of new network service models.

### 7.1.1.2 Deployment Positions of Network Controllers

Network controllers are the management and control centers used to undertake the service requirements of higher-level systems and to manage and control lower-level physical networks. Figure 7.1 shows the deployment positions of network controllers.

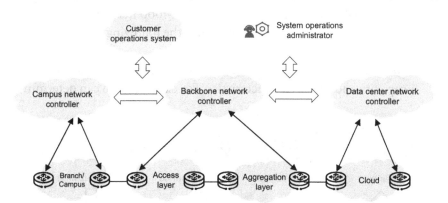

FIGURE 7.1 Deployment positions of network controllers.

A network controller is capable of performing the following operations over interfaces in different directions:

- Over the management and control interface connected to a device: The network controller obtains information about the management plane, control plane, and forwarding plane on the device, including configurations, routes, and forwarded traffic; it also delivers configurations and control data to the device to control the behaviors of the preceding three planes.

- Over the interface connected to a neighboring network controller: The network controller collaborates with the neighbor to implement cross-domain or composite service management.

- Over the interface connected to a higher-level system, such as a customer operations system: The network controller receives service requirements from the customer operations system and provides the system with network information.

- Over a human-machine interface: The network controller allows system administrators to manage and maintain the network.

### 7.1.1.3 Key Functions of a Network Controller

As shown in Figure 7.2, a network controller provides four types of functions — network planning, construction, maintenance, and optimization — to fulfill the full-lifecycle network service. The four types of functions work together to provide closed-loop network services.

The four types of functions help you with the following tasks:

- Network planning: Design network capabilities based on network capacity and service characteristics. For example, you can determine

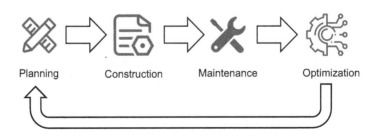

FIGURE 7.2   Key functions of a network controller.

schemes for IP address allocation and Interior Gateway Protocol (IGP) domain division.

- Network construction: Deploy a network based on construction intents. For example, you can configure devices to provide networking services and deploy private line services.

- Network maintenance: Monitor and check the running states of a network, and quickly respond to and rectify faults or errors.

- Network optimization: Optimize and adjust a network based on the network's operating state, as well as analysis of network traffic and quality, to ensure it runs as expected.

To complete the tasks involved in the preceding functions, a network controller requires full-lifecycle function modules. As shown in Figure 7.3, an intelligent network controller generally consists of five modules: business service, management service, control service, analysis service, and platform service modules.

The five modules are described as follows:

- Business service: It receives service requests delivered by higher-level systems, orchestrates the management, control, and analysis service

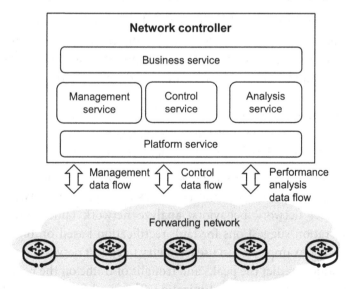

FIGURE 7.3 Modules of a network controller.

modules to execute corresponding functions based on service characteristics, determines the function execution results, and drives subsequent function execution to meet service requirements.

- Management service: It provides network management capabilities, including the FCAPS capabilities available on a traditional NMS. It also enables external systems to obtain information such as NE data, network data, topology information, and physical inventory data through application programming interfaces. Furthermore, this module provides intent-level interfaces, converts user intents into network functions and deploys them, and continuously maintains intent states after the network topology or configuration changes. In the network planning phase, after receiving the network design from a customer, the management service module defines network resource and service deployment schemes — for example, IP address resource planning and routing domain division policies — to support subsequent network construction. In the network construction phase, this module completes network provisioning, such as enabling IGP, BGP, and Segment Routing over IPv6 (SRv6) capabilities on the network. It also completes service configuration, such as configuring a policy for steering Virtual Private Network (VPN) traffic to an SRv6 domain. And in the network maintenance phase, the module displays alarms, states, and more.

- Control service: As the network-level control plane, it works with the control planes of devices to control traffic. In the network construction phase, the control service module is responsible for controlling services. For example, it learns network routes and topologies through BGP-Link State (BGP-LS), delivers SRv6 Policy routes through BGP, and controls the forwarding paths of network devices. In the network optimization phase, this module implements optimization functions. For example, it adjusts the paths of SRv6 Policies for a congested network.

- Analysis service: It uses the network performance and running data obtained by various network probes to display the network states, predict network behaviors, analyze network faults, and provide operation suggestions for fault rectification based on big data and AI. For example, it can use telemetry to collect network traffic information, predict the peaks and troughs of traffic on the network, and drive network traffic optimization. This module can also determine a fault's root cause based on information such as alarms, service paths, and service traffic, facilitating fault rectification.

- Platform service: As a universal platform for application services, it provides unified service governance, security, user management, log, and alarm capabilities and unified data services to implement data flow among the management, control, and analysis service modules. After the management service module creates a service object, the platform associates itself with the control service module to optimize the object and with the analysis service module to collect and analyze the performance of the object.

The preceding service modules can be deployed individually or together in a combination. For example, you can deploy only the management service module to provide traditional FCAPS capabilities, or you can deploy it together with the control and analysis service modules to provide a complete set of network management and control capabilities. Network controllers hugely benefit End-to-End (E2E) IPv6 network slicing solutions, bringing more innovations and applications.

### 7.1.2 Architecture of an IPv6 Network Slice Controller

As shown in Figure 7.4, the IPv6 network slice controller is between the customer's upper-layer management system and IP transport network; it receives network slice requests from the customer and manages network slices on the IPv6 network. This section details the IPv6 network slice controller.

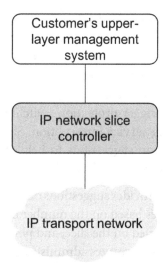

FIGURE 7.4    Overall architecture of IPv6 network slicing.

IPv6 network slices are categorized as service slices or resource slices. Service slices are implemented based on traditional VPN technologies, which are explained in detail in many other books and documents. As such, this section focuses on resource slices to describe the architecture of the IPv6 network slice controller. Unless otherwise specified, "network slices" or "slices" mentioned in the following sections of this chapter all refer to resource slices.

As a sub-feature of network controllers, network slicing provides slice planning, deployment, O&M, and optimization functions and is involved in all networking phases — planning, construction, maintenance, and optimization.

- Slice planning: Creates a deployment template for the constraints and technical parameters of network slice resources according to the planning of network resource allocation and choice of network technologies received from administrators. This template is used as the execution criteria for subsequent actions such as slice deployment and optimization.

- Slice deployment: Determines the devices involved in network slicing based on slice deployment requirements, generates configurations according to the format requirement of the southbound interface model, and delivers configurations to each involved network device, allowing slicing functions to take effect on the network.

- Slice O&M: Monitors and displays the traffic forwarding performance of slices and the bandwidth usage of slices in real time, facilitating the normal running of slice instances. For example, if a slice fails due to a faulty device, port, or link, slice O&M can locate and display the root cause and either recompute resources and allocate a suitable slice or trigger protection switching to an existing slice, thereby minimizing service interruption. Slice O&M can also provide fault-rectification suggestions to help O&M personnel rectify faults and restore services.

- Slice optimization: Provides suggestions on slice scaling or adjustment of occupied resources based on the number of services deployed on a slice, data traffic carried on the slice, and physical network resources. Slice optimization also executes administrator-provided optimization instructions to complete slice optimization.

Like the network controller described earlier, an IPv6 network slice controller also consists of the platform service, management service, control service, analysis service, and business service modules, as shown in Figure 7.5. Table 7.1 describes the services provided by each module.

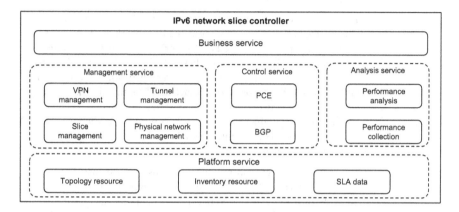

FIGURE 7.5  Modules of an IPv6 network slice controller.

TABLE 7.1  Modules and Service Types of an IPv6 Network Slice Controller

| Module | Service Type |
|---|---|
| Platform service | The platform service module is composed of three sub-modules: topology resource, inventory resource, and SLA data sub-modules. |

- The topology resource sub-module provides different layers of topology services, including those for Layer 1 physical topologies, Layer 2 link topologies, Layer 3 IGP topologies, tunnel topologies, and VPN topologies. It allows users to add, delete, modify, and query topology instances as well as nodes and links in a topology.

- The inventory resource sub-module allows users to add, delete, modify, and query physical-layer objects (e.g., Layer 1 chassis, slots, boards, subcards, and optical modules) and logical objects (e.g., Layer 2 NEs and interfaces). Because these objects are public and necessary for almost all services in the system, they need to be identified in a unified manner. The inventory resource sub-module achieves this by uniformly managing public resource objects in the system and providing the unified-ID mapping service. This sub-module maps a resource object's service ID (e.g., an interface name) to a uniformly managed resource ID (e.g., an interface's Universal Unique Identifier, or UUID for short).

- The SLA data sub-module provides functions to add, delete, modify, and obtain SLA data, such as traffic, delay, and bandwidth of interfaces to be analyzed and processed by the higher-level management, control, analysis, and business service modules.

*(Continued)*

TABLE 7.1 (*Continued*)   Modules and Service Types of an IPv6 Network Slice Controller

| Module | Service Type |
|---|---|
| Management service | The management service module is composed of four sub-modules: physical network management, slice management, VPN management, and tunnel management sub-modules. |

- The physical network management sub-module is responsible for establishing basic connectivity across the IP network. It configures IP addresses based on the Layer 2 (link-layer) network, deploys routing protocols (e.g., IGPs), and enables basic capabilities (e.g., SRv6), thereby providing Layer 3 connectivity atop a Layer 2 network. Such connectivity must be established before services such as VPNs and tunnels can be deployed. Basic network parameters must be configured to add new logical interfaces to the existing network control plane when new Layer 2 and Layer 3 networks are built. This sub-module is indispensable in the overall network slicing solution.

- The slice management sub-module is responsible for managing resource slices (i.e., allocating Layer 2 resources and connecting the Layer 2 networks formed by these resources). For example, it can create FlexE interfaces, channelized sub-interfaces, and Flex-Channels. It can also drive physical network management, deploy control protocols for slices, and construct the control plane of slices. In addition, the slice management sub-module can restore services for, and manage and monitor the states of slices deployed on a live network.

- The VPN management sub-module deploys, manages, and monitors VPN services, such as L2VPN, L3VPN, and Ethernet VPN (EVPN), on slices.

- The tunnel management sub-module deploys, manages, and monitors various types of tunnels, such as SR/SRv6 Policies, Resource Reservation Protocol-Traffic Engineering (RSVP-TE) tunnels, and static tunnels.

| Control service | The control service module is composed of two sub-modules: PCE and BGP sub-modules. |
|---|---|

- The PCE sub-module provides path computation and control services. Specifically, it computes and delegates tunnel paths to support tunnel path establishment and optimization within the resource slice scope; computes and delegates hierarchical slices to support resource partitioning for hierarchical slices within the resource slice scope; and responds to network topology changes and SLA changes (e.g. bandwidth and delay changes), computes better paths for tunnels and hierarchical slices, and drives the release of computation results to network devices.

- The BGP sub-module sets up BGP connections with network devices, obtains the Layer 3 network topology information through BGP-LS, and delivers tunnel paths through BGP-SRv6 Policies.

*(Continued)*

TABLE 7.1 (*Continued*)   Modules and Service Types of an IPv6 Network Slice Controller

| Module | Service Type |
|---|---|
| Analysis service | The analysis service module is composed of two sub-modules: performance collection and performance analysis sub-modules. |

- The performance collection sub-module collects traffic data (including those of physical interfaces, tunnels, sub-interfaces partitioned by resource slices, and hierarchical slices) and performance data (e.g., link delay) in real time and converts the data into a unified format (containing the NEs of data, data objects, data values, and data creation time), providing standardized data to other services such as network traffic optimization and network health analysis and display. This sub-module supports various protocols for collecting data, including telemetry and Simple Network Management Protocol (SNMP).

- Based on the performance data collected on the network controller's managed objects (e.g., service slices, resource slices, hierarchical slices, and slice-specific tunnels), the performance analysis sub-module analyzes the service running states in multiple dimensions, and then displays the state information.

| Module | Service Type |
|---|---|
| Business service | The business service module receives service requests delivered by higher-level systems, orchestrates the management, control, and analysis service modules to execute corresponding functions based on service characteristics, determines the function execution results, and drives subsequent function execution to meet service requirements. For example, the slice planning sub-module of the business service module provides optimization recommendations for physical network construction and resource slice partitioning by learning the traffic analysis information of resource slices from the analysis service module and the service deployment information of slices from the management service module. The slice maintenance sub-module of the business service module locates and diagnoses faults by learning the slice and service deployment information and alarm information from the management service module, and the topology and tunnel path information from the control service module. |

## 7.2 FUNCTIONS OF AN IPV6 NETWORK SLICE CONTROLLER

The basic functions of an IPv6 network slice controller include slice planning, deployment, O&M, and optimization. In addition, the IPv6 network slice controller provides the function of slice restoration. This section describes the key technologies and processes for implementing these functions.

### 7.2.1 Network Slice Planning

Network slice planning, part of the overall network service planning, relies on information provided by the network and service model to function. This section describes the key information that needs to be determined for network slice planning. Such information is also necessary for subsequent slice deployment.

- Slice resource planning information: This includes information about the number of slice instances, SLA requirements (bandwidth and delay) of each slice instance, and more. A physical network's basic information and service information are used — through either computation or manual setting — to determine the resource requirements of a slice on the network. The basic information of the physical network includes the topology, board types, link bandwidth, node delay, link delay, and Shared Risk Link Groups (SRLGs) of nodes and links. Service information includes service types, the access point of each service, traffic, reliability requirements, and the convergence ratio of service bandwidth to physical network bandwidth.

- Slicing technology selection information: To enable slicing, both forwarding- and control-plane slicing technologies are required. The former divides a physical network into smaller-grained virtual forwarding networks — the basis for implementing all forwarding and control functions; the latter implements control plane deployment for the network and leverages control protocols (e.g., IGP and BGP) to calculate slice routes in the control plane in addition to advertising and negotiating slice information. Forwarding- and control-plane technologies need to be selected for slice planning. Table 7.2 lists eight options that combine network slicing technologies. You

TABLE 7.2   Slicing Technology Options

| Technology Selection Option | Control-Plane Technology | | Forwarding-Plane Technology | | |
|---|---|---|---|---|---|
| | SRv6 SID Mode | Slice ID Mode | FlexE | Channelized Sub-Interface | Flex-Channel |
| Option 1 | √ | X | √ | X | X |
| Option 2 | X | √ | √ | X | X |
| Option 3 | √ | X | X | √ | X |
| Option 4 | X | √ | X | √ | X |
| Option 5 | √ | X | √ | X | √ |
| Option 6 | X | √ | √ | X | √ |
| Option 7 | √ | X | X | √ | √ |
| Option 8 | X | √ | X | √ | √ |

*Remarks:* √ indicates selected, and X indicates unselected.

can use the table, from which you can select the best option according to the features supported by network devices' boards and slicing technology evolution status. Options 5 to 8 can be used as hierarchical slicing solutions in large-grained industry slicing scenarios.

### 7.2.2 Network Slice Deployment

Because network slice configurations are diversified, network slice controllers can be used to simplify user operations and minimize configuration errors. These controllers convert users' slice intents into specific slice configurations on network devices, allowing users to focus more on providing services on slices.

Network slice deployment can be driven in several ways:

- By the system administrator, who directly sets parameters through the user interface.

- By a network slice controller's higher-level system, for example, an E2E network slice controller.

- By the business service module of the IPv6 network slice controller. For example, when the user needs to create a VPN private line to bear the intelligent grid control service, the business service of the private line can trigger the creation of a low-delay slice that meets SLA requirements.

Network slices can be deployed based on slice IDs or SRv6 SIDs. After a resource slice is deployed, some typical services can be deployed on it, or hierarchical slicing can be further deployed. Regardless of the mode in which a slice is deployed, the primary aim is to ensure that the slice functions properly on the network. Slice deployment mainly involves the following two parts:

- Network device: The forwarding plane divides physical interface resources into different slices' resources. The control plane then advertises these slice resources using routing protocols to form a forwarding table, and the data plane performs packet encapsulation and intra-slice packet forwarding.

- Controller: It instructs the device to perform the preceding operations by interworking with the device's management plane and provides optimal paths for intra-slice data packet forwarding by interworking with the device's control plane.

The following describes the modes for deploying slices and services:

### 7.2.2.1 Slice Deployment in Slice ID-Based Mode

Figure 7.6 shows slice deployment in slice ID-based mode.

Before slice deployment, the operations in steps a, b, and c need to be performed.

Step a: Manage devices. After devices are connected to the network, the physical network management module completes basic network configuration, including establishing protocol neighbor relationships between devices, setting up management channels between the devices and network controller, and creating the default network slice. These are necessary in order for the devices to meet basic connectivity and service deployment requirements.

Step b: Obtain the basic network topology. The topology resource submodule obtains the Link Layer Discovery Protocol neighbor relationships of the devices through a general protocol (e.g., NETCONF

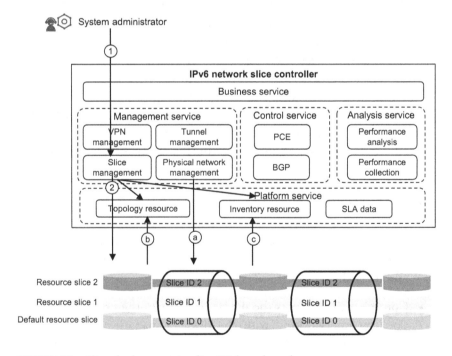

FIGURE 7.6   Slice deployment in slice ID-based mode.

or SNMP) and establishes a Layer 2 topology, providing data on topology connection relationships for subsequent slice calculation.

Step c: Obtain device information. After the devices are managed by the network controller, the inventory resource sub-module reads device configurations to obtain the device names, router IDs, interface names, interface types, and more, providing topology node attribute data for subsequent slice calculation.

After the preceding steps are complete, a slice can be deployed in two steps:

Step 1: Input a slice establishment intent. Using the network controller's interface or an open northbound interface, the system administrator enters the intent of establishing a slice, as well as the site scope and SLA requirements of the slice. The slice management sub-module saves the entered information and starts slice deployment.

Step 2: Partition slices in the forwarding plane of the devices. The slice management sub-module determines the devices and interfaces through which a slice passes based on information about the Layer 2 topology, physical inventory resources, etc. This sub-module also deploys the required FlexE interfaces or channelized sub-interfaces on all slice-related nodes to form a Layer 2 slicing network. The configuration includes creating FlexE interfaces or channelized sub-interfaces, mapping sub-interfaces with main interfaces, configuring interface bandwidth, and configuring slice IDs for interfaces.

### 7.2.2.2 Slice Deployment in SRv6 SID-Based Mode

Figure 7.7 shows the slice deployment process in SRv6 SID-based mode. This mode is similar to slice ID-based deployment. In SRv6 SID-based deployment, the physical network management sub-module deploys control plane-related basic configurations on Layer 2 interfaces, ensuring that slice interfaces are controlled by network control-plane protocols. The configuration includes configuring IP addresses, IGP capabilities, and SRv6 capabilities on interfaces. If a control-plane technology with an affinity attribute is used, the corresponding link administrative group needs to be configured.

Compared with the slice ID-based deployment mode, the SRv6 SID-based mode requires an additional step — step 3, shown in Figure 7.7. The slice

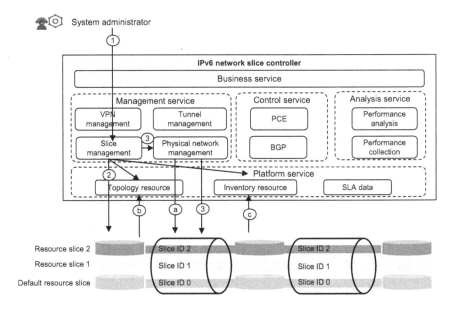

FIGURE 7.7    Slice deployment in SRv6 SID-based mode.

management sub-module adds the sub-interfaces created by the network slices to the deployment scope of the physical network management sub-module. The physical network management sub-module then deploys the configurations for IP addresses, IGP neighbor relationships, and more on the slice sub-interfaces at both ends of a link according to the process of adding a Layer 2 link. This sub-module also adds the new link to the IGP Link State Database.

### 7.2.2.3 Typical Service Deployment on Resource Slices

Various services can be deployed after resource slices are deployed. Typical services include VPN and tunnel services, which are representatives of user-side and network-side services, respectively. A route or tunnel policy can be deployed to steer VPN service traffic to a tunnel, associating the user-side and network-side services. Figure 7.8 shows the deployment process.

Before service deployment, the IPv6 network slice controller needs to obtain the network topology information that contains the traffic engineering information through the control service module. The BGP sub-module of the control service module needs to obtain the device-advertised link state information and TE attribute information over BGP-LS connections,

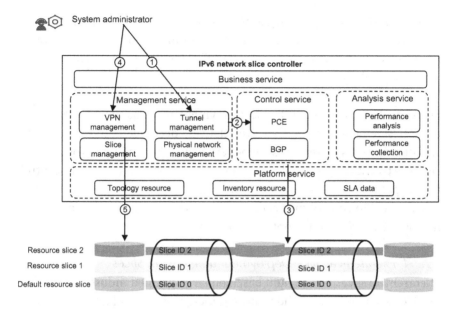

FIGURE 7.8 Typical service deployment.

and the PCE sub-module parses the information into the network topology information and slice information so it can maintain the Traffic Engineering Database and prepare data for subsequent service path computation. The service deployment process is as follows:

1. Network-side tunnel deployment: Deploy a tunnel in a slice and specify the tunnel's source and destination nodes, SLA constraints, etc.

2. Tunnel path computation: The tunnel management sub-module drives the PCE sub-module to compute the forwarding path of a tunnel in a slice based on the tunnel's source and destination nodes, SLA constraints, etc.

3. Tunnel path delivery: The PCE sub-module delivers a computed tunnel path to the tunnel ingress over SRv6 Policy connections to create an SRv6 Policy on the ingress.

4. User-side service deployment (e.g., VPN service): Determine the target resource slice for the VPN service, and determine the forwarding policy (BE path forwarding or tunnel forwarding) in the slice.

5. User-side service configuration delivery: The VPN management sub-module delivers VPN service configurations to corresponding service access devices over NETCONF, Secure Shell, or other protocols.

Steps 1 to 3 focus on network-side deployment, whereas steps 4 and 5 focus on user-side deployment. They are relatively decoupled, allowing you to choose network-side service schemes as needed. For example, you can use either network slice controllers or Flex-Algo-capable forwarders to control tunnel paths. The above steps are all needed when network slice controllers are used to control tunnel paths. However, steps 1 to 3 are not needed if forwarders are used to control tunnel paths.

*7.2.2.4 Hierarchical Slice Deployment on Network Slices*
Hierarchical slices can be built based on large-grained industry slices, but use Flex-Channels to provide finer-grained resource isolation for typical services. In most cases, the creation of a hierarchical slice is driven by a service instance deployed on an industry slice when fine-grained SLA assurance is needed. Figure 7.9 shows the deployment process of hierarchical slices for the VPN service.

- Hierarchical slice deployment: Select a network slice and create VPNs for fine-grained resource isolation on the network slice. The VPN service then drives the establishment of network-side tunnels among involved sites and configures a tunnel policy for the VPN to implement VPN traffic forwarding over hierarchical slices.

- Path computation for hierarchical slices: The tunnel management sub-module drives the PCE sub-module to compute the forwarding path of a tunnel based on the tunnel's source and destination nodes, SLA constraints, etc.

- Slice forwarding path delivery: The PCE sub-module delivers a computed tunnel path to the tunnel ingress over SRv6 Policy connections to create an SRv6 Policy on the ingress.

- Delivery of configurations related to slice path resource isolation: The tunnel management sub-module creates Flex-Channels on the interfaces that a tunnel path passes and delivers the corresponding

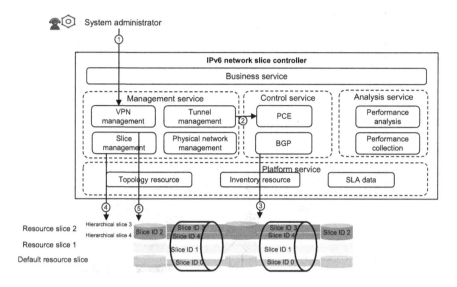

FIGURE 7.9   Deployment process of hierarchical slices.

configurations to devices over NETCONF channels. During data forwarding, slice IDs are used to control forwarding resource isolation, and the forwarding paths delivered in step 3 are used for forwarding packets, implementing resource isolation among hierarchical slices.

- User-side service configuration delivery: The VPN management submodule delivers VPN service configurations to corresponding service access devices over NETCONF, Secure Shell, or other protocols.

### 7.2.3  Network Slice O&M

O&M involves a wide range of activities, including state visualization, troubleshooting, cutover, and upgrade. This section focuses on how to build the visualization capability of network slicing.

After slices are deployed, a network controller can collect data such as logs, alarms, and network traffic statistics to display the running states of slice objects and services in multiple dimensions, helping O&M personnel better manage and maintain the slices.

Figure 7.10 shows a visualized network slice topology — composed of the default slice, network slice 1, and network slice 2 — which is clearly displayed on a network controller.

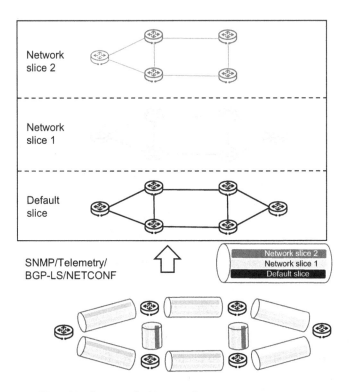

FIGURE 7.10   Visualized network slice topology.

The network controller also clearly displays the visualized tunnel paths of the three slices, as shown in Figure 7.11.

Furthermore, the network controller clearly displays the visualized Quality of Services (QoS) — including VPN performance and service performance — in the three slices, as shown in Figure 7.12.

In addition to multi-dimensional state visualization, network slice O&M provides numerous other functions, such as fault diagnosis, rectification and closure, analysis of running state exceptions, and fault prediction. While these functions have similar dependencies and interaction modes, they are continuously enhanced or expanded to meet user and network requirements. Generally, the implementation of common O&M functions involves the following operations:

- Data collection: The performance collection sub-module collects raw performance, alarm, and running state data of devices through various data collection methods, such as telemetry and SNMP.

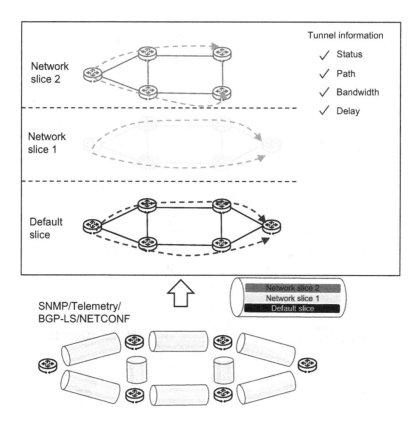

FIGURE 7.11   Visualized tunnel paths in slices.

- Data analysis and decision-making: As different O&M functions require different types of data for analysis, an O&M function module selects and analyzes corresponding data. For example, the running state exception analysis module reads the traffic data of interfaces and tunnels in different time segments, analyzes the data, and displays abnormal traffic and alarms.

- Maintenance action execution: After data analysis and decision-making are completed, the slice management sub-module delivers configurations to devices and performs connectivity tests and failovers to complete maintenance actions.

## 7.2.4  Network Slice Optimization

When network slices are added or deleted, some existing network slices may not be allocated the most appropriate resources because of the deployment

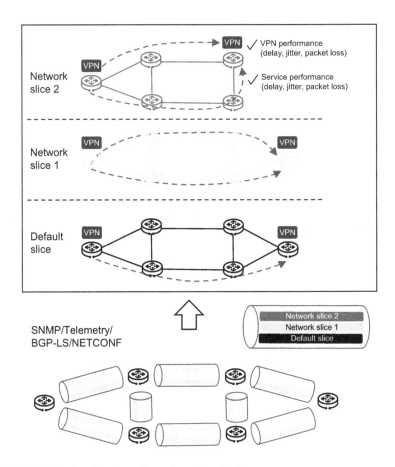

FIGURE 7.12   Visualized quality of services in slices.

time sequence of network slices. To address this issue, as well as to meet the scale-in and scale-out requirements of existing slices, the network slice controller adjusts the usage of existing network slice resources based on global calculation results. This enables the network to carry more slice services and minimizes the impact of new network slice sites on existing ones.

Figure 7.13 shows a typical path change scenario: the path carried on the existing slice link d2 is changed when a new slice link d1 is added. The network slice controller implements the change by using a network slicing algorithm to calculate better slice paths based on existing network slice links, optimizing resource utilization.

During network slice deployment, the resources required by a network slice need to be determined through calculation. Similarly, during

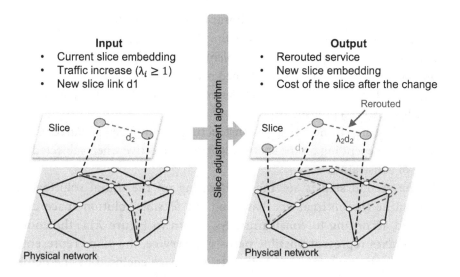

**Input**
- Current slice embedding
- Traffic increase ($\lambda_i \geq 1$)
- New slice link d1

**Output**
- Rerouted service
- New slice embedding
- Cost of the slice after the change

FIGURE 7.13    Slice optimization when a new slice link is added.

network slice optimization, slice resource adjustment also needs to be determined through calculation. The algorithm is key in both cases — a better algorithm helps a network utilize network resources and meet user requirements more effectively.

A network slicing algorithm is expected to achieve the following objectives: To find a better resource allocation manner for existing network slice services and to find a new resource allocation manner for new services when given a communications network, a group of deployed network slice requests, a group of new network slice requests, deployment results, and requirements contained in the network slice requests. The constraints are as follows: A deployed network slice resource reservation solution involves minimal change; new slice sub-interfaces are divided into as few as possible, and the minimal amount of network resources is consumed. Network slicing requirements include source nodes, destination nodes, and QoS requirements (protection mode, E2E delay, bandwidth, convergence ratio, and resource partitioning capability of interfaces). Protection modes include no protection, 1:1 protection, and 1+1 protection. The convergence ratio defines the proportion of the actual physical bandwidth that can be occupied by slice services.

The problem involved in network slicing algorithms is a typical Multi-Commodity Flow (MCF) problem. A general solution to the multi-commodity flow problem is linear programming. In linear programming, the column generation algorithm is often used to efficiently solve large-scale linear optimization problems — this algorithm can also be used to solve the previously mentioned network slice calculation problems. Figure 7.14 shows the basic principles of a column generation algorithm, which can solve a problem in two steps.

The first step is modeling — constructing a minimized resource usage function, depending on the slicing algorithm objective when subjected to a set of constraints.

The second step is solving — iterating on the initial solution to determine the optimal one based on the feasible solution space calculated according to constraints. As shown in Figure 7.14, the coordinate axes represent possible paths of a service, the plane represents a combination of service constraints, the space enclosed by the plane represents a feasible solution space, and X(n) represents a service path combination after n iterations (that is, several relatively optimized feasible slice solutions).

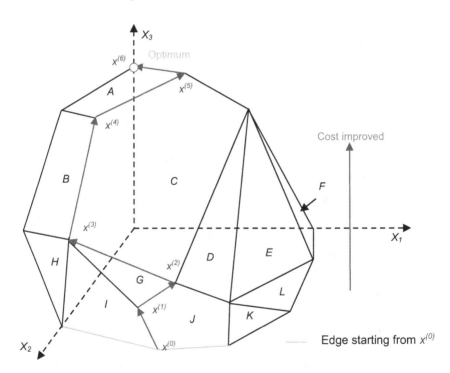

FIGURE 7.14   Basic principles of a column generation algorithm.

The network slicing algorithm involves complex mathematical problems. For details about the algorithm, refer to professional books such as *Column Generation*.[1]

### 7.2.5 Network Slice Restoration

In scenarios where slices are deployed before a network controller is employed, the network controller can restore the slices in order to manage deployed slice services.

The network controller can restore discrete slice configurations on network devices to slice services based on the collected network device configurations (configurations involved in the slice deployment phase), network topology, SRv6 Policies, and slice planning policies. This makes it possible to perform modification, O&M, and optimization of network slice services.

## 7.3 EXTERNAL INTERFACES OF AN IPV6 NETWORK SLICE CONTROLLER

To define the external interfaces of IPv6 network slice controllers, the IETF defined hierarchical network slice management and control functions.[2] As shown in Figure 7.15, an IP network slice controller consists of two layers — a Network Slice Controller (NSC) and Network Controllers (NCs). The NSC undertakes technology-independent network slicing service requirements and implements multi-domain and multi-vendor slicing function decomposition. The NCs convert a domain's slicing service requirements into configurations and deploy the configurations on the network.

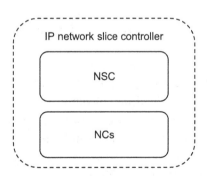

FIGURE 7.15    IETF's definition of IP network slice controller functions.

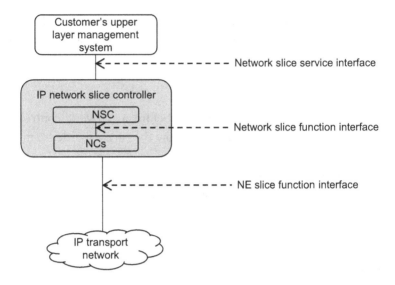

FIGURE 7.16   External interfaces of the IP network slice controller.

As shown in Figure 7.16, three types of interfaces are related to the IP network slice controller.

- Network slice service interface: takes slices as management objects and provides management and maintenance services for them. Such an interface is unaware of the slicing techniques used.

- Network slice function interface: distinguishes between a service slice and a resource slice and implements corresponding management and maintenance functions. Such an interface needs to be aware of the slicing techniques used.

- NE slice function interface: deploys and maintains network slices. Such an interface is also a configuration interface provided by a network device.

The IETF is currently discussing and formulating standards related to network slice interfaces. As such, different vendors implement such interfaces in different ways. This section follows best practices to describe the interfaces to help you understand technical fundamentals.

7.3.1 Network Slice Service Interfaces

*draft-ietf-teas-ietf-network-slice-nbi-yang* defines network slice service interfaces as follows[3]:

```
module: ietf-network-slice
+--rw network-slices
+--rw ns-slo-sle-templates
| +--rw ns-slo-sle-template* [id]
| +--rw id string
| +--rw template-description? string
+--rw network-slice* [ns-id]
+--rw ns-id string
+--rw ns-description? string
+--rw customer-name* string
+--rw ns-connectivity-type? identityref
+--rw (ns-slo-sle-policy)?
| +--:(standard)
| | +--rw slo-sle-template? leafref
| +--:(custom)
| +--rw slo-sle-policy
| +--rw policy-description? string
| +--rw ns-metric-bounds
| | +--rw ns-metric-bound* [metric-type]
| | +--rw metric-type identityref
| | +--rw metric-unit string
| | +--rw value-description? string
| | +--rw bound? uint64
| +--rw security* identityref
| +--rw isolation? identityref
| +--rw max-occupancy-level? uint8
| +--rw mtu uint16
| +--rw steering-constraints
| +--rw path-constraints
| +--rw service-function
+--rw status
| +--rw admin-enabled? boolean
| +--ro oper-status? operational-type
+--rw ns-endpoints
| +--rw ns-endpoint* [ep-id]
| +--rw ep-id string
| +--rw ep-description? string
| +--rw ep-role? identityref
| +--rw location
| | +--rw altitude? int64
| | +--rw latitude? decimal64
| | +--rw longitude? decimal64
| +--rw node-id? string
```

```
| +--rw ep-ip? inet:host
| +--rw ns-match-criteria
| | +--rw ns-match-criterion* [match-type]
| | +--rw match-type identityref
| | +--rw values* [index]
| | +--rw index uint8
| | +--rw value? string
| +--rw ep-peering
| | +--rw protocol* [protocol-type]
| | +--rw protocol-type identityref
| | +--rw attribute* [index]
| | +--rw index uint8
| | +--rw attribute-description? string
| | +--rw value? string
| +--rw ep-network-access-points
| | +--rw ep-network-access-point* [network-access-id]
| | +--rw network-access-id string
| | +--rw network-access-description? string
| | +--rw network-access-node-id? string
| | +--rw network-access-tp-id? string
| | +--rw network-access-tp-ip? inet:host
| | +--rw mtu uint16
| | +--rw ep-rate-limit
| | +--rw incoming-rate-limit?
| | | te-types:te-bandwidth
| | +--rw outgoing-rate-limit?
| | te-types:te-bandwidth
| +--rw ep-rate-limit
| | +--rw incoming-rate-limit? te-types:te-bandwidth
| | +--rw outgoing-rate-limit? te-types:te-bandwidth
| +--rw status
| | +--rw admin-enabled? boolean
| | +--ro oper-status? operational-type
| +--ro ep-monitoring
| +--ro incoming-utilized-bandwidth?
| | te-types:te-bandwidth
| +--ro incoming-bw-utilization decimal64
| +--ro outgoing-utilized-bandwidth?
| | te-types:te-bandwidth
| +--ro outgoing-bw-utilization decimal64
```

```
+--rw ns-connections
+--rw ns-connection* [ns-connection-id]
+--rw ns-connection-id uint32
+--rw ns-connection-description? string
+--rw src
|  +--rw src-ep-id? leafref
+--rw dest
|  +--rw dest-ep-id? leafref
+--rw (ns-slo-sle-policy)?
|  +--:(standard)
|  |  +--rw slo-sle-template? leafref
|  +--:(custom)
|  +--rw slo-sle-policy
|  +--rw policy-description? string
|  +--rw ns-metric-bounds
|  |  +--rw ns-metric-bound* [metric-type]
|  |  +--rw metric-type identityref
|  |  +--rw metric-unit string
|  |  +--rw value-description? string
|  |  +--rw bound? uint64
|  +--rw security* identityref
|  +--rw isolation? identityref
|  +--rw max-occupancy-level? uint8
|  +--rw mtu uint16
|  +--rw steering-constraints
|  +--rw path-constraints
|  +--rw service-function
+--rw monitoring-type? ns-monitoring-type
+--ro ns-connection-monitoring
+--ro latency? yang:gauge64
+--ro jitter? yang:gauge32
+--ro loss-ratio? decimal64
```

The ietf-network-slice model contains two main nodes: ns-slo-sle-templates (container object) and ietf-network-slice (sequence object).

The container object ns-slo-sle-templates defines and maintains common attributes of all network slice objects, including two types of attribute definitions: SLO and SLE2. These attributes can be applied to specific network slice instances, allowing these instances to inherit attributes from ns-slo-sle-templates.

The sequence object ietf-network-slice defines a group of slice instances. Each ietf-network-slice data structure is the model expression of the slice object. The main sub-objects of ietf-network-slice are as follows:

- ns-id: uniquely identifies a slice service.

- ns-connectivity-type: defines the network connectivity type for nodes in a network slice topology. The type can be any-to-any, hub-and-spoke, or custom.

- ns-slo-sle-policy: defines SLO and SLE policies for a network slice instance. Such policies include ns-slo-bandwidth (guaranteed minimum bidirectional bandwidth), network-slice-slo-latency (maximum permissible one-way/round-trip latency), ns-slo-delay-variation (maximum permissible unidirectional/bidirectional traffic jitter), ns-slo-packet-loss (maximum permissible packet loss rate), and ns-slo-availability (maximum permissible link availability).

- status: defines the operating and administrative status of a network slice instance. It is used for slice management and maintenance.

- ns-endpoints: defines the ingresses and egresses in a network slice instance and the attributes of these nodes, including the rate limits on incoming and outgoing traffic, control-plane routing protocols used by the access node, and service access interfaces of the access node.

- ns-connections: defines the connections between the ingress and egress of network slice traffic and the attributes of the connections, including the source and destination nodes of the connections, SLO and SLE traffic policies of each connection, and SLA monitoring modes for the connections.

For details about the model, refer to the IETF draft for the network slice service interface model.[3]

### 7.3.2 Network Slice Function Interfaces

Currently, the IETF draft *draft-wd-teas-nrp-yang* defines network slice function interfaces as follows[4]:

```
module: ietf-nrp
augment /nw:networks/nw:network/nw:network-types:
+--rw nrp!
augment /nw:networks/nw:network:
+--rw nrp
+--rw nrp-id? uint32
+--rw nrp-name? string
+--rw bandwidth-reservation
| +--rw (bandwidth-type)?
| +--:(bandwidth-value)
| | +--rw bandwidth-value? uint64
| +--:(bandwidth-percentage)
| +--rw bandwidth-percent? rt-types:percentage
+--rw control-plane
| +--rw topology-ref
| +--rw igp-topology-ref
| | +--rw network-ref?
| | | -> /nw:networks/network/network-id
| | +--rw multi-topology-id? uint32
| | +--rw flex-algo-id? uint32
| +--rw te-topology-identifier
| +--rw provider-id? te-global-id
| +--rw client-id? te-global-id
| +--rw topology-id? te-topology-id
+--rw data-plane
| +--rw global-resource-identifier
| | +--rw nrp-dataplane-ipv6-type
| | | +--rw nrp-dp-value? inet:ipv6-address
| | +--rw nrp-dataplane-mpls-type
| | +--rw nrp-dp-value? uint32
| +--rw nrp-aware-dp
| +--rw nrp-aware-srv6-type!
| +--rw nrp-aware-sr-mpls-type!
+--rw steering-policy
+--rw color-id* uint32
+--rw acl-ref* -> /acl:acls/acl/name
augment /nw:networks/nw:network/nw:node:
+--rw nrp
+--rw nrp-aware-srv6
| +--rw nrp-dp-value? srv6-types:srv6-sid
+--rw nrp-aware-sr-mpls
+--rw nrp-dp-value? rt-types:mpls-label
```

```
augment /nw:networks/nw:network/nt:link:
+--rw nrp
| +--rw link-partition-type? identityref
| +--rw bandwidth-reservation
|     | | +--rw (bandwidth-type)?
| | +--:(bandwidth-value)
| | | +--rw bandwidth-value? uint64
| | +--:(bandwidth-percentage)
| | +--rw bandwidth-percent? rt-types:percentage
| +--rw nrp-aware-srv6
| | +--rw nrp-dp-value? srv6-types:srv6-sid
| +--rw nrp-aware-sr-mpls
| +--rw nrp-dp-value? rt-types:mpls-label
+--ro statistics
+--ro admin-status? te-types:te-admin-status
+--ro oper-status? te-types:te-oper-status
+--ro one-way-available-bandwidth?
| rt-types:bandwidth-ieee-float32
+--ro one-way-utilized-bandwidth?
| rt-types:bandwidth-ieee-float32
+--ro one-way-min-delay? uint32
+--ro one-way-max-delay? uint32
+--ro one-way-delay-variation? uint32
+--ro one-way-packet-loss? decimal64
```

This interface model defines each network slice as a Virtual Transport Network (VTN) instance and uses the topology model defined in RFC 8345[5] to express the virtual network object. A new network type, VTN, is defined in the VTN slice model. When the network type field (/nw:networks/nw:network/nw:network-types) of an RFC 8345-compliant network instance is set to VTN, this network object indicates a VTN slice instance.

VTN data node objects defined on the model's root node are used to define global parameters of a network slice, including the bandwidth reservation policy of the slice instance, protocol and technology options used by the slice control plane, protocol and technology options used by the slice data plane, and policy for steering service traffic to the slice. The VTN data nodes are described as follows:

- vtn-id: uniquely identifies a VTN instance on a network.

- vtn allocation resources: identifies resources allocated to a VTN instance. bandwidth-reservation specifies the bandwidth allocated to the VTN instance, and interface-partition-capability specifies the resource partitioning capability of the physical interface associated with the VTN instance.

- vtn control plane: indicates the VTN control plane and defines the control mode of a network slice instance — slice ID-based control mode or SRv6 SID-based control mode. The selected mode determines the control plane-related configurations to be delivered to devices during slice deployment.

- vtn data plane: indicates the VTN data plane and defines the encapsulation type — IPv6, MPLS, SR-MPLS, or SRv6 — for data packets in the slice data plane.

- vtn steering policy: specifies the traffic steering policy. It can specify a VTN color ID-based traffic steering policy so that VPN traffic with the same color ID is steered to the slice with the corresponding color attribute.

Each VTN instance is composed of a group of nodes and a group of connections. Different nodes and links have different attributes that define the slice management and control parameters of the node and interface, for example, the bandwidth reservation mode of the interface.

While inheriting the node object definition in RFC 8345, the model extends the following link objects:

- interface-partition-capability: defines the resource partitioning technology, which can be FlexE interfaces or channelized sub-interfaces, for the forwarding plane of interfaces. The forwarding-plane technology of interfaces determines the forwarding-plane resource partitioning configurations of devices.

- bandwidth-reservation: defines the bandwidth that needs to be reserved on a physical link of a slice instance.

- statistics: defines the query interface for the traffic of slice links, providing data for various maintenance functions.

For details about the model, see the IETF draft *draft-wd-teas-nrp-yang.*[4]

The above network function interfaces are used by network resource slices. Network service slices are generally implemented using VPNs.

Correspondingly, an IPv6 network slice controller may directly use VPN-related network function interfaces to support network service slices. These network function interfaces include L3NM function interfaces defined in RFC 9182 and L2NM function interfaces defined in *draft-ietf-opsawg-l2nm*. They were previously used to support common L3VPN/L2VPN, and later they became applicable to network slice services after simple extensions. For details, see related documents.

### 7.3.3 NE Slice Function Interfaces

A southbound interface of a network controller is also a northbound interface provided by a network device. While northbound interfaces vary with vendors, they are all designed based on configuration objects.

Slice deployment requires the following types of technical models:

- In the slice deployment phase, a specific resource slicing technology is required to partition a physical network into multiple slice networks. As such, a corresponding physical network partitioning technical model is required.

- After a physical network is partitioned, a technical model for deploying slice instances on the sliced network is required.

- Traditional models such as interface management and IGP models are required to deploy IP addresses and IGPs on the sliced network.

- The traditional VPN model needs to be modified in order to add policies for steering traffic to slices.

Network devices provide slice-related functions and services by providing the preceding objects and corresponding models. After being orchestrated and combined by the network controller, the functions and services are delivered to network devices for them to take effect.

## 7.4 STORIES BEHIND NETWORK SLICING
### 7.4.1 Network Slicing Increases the Value of Controllers

SDN was initially designed to separate the control and forwarding planes and implement flexible forwarding by controlling the programming of flow tables. This gave rise to the concept of network controllers.

SDN controllers were first widely applied to data center networks. Because Virtual Extensible LAN (VXLAN)-based forwarding is relatively simple, SDN controllers can quickly establish forwarding paths by delivering forwarding entries to service endpoints only. SDN controllers greatly simplify service deployment on data center networks and demonstrate the value of centralized control.

However, a number of factors have hindered the use of SDN controllers on carriers' Wide Area Networks (WANs). First, there are not enough requirements for global traffic optimization through centralized control. Second, the services, topologies, and technologies on carriers' IP networks are much more complex than those on data center networks, making many difficulties in the controller's design, implementation, and deployment. And third, because a carrier's IP network often involves device interworking across multiple vendors, a controller needs to interconnect with third-party devices — a requirement that is always troublesome.

The application of SDN controllers on WANs started with the emergence of technologies such as SR[6] and stateful PCE.[7] The Google B4 network's practice of global optimization[8] attracted major attention worldwide at the beginning. However, it took around 10 years for large-scale commercial use of SDN controllers on WANs to occur. There are several main technologies that drive the commercial use of SDN controllers. First is SR, which is used to simplify path optimization. SR is easy to deploy and extend, as it requires programming only on an ingress when implementing path optimization, resolving the issues facing RSVP-TE. Unlike SR-MPLS, SRv6 supports native IP, enabling it to further simplify the deployment of network services. However, the implementation of SR and SRv6 depends on the support of powerful programmable chips, requiring the industry to keep up. Second are BGP and PCEP, which are used as the standardized southbound protocols of controllers. Using BGP/PCEP for this purpose is another milestone for the deployment of controllers on WANs, as they provide better performance and interoperability than using traditional command lines or NETCONF/YANG. However, the process from technological innovation and standardization of BGP/PCEP to final multi-vendor interoperability also took a long time.

Although the preceding technologies have resolved many of the problems hindering the use of controllers on WANs, the lack of path optimization requirements through centralized control is still a major obstacle to their deployment. For example, centralized path optimization via a controller is not in high demand on carrier networks because this task can be easily completed by upgrading hardware to expand bandwidth. Besides, automatic path optimization brings risks, and carriers are therefore reluctant to deploy controllers. The more a new technology is applied and optimized, the more complete it becomes. Conversely, the less a technology is applied, the slower it develops. Although controller-based automatic path optimization has certain advantages, it is not satisfactory due to requirements and technical challenges.

Fortunately, the development of network slicing brings new opportunities for controllers. Managing a single physical network is a complex task. Managing hundreds or even thousands of network slices — each similar to a single network — becomes impractical when done manually. That is, the control and management of network slices become impossible if automation methods are not introduced. Consequently, network slicing brings strong demand for network controllers.

Although it has been difficult to apply controllers to IP networks, the concepts of SDN and controllers have been deeply ingrained in people's minds. This is why controllers have been introduced to carriers' IP networks, to varying degrees, over the past decade. These controller deployments lay the foundation for implementing automatic network slicing, and network slicing further improves the value of controllers and creates new opportunities for their large-scale deployment.

### 7.4.2 New Opportunities Brought by Network Slicing to PCECC/BGPCC

During the emergence and development of SDN technologies, we proposed a new central-control technology — the Path Computation Element for Central Control (PCECC).[9] Later, we developed another such technology — the Border Gateway Protocol for Central Control (BGPCC).[10] The basic idea of these technologies is to use a controller for allocating and advertising labels (common MPLS labels) or SIDs (SR-MPLS or SRv6 SIDs) to network devices. In a classic SR solution, node and link segments are configured on a local device and flooded to other network devices through IGP. The segment information can then be reported to a controller through BGP-LS. The PCECC/BGPCC solution is completely different, which uses a controller to allocate and advertise SR SIDs in a centralized manner. The centralized method reduces the need for flooding SR SIDs through IGP. Either PCE or BGP is used by the controller as the southbound protocol to advertise SR SIDs to network devices. This is the reason why the solution is called PCECC or BGPCC.

Some IETF experts have concerns about the requirements of PCECC/ BGPCC. They think that node and link segments used in SR should be statically configured using command lines or NETCONF/YANG rather than being dynamically generated by PCEP/BGP-like control protocols, as these segments seldom change after being allocated. They are of the opinion that binding SIDs should be dynamically generated by PCEP/ BGP based on network path changes. PCECC/BGPCC is becoming a generalized method used by a controller to allocate identifier resources and advertise the resources to network devices through PCE/BGP. Here, identifier resources include not only MPLS labels and SR SIDs but also slice IDs of network slices.

Compared with the traditional approach of using the command line or NETCONF/YANG method for configuration delivery, identifier allocation using PCECC/BGPCC provides better performance. With the large-scale deployment of network slices, massive amounts of information about binding relationships between slice IDs/SR SIDs and resources need to be deployed across the network. Using the traditional approach for configuration delivery is hard to meet performance requirements — high-performance control protocols such as PCEP and BGP therefore need to be used. This not only requires controllers to automatically deploy network slices but also requires control protocols with better performance to allocate network slices, bringing a new development opportunity for PCECC/BGPCC.

## REFERENCES

[1] Desaulniers G, Desrosiers J, Solomon MM. Column Generation. 1. Springer, Vol. 5. 2005.

[2] Farrel A, Gray E, Drake J, et al. A Framework for IETF Network Slices [EB/ OL]. (2022-12-21)[2022-12-30]. draft-ietf-teas-ietf-network-slices-17.

[3] Wu B, Dhody D, Rokui R, et al. IETF Network Slice Service YANG Model [EB/OL]. (2022-11-07)[2022-11-30]. draft-ietf-teas-ietf-network-slice-nbi-yang-03.

[4] Wu B, Dhody D, Cheng Y. A YANG Data Model for Network Resource Partition (NRP) [EB/OL]. (2022-09-25)[2022-09-30]. draft-wd-teas-nrp-yang-02.

[5] Clemm A, Medved J, Varga R, et al. A YANG Data Model for Network Topologies [EB/OL]. (2018-03)[2022-09-30]. RFC 8345.

[6] Filsfils C, Previdi S, et al. Segment Routing Architecture [EB/OL]. (2018-07) [2022-09-30]. RFC 8402.

[7] Crabbe E, Minei I, Medved J, et al. Path Computation Element Communication Protocol (PCEP) Extensions for Stateful PCE [EB/OL]. (2017-09) [2022-09-30]. RFC 8231.

[8] Jain S, Kumar A, Mandal S, et al. B4: Experience with a globally-deployed software defined WAN. *ACM SIGCOMM Computer Communication Review*, 2013, 43(4): 3–14.

[9] Farrel A, Zhao Q, Li Z, et al. An architecture for use of PCE and the PCE communication protocol (PCEP) In a Network with Central Control [EB/OL]. (2017-12)[2022-09-30]. RFC 8283.

[10] Luo Y, Qu L, Huang X, et al. Architecture for Use of BGP as Central Controller [EB/OL]. (2022-08-15)[2022-09-30]. draft-cth-rtgwg-bgp-control-09.

# CHAPTER 8

# Inter-Domain IPv6 Network Slicing Technologies

A N IPv6 NETWORK SLICE can be used as a 5G Transport Network (TN) slice and combined with a Radio Access Network (RAN) slice and a Core Network (CN) slice to form a 5G end-to-end (E2E) network slice. And as network slice services are being deployed on a larger scale, an IPv6 network slice itself may span multiple IP network domains. As such, IPv6 networks need to support inter-domain slices. This chapter starts by describing the framework, procedure, and implementation of mapping 5G E2E network slices to IPv6 network slices. It then introduces the technologies involved in inter-domain IPv6 network slicing and SRv6-based inter-domain IPv6 network slicing. Finally, it explains the intent-based routing mechanism, which can be used to steer traffic to IPv6 network slices in different network domains.

## 8.1 5G E2E NETWORK SLICING

### 8.1.1 Framework and Procedure for 5G E2E Network Slice Mapping

A 5G E2E network slice is composed of RAN slices, CN slices, and TN slices. A TN slice provides the connection between a RAN slice and a CN slice and, together with them, provides guarantees for differentiated services, security isolation, and more. The Internet Engineering Task Force

DOI: 10.1201/9781032699868-10

257

(IETF) refers to the TN slice as the IETF network slice because it employs IETF-defined technologies. This book refers to it as the IPv6 network slice when it is used on IPv6 networks.

The IETF draft "IETF Network Slice Application in 5G End-to-End Network Slice[1]" describes the framework and procedure for mapping 5G E2E network slices to IPv6 network slices. This section focuses on how this mapping is implemented in the management plane, control plane, and data plane.

In 3GPP,[2] the term "Network Slice Instance (NSI)" describes a set of network function instances and the required resources (e.g., compute, storage, and networking resources) that form a deployed network slice. "Network Slice Subnet Instance (NSSI)" describes an instance of a network slice subnet representing the management aspects of a set of managed function instances and the used resources (e.g., compute, storage, and networking resources). "Single Network Slice Selection Assistance Information (S-NSSAI)" uniquely identifies a 5G E2E network slice.

Figure 8.1 shows the mapping from 5G E2E network slices to slices of technology-specific domains (i.e., RAN, CN, and TN slices). In this figure, three 5G E2E network slices (identified by S-NSSAIs 01111111, 02222222,

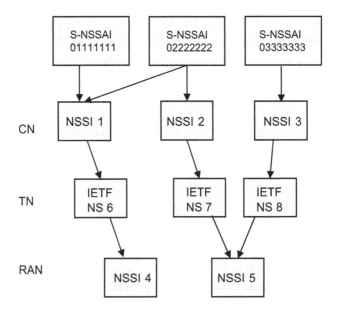

FIGURE 8.1   Mapping from 5G E2E network slices to slices of technology-specific domains.

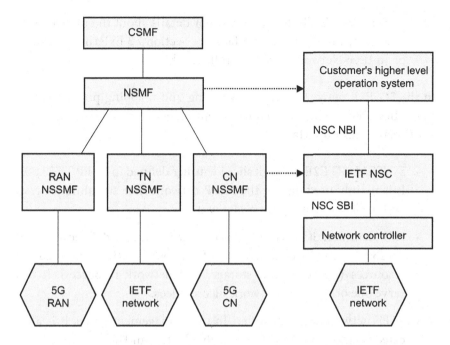

FIGURE 8.2    Mapping between the management frameworks of the 5G E2E network slice and IETF network slice.

and 03333333) are mapped to the RAN, CN, and TN NSSIs. Note that the TN NSSI in a 3GPP 5G E2E slice is equivalent to the IETF network slice.

Figure 8.2 illustrates the mapping between the terms used in the management frameworks of the 5G E2E network slice and the IETF network slice. Details are as follows:

- The Network Slice Management Function (NSMF) in the 5G E2E network slice corresponds to the customer's higher-level operation system in the IETF-defined network slice.

- The TN NSSMF in the 5G E2E network slice corresponds to the IETF-defined Network Slice Controller (NSC). The NSC can be used to deploy and manage IETF network slices through a network controller. Because both the NSC and network controller are logical network elements, their functions can be implemented by a unified IPv6 NSC.

- The management interface between the NSMF and the TN NSSMF in the 5G E2E network slice corresponds to the Northbound Interface

(NBI) of the IETF-defined NSC. For details about the implementation of the management interface, see Section 7.3 External Interfaces of an IPv6 Network Slice Controller in this book.

In the 5G E2E network slice interworking and mapping processes, network slice identifiers in the management plane, control plane, and data (user) plane play important roles.

- S-NSSAI: 5G E2E network slice identifier defined in 3GPP TS 23.501. It is mainly used during the 3GPP network slice signaling process, and the TN is usually not aware of it.

- NSI identifier: 5G network slice instance identifier defined in 3GPP TS 23.501. An NSI contains a set of network functions and required resources (e.g., compute, storage, and network resources). It can serve one or more 5G network slice services.

- IETF network slice identifier: In the management plane, it is allocated by the IETF NSC to uniquely identify an IETF network slice. In the data plane, it can reuse an existing identifier (e.g., an SR SID) or be a newly defined one (e.g., a slice ID).

- IETF network slice Interworking Identifier (IID): an identifier encapsulated by a RAN or CN network element into a data packet to be sent to the TN. A slice IID is used to map the traffic of the 5G E2E network slice to a specific IETF network slice. It can reuse an existing data plane identifier (e.g., a VLAN ID) or be a newly defined one.

Figure 8.3 shows the mapping between 5G E2E network slice identifiers and IETF network slice identifiers in the management plane, control plane, and data plane.

The overall procedure for 5G E2E network slice mapping is as follows:

- The NSMF receives a request to create or allocate an E2E network slice from the Communication Service Management Function (CSMF). This request contains the requirements of the network slice service.

- The NSMF parses the request to discover service requirements on the RAN, CN, and TN NSSIs. It then determines the network functions and resources that each NSSI needs to provide.

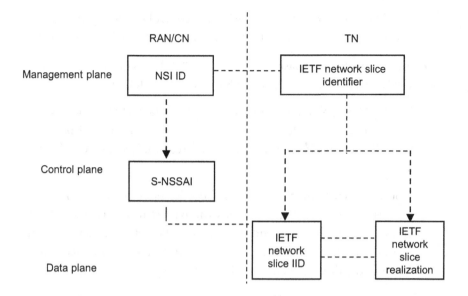

FIGURE 8.3    Mapping between network slice identifiers.

- The NSMF determines the IETF network slice IIDs between the RAN and TN and between the CN and TN.

- The NSMF sends a request to the RAN NSSMF for the creation of a RAN slice.

- The NSMF sends a request to the CN NSSMF for the creation of a CN slice.

- The NSMF sends a request to the IETF NSC for the creation of an IETF network slice. The request contains the IETF network slice IID and the attribute information required by the IETF network slice, including the endpoints, Service-Level Agreement (SLA)/Service-Level Objective (SLO), and more.

- The NSC, through the network controller, creates an IETF network slice that meets the requirements of specified endpoints (RAN and CN border nodes), allocates an IETF network slice identifier, and then returns the creation result to the NSMF.

- The NSMF maintains the mapping from the E2E network slice to the IETF network slice.

- A 5G User Equipment (UE), using 5G control signaling, requests to connect to an E2E network slice identified by a specified S-NSSAI.

- The UE uses the Protocol Data Unit (PDU) session in the E2E network slice identified by the S-NSSAI to send a data packet.

- The RAN or CN node, before sending the data packet to the TN border node, encapsulates the IETF network slice IID into it based on the E2E network slice information corresponding to the PDU session information.

- Upon receiving the packet, the TN border node parses the network slice IID in the packet and maps the packet to the corresponding IETF network slice. Depending on how IETF network slicing is realized, the node encapsulates the corresponding network slice identifier into the data packet.

### 8.1.2 Realization of 5G E2E Network Slice Mapping

This section describes how 5G E2E network slice mapping is realized in the management plane, control plane, and data plane.

#### 8.1.2.1 E2E Network Slice Mapping in the Management Plane

The TN slice management system TN-NSSMF (equivalent to the IETF NSC) provides a management interface for the NSMF to implement the following functions:

- Ensures that an IPv6 network slice can provide connections and SLAs required by the RAN and CN slices in 5G E2E network slices.

- Maps 5G E2E network slice identifiers to IPv6 network slice identifiers.

- Provides management and maintenance functions for IPv6 network slices in 5G E2E network slices.

The service profile defined in 3GPP TS 28.530 contains the requirements of services or users on 5G E2E NSIs, involving parameters such as the delay, resource sharing level, and resource availability. Learning what the IPv6 network slice requirements are from the 5G E2E NSI requirements is one of the key tasks that need to be completed in network slice requirement mapping. To realize this goal, the Global System for Mobile Communications Association (GSMA) has defined a Generic Network Slice Template (GST) that describes network slice requirements from the perspective of carriers. The parameters involved in network slice requirements are also necessary for defining an NBI for a TN slice.

The IPv6 NSC is responsible for maintaining connections and attributes such as SLAs for an IPv6 network slice. If the attributes of an existing IPv6 network slice meet the requirements placed on the TN slice by a 5G E2E network slice, the NSC selects the existing slice and completes the mapping from the 5G E2E network slice to the existing slice. Otherwise, the NSC creates a new IPv6 network slice and completes the mapping from the 5G E2E network slice to the new IPv6 network slice.

The IPv6 NSC then provides the identifier of the IPv6 network slice to the NSMF. Both the NSMF and IPv6 NSC need to maintain the mapping from the 5G E2E network slice identifier to the IPv6 network slice identifier. The NBI service model of the IPv6 NSC can be used by the higher-level 5G E2E slice management system to create and manage the IPv6 network slice.

### 8.1.2.2 E2E Network Slice Mapping in the Control Plane

An S-NSSAI is used by a UE to register to a 5G E2E network slice and establish a PDU session in the specified 5G E2E network slice. Mapping from the 5G E2E network slice to the IPv6 network slice is mainly realized in the management plane — the TN does not directly participate in the interaction between the RAN and the CN in the control plane.

### 8.1.2.3 E2E Network Slice Mapping in the Data Plane

If RAN slices or CN slices connect to the TN through different physical interfaces, they can be distinguished according to the physical interfaces they use. They can then be mapped and bound to IPv6 network slices accordingly. Conversely, if they connect to the TN through the same physical interface and need to be mapped to different IPv6 network slices, a field in packets needs to be used as the IPv6 network slice IID to distinguish between these slices.

8.1.2.3.1 Basic Procedure for E2E Network Slice Mapping in the Data Plane    In order to realize E2E network slice mapping in the data plane, nodes need to maintain the mapping between different identifiers. Specifically, the RAN and CN nodes need to maintain the mapping between the 5G E2E network slice identifiers and IPv6 network slice IIDs, and the TN border nodes need to maintain the mapping between IPv6 network slice IIDs and IPv6 network slice identifiers. In this way, a RAN node can add the corresponding IPv6 network slice IID into a 5G service packet before sending the packet upstream to the TN. After receiving this packet, a TN border node then maps it to the corresponding IPv6 network slice based on the IPv6 network slice IID carried in the packet. A similar procedure is used for a downstream 5G service packet sent from the CN to the TN.

8.1.2.3.2 Network Slice IID Options in the Data Plane    Figure 8.4 shows the data plane connections of 5G E2E network slices. Mapping from the 5G E2E network slices to IPv6 network slices may occur on the RAN nodes (e.g., gNBs) and the CN User Plane Functions (UPFs). Specifically, the RAN nodes and UPFs, respectively, map user data packets from the RAN slices and CN slices to IPv6 network slices by encapsulating IPv6 network slice IIDs into these packets.

Figure 8.5 shows the user plane protocol stack in a 5G E2E system. The RAN node sends a 5G service packet to the UPF over the N3 interface after it encapsulates a GPRS Tunnelling Protocol for the User Plane (GTP-U) packet header and then a UDP/IP header into the packet. The TN is mainly responsible for providing N3 interface connections (between RAN nodes and UPFs) and N9 interface connections (between different UPFs).

In the PDU layer, PDUs are transmitted between the UE and Packet Data Network (PDN) over a PDU session. Such a session can be of the IP or Ethernet type (for IP or Ethernet packet transmission, respectively).

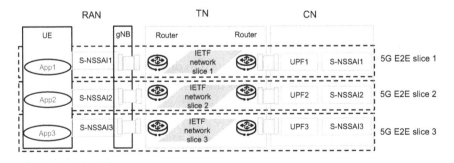

FIGURE 8.4    5G E2E network slice mapping in the data plane.

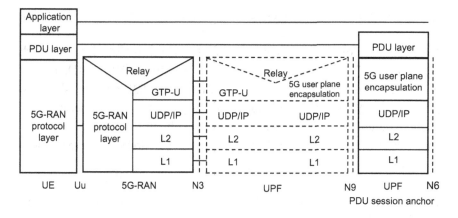

FIGURE 8.5    User plane protocol stack in an E2E 5G system.

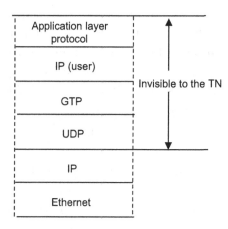

FIGURE 8.6    Typical data packet encapsulation on the N3 interface.

The N3 interface uses GTP-U tunnels to carry all user data packets from different PDU sessions.

Figure 8.6 shows how a data packet is encapsulated on the N3 interface. Identifiers are usually provided in either the IP header or Ethernet header for interworking between RAN/CN slices and IPv6 network slices. This is because the encapsulated content above the IP layer is typically invisible to TN devices.

8.1.2.3.3  Layer 2 Encapsulation    In an Ethernet packet, a VLAN ID can be used as an IPv6 network slice IID. On the TN of the 3G and 4G networks, VLAN IDs are widely used to achieve interworking between RAN/

CN nodes and TN border nodes as they enable different RAN/CN services to access different VPNs on the TN. In 5G E2E network slices, RAN and CN slices can continue to use VLAN IDs to interwork with IPv6 network slices on the TN. However, the maximum number of VLAN IDs is only 4096, which may not be enough to identify all 5G E2E network slices. In addition, VLAN IDs have only local significance on a Layer 3 network. As such, different VLAN IDs may be used on different network devices for interworking with the same IPv6 network slice, making the management complex.

8.1.2.3.4 Layer 3 Encapsulation  The following fields in an IP packet header may be used to function as the network slice IID:

- DSCP: Certain values (e.g., unassigned code points) can be borrowed from the DSCP field for network slice mapping. However, doing so will cause confusion between QoS mapping and network slice mapping because this field is usually used for QoS mapping between the RAN/CN and the TN. As such, using this field to function as the network slice IID is not recommended.

- Destination address: Different IP addresses can be allocated to RAN or CN nodes for different network slices. In this case, destination addresses in IP packets can be used as the IPv6 network slice IIDs. However, this poses additional requirements on IP address planning. In some cases, different RAN or CN network slices may require independent address spaces. Consequently, there may be duplicate IP addresses in different 5G E2E network slices, meaning that IP addresses cannot be used to uniquely determine network slices in such cases.

- IPv6 extension header: If RAN and CN nodes support IPv6, an IPv6 extension header can be used to carry an IPv6 network slice IID. This overcomes the conflicts and limitations caused by reusing an existing packet field as the network slice IID. However, the tradeoff is that new extensions need to be introduced to the IPv6 data plane. As described in the IETF draft *draft-li-teas-e2e-ietf-network-slicing*,[3] a 5G E2E network slice identifier is introduced to the data plane and can be carried in an IPv6 extension header to map a 5G E2E network slice to an IPv6 network slice.

8.1.2.3.5 Above Layer 3 Encapsulation  If the encapsulated content in packet headers above the IP layer is visible to TN border nodes, using such content to carry the IPv6 network slice IID is possible. For example, a UDP header can be used to carry such an identifier.

One possible way is to use the UDP source port number field in the UDP header to carry it. Although the source port number remains unchanged during packet transmission, it is usually used for load balancing. The load balancing function has to be disabled if this field is used for network slice mapping. This may affect network deployment and usage. As such, using this field to carry IPv6 network slice IIDs is not recommended.

In summary, although there are some drawbacks involved in using VLAN IDs as IPv6 network slice IIDs, it currently remains the most feasible solution. As IPv6 deployment and application become more widespread, using the IPv6 extension header instead is considered a very promising solution.

## 8.2 E2E INTER-DOMAIN IPV6 NETWORK SLICING

Because an IPv6 network slice may span multiple network administrative domains and a 5G E2E network slice consists of different technology-specific domains, service data packets can carry the identifiers of 5G E2E network slices, inter-domain IP network slices, and intra-domain IP network slices in order to facilitate network slice mapping and interworking between the different domains.

### 8.2.1 E2E IPv6 Network Slicing Architecture

The IETF draft *draft-li-teas-e2e-ietf-network-slicing*[3] introduces the architecture of E2E IP network slicing, including the network slice interworking framework across different technology-specific domains and network administrative domains. It also defines multiple identifiers related to network slicing and the functions of these identifiers in packet forwarding.

Figure 8.7 shows an E2E IP network slice that can be used in two scenarios:

- 5G E2E network slice: This slice is composed of RAN, CN, and TN slices. It is identified by a 3GPP-defined S-NSSAI, which was originally used only in the management and control planes of a 5G network. To map the RAN slice and CN slice to the TN slice (which can

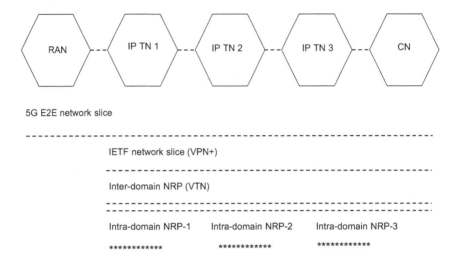

FIGURE 8.7    Typical scenarios of an E2E IP network slice.

be an IPv6 network slice), the RAN nodes and CN nodes need to add an IPv6 network slice IID to data packets that will be sent to the TN. After receiving such packets, the TN border nodes map the data packets to the corresponding IPv6 network slice based on the IPv6 network slice IID. The VLAN ID is typically used as the IPv6 network slice IID. Alternatively, the IETF draft *draft-li-teas-e2e-ietf-network-slicing*[3] proposes to carry the S-NSSAI in data packets. In this approach, the RAN nodes and CN nodes directly add an S-NSSAI to a data packet to be sent to the TN. After receiving such a packet, a TN border node maps the 5G E2E network slice to the corresponding IPv6 network slice based on the S-NSSAI according to the local mapping relationship between the S-NSSAI-identified 5G E2E slice and the IPv6 network slice.

- Inter-domain IP network slice: On an IP network crossing multiple administrative domains, an inter-domain IP network slice can be a service slice (VPN+ service) that spans multiple domains. Such a service slice is underpinned by an inter-domain network resource slice, which itself is composed of several intra-domain network resource slices. This is similar to inter-AS VPN,[4] which can be provided using Option A, Option B, or Option C. This book focuses on the Option C-based realization of inter-domain network slicing.

An inter-domain IP network slice can be realized using the slice ID-based network slicing solution, in which data packets from each domain are encapsulated with a domain-wide network slice identifier. This identifier helps network nodes in each domain determine the network resources required by the network slice and then use the resources to process and forward the data packets.

To form one inter-domain network slice based on multiple intra-domain network slices, an inter-domain network slice identifier can be carried in data packets. The border nodes of each domain then map this identifier to the intra-domain network slice identifier.

In the preceding typical scenarios of an E2E IP network slice, three network slice-related identifiers are available in the data plane:

Intra-domain Network Resource Partition (NRP) ID: uniquely identifies a network resource slice in a single domain. Network nodes use this ID to determine the set of network resources that they reserve for the network slice. The intra-domain NRP ID needs to be parsed and processed by each intra-domain network node along the forwarding path of the data packet that carries this ID.

Inter-domain NRP ID: uniquely identifies a network resource slice that spans multiple domains. In each network domain, the border nodes map this ID to the intra-domain NRP ID in order to guide data packet forwarding within the domain.

S-NSSAI: uniquely identifies a 5G E2E network slice and can be carried in data packets through an IPv6 extension header to realize interworking and mapping between a RAN/CN slice and an IPv6 network slice. When the border nodes of the TN receive the packets from the RAN/CN, they encapsulate the outer tunnel header (e.g., the outer IPv6 header) into the packets and copy the S-NSSAI to the outer tunnel header to associate the S-NSSAI with the IPv6 network slice identifier. This association can be used to provide traffic monitoring and SLA guarantee for different 5G E2E network slices.

Among these three network slice identifiers, the intra-domain NRP ID is mandatory for data packets in all scenarios, whereas the inter-domain NRP ID and S-NSSAI are carried in data packets only in some scenarios. The presence of the inter-domain NRP ID depends on whether an IPv6 network slice spans different administrative domains of a TN. If it does, but the intra-domain NRP IDs of different domains are uniformly planned and allocated (i.e., the same intra-domain NRP ID is used across different domains for the same inter-domain network slice), the inter-domain NRP ID can be the same as the intra-domain NRP ID. This means that data packets need to carry only one NRP ID, and mapping NRP IDs on the border nodes of domains is not necessary. A 5G E2E network slice identifier is carried in packets if both the following conditions are true: (1) the IPv6 network slice provides the TN slice function as a part of the 5G E2E network slice, and (2) the TN border nodes maintain the mapping from the 5G E2E network slice to the IPv6 network slice.

### 8.2.2 E2E IPv6 Network Slicing Realization

E2E IPv6 network slicing can be realized as follows:

- Data plane: To facilitate mapping from 5G E2E network slices to IPv6 network slices and from inter-domain IP network slices to intra-domain IP network slices, network slice identifiers (including S-NSSAIs, inter-domain NRP IDs, and intra-domain NRP IDs) need to be carried in data packets. Specifically, in an inter-domain IP network slice, the border nodes of each domain must be able to map the inter-domain NRP ID to the intra-domain NRP ID in the data plane. Similarly, in a 5G E2E network slice, if an S-NSSAI is used for network slice interworking, the border nodes of the TN must be able to map the S-NSSAI to the inter-/intra-domain NRP ID of the TN. And for packets sent from the RAN/CN, if an S-NSSAI needs to be associated with an IPv6 network slice, the border nodes of the TN must be able to copy the S-NSSAI in the packets to the outer tunnel encapsulation information.

- Management plane/Control plane: For an inter-domain IPv6 network slice, the IPv6 NSC is responsible for allocating the inter-domain and intra-domain NRP IDs and delivering the mapping between them to the border nodes in different network domains. And for the S-NSSAI-based interworking between a 5G E2E network slice and an IPv6 network slice, the IPv6 NSC needs to deliver the mapping between the S-NSSAI and the inter-/intra-domain NRP IDs to the border nodes of the IP network. In addition, the network devices need to distribute and report inter- and intra-domain NRP topologies and TE attribute information through control plane protocols. For details, see the related description in Section 6.2 BGP-LS Extensions for Network Slicing.

### 8.2.3 E2E IPv6 Network Slicing Encapsulation

To realize E2E IPv6 network slicing, the IETF draft *draft-li-6man-e2e-ietf-network-slicing*[5] defines a couple of methods for encapsulating E2E network slice identifiers into IPv6 data packets.

One method is to define a new IPv6 extension header option for the inter-domain NRP ID and another for the S-NSSAI. In this way, network slice identifiers applying to different network scopes are carried using separate IPv6 options.

Another method is to define only one IPv6 extension header option for the IPv6 network slice and use separate TLVs or fields in the IPv6 extension header option to represent the network slice identifiers applying to different scopes. This requires a variable-length extension header option.

Whether the inter-domain NRP ID and S-NSSAI exist in data packets depends on whether the IPv6 network slice spans multiple network domains and forms part of the 5G E2E network slice.

## 8.3 SRV6-BASED E2E IPV6 NETWORK SLICING

### 8.3.1 SRv6 BSID for E2E IPv6 Network Slicing

In each of the network administrative domains that an IPv6 network slice spans, traffic of the E2E IPv6 network slice needs to be mapped to the intra-domain slice for forwarding.

- If the SRv6 SID-based network slicing solution is used within the domain, the domain border nodes need to steer the service traffic from the E2E IPv6 network slice to the SRv6 forwarding path specified using the resource-aware SIDs associated with the network slice in the domain.

- If the slice ID-based network slicing solution is used within the domain, the domain border nodes need to determine the intra-domain network slice ID for the E2E IPv6 network slice, add this ID to data packets, and forward the packets using the network resources reserved for this network slice.

In scenarios where inter-domain forwarding paths for an E2E IPv6 network slice are established using SRv6, the SRv6 binding SID (BSID) mechanism can be used to assign different BSIDs to SRv6 Policies in the network slice of each domain. BSIDs in different domains can form an SRv6 SID list to implement inter-domain SRv6 network path programming for the E2E IPv6 network slice. The following describes the main steps involved in this process:

- When the ingress of a local domain receives an SRv6 packet from another network domain, the ingress obtains the SID list of the SRv6 Policy in the local domain based on the corresponding BSID carried in the packet. The ingress then adds a new outer IPv6 packet header to the packet and encapsulates the SID list of the SRv6 Policy in the local domain into the SRH, steering packet forwarding in the local domain along the path specified using the SID list.

- When the packet arrives at the egress of the domain, the egress (which is the egress of the SID list in the local domain) removes the outer IPv6 packet header and SRH. The egress then forwards the packet to the next domain based on the SID list in the original SRv6 packet.

Section 6.4 SR Policy Extensions for Network Slicing of this book describes the extensions used to associate SR Policies with network slices based on slice IDs. Such association enables data packets to be forwarded along specific SRv6 Policy paths, with service performance guaranteed using the resources reserved for the slices specified by slice IDs. A BSID can also be allocated to an SRv6 Policy associated with a slice ID and used by other domains to establish an inter-domain SRv6 path for an E2E IPv6 network slice. In this case, when the ingress of a network domain receives an SRv6 data packet containing BSIDs, the ingress obtains the SID list of the SRv6 Policy in the local domain and the Policy-associated slice ID based on the corresponding BSID. It then encapsulates the SID list and the slice ID into the outer IPv6 packet header to respectively indicate the forwarding path of the packet and the resources reserved for the network slice.

For SRv6 Policies that are associated with slice IDs, the use of BSIDs facilitates inter-domain SRv6 path orchestration in E2E IPv6 network slices while also ensuring compatibility with existing SRv6 Policies. However, there is a drawback: Slices cannot be flexibly selected because an SRv6 Policy is bound to a specific intra-domain network slice. If services need to be switched to another network slice in the domain because resources in the network slice change or the network slice interworking policy changes, the domain border nodes have to be reconfigured. This is necessary for the border nodes to generate a new SRv6 Policy, assign a new BSID, associate the SRv6 Policy with the new network slice ID, and advertise the BSID so that network nodes in other domains can orchestrate inter-domain paths for the E2E IPv6 network slice. Adjustment of an E2E IPv6 network slice is therefore complex and requires new states to be added on the transit nodes.

To increase the flexibility of E2E IPv6 network slices, a special type of SRv6 BSID—NRP BSID[6]—needs to be introduced to SRv6 to indicate network slice information in each domain. In this way, a network slice that spans multiple domains can be specified by adding an NRP BSID list to data packets. Each NRP BSID in the BSID list is parsed by the corresponding domain border node, which then encapsulates the SID list of the NRP BSID (with or without the intra-domain NRP ID) into packets. This allows the service traffic of the E2E network slice to be processed and forwarded in the intra-domain network slice.

With SRv6, there are multiple approaches to steering service traffic of an E2E IPv6 network slice to an intra-domain network slice. These approaches can be classified into two types.

Type 1: An NRP BSID of a specific type — NRP TE BSID — is used to steer the service traffic of an E2E IPv6 network slice to an SRv6 Policy associated with a specific intra-domain network slice. According to the packet encapsulation behavior, the NRP TE BSID has two variants:

- Variant 1: A type of NRP TE BSID is used to instruct a domain border node to steer traffic to an SRv6 Policy associated with an intra-domain network slice. The explicit paths of the SRv6 Policy consist of a group of resource-aware SIDs.

- Variant 2: A type of NRP TE BSID is used to instruct a domain border node to steer a data packet to an SRv6 Policy associated with a network slice in a specific domain. This SRv6 Policy instructs the ingress to encapsulate both the SID list and the slice ID of the network slice into the data packet.

Type 2: An NRP BSID of a specific type—NRP BE BSID—is used to steer the service traffic of an E2E IPv6 network slice to the shortest forwarding path associated with a specific intra-domain network slice.

According to the packet encapsulation behavior, the NRP BE BSID also has two variants:

- Variant 1: A type of NRP BE BSID is used to instruct a domain border node to determine the intra-domain network slice and encapsulate the corresponding slice ID into data packets.

- Variant 2: A type of NRP BE BSID is used to instruct a domain border node to encapsulate the slice ID of a specific network slice in the local domain into data packets. The slice ID in the domain is specified by the ingress node of the E2E IPv6 network slice and is carried in a specific field in the packets.

The second variant of the NRP TE BSID and both variants of the NRP BE BSID have different behaviors from those of the existing SRv6 BSIDs. Therefore, new SRv6 binding behaviors need to be defined. The following sections delve into the details of these NRP BSIDs.

### 8.3.2 SRv6 NRP-Binding Behaviors

#### 8.3.2.1 End.B6.Encaps Behavior

RFC 8986[7] defines the concepts and framework of SRv6 network programming and provides a basic set of SRv6 network behaviors. The SRv6 End.B6.Encaps behavior is one of the SRv6 instantiations of a BSID.

The first variant of the NRP TE BSID is similar to the SRv6 End.B6.Encaps SID in terms of processing behavior. That is, they both obtain an SRv6 Policy based on a BSID and encapsulate the corresponding SID list into data packets. They differ in that the NRP TE BSID is associated with a specific network slice. Therefore, when the NRP TE explicit path is implemented based on End.B6.Encaps, the corresponding SID list needs to contain resource-aware SIDs corresponding to the intra-domain network slice.

#### 8.3.2.2 End.B6NRP.Encaps Behavior

End.B6NRP.Encaps is a variant of the SRv6 End behavior and is used to steer packets to an SRv6 Policy in a specified IPv6 network slice. This SRv6 behavior instructs an SRv6 endpoint to determine the IPv6 network slice and SRv6 Policy corresponding to the SRv6 BSID, and then to encapsulate the corresponding NRP ID and the SID list of the SRv6 Policy into a new IPv6 header.

The pseudocode of the End.B6NRP.Encaps behavior is as follows:

```
Any SID instance of this behavior is associated with
an SR Policy B,
an NRP-ID V and a source address A.
When node N receives a packet whose IPv6 DA is S, and
S is a local
End.B6NRP.Encaps SID, N does the following:
S01. When an SRH is processed {
S02. If (Segments Left == 0) {
S03. Stop processing the SRH, and proceed to process
the next
header in the packet, whose type is identified by
the Next Header field in the routing header.
S04. }
S05. If (IPv6 Hop Limit <= 1) {
S06. Send an ICMP Time Exceeded message to the Source
Address
with Code 0 (Hop limit exceeded in transit),
interrupt packet processing, and discard the packet.
S07. }
S08. max_LE = (Hdr Ext Len / 2) -1
S09. If ((Last Entry > max_LE) or (Segments Left >
Last Entry+1)) {
S10. Send an ICMP Parameter Problem to the Source
Address
with Code 0 (Erroneous header field encountered)
and Pointer set to the Segments Left field,
interrupt packet processing, and discard the packet.
S11. }
S12. Decrement IPv6 Hop Limit by 1
S13. Decrement Segments Left by 1
S14. Update IPv6 DA with Segment List [Segments Left]
S15. Push a new IPv6 header with its own SRH
containing B, and
set the NRP-ID in the HBH header to V
S16. Set the outer IPv6 SA to A
S17. Set the outer IPv6 DA to the first SID of B
```

S18. Set the outer Payload Length, Traffic Class, Flow Label,
Hop Limit, and Next Header fields
S19. Submit the packet to the egress IPv6 FIB lookup for transmission to the new destination
S20. }

### 8.3.2.3 End.NRP.Encaps Behavior

End.NRP.Encaps is a variant of the SRv6 End behavior. The SRv6 end-point corresponding to the End.NRP.Encaps SID maintains the mapping between the SID and the intra-domain NRP ID. After receiving a data packet carrying an End.NRP.Encaps SID allocated by itself, the SRv6 end-point can determine the corresponding NRP ID according to the End.NRP.Encaps SID. It then encapsulates the NRP ID into the IPv6 HBH Options header of the data packet.

The pseudocode of the End.NRP.Encaps behavior is as follows:

Any SID instance of this behavior is associated with one NRP-ID V.
When node N receives a packet whose IPv6 DA is S, and S is a local
End.NRP.Encaps SID, N does the following:
S01. When an SRH is processed {
S02. If (Segments Left == 0) {
S03. Stop processing the SRH and proceed to process the next
header in the packet, whose type is identified by ·
the Next Header field in the routing header.
S04. }
S05. If (IPv6 Hop Limit <= 1) {
S06. Send an ICMP Time Exceeded message to the Source Address
with Code 0 (Hop limit exceeded in transit),
interrupt packet processing, and discard the packet.
S07. }
S08. max_LE = (Hdr Ext Len / 2) -1
S09. If ((Last Entry > max_LE) or (Segments Left > Last Entry+1)) {
S10. Send an ICMP Parameter Problem to the Source Address

with Code 0 (Erroneous header field encountered)
and Pointer set to the Segments Left field,
interrupt packet processing, and discard the packet.
S11. }
S12. Decrement IPv6 Hop Limit by 1
S13. Decrement Segments Left by 1
S14. Update IPv6 DA with Segment List [Segments Left]
S15. Set the NRP-ID in the HBH header to V
S16. Submit the packet to the egress IPv6 FIB lookup
for
transmission to the new destination
S17. }

### 8.3.2.4 End.BNRP.Encaps Behavior

End.BNRP.Encaps is a variant of the SRv6 End behavior and is used to send packets to an IPv6 network slice based on slice ID encapsulation. The intra-domain NRP ID corresponding to the End.BNRP.Encaps SID is specified by the ingress of an E2E SRv6 path and carried in the SRH. This SID instructs the involved SRv6 endpoint to obtain the corresponding NRP ID from the packet encapsulation information and encapsulate the NRP ID into the IPv6 HBH Options header.

End.BNRP.Encaps differs from End.NRP.Encaps in the following aspects:

- They use different methods to obtain the intra-domain NRP ID. For End.NRP.Encaps, the SRv6 endpoint specified by the End.NRP. Encaps SID obtains the intra-domain NRP ID according to the locally maintained mapping between the End.NRP.Encaps SID and the NRP ID. For End.BNRP.Encaps, the ingress of an inter-domain SRv6 path encapsulates the End.BNRP.Encaps SID of an SRv6 endpoint into a packet while also inserting the specified intra-domain NRP ID of the SRv6 endpoint into the packet. When the SRv6 endpoint specified by the End.BNRP.Encaps SID receives the packet, it directly obtains the intra-domain NRP ID from the packet encapsulation information.

- They require different conditions to establish a path in an inter-domain NRP. When End.NRP.Encaps is used to establish such a path, other domain nodes only need to know the End.NRP.Encaps

SID (they do not need to know the intra-domain NRP ID of the SRv6 endpoint corresponding to the End.NRP.Encaps SID). However, when End.BNRP.Encaps is used to establish such a path, the ingress of the E2E SRv6 path needs to know both the End.NRP.Encaps SID and the intra-domain NRP ID of the SRv6 endpoint.

- They use different methods for intra-domain NRP ID mapping. The SRv6 endpoint specified by the End.NRP.Encaps SID maps the End.NRP.Encaps SID to a unique intra-domain NRP ID. In contrast, when the ingress of an E2E SRv6 path encapsulates the End.BNRP.Encaps SID, it can insert different NRP IDs in the SRH based on service requirements. By doing so, the ingress can instruct the SRv6 endpoint specified by the End.BNRP.Encaps BSID to obtain and encapsulate the intra-domain NRP ID of the SRv6 endpoint. In other words, End.BNRP.Encaps enables the ingress of an SRv6 path in an inter-domain NRP to flexibly specify the intra-domain NRPs that are required for packet forwarding in different domains.

There are several options for carrying the intra-domain NRP ID of the SRv6 endpoint corresponding to the End.BNRP.Encaps SID in packets:

- In the Arguments part of an End.BNRP.Encaps SID (this is currently the preferred option)

- In the TLV field of an SRH

- In the next SID following the End.BNRP.Encaps SID that is being processed in the SID list

When the ingress of an inter-domain SRv6 path in an E2E IPv6 network slice encapsulates an End.BNRP.Encaps SID into a data packet, it needs to put the intra-domain NRP ID that the packet should be steered to into the Arguments part of the SRv6 SID.

The pseudocode of the End.BNRP.Encaps behavior is as follows:

```
Any SID instance of this behavior contains one NRP-ID
V in its argument.
When node N receives a packet whose IPv6 DA is S, and
S is a local
End.BNRP.Encaps SID, N does the following:
```

```
S01. When an SRH is processed {
S02. If (Segments Left == 0) {
S03. Stop processing the SRH, and proceed to process
the next
header in the packet, whose type is identified by
the Next Header field in the routing header.
S04. }
S05. If (IPv6 Hop Limit <= 1) {
S06. Send an ICMP Time Exceeded message to the Source
Address
with Code 0 (Hop limit exceeded in transit),
interrupt packet processing, and discard the packet.
S07. }
S08. max_LE = (Hdr Ext Len / 2) -1
S09. If ((Last Entry > max_LE) or (Segments Left >
Last Entry+1)) {
S10. Send an ICMP Parameter Problem to the Source
Address
with Code 0 (Erroneous header field encountered)
and Pointer set to the Segments Left field,
interrupt packet processing, and discard the packet.
S11. }
S12. Obtain the NRP-ID V from the argument part of the
IPv6 DA
S13. Decrement IPv6 Hop Limit by 1
S14. Decrement Segments Left by 1
S15. Update IPv6 DA with Segment List [Segments Left]
S16. Set the NRP-ID in the HBH header to V
S17. Submit the packet to the egress IPv6 FIB lookup
for
transmission to the new destination
S18. }
```

## 8.4 INTENT-BASED ROUTING COMBINED WITH E2E IPV6 NETWORK SLICING

### 8.4.1 Fundamentals of Intent-Based Routing

The IETF draft *draft-hr-spring-intentaware-routing-using-color*[8] describes the requirements for establishing E2E intent-aware paths that span network domains. To set up such paths for meeting different service SLA requirements, BGP-based control protocol mechanisms are discussed in multiple IETF drafts.[9,10] On an SR network, these inter-domain E2E paths require SR Policies to be set up according to different <color, endpoint> pairs. This will result in many SR Policies being introduced into an inter-domain network, compromising network scalability.

To address this issue, the IETF draft *draft-li-apn-intent-based-routing*[11] defines an intent-based routing mechanism that allows data packets to carry intent information. Based on this mechanism, network nodes steer the data packets to the corresponding intra-domain SR Policies in order to meet service requirements (i.e., to meet specific intents). When the intent-based routing mechanism is used, there is no need for network nodes to maintain fine-grained E2E connection states to each endpoint for different intents in the control plane, significantly improving the E2E routing scalability.

In addition to steering data packets to SR Policies, the intent-based routing mechanism can steer service traffic to network slices in order to meet specific intents. This mechanism can also be used to enforce policies for other intents such as network measurement and security. It is worth pointing out here that different solutions can be used to meet the same intent in different network domains. For example, the low-delay intent of a service can be met by SR Policy or network slicing. Given this, intent-based routing can combine the solutions of different domains to ensure the consistency of intents across the entire inter-domain network, allowing an inter-domain network to more flexibly meet service requirements.

To represent the service requirements of a data packet destined to a specific address, intent-based routing needs to introduce intent information in the data plane. This intent can be associated with a series of service requirements, such as low delay and high bandwidth, and its ID in the data plane can be allocated by a network administrator based on service requirements. Note that intent IDs must be consistent across the entire inter-domain network.

The IETF's RFC 9256 "Segment Routing Policy Architecture" defines the color attribute used for SR Policies.[12] A color is a 32-bit control plane identifier that associates an SR Policy with an intent (e.g., low delay). To divert traffic to SR Policies based on intent information, network devices need to maintain the mapping between colors and intents. If intent IDs in the data plane and the colors of SR Policies can be designed and allocated consistently (i.e., the color values of SR Policies are the same as intent IDs), the mapping between them does not need to be stored in the data plane.

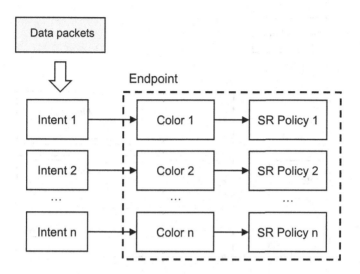

FIGURE 8.8   SR Policy group.

As shown in Figure 8.8, in an intent-based inter-domain routing scenario, SR Policies with different colors destined to a specific endpoint only need to be established in the local network domain. That is, there is no need to advertise or establish an E2E inter-domain SR Policy corresponding to each <color, endpoint> pair in the intent-based routing mechanism. The border node of a network domain, after receiving a data packet carrying an intent ID, can find the next hop of a route according to the destination address of the packet. The node then matches the <color, endpoint> pair of SR Policies against the intent ID and the next hop in the packet, determines the corresponding intra-domain SR Policy, and steers the data packet to the SR Policy for forwarding.

As shown in Figure 8.9, in an inter-domain network slicing scenario, a mapping between a color and an intra-domain network slice can be established in each domain. After receiving a data packet that carries an intent ID, the border node of a network domain can steer the packet into the domain's network slice according to the mapping between the color and intent and between the color and network slice.

Because a given intent can be met by an SR Policy, network slice, or other solution, a different solution can be chosen for different network domains. This improves inter-domain routing flexibility.

Figure 8.10 shows an example of intent-based inter-domain routing. In this example, a carrier network is composed of AS1 and AS2. Assume that

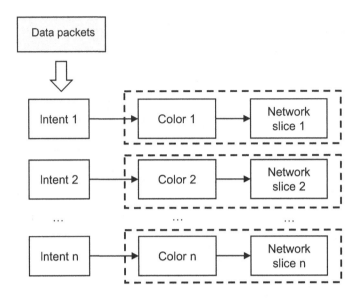

FIGURE 8.9   Mapping between colors and intra-domain network slices.

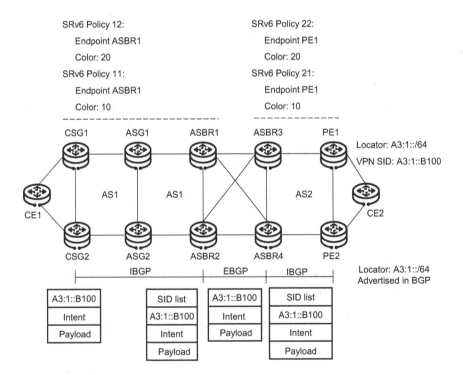

FIGURE 8.10   Intent-based inter-domain routing.

the following configurations are applied on the network and that a customer requests a private line service with guaranteed bandwidth from CSG1 to PE1:

- An independent IGP instance is deployed in AS1.

- An independent IGP instance is deployed in AS2.

- BGP is deployed between Autonomous System Boundary Routers (ASBRs).

- PE1's SRv6 locator is A3:1::/64, and the SRv6 VPN SID of the VPN instance on PE1 is A3:1::B100.

- On CSG1 in AS1, two SRv6 Policies are established with the same endpoint (ASBR1) but different color values. One is associated with color value 10 (low delay), and the other is associated with color value 20 (high bandwidth).

- On ASBR3 in AS2, two SRv6 Policies are established with the same endpoint (PE1) but different color values. One is associated with color value 10 (low delay), and the other is associated with color value 20 (high bandwidth).

- PE1's SRv6 locator A3:1::/64 is used as the route prefix and advertised through BGP. The ASBR changes the next hop of the route and then advertises the updated route.

PE1 advertises a VPN route with the color extended community attribute of 10 to CSG1. The route carries the SRv6 VPN SID A3:1::B100. After receiving the VPN route, CSG1 maps the color value to an intent ID and then generates the mapping between the VPN route with the VPN SID of A3:1::B100 and the corresponding intent ID. When it receives a data packet from CE1, CSG1 performs VPN route matching, packet encapsulation, and packet forwarding. The details are as follows:

- CSG1 encapsulates an outer IPv6 header into the data packet, sets the destination IPv6 address to the VPN SID A3:1::B100 of the VPN route, and adds the corresponding intent ID to the packet.

- CSG1 looks up the destination IPv6 address A3:1::B100 in the IPv6 routing table and finds the matching route to PE1's locator A3:1::/64, with the next hop being ASBR1.

- CSG1 resolves PE1's locator route onto SRv6 Policy 11 with color value 10 and endpoint ASBR1 based on the next hop ASBR1 and intent ID. It then adds the SID list of the SRv6 Policy into the outer IPv6 header.

- CSG1 and other network nodes in AS1 forward the data packet to ASBR1 based on the SID list of SRv6 Policy 11. When ASBR1 receives the packet, it removes the outer IPv6 header and the SID list of SRv6 Policy 11.

- ASBR1 looks up the destination IPv6 address A3:1::B100 in the IPv6 routing table and sends the data packet to its next hop, ASBR3.

- ASBR3 looks up the destination IPv6 address A3:1::B100 in the IPv6 routing table and finds the matching route to PE1's locator A3:1::/64, with the next hop being PE1.

- ASBR3 resolves PE1's locator route onto SRv6 Policy 21 with color value 10 and endpoint PE1 based on the next hop PE1 and intent ID. It then encapsulates a new IPv6 header containing the SID list of SRv6 Policy 21 into the packet.

- ASBR3 and other network nodes in AS2 forward the data packet to PE1 based on the SID list of SRv6 Policy 21. When PE1 receives the packet, it removes the outer IPv6 header and the SID list of SRv6 Policy 21.

- PE1 determines the VPN routing table identified by the VPN SID A3:1::B100 and then performs a lookup to forward the data packet.

### 8.4.2 IPv6 Encapsulation in Intent-Based Routing

An intent ID can be encapsulated using different data plane protocols. To support intent-based routing in IPv6, a new IPv6 extension header option—called the intent option—needs to be defined. Figure 8.11 shows the format of the intent option. Table 8.1 describes the fields in the intent option.

The intent option can be carried in either of the following IPv6 packet headers, depending on the scenario and implementation requirements.

- HBH Options header: When this type of header is used, each node on a path can read the intent information carried in data packets.

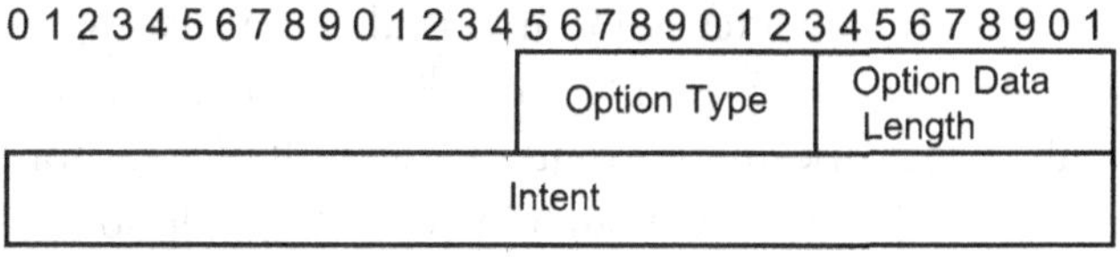

```
0 1 2 3 4 5 6 7 8 9 0 1 2 3 4 5 6 7 8 9 0 1 2 3 4 5 6 7 8 9 0 1
```

| Option Type | Option Data Length |
|:---:|:---:|
| Intent | |

FIGURE 8.11   Intent option.

TABLE 8.1   Fields in the Intent Option

| Field | Description |
|---|---|
| Option Type | Type of option. It is an 8-bit unsigned integer. The value of the IPv6 intent option type is to be allocated by the IANA. |
| Option Data Length | Length of the intent ID. The value is 4 bytes. |
| Intent | Intent ID with a length of 32 bits |

- Destination Options Header (DOH): When this type of header is used, only the destination node on a path can read the intent information carried in data packets.

## 8.5 STORIES BEHIND NETWORK SLICING

### 8.5.1 Evolution of Inter-Domain Network Technologies

The development of IP technologies has always had a particular focus on inter-domain networks—after all, IP itself was first designed for interconnection between different networks. Due to the prevalence of Multiprotocol Label Switching (MPLS), networks running protocols such as Asynchronous Transfer Mode (ATM), Frame Relay (FR), and Time Division Multiplexing (TDM) are gradually becoming IP-based. However, while MPLS has achieved great success, it introduces complexity for inter-domain connections, negatively impacting E2E service deployment.

MPLS-based inter-domain connections can be provided with inter-AS VPN technologies such as Option A, Option B, and Option C.[4] While Option A and Option B are widely used, their VPN service deployment is complex. They also require edge VPN routes to be advertised to ASBRs, increasing the workload that ASBRs need to handle. Conversely, Option C simplifies VPN service deployment because VPN is only deployed on the edge routers, and VPN routes are only advertised between these edge routers without involving ASBRs, requiring connections to be set up between only these edge routers. The key technology involved in Option C — namely, BGP-Labeled Unicast (BGP-LU)[13] — distributes labels for BGP public network unicast routes. Option C is also the basis for developing the seamless MPLS network architecture,[14] which uses BGP to distribute labels for public network unicast routes between IGP areas for establishing E2E inter-domain LSPs. Although inter-AS VPN Option C simplifies VPN service deployment, using BGP to distribute labels for segment-by-segment stitching within and between ASs is still complex.

As SR gained popularity, BGP Prefix Segment[15]—similar to BGP-LU—was developed to allocate segments to inter-domain routes. Further developments were made in terms of BGP, with BGP Egress Peer Engineering (EPE)[16] emerging to support inter-domain route selection. It allows different types of segments (e.g., segments for an inter-domain link, a peer ASBR, and a set of peer ASBRs) to be generated between domains in order to steer traffic. By using these segments, the ingress can program and generate E2E inter-domain paths. Unlike BGP-LU, BGP EPE does not need to maintain the state of each LSP or stitch LSPs segment by segment.

In contrast to SR-MPLS, SRv6 can directly use IPv6 route reachability to achieve inter-domain connections, meaning it does not require additional control signaling to distribute labels for inter-domain reachability. It also enables the aggregation of inter-domain routes, thereby reducing the number of forwarding entries and consequently improving network scalability. Because SRv6 SIDs are routable across the network, which the SR-MPLS SIDs lack, this difference must be considered in protocol design. A prime example of this difference can be seen in inter-domain scenarios. Because SRv6 drastically simplifies inter-domain connections, improves inter-domain network connection scalability, and facilitates E2E service deployment, it has become the go-to option for many carriers.

Traditionally, BGP can establish only one E2E inter-domain path for a specific prefix. However, if carriers want to provide differentiated inter-domain connection services, they need to establish different inter-domain paths to the same destination. The ability to do so signals a notable improvement for inter-domain technologies. To date, this requirement can be met in two ways: one is to use BGP in the control plane to distribute a different segment[9,10] for each <prefix, color> pair and match different intra-domain tunnels against the color and BGP next hop, resulting in multiple E2E paths becoming available; the other is to use the intent-based routing mechanism[11]—described earlier in this chapter—to establish an intra-domain SR Policy group for a specific route. In this group, SR Policies can be matched according to the mapping between the intent ID and color.

## 8.5.2 Intent-Based Routing and APN

By matching the 5-tuple information (source IP address, destination IP address, protocol number, source port number, and destination port number) in packets, services can be mapped to the intent-compliant SR Policies or network slices. But after packets are mapped to an SR Policy at the border of a network domain and encapsulated with an outer SRH, the 5-tuple information they contain is no longer visible. If further mapping is required (e.g., in inter-domain scenarios), a network service policy that steers traffic to SR Policies or network slices cannot be enforced based on the 5-tuple information of packets without involving deep parsing of the inner packet header, giving rise to network security and forwarding performance problems.

Back in early 2019, we proposed Application-aware Networking (APN),[17] which can be used to solve the preceding problems. APN enables applications or network edge devices to encapsulate application-related information (APN attributes) into packets and advertise the information throughout the network, making it possible to provide finer-grained, differentiated network services. Similar to IPv6 network slicing, APN can also use the IPv6 extension header to carry APN attributes.[18]

Specifically, APN maps the 5-tuple of original packets to APN attributes (including the APN ID and related parameters) and encapsulates these attributes into the outer tunnel header. In this way, the nodes along the tunnel can continue to enforce the network service policy (e.g., steering traffic to an SR Policy or network slice) according to the APN attributes.

Because the intent ID carried in packets can represent a set of service requirement parameters associated with an application group or user group, intent-based routing in this chapter can be considered a simplified implementation of APN. A network edge node can perform intent ID mapping by using information such as the 5-tuple, or it can establish the mapping between a destination address and intent ID according to the color attribute carried in the service route and the mapping between the color and intent ID. The latter can be considered a simplified implementation of the former. Note that the intent ID does not reflect application- or user-level differences—if network service policies need to be enforced based on the intent of an application group or user group, more APN attributes are required.

## REFERENCES

[1] Geng X, Contreras L, Dong J, et al. IETF Network Slice Application in 5G End-to-End Network Slice [EB/OL]. (2022-10-24)[2022-10-30]. draft-gcdrb-teas-5g-network-slice-application-01.

[2] 3 GPP. System architecture for the 5G System (5GS) [EB/OL]. (2022-03-23) [2022-09-30]. 3GPP TS 23.501.

[3] Li Z, Dong J. Framework for End-to-End IETF Network Slicing [EB/OL]. (2022-09-08)[2022-09-30]. draft-li-teas-e2e-ietf-network-slicing-02.

[4] Rosen E, Rekhter Y. BGP/MPLS IP Virtual Private Networks (VPNs) [EB/OL]. (2006-02)[2022-09-30]. RFC 4364.

[5] Li Z, Dong J. Encapsulation of End-to-End IETF Network Slice Information in IPv6 [EB/OL]. (2021-10-16)[2022-09-30]. draft-li-6man-e2e-ietf-network-slicing-00.

[6] Li Z, Dong J, Pang R, et al. Segment Routing for End-to-End IETF Network Slicing [EB/OL]. (2022-10-24)[2022-10-30]. draft-li-spring-sr-e2e-ietf-network-slicing-05.

[7] Filsfils C, Camarillo P, Li Z, et al. Segment Routing over IPv6 (SRv6) Network Programming [EB/OL]. (2021-02)[2022-09-30]. RFC 8986.

[8] Hegde S, Rao D, Sangli SR, et al. Problem Statement for Inter-Domain Intent-Aware Routing Using Color [EB/OL]. (2022-07-15)[2022-09-30]. draft-hr-spring-intentaware-routing-using-color-00.

[9] Vairavakkalai K, Venkataraman N. BGP Classful Transport Planes [EB/OL]. (2022-09-06)[2022-09-30]. draft-ietf-idr-bgp-ct-00.

[10] Rao D, Agrawa S. BGP Color-Aware Routing (CAR) [EB/OL]. (2022-09-06) [2022-09-30]. draft-ietf-idr-bgp-car-05.

[11] Li Z, Hu Z, Dong J. Intent-based Routing [EB/OL]. (2022-09-06)[2022-09-30]. draft-li-apn-intent-based-routing-00.

[12] Filsfils C, Talaulikar K, Voyer D. Segment Routing Policy Architecture [EB/OL]. (2022-07-24)[2022-09-30]. RFC 9256.

[13] Rosen E. Using BGP to Bind MPLS Labels to Address Prefixes [EB/OL]. (2017-10)[2022-09-30]. RFC 8277.

[14] Leymann N, Decraene B, Filsfils C, et al. Seamless MPLS Architecture [EB/OL]. (2014-06-28)[2022-09-30]. draft-ietf-mpls-seamless-mpls-07.

[15] Filsfils C, Previdi S, Lindem A, et al. Segment Routing Prefix Segment Identifier Extensions for BGP [EB/OL]. (2019-12)[2022-09-30]. RFC 8669.

[16] Filsfils C, Previdi S, Talaulikar K, Filsfils C, Dawra G, et al. Border Gateway Protocol – Link State (BGP-LS) Extensions for Segment Routing BGP Egress Peer Engineering[EB/OL]. (2021-08)[2022-09-30]. RFC 9086.

[17] Li Z, Peng S, et al. Application-Aware Networking (APN) Framework [EB/OL]. (2022-09-30)[2022-10-30]. draft-li-apn-framework-06.

[18] Li Z, Peng S, Xie C. Application-Aware IPv6 Networking (APN6) Encapsulation [EB/OL]. (2022-12-09)[2022-12-30]. draft-li-apn-ipv6-encap-06.

# CHAPTER 9

# IPv6 Network Slicing Deployment

THIS CHAPTER FOCUSES ON the deployment of IPv6 network slicing. It starts by introducing the network slicing solutions designed for smart healthcare, smart government, smart port, smart grid, and smart enterprise scenarios. Next, it describes how to configure resource partitioning in network slicing solutions and how to deploy such solutions based on Segment Routing over IPv6 (SRv6) Segment Identifiers (SIDs) and slice IDs. Then, it explains how to deploy single-layer slicing, hierarchical slicing, and inter-domain slicing solutions using controllers.

## 9.1 DESIGN OF IPV6 NETWORK SLICING SOLUTIONS

Network slicing enables carriers to provide customized services and meet the differentiated SLA requirements of various network services in the 5G and cloud era, thereby facilitating the digital transformation of industries and enterprises. The following sections introduce the network slicing solutions designed for five different scenarios: smart healthcare, smart government, smart port, smart grid, and smart enterprise.

### 9.1.1 Smart Healthcare

#### 9.1.1.1 Requirement Introduction

Smart healthcare — a healthcare service system — uses network technologies to provide a full range of health-related services, from illness

DOI: 10.1201/9781032699868-11

prevention, consultation, and diagnosis all the way through to treatment and rehabilitation. As such, high-speed broadband networks and site-to-site private lines that cover both urban and rural healthcare organizations are crucial in enabling smart healthcare.

In order for all levels of hospitals in both urban and rural areas to cloudify and interconnect their services and to implement telemedicine anytime and anywhere, the healthcare private network needs to provide the following capabilities:

- Any-to-any connection: City-level hospitals serving as healthcare centers need to establish hub-spoke interconnections with county-level hospitals. This is necessary for quickly establishing service channels between any two healthcare organizations.

- High bandwidth: Healthcare organizations at the village-level, township-level, and county-level and higher need bandwidths of up to 300 Mbit/s, 500 Mbit/s, and 1 Gbit/s, respectively.

- Ultra-low delay: The service delay of core healthcare systems — such as the Picture Archiving and Communication System and Hospital Information System — migrated to the cloud needs to be lower than 20 ms and remain stable so that the service experience is the same as that provided by local service systems.

### 9.1.1.2 Smart Healthcare Based on Network Slicing

The healthcare cloud network — a slice-based private network solution for healthcare — enables one-network for multi-purpose use, as shown in Figure 9.1.

The network slicing-based smart healthcare solution has the following characteristics:

- Network slicing for hard isolation: Because the resources of different network slices are independent of each other, the SLAs of services — such as bandwidth-hungry Picture Archiving and Communication System (PACS) services and delay-sensitive Hospital Information System (HIS) services — in the healthcare slice can be guaranteed even if other slices are congested.

- Fast provisioning and agile O&M: The Network Slice Controller (NSC) provides E2E lifecycle management of network slices and allows slices and service SLAs to be visualized and controlled.

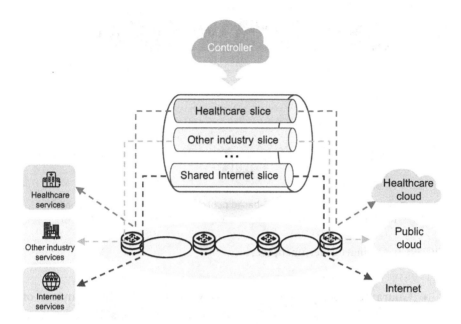

FIGURE 9.1   Slice-based smart healthcare private network.

- One network for multiple purposes: One healthcare private network slice can be further sliced to provide multiple hierarchical sub-slices, enabling one network to be used for multiple purposes and thereby achieving a high Return on Investment.

## 9.1.2  Smart Government

### 9.1.2.1  Requirement Introduction

5G networks play a major role in enabling smart government services such as emergency rescue and video security, as shown in Figure 9.2. Through multi-dimensional patrol covering both ground and air within a given jurisdiction, smart government improves emergency rescue and government working efficiency.

To provide smart government services, networks need to provide the following capabilities:

- Security isolation: Transmission of video security data has high security requirements and must be fully isolated from public data.

- High bandwidth: Emergency rescue, public service booths, and video security use 4K High Definition (HD) cameras and need real-time transmission, requiring per-channel uplink bandwidth of 20–40 Mbit/s.

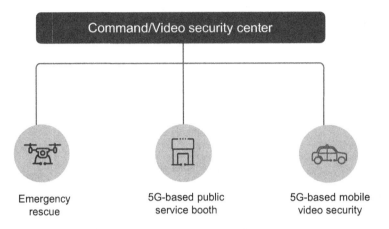

FIGURE 9.2    Smart government services.

- Guaranteed delay: In hotspot areas where there is a huge amount of 2C user traffic, the delay of government services must be guaranteed through E2E resource reservation.

### 9.1.2.2 Smart Government Based on Network Slicing

E2E network slicing can provide a smart government private network capable of isolating government services from public user services, as shown in Figure 9.3.

The network slicing-based smart government solution has the following characteristics:

- High security and reliability: An independent E2E government service slice is deployed to isolate government services from public services and ensure the security of government data. In this slice, Radio Bearer (RB) or Allocation and Retention Priority (ARP) is employed on the Radio Access Network (RAN) to reserve radio resources, FlexE is employed on the IP Transport Network (TN) to reserve transport resources, and standalone UPFs are deployed on the Core Network (CN).

- High bandwidth: To meet the upstream bandwidth requirements of video services and enable real-time uploading of multi-channel HD video streams, 10 Gbit/s, 50 Gbit/s, and 100 Gbit/s bandwidths are provided for the access layer, aggregation layer, and core layer, respectively.

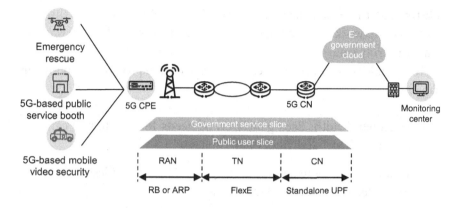

FIGURE 9.3   Slice-based smart government private network.

- E2E network slicing: E2E network slices are deployed across the RAN, TN, and CN. VLAN IDs are used on the RAN and CN to differentiate network slices, and a separate VLAN sub-interface is used on the TN to identify the government service slice.

- Guaranteed delay: FlexE is deployed to provide hard isolation between slices and guarantee deterministic delay for government services.

- Visualized network slice SLAs: In-situ Flow Information Telemetry (IFIT) is deployed to visualize the SLAs of network slice services, enabling network faults to be quickly located.

### 9.1.3  Smart Port

*9.1.3.1 Requirement Introduction*

Ports involve a lot of heavy machinery and operate predominantly in large outdoor yards that are covered by containers, cranes, and container trucks. Gantry cranes are used for hoisting containers to specified locations and are traditionally connected to a central control room through optical fibers or Wi-Fi for remote control. However, these connection methods have problems such as high optical fiber costs, limited Wi-Fi coverage, difficulty in isolating the production network, and high labor costs.

The advent of 5G has made it necessary to make ports smart. To achieve this, it is necessary to equip gantry cranes with multiple HD cameras that stream HD video feeds to the control room. Workers can then view the site through these video feeds and remotely control gantry cranes through low-delay network connections. This represents a major leap forward in realizing truly smart ports, accelerating their construction.

To provide smart port services, networks need to provide the following capabilities:

- High bandwidth: Each gantry crane needs 18 HD (1080p) cameras and an uplink bandwidth of 30 Mbit/s.

- Low delay: Remote control requires an E2E delay of less than 18 ms and a delay of less than 3 ms on the TN.

- High availability: The availability must reach 99.999%, which is equivalent to less than one outage per month.

### 9.1.3.2 Smart Port Based on Network Slicing

As shown in Figure 9.4, remote control and video security have different network requirements, which can be met by respectively deploying

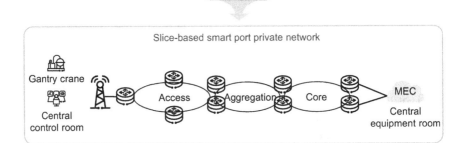

FIGURE 9.4   Slice-based smart port private network.

a low-delay slice and a high-bandwidth slice through the network slice management system. This provides differentiated E2E SLA guarantees, effectively meeting the remote operation requirements of gantry cranes.

The network slicing-based smart port solution has the following characteristics:

- Low delay: A low-delay network slice is deployed based on FlexE to carry control services. This provides hard isolation and meets ultra-low delay requirements.

- High bandwidth: A high-bandwidth network slice is deployed to carry video services, meeting uplink bandwidth requirements without affecting control services.

- High reliability: Fast Reroute (FRR) is used in slices to switch service traffic within 50 ms in the case of a fault.

- Visualized network slice SLAs: IFIT is deployed to visualize the SLAs of network slice services, enabling network faults to be located within minutes.

By adopting remote control and video security, smart ports can slash labor costs by 75% and enable unattended operation of gantry cranes, reducing the risk of accidents.

### 9.1.4 Smart Grid

#### *9.1.4.1 Requirement Introduction*

To achieve targets related to reliability, safety, costs, efficiency, and carbon neutrality, smart grids — built on communications networks — use sensing and measurement technologies, device technologies, control methods, and decision-making support systems.

Smart grids involve control and collection services, which are described in the following table (Table 9.1).

To provide smart grid services, networks need to provide the following capabilities:

- Ultra-low delay: Intelligent decentralized power distribution and power load demand response services require precise control and millisecond-level response.

TABLE 9.1    Smart Grid Service Scenarios

| Service Type | Typical Scenario | Scenario Description |
|---|---|---|
| Control | Intelligent decentralized power distribution | Implements protection and control of the power distribution network. Automatic relay protection devices are used to monitor the status of lines and devices on the power distribution network so that related faults can be rapidly and accurately located and isolated without affecting power supply in fault-free areas. This scenario requires ultra-low delay and high reliability. |
| | Power load demand response | Adjusts the power load as necessary to meet demand and ensure stability of the power grid. This scenario requires ultra-low delay and high reliability. |
| | Distributed energy control | Controls the utilization of various energy resources, including solar, wind, fuel cell, and Combined Cooling, Heating, and Power (CCHP) resources. Such resources are distributed across user/load sites and adjacent sites in scattered locations. This scenario requires massive connections and real-time statistics collection. |
| Collection | Advanced metering | Collects power consumption information from smart meters to enable smart power consumption and personalized customer service. In this scenario, a large amount of data is frequently collected, requiring massive connections and real-time statistics collection. |
| | Big video applications | Transmits real-time videos and images, covering substation inspection robots, drone patrol for power transmission lines, comprehensive video security for power distribution rooms, and mobile management and control for onsite construction activities. This scenario requires high communication bandwidth. |

- Massive connections: The power distribution network spans a wide area and involves large numbers of smart meters and distributed energy resources, requiring massive connections.

- High bandwidth: Monitoring and inspection services require high bandwidth.

- High availability: Video services require 99.9% availability, and control services require 99.999% availability.

- Service isolation: Production services and management services require isolation.

### 9.1.4.2 Smart Grid Based on Network Slicing

Smart grid services have a wide range of communication and transmission requirements, which can be met by using different types of network slices. As shown in Figure 9.5, different types of network slices are deployed for different service scenarios.

- The Ultra-Reliable Low-Latency Communication (URLLC) slice mainly carries intelligent decentralized power distribution and power load demand response services.

- The Massive Machine-Type Communications (mMTC) slice mainly carries distributed energy control and advanced metering services.

- The Enhanced Mobile Broadband (eMBB) slice mainly carries big video applications, such as substation inspection robots and drone patrol for power transmission lines.

Multiple Network Slice Instances (NSIs) can be created for each type of slice as required. Power grid enterprises can be provided with differentiated network slice services to meet the requirements of their different power services.

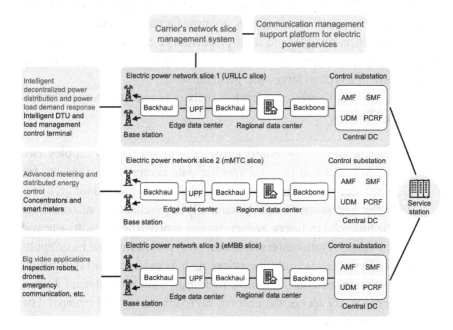

FIGURE 9.5   Slice-based smart grid private network.

The network slicing-based smart grid solution has the following characteristics:

- Deterministic guaranteed delay: MEC is deployed downwards on demand, and FlexE for resource partitioning is introduced on the IP network. The resulting benefit is that the IP network delay is less than 2 ms.

- Security isolation: The IP network uses FlexE to reserve resources — including both physical and logical resources — for services in different zones of the power grid, meeting different security isolation requirements for production and management power services.

- High reliability of services: Comprehensive protection mechanisms, such as FRR, are deployed in network slices to ensure the high-quality bearing of power grid services.

### 9.1.5 Smart Enterprise

#### 9.1.5.1 Requirement Introduction

As enterprise informatization deepens, the informatization infrastructure has a significant bearing on how efficiently enterprises can operate. Large enterprises, well aware of this, are now focusing strategic efforts on building a secure, reliable, and high-performance network infrastructure to support their intelligent informatization. Figure 9.6 shows the logical architecture of a typical large enterprise network.

To provide smart enterprise services, networks need to provide the following capabilities:

- Multi-site and multi-center: Large enterprises usually employ two data centers in one city and another data center in another city for disaster recovery, forming a highly reliable geo-redundant architecture. Enterprises that require extremely high reliability, such as those in the financial industry, are starting to evolve toward multi-site and multi-center. Data centers house an enterprise's internal basic application systems and public services such as external portal websites, involving numerous modules, including external Internet access, internal WAN access, data center interconnection, and internal data center network.

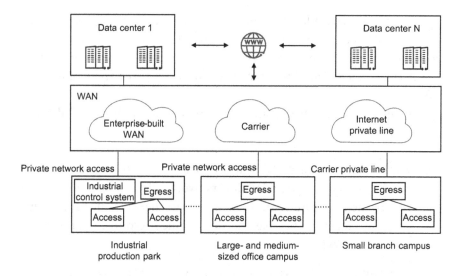

FIGURE 9.6    Logical architecture of a typical large enterprise network.

- Multi-branch flexible access: An enterprise's branches (including business units and subsidiaries) are dispersed across a wide geographical area, and their production and office campus networks vary in scale. Generally, enterprise branches are connected to both the enterprise private WAN and the Internet. Enterprises that impose strict security management on Internet access use a unified Internet gateway that is usually deployed in a data center for centralized security protection and access control.

- WAN service guarantee: Branch campuses of an enterprise need to access internal data center services through the WAN. As such, the WAN must provide an SLA guarantee for related key services.

### 9.1.5.2  Smart Enterprise Based on Network Slicing

By allocating network resources to different network slices, it is possible to meet the SLA requirements of different enterprise services, ensure service isolation, and provide an on-demand SLA guarantee for key enterprise services that have strict requirements on delay and jitter (e.g., video and production services). Each network slice can be regarded as an independent network, and different types of services can be steered into different slices for transport based on steering policies.

One or more network slices can be deployed for an enterprise to match its service characteristics. For example, all of the enterprise's services can be carried in one network slice, or each service can be carried in a separate network slice. Figure 9.7 shows how network slices are deployed for enterprise services.

The network slicing-based smart enterprise solution has the following characteristics:

- On-demand resource allocation: Shared or dedicated network resources can be provided for network slices based on service requirements. More than 1000 enterprise network slices are supported to meet the flexible and fine-grained resource requirements of various services.

- Deterministic latency: Dedicated network slice resources can be allocated based on the deterministic latency requirements of specific services to achieve committed delay.

- High reliability: Technologies such as FRR can be deployed in network slices to achieve high reliability.

- Intelligent slicing management: Network slicing management interfaces enable slice users to operate slices, streamlining the entire process from user intent identification to service provisioning. Slice planning and deployment, flexible slicing mapping, and service SLA visualization are supported to achieve optimal resource allocation and improve network utilization.

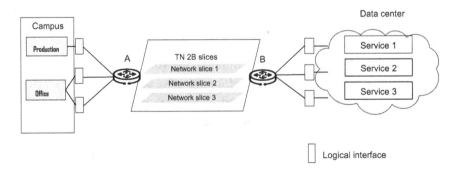

FIGURE 9.7    Slice-based smart enterprise private network.

## 9.2 RESOURCE PARTITIONING CONFIGURATION FOR IPV6 NETWORK SLICES

Fine-grained management of physical network resources is fundamental to IPv6 network slicing. It involves using multiple resource reservation technologies to properly plan resources based on enterprise application scenarios and service requirements, thereby enabling different services to be isolated and provided with guaranteed SLAs. The following uses the example of a physical network that uses 10 Gbit/s links at the access layer and 100 Gbit/s links at the aggregation layer and core layer. In order to meet the isolation and deterministic latency requirements of a service on this network, FlexE resource partitioning technology can be used to provide an E2E network slice with 1 Gbit/s bandwidth. In this slice, QoS technology can be used to provide differentiated scheduling for slice services with different priorities, maximizing the statistical multiplexing gain.

In addition to isolating microburst interference between different service flows and thereby ensuring the deterministic latency of flows with a constant rate, network slice resource reservation provides differentiated SLA capabilities for network administrators. In real-world applications, mapping between service requirements and resource allocation must be planned appropriately to strike a better balance between statistical multiplexing and the service SLA guarantee.

- Services that require isolation and deterministic latency require the allocation of dedicated network resources. For example, FlexE is preferred to provide exclusive resources for mission-critical services in vertical industries, such as differential protection services in the electric power industry.

- Large-burst services can be planned in a high-bandwidth network slice, in which service differentiation can also be achieved based on different QoS priorities.

During network deployment, different resource partitioning and reservation technologies — such as the FlexE interface, channelized sub-interface, and Flex-Channel — can be used flexibly based on different service requirements. Once such a technology is selected for use, corresponding resource partitioning needs to be configured on network devices. The following sections introduce several typical configuration methods.

## 9.2.1 FlexE Interface Configuration

FlexE technology uses the FlexE shim layer to partition the physical interface resources into a pool of timeslots. Through this pool, a high-bandwidth physical interface can be flexibly partitioned into several FlexE interfaces that each function like a physical interface with strictly isolated bandwidth resources. This makes it possible to manage interface resources in a flexible and fine-grained way. In terms of delay, because the interference between FlexE interfaces is negligible, the interfaces can provide a committed delay. As such, these interfaces are suitable for carrying URLLC services (e.g., differential protection services of power grids), which have strict requirements on the delay SLA.

When it comes to configuration, first set a sub-timeslot granularity for a FlexE subcard on a device. The minimum configurable sub-timeslot granularity is 1 Gbit/s, and the maximum is 5 Gbit/s (the default granularity). In addition, enable the FlexE mode on the interface. An example of the configuration is as follows:

```
<HUAWEI> system-view
[~HUAWEI] set flexe sub-time-slot granula slot 1 card
0 1G   //Set a sub-timeslot granularity for a FlexE
subcard.
[*HUAWEI] flexe enable port 1/0/1
[*HUAWEI] commit
```

To ensure that interconnected devices can communicate with each other through FlexE physical interfaces, configure the same PHY number for these interfaces. An example of the configuration is as follows:

```
<HUAWEI> system-view
[~HUAWEI] interface FlexE-50G 1/0/1
[~HUAWEI-FlexE-50G1/0/1] phy-number 5   //Configure a
PHY number for the FlexE physical interface.
[*HUAWEI-FlexE-50G1/0/1] commit
```

A FlexE physical interface must be bound to a FlexE group. As such, create a FlexE group and bind a FlexE physical interface to it. The bandwidth of a FlexE group is the total bandwidth of all FlexE physical interfaces bound to the group. To ensure that interconnected devices can communicate with each other, configure the same group number for the FlexE groups to which the interconnected FlexE physical interfaces are bound. An example of the configuration is as follows:

```
<HUAWEI> system-view
[~HUAWEI] flexe group 1
[*HUAWEI-flexe-group-1] binding interface FlexE-50G
1/0/1
[*HUAWEI-flexe-group-1] flexe-groupnum 1    //Configure
a group number for the FlexE group.
[*HUAWEI-flexe-group-1] commit
```

A FlexE interface functions the same as a physical Ethernet interface and can run network protocols. Each FlexE interface can flexibly obtain bandwidth from a FlexE group and supports bandwidth adjustment. A FlexE client instance needs to be created before a FlexE interface can be generated. In the system view, set **flexe-type** to **full-function (port-id** is optional). Then, in the FlexE client instance view, set a client ID and bandwidth value in Gbit/s. An example of the configuration is as follows:

```
<HUAWEI> system-view
[~HUAWEI] flexe client-instance 129 flexe-group 1
flexe-type full-function port-id 129
[*HUAWEI-flexe-client-129] flexe-clientid 129
[*HUAWEI-flexe-client-129] flexe-bandwidth 4
[*HUAWEI-flexe-client-129] commit
```

After the FlexE client instance is configured, a FlexE interface, FlexE 1/0/129, is generated. You can enter the FlexE interface view to configure the interface using the same command formats as those used for configuring a physical Ethernet interface.

```
<HUAWEI> system-view
[~HUAWEI] interface FlexE 1/0/129
[*HUAWEI-FlexE1/0/129] ipv6 enable
[*HUAWEI-FlexE1/0/129] commit
```

### 9.2.2 Channelized Sub-Interface Configuration

Channelized sub-interfaces, based on the HQoS mechanism, can be configured using the sub-interface configuration model for network slices to achieve flexible bandwidth allocation. After the configuration, each channelized sub-interface is allocated exclusive bandwidth and a dedicated scheduling tree to reserve resources for slice services. On each channelized sub-interface, additional differentiated scheduling can be performed based on packet priorities.

Channelized sub-interfaces are independent logical interfaces that reside on physical interfaces, making them ideal for creating logical networks. They are usually used to provide Multipoint-to-Multipoint (MP2MP) network slice services with guaranteed bandwidth. Using channelized sub-interfaces for slice resource reservation has the following characteristics:

- Resource isolation: Dedicated resources are reserved for network slices to prevent slice services from preempting resources when traffic bursts occur.

- Flexible bandwidth granularity: The minimum slice bandwidth can reach 10 Mbit/s with a granularity of 1 Mbit/s.

To configure a channelized sub-interface, create a sub-interface on an Ethernet main interface, set the encapsulation type of the sub-interface to Dot1q, and enable channelization. Then, configure the bandwidth (in Mbit/s) based on the slice requirement. An example of the configuration is as follows:

```
<HUAWEI> system-view
[~HUAWEI] interface GigabitEthernet0/1/7.1
[*HUAWEI-GigabitEthernet0/1/7.1] vlan-type dot1q 1
[*HUAWEI-GigabitEthernet0/1/7.1] mode channel enable
//Enable channelization for the sub-interface.
[*HUAWEI-GigabitEthernet0/1/7.1] mode channel
bandwidth 100 //Configure bandwidth for the
channelized sub-interface.
[*HUAWEI-GigabitEthernet0/1/7.1] commit
```

### 9.2.3 Flex-Channel Configuration

In a hierarchical network slicing solution, a level-1 network slice (also referred to as a main slice) can use FlexE interfaces or channelized sub-interfaces for resource partitioning, and a level-2 network slice (also referred to as a sub-slice) can use Flex-Channel for additional resource partitioning within the FlexE interfaces or channelized sub-interfaces of the level-1 network slice.

Flex-Channel enables interface resources to be reserved in a flexible and fine-grained manner without involving a sub-interface model. As such, it is easier to configure than a channelized sub-interface and better suited to scenarios where network slices need to be quickly created on demand.

Using Flex-Channel to partition slice resources has the following characteristics:

- On-demand slicing: Based on the network slicing requirements of services, an NSC delivers slices together with services to realize on-demand slicing.

- Massive flexible slices: Flex-Channel supports a minimum bandwidth granularity of 1 Mbit/s and thousands of network slices, meeting enterprises' requirements for network slice bandwidth and quantity.

The following is a configuration example where the main slice uses a FlexE interface and the sub-slices use Flex-Channel:

```
<HUAWEI> system-view
[~HUAWEI] interface FlexE1/0/129
[~HUAWEI-FlexE1/0/129] network-slice 101 data-plane
//101 indicates the main slice.
[*HUAWEI-FlexE1/0/129] network-slice 10001
flex-channel 800    //Reserve 800 Mbit/s bandwidth for
sub-slice 10001.
[*HUAWEI-FlexE1/0/129] network-slice 10002
flex-channel 500    //Reserve 500 Mbit/s bandwidth for
sub-slice 10002.
[*HUAWEI-FlexE1/0/129] commit
```

The following is a configuration example where the main slice uses a channelized sub-interface and the sub-slices use Flex-Channel:

```
<HUAWEI> system-view
[~HUAWEI] interface GigabitEthernet0/1/7.1
```

[*HUAWEI-GigabitEthernet0/1/7.1] **network-slice 102 data-plane**...//102 indicates the main slice.
[*HUAWEI-GigabitEthernet0/1/7.1] **network-slice 20001 flex-channel 800** //Reserve 800 Mbit/s bandwidth for sub-slice 20001.
[*HUAWEI-GigabitEthernet0/1/7.1] **network-slice 20002 flex-channel 500** //Reserve 500 Mbit/s bandwidth for sub-slice 20002.
[*HUAWEI-GigabitEthernet0/1/7.1] **commit**

## 9.3 DEPLOYMENT OF THE SRV6 SID-BASED NETWORK SLICING SOLUTION

### 9.3.1 Deployment with the Affinity Attribute Used in the Control Plane

#### 9.3.1.1 Solution Description

For the SRv6 SID-based network slicing solution with the affinity attribute used in the control plane, logical interfaces need to be created and assigned bandwidth resources for network slices. Furthermore, attributes — such as IP addresses and link administrative groups (colors) — need to be configured for the logical interfaces.[1] The NSC uses affinity and other attributes as constraints to compute explicit paths for SRv6 Policies in network resource slices and binds VPN instances of service slices to these SRv6 Policies. In this way, traffic of the service slices can be forwarded using reserved resources of the corresponding network resource slices. A default network slice usually needs to be created on the network to carry service traffic that is not assigned to a dedicated network slice. To prevent logical links of a non-default network slice from being selected for traffic of the default slice during path selection (thereby preventing the traffic from pre-empting bandwidth resources of the non-default slice), the metric of the logical links in the non-default network slice must be set to a value larger than that of the links in the default slice.

This solution has the following characteristics:

- Uses link colors as the control plane identifier of network slices, with each color corresponding to one network slice.

- Uses link colors to identify Layer 3 resource interfaces or sub-interfaces of different network slices.

- Uses the affinity attribute (in the control plane) as the constraint to compute SRv6 Policy explicit paths in each network slice for carrying the service traffic of that network slice.

- Uses SRv6 SRHs (in the data plane) to encapsulate the SID lists of SRv6 Policies in the network slices for hop-by-hop service packet forwarding. In this way, packets are forwarded by the corresponding interfaces of the network slices, guaranteeing service SLAs.

This solution takes advantage of the technically mature affinity attribute to ensure that service packets are forwarded based on the topologies and resources of network slices, thereby guaranteeing the SLAs of slice services. In this solution, an IP address needs to be configured and IGP needs to be enabled for the resource interfaces or sub-interfaces of each network slice so that the control plane can distribute and report the topology and link attribute information of each network slice to the NSC for path calculation. Consequently, this solution does not support a large number of network slices, typically no more than 10.

### 9.3.1.2 Network Slicing Solution Deployment Example

Figure 9.8 shows an example for deploying the SRv6 SID-based network slicing solution with the affinity attribute used in the control plane.

In this example,

- Network slice resources are partitioned using different FlexE interfaces. The default network slice uses FlexE 1/0/129, network slice 1 uses FlexE 1/0/130, and network slice 2 uses FlexE 1/0/131. IP addresses are configured, and IGP is enabled for the network slice interfaces. See Figure 9.8 for the interface IP address plan. The access and aggregation layers use IGP to ensure route reachability throughout the network.

- Different link administrative group (color) attributes are configured for the FlexE interfaces of the non-default network slices. Specifically, green is configured for the FlexE interface of network slice 1, and blue is configured for the FlexE interface of network slice 2.

- To prevent BE (shortest path-based) traffic in the default network slice from being forwarded using the links of other network slices,

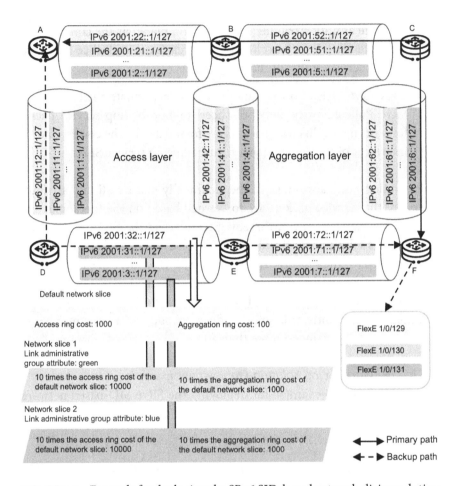

FIGURE 9.8 Example for deploying the SRv6 SID-based network slicing solution with the affinity attribute used in the control plane.

the IGP cost of the links in the non-default network slices is set to 10 times that of the links in the default network slice (see Figure 9.8 for the costs). This ensures that network devices always select the links of the default network slice for BE traffic forwarding when calculating the shortest path.

- SRv6 and SRv6 locators are configured on network devices. In the SRv6 SID-based network slicing solution with the affinity attribute used in the control plane, all network slices use the same locator on each device. Each device automatically generates an End.X SID for each IS-IS IPv6-enabled interface or sub-interface.

The link attribute information — including the End.X SID, delay, TE metric, and link administrative group (color) — in the IGP domain is reported to the NSC through BGP-LS. The NSC generates network slice topologies with different link color attributes based on the affinity attributes of the network slices and computes explicit paths for SRv6 Policies in these topologies. In addition, it instructs the headends of the SRv6 Policies in these network slices to associate these Policies with specific color attributes of VPN services. In this way, the explicit paths of these SRv6 Policies are used to forward service packets with specific SLA requirements. In order to ensure that a network slice provides a hop-by-hop SLA guarantee for services, the SRv6 Policy in the network slice supports only the strict explicit path. The SRv6 BE path in the default network slice can be used as the protection path for service packets in other network slices.

### 9.3.1.3 Network Slicing Solution Deployment — Topology Creation and Link Addition

In the SRv6 SID-based network slicing solution with the affinity attribute used in the control plane, IPv6 addresses and IGP need to be configured for resource interfaces of network slices. An example of the configuration is as follows:

```
<HUAWEI> system-view
[~HUAWEI] interface FlexE1/0/129
[~HUAWEI-FlexE1/0/129] ipv6 enable
[*HUAWEI-FlexE1/0/129] ipv6 address 2001:6::1 127
[*HUAWEI-FlexE1/0/129] isis ipv6 enable 1
[*HUAWEI-FlexE1/0/129] isis circuit-type p2p
[*HUAWEI-FlexE1/0/129] isis ipv6 cost 100
[*HUAWEI-FlexE1/0/129] commit
[~HUAWEI-FlexE1/0/129] quit
[~HUAWEI] interface FlexE1/0/130
[~HUAWEI-FlexE1/0/130] ipv6 enable
[*HUAWEI-FlexE1/0/130] ipv6 address 2001:61::1 127
[*HUAWEI-FlexE1/0/130] isis ipv6 enable 1
[*HUAWEI-FlexE1/0/130] isis circuit-type p2p
[*HUAWEI-FlexE1/0/130] isis ipv6 cost 1000
[*HUAWEI-FlexE1/0/130] commit
[~HUAWEI-FlexE1/0/130] quit
[~HUAWEI] interface FlexE1/0/131
[~HUAWEI-FlexE1/0/131] ipv6 enable
```

```
[*HUAWEI-FlexE1/0/131] ipv6 address 2001:62::1 127
[*HUAWEI-FlexE1/0/131] isis ipv6 enable 1
[*HUAWEI-FlexE1/0/131] isis circuit-type p2p
[*HUAWEI-FlexE1/0/131] isis ipv6 cost 1000
[*HUAWEI-FlexE1/0/131] commit
```

Once the preceding configuration is complete, the link administrative group (color) attribute needs to be set for the resource interfaces of network slices. This attribute is a 32-bit bit mask, in which each bit represents a different link color. In this way, different colors can be configured for interfaces by setting different values for the bits in the link administrative group. An example of the configuration is as follows:

```
<HUAWEI> system-view
[~HUAWEI] interface FlexE1/0/130
[~HUAWEI-FlexE1/0/130] te link administrative
group 80000000   //Set bit 0 of the link
administrative group attribute to 1 for the interface,
representing the link color green.
[*HUAWEI-FlexE1/0/130] commit
[~HUAWEI-FlexE1/0/130] quit
[~HUAWEI] interface FlexE1/0/131
[~HUAWEI-FlexE1/0/131]  te link administrative
group 40000000 // Set bit 1 of the link administrative
group attribute to 1 for the interface, representing
the link color blue.
[*HUAWEI-FlexE1/0/131] commit
```

When network slices share link resources, the bit mask values of the link administrative group attribute corresponding to the network slices need to be configured for interfaces or sub-interfaces. For example, in the case of two network slices — whose affinity attributes are respectively green and blue — sharing a link, both bits 0 and 1 of the link administrative group attribute need to be set to 1. In other words, the value of the link administrative group attribute is 0xC0000000.

*9.3.1.4 Network Slicing Solution Deployment — SRv6 Configuration*
In the SRv6 SID-based network slicing solution, with the affinity attribute used in the control plane, SRv6 is used in the data plane. SRv6 path

programmability allows service packets to be forwarded along the explicit path of a specific network slice using the reserved resources of the network slice.

After SRv6 is enabled, a source address (used for outer IPv6 header encapsulation) and an SRv6 locator need to be specified. In this solution, all slices share one locator. The locator configuration includes specifying an IPv6 prefix, length reserved for the Function part of static SIDs, and length of the Args part. An example of the configuration is as follows:

```
[~HUAWEI] segment-routing ipv6
[*HUAWEI-segment-routing-ipv6] encapsulation
source-address 1::6
[*HUAWEI-segment-routing-ipv6] locator SRv6_locator
ipv6-prefix A6:: 64 static 8 args 16
[*HUAWEI-segment-routing-ipv6] commit
```

In this example, the encapsulated source address in the IPv6 header is **1::6**, the locator name is **SRv6_locator**, the corresponding IPv6 prefix is **A6::/64**, **static 8** indicates that 8 bits are reserved for the Function part of static SIDs, and **args 16** indicates that 16 bits are reserved for the Args part.

After the configuration is complete, the following command can be run to check the SRv6 locator information:

```
[~HUAWEI] display segment-routing ipv6 locator verbose
            Locator Configuration Table
            - - - - - - - - - - - - - - - - - - - - - - - - - -
LocatorName   : SRv6_locator        LocatorID    : 1
IPv6Prefix    : A6::                 PrefixLength : 64
StaticLength  : 8                    Reference    : 4
Default       : N                    ArgsLength   : 16
AutoSIDBegin  : A6::1:0
AutoSIDEnd    : A6::FFFF:FFFF:FFFF:0
Total Locator(s) : 1
```

The command output shows the configured locator name, IPv6 prefix, length reserved for the Function part of static SIDs, and start and end of dynamic SIDs.

After an SRv6 locator is configured on a device, the device dynamically allocates an End SID, which is shared by all network slices. The following command can be run to check the End SID of the device:

```
<HUAWEI> display segment-routing ipv6 local-sid end
forwarding
            My Local-SID End Forwarding Table
        ---------------------------------
SID          : A6::1:0/128           FuncType    : End
Flavor       : PSP
LocatorName : SRv6_locator           LocatorID   : 1
ProtocolType: ISIS                   ProcessID   : 1
UpdateTime   : 2022-02-26 10:42:24.216
Total SID(s): 1
```

The device also allocates dynamic End.X SIDs to IGP-enabled interfaces or sub-interfaces. The following command can be run to check the End.X SIDs of links on the device:

```
[~HUAWEI] display segment-routing ipv6 local-sid end-x
forwarding
            My Local-SID End.X Forwarding Table
        ---------------------------------
SID          : A6::61:0/128 FuncType    : End.X
Flavor       : PSP
LocatorName : SRv6_locator LocatorID   : 1
ProtocolType: ISIS         ProcessID   : 1
UpdateTime   : 2022-02-26 10:42:24.217
NextHop      :              Interface :     ExitIndex
FE80::3AD5:E4FF:FE21:100    FlexE1/0/129    0x00000001
SID          : A6::62:0/128 FuncType    : End.X
Flavor       : PSP
LocatorName : SRv6_locator LocatorID   : 1
ProtocolType: ISIS         ProcessID   : 1
UpdateTime   : 2022-02-26 10:42:24.217
NextHop      :              Interface :     ExitIndex
FE80::3AD5:E4FF:FE21:200    FlexE1/0/130    0x00000002
SID          : A6::63:0/128 FuncType    : End.X
Flavor       : PSP
LocatorName : SRv6_locator LocatorID   : 1
ProtocolType: ISIS         ProcessID   : 1
```

```
UpdateTime  : 2022-02-26 10:42:24.217
NextHop     :                Interface :    ExitIndex
FE80::3AD5:E4FF:FE21:300     FlexE1/0/131   0x00000003
Total SID(s): 3
```

### 9.3.1.5 Network Slicing Solution Deployment — Network Slicing Path Establishment

The link administrative group (color) attribute information of links in a network slice is reported to the NSC through BGP-LS. The NSC, after matching the affinity attribute of the network slice, selects the links that belong to the corresponding network slice in order to form a network slice topology. Based on the topology, the NSC can compute SRv6 Policy explicit paths — comprised of the End.X SIDs of hop-by-hop links in the network slice topology — that meet service requirements. This enables service packets to be forwarded along the SRv6 Policy explicit paths in this network slice.

As shown in Figure 9.8, the NSC computes SRv6 Policy paths from A to F for network slice 1. Table 9.2 shows the SRv6 Policy path information.

The following command can be run to check the status of the SRv6 Policies delivered by the NSC:

TABLE 9.2   SRv6 Policy Path Information from A to F Computed by the NSC for Network Slice 1

| Item | Details |
| --- | --- |
| Color | 100 |
| Endpoint | 1::6 |
| Candidate path and SID list | **Path preference: 110**<br>BSID: A1::1:0:100:0<br>SID list:<br>A1::1:0:11:0 (A End.X)<br>A2::1:0:21:0 (B End.X)<br>A3::1:0:31:0 (C End.X)<br>A6::1:0:1:0 (F End)<br>**Path preference: 100**<br>BSID: A1::1:0:100:0<br>SID list:<br>A1::1:0:12:0 (A End.X)<br>A4::1:0:42:0 (D End.X)<br>A5::1:0:52:0 (E End.X)<br>A6::1:0:1:0 (F End) |

```
<HUAWEI> display srv6-te policy endpoint 1::6 color
100
PolicyName : Policy1
Color : 100 Endpoint : 1::6
TunnelId : 1 Binding SID : A1::1:0:100:0
TunnelType : SRv6-TE Policy DelayTimerRemain : -
Policy State : Up State Change Time : 2022-02-21
09:39:52
Admin State : Up Traffic Statistics : Disable
Backup Hot-Standby : Disable BFD : Disable
Interface Index : 87 Interface Name : SRv6TE-Policy-1
Interface State : Up Encapsulation Mode : Encaps
Candidate-path Count : 2
Candidate-path Preference : 110
Path State : Active Path Type : Primary
Protocol-Origin : Configuration(30) Originator :
0, 0.0.0.0
Discriminator : 200 Binding SID : -
GroupId : 2 Policy Name : 1
Template ID : 0 Path Verification : Disable
DelayTimerRemain : - Network Slice ID : -
Segment-List Count : 1
Segment-List : 1
Segment-List ID : 2 XcIndex : 2
List State : Up DelayTimerRemain : -
Verification State : - SuppressTimeRemain : -
PMTU : 9600 Active PMTU : 9600
Weight : 1 BFD State : -
Network Slice ID : -
SID :
A1::1:0:11:0
A2::1:0:21:0
A3::1:0:31:0
A6::1:0:1:0
Candidate-path Preference : 100
Path State : Inactive (Valid) Path Type : -
Protocol-Origin : Configuration(30) Originator :
0, 0.0.0.0
Discriminator : 100 Binding SID : -
GroupId : 1 Policy Name : 1
Template ID : 0 Path Verification : Disable
```

```
DelayTimerRemain : - Network Slice ID : -
Segment-List Count : 1
Segment-List : 1
Segment-List ID : 1 XcIndex : -
List State : Down(Valid) DelayTimerRemain : -
Verification State : - SuppressTimeRemain : -
PMTU : 9600 Active PMTU : 9600
Weight : 1 BFD State : -
Network Slice ID : -
SID :
A1::1:0:12:0
A4::1:0:42:0
A5::1:0:52:0
A6::1:0:1:0
```

### 9.3.1.6 Network Slicing Solution Deployment — Mapping Service Slices to Resource Slices

In the SRv6 SID-based network slicing solution with the affinity attribute used in the control plane, the tunnel policy of using SRv6 Policies and the color attribute can be configured for VPN instances to associate the service slices of the VPN instances with the SRv6 Policies in resource slices. The NSC uses <Headend, Color, Endpoint> to uniquely identify an SRv6 Policy and delivers the computed SRv6 SID lists to the headend. A default color value can be configured for a VPN instance on the headend PE so that the VPN service can be associated with the corresponding SRv6 Policy based on the default color value. An example of the configuration is as follows:

```
//Configure the tunnel policy of using SRv6 Policies.
<HUAWEI> system-view
[~HUAWEI] tunnel-policy SRv6-policy
[*HUAWEI-tunnel-policy-SRv6-policy] tunnel select-seq
ipv6 srv6-te-policy load-balance-number 1
[*HUAWEI-tunnel-policy-SRv6-policy] commit
//Set the default color value to 100 for EVPN VPWS
services in an EVPN instance in VPWS mode.
<HUAWEI> system-view
[~HUAWEI] evpn vpn-instance evrf1 vpws
[*HUAWEI-vpws-evpn-instance-evrf1] tnl-policy
SRv6-policy  //Associate the VPN instance with the
tunnel policy.
```

```
[*HUAWEI-vpws-evpn-instance-evrf1] default-color 100
//Set the default color value to 100 for instance
evrf1.
[*HUAWEI-vpws-evpn-instance-evrf1] commit
//Set the default color value to 100 for EVPN L3VPN
services in the IPv4 address family of the VPN
instance.
<HUAWEI> system-view
[~HUAWEI] ip vpn-instance vrf1
[*HUAWEI-vpn-instance-vrf1] ipv4-family
[*HUAWEI-vpn-instance-vrf1-ipv4] tnl-policy
SRv6-policy evpn    //Associate the VPN instance with
the tunnel policy.
[*HUAWEI-vpn-instance-vrf1-ipv4] default-color 100
evpn   //Set the default color value to 100 for
instance vrf1.
[*HUAWEI-vpn-instance-vrf1-ipv4] commit
```

## 9.3.2 Deployment with IGP Flex-Algo Used in the Control Plane

### 9.3.2.1 Solution Description

IPv6 network slicing solutions can use the Flexible Algorithm (Flex-Algo) in the control plane[2] to provide distributed route calculation based on network slice topologies. Flex-Algo can define different topology constraints for path computation based on the link color attribute on a physical or logical network. Using the metric type (IGP cost, link delay, or TE metric) and route computation algorithm specified by Flex-Algo, distributed constraint-based routes can be computed. In the SRv6 SID-based network slicing solution with IGP Flex-Algo used in the control plane, each network slice corresponds to a Flex-Algo. This means that a network slice can be identified by a unique Flex-Algo ID in the control plane without needing to introduce a new control plane identifier. Flex-Algo delivers the following benefits:

- Supports SRv6 BE for path computation and forwarding. The forwarding paths can be computed according to not only the minimum IGP cost but also the minimum delay or TE metric, meeting different service requirements.

- Supports path computation with the link administrative group (color) attribute used as the constraint on the Layer 3 interfaces or sub-interfaces of network slices. If the color attribute is included in the constraints of the Flex-Algo used by a network slice, this slice's resource interfaces or sub-interfaces are included in the constrained topology of the Flex-Algo. As such, when Flex-Algo is used to compute a forwarding path, only the topology that contains the specific resource interfaces or sub-interfaces is involved. In this way, services that need to be forwarded using the shortest path in different network slices can exclusively use the resources reserved for these network slices, thereby achieving resource isolation between services.

- Supports the configuration of SRLG constraints to exclude risky links during the computation of protection paths, thereby improving service reliability.

Topologies used by Flex-Algo for path computation are classified into two types:

- Physical topology: Flex-Algo defines path computation constraints based on the physical topology. Specifically, colors corresponding to different Flex-Algos are configured on physical interfaces. When multiple Flex-Algos are configured on the same physical interface, network slices associated with different Flex-Algos share this interface's resources. This approach offers differentiated forwarding paths for services of different network slices but lacks resource isolation between network slices. As such, it is unable to provide an SLA guarantee.

- Logical topology: Each Flex-Algo uses a separate logical topology. To achieve this, colors corresponding to different Flex-Algos are configured on different FlexE interfaces or channelized sub-interfaces. Because the Flex-Algo associated with each network slice has a separate logical topology and exclusive interface resources, this approach provides better resource isolation and SLA guarantee for services in different network slices.

In the SRv6 SID-based network slicing solution with IGP Flex-Algo used in the control plane, both SRv6 BE and SRv6 Policy modes are supported for path computation. In SRv6 BE mode, a device can perform distributed path computation in a network slice topology based on the topology constraints of the associated Flex-Algo. In SRv6 Policy mode, an NSC can be deployed to compute SRv6 Policy explicit paths in a network slice topology based on the topology information reported by network devices through BGP-LS.

By using IGP Flex-Algo instead of the affinity attribute in the control plane, this solution offers the following advantages:

- Both SRv6 BE and SRv6 Policy modes are supported for path computation and traffic forwarding in network slices.

- Traffic of non-default network slices can be isolated from SRv6 BE traffic of the default network slice without needing to configure a larger cost for the network slice interfaces or sub-interfaces.

- If an SRv6 Policy in a network slice fails, the adopted SRv6 BE-based protection path is still in the same network slice.

*9.3.2.2 Network Slicing Solution Deployment Example*

Figure 9.9 shows an example for deploying the SRv6 SID-based network slicing solution with IGP Flex-Algo used in the control plane.

In this example,

- Network slice resources are partitioned using channelized sub-interfaces, whose bandwidth is allocated from the total bandwidth of a physical interface (the remaining bandwidth of the physical interface is used for the default network slice). As shown in Figure 9.9, the total bandwidth of the physical interface GE 1/0/0 is 10 Gbit/s. Network slices 1, 2, and 3 use channelized sub-interfaces GE 1/0/0.1 (assigned 3 Gbit/s bandwidth), GE 1/0/0.2 (assigned 2 Gbit/s bandwidth), and GE 1/0/0.3 (assigned 500 Mbit/s bandwidth), respectively. The remaining bandwidth of the default network slice is 4.5 Gbit/s (10 Gbit/s – 3 Gbit/s – 2 Gbit/s – 500 Mbit/s = 4.5 Gbit/s).

- IP addresses are configured, and IGP is enabled for the default network slice's physical interfaces and other network slices' channelized sub-interfaces. Using IGP enables the access and aggregation layers to achieve network-wide reachability. In addition, parameters including the link administrative group (color) attribute and metric are configured for the channelized sub-interfaces of the network slices.

- Flex-Algo Definitions (FADs) are provided for the three network slices, as listed in Table 9.3.

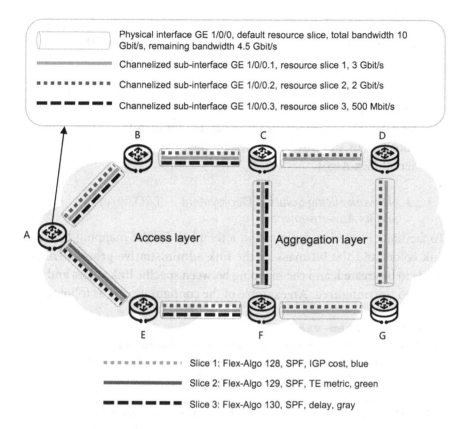

FIGURE 9.9 Example for deploying the network slicing solution with IGP Flex-Algo used in the control plane.

TABLE 9.3 FADs in the SRv6 SID-Based Network Slicing Solution with IGP Flex-Algo Used in the Control Plane

| Network Slice | Flex-Algo ID | Algorithm Type | Metric Type | Color | Topology Scope |
|---|---|---|---|---|---|
| 1 | 128 | SPF | IGP cost | Blue | Network-wide topology |
| 2 | 129 | SPF | TE metric | Green | Network-wide topology |
| 3 | 130 | SPF | Delay | Gray | Access-layer network topology |

- SRv6 and SRv6 locators are configured on network devices. In this network slicing solution, each network slice uses a separate locator. That is, locator_128, locator_129, and locator_130 need to be created for Flex-Algo 128 of network slice 1, Flex-Algo 129 of network slice 2, and Flex-Algo 130 of network slice 3, respectively. If some services are expected to run in the default network slice, locator_0 needs to be created for the default network slice. SRv6 locator information of different network slices can be advertised throughout the network using IGP.

- After SRv6 locators are configured, multiple End SIDs are dynamically assigned to each device based on locator prefixes, and multiple End.X SIDs are automatically generated for each IS-IS IPv6-enabled interface or sub-interface based on the SRv6 locator prefixes of different Flex-Algos.

### 9.3.2.3 Network Slicing Solution Deployment — FAD and Its Advertisement

To facilitate Flex-Algo deployment, a template for the mapping between link colors and the bit mask of the link administrative group attribute needs to be created, and the mapping between specific link colors and bits needs to be configured. An example of the configuration is as follows:

```
<HUAWEI> system-view
[~HUAWEI] path-constraint affinity-mapping
//Configure a template for the mapping between link
colors and the bit mask of the link administrative
group attribute.
[*HUAWEI-pc-af-map] attribute blue bit-sequence 5
//Configure the mapping between color blue and bit 5
of the link administrative group attribute.
[*HUAWEI-pc-af-map] attribute green bit-sequence 6
//Configure the mapping between color green and bit 6
of the link administrative group attribute.
[*HUAWEI-pc-af-map] attribute grey bit-sequence 7
//Configure the mapping between color gray and bit 7
of the link administrative group attribute.
[*HUAWEI-pc-af-map] commit
```

To deploy the SRv6 SID-based network slicing solution with IGP Flex-Algo used in the control plane, it is necessary to assign Flex-Algo IDs and specify the metric type, calculation type, and topology constraints of each Flex-Algo.

The following configuration example shows how to create three SRv6 SID-based network slices with IGP Flex-Algo used in the control plane:

```
<HUAWEI> system-view
[~HUAWEI] flex-algo identifier 128    //Set Flex-Algo
ID to 128.
[~HUAWEI-flex-algo-128] metric-type igp
//Configure Flex-Algo 128 to use the IGP cost for path
computation.
[*HUAWEI-flex-algo-128] affinity include-any blue
//Configure Flex-Algo 128 to include all links whose
color is blue when it computes a path.
[*HUAWEI-flex-algo-128] commit
[~HUAWEI-flex-algo-128] quit
[~HUAWEI] flex-algo identifier 129    //Set Flex-Algo
ID to 129.
[~HUAWEI-flex-algo-129] metric-type te    //Configure
Flex-Algo 129 to use TE metric for path computation.
[*HUAWEI-flex-algo-129] affinity include-any green
//Configure Flex-Algo 129 to include all links whose
color is green when it computes a path.
[*HUAWEI-flex-algo-129] commit
[~HUAWEI-flex-algo-129] quit
[~HUAWEI] flex-algo identifier 130    //Set Flex-Algo
ID to 130.
[~HUAWEI-flex-algo-130] metric-type delay    //
Configure Flex-Algo 130 to use delay for path
computation.
[*HUAWEI-flex-algo-130] affinity include-any grey    //
Configure Flex-Algo 130 to include all links whose
color is gray when it computes a path.
[*HUAWEI-flex-algo-130] commit
[~HUAWEI-flex-algo-130] quit
```

IGP needs to be enabled to advertise Flex-Algos. The following uses IS-IS as an example:

```
<HUAWEI> system-view
[~HUAWEI] isis 1
[*HUAWEI-isis-1] flex-algo 128    //Enable IS-IS to
advertise Flex-Algo 128.
[*HUAWEI-isis-1] flex-algo 129    //Enable IS-IS to
advertise Flex-Algo 129.
```

```
[*HUAWEI-isis-1] flex-algo 130    //Enable IS-IS to
advertise Flex-Algo 130.
[*HUAWEI-isis-1] ipv6 traffic-eng    //Enable TE for
IS-IS.
[*HUAWEI-isis-1] ipv6 metric-delay advertisement
enable    //Enable IS-IS to advertise IPv6 link delay.
[*HUAWEI-isis-1] commit
```

### 9.3.2.4 Network Slicing Solution Deployment — Topology Creation and Link Addition

According to the preceding deployment example, independent channelized sub-interfaces need to be created for the network slices, and link attributes used by Flex-Algos — such as the link administrative group (color) attribute, TE metric, and link delay — need to be configured for these channelized sub-interfaces.

• Link administrative group (color) attribute: This attribute needs to be configured on channelized sub-interfaces for the corresponding network slices. In Figure 9.9, the color attributes blue, green, and gray are configured for the channelized sub-interfaces of network slices 1, 2, and 3, respectively.

• TE metric: In this deployment example, a TE metric value needs to be configured on the channelized sub-interface of network slice 2 for path computation in Flex-Algo 129.

• Link delay: Generally, it is possible to obtain an accurate link delay by using a dynamic link delay measurement feature such as the Two-Way Active Measurement Protocol (TWAMP). With this feature, devices can dynamically update link states according to link delay changes. In scenarios where dynamic link delay measurement cannot be used, a static delay value needs to be configured for links. In this deployment example, a delay value needs to be configured on the channelized sub-interface of network slice 3.

Link attributes used by Flex-Algo need to be configured for the channelized sub-interfaces. An example of the configuration is as follows:

```
<HUAWEI> system-view
[~HUAWEI] interface GigabitEthernet 1/0/0.1
```

```
[~HUAWEI-GigabitEthernet1/0/0.1] te link-attribute-
application flex-algo
[*HUAWEI-GigabitEthernet1/0/0.1-te-link-attribute-
application] link administrative group name blue
//Set the link color to blue.
[*HUAWEI-GigabitEthernet1/0/0.1-te-link-attribute-
application] commit
[~HUAWEI-GigabitEthernet1/0/0.1-te-link-attribute-
application] quit
[~HUAWEI-GigabitEthernet1/0/0.1] quit
[~HUAWEI] interface GigabitEthernet 1/0/0.2
[~HUAWEI-GigabitEthernet1/0/0.2] te link-attribute-
application flex-algo
[*HUAWEI-GigabitEthernet1/0/0.2-te-link-attribute-
application] link administrative group name green
//Set the link color to green.
[*HUAWEI-GigabitEthernet1/0/0.2-te-link-attribute-
application] metric 200000    //Configure a TE metric
value for the link.
[*HUAWEI-GigabitEthernet1/0/0.2-te-link-attribute-
application] commit
[~HUAWEI-GigabitEthernet1/0/0.2-te-link-attribute-
application] quit
[~HUAWEI-GigabitEthernet1/0/0.2] quit
[~HUAWEI] interface GigabitEthernet 1/0/0.3
[~HUAWEI-GigabitEthernet1/0/0.3] te link-attribute-
application flex-algo
[*HUAWEI-GigabitEthernet1/0/0.3-te-link-attribute-
application] link administrative group name grey
//Set the link color to gray.
[*HUAWEI-GigabitEthernet1/0/0.3-te-link-attribute-
application] delay 20    //Set the link delay to
20 microseconds.
[*HUAWEI-GigabitEthernet1/0/0.3-te-link-attribute-
application] commit
[~HUAWEI-GigabitEthernet1/0/0.3-te-link-attribute-
application] quit
[~HUAWEI-GigabitEthernet1/0/0.3] quit
```

*9.3.2.5 Network Slicing Solution Deployment — SRv6 Configuration*
In the SRv6 SID-based network slicing solution with IGP Flex-Algo used
in the control plane, an SRv6 locator needs to be configured for each

Flex-Algo. The locator configuration includes specifying the locator name, IPv6 prefix, length reserved for the Function part of static SIDs, length reserved for the Args part, and Flex-Algo ID. In addition, IS-IS SRv6 needs to be enabled for each Flex-Algo in the IS-IS process. An example of the configuration is as follows:

```
<HUAWEI> system-view
[~HUAWEI] segment-routing ipv6
[*HUAWEI-segment-routing-ipv6] locator locator_128
ipv6-prefix 2001:DB8:111:1:: 64 static 8 args 16
flex-algo 128    //Configure a locator for
Flex-Algo 128.
[*HUAWEI-segment-routing-ipv6] locator locator_129
ipv6-prefix 2001:DB8:111:2:: 64 static 8 args 16
flex-algo 129    //Configure a locator for
Flex-Algo 129.
[*HUAWEI-segment-routing-ipv6] locator locator_130
ipv6-prefix 2001:DB8:111:3:: 64 static 8 args 16
flex-algo 130    //Configure a locator for Flex-Algo
130.
[*HUAWEI-segment-routing-ipv6] quit
[*HUAWEI] isis 1
[*HUAWEI-isis-1] segment-routing ipv6 locator
locator_128    //Enable IS-IS SRv6 for Flex-Algo 128.
[*HUAWEI-isis-1] segment-routing ipv6 locator
locator_129    //Enable IS-IS SRv6 for Flex-Algo 129.
[*HUAWEI-isis-1] segment-routing ipv6 locator
locator_130    //Enable IS-IS SRv6 for Flex-Algo 130.
[*HUAWEI-isis-1] commit
[~HUAWEI-isis-1] quit
```

After an SRv6 locator is configured on a device, the device allocates a dynamic End SID. Three locators are configured in this example, so three End SIDs are dynamically generated. The following command can be run to check the End SIDs of the device:

```
[~HUAWEI] display segment-routing ipv6 local-sid end
forwarding
          My Local-SID End Forwarding Table
          --------------------------------
SID          : 2001:DB8:111:1::1:0/128  FuncType : End
```

```
Flavor       : PSP
LocatorName : locator_128              LocatorID   : 1
ProtocolType: ISIS                     ProcessID   : 1
UpdateTime   : 2022-02-26 10:42:24.216
SID          : 2001:DB8:111:2::1:0/128  FuncType : End
Flavor       : PSP
LocatorName : locator_129     LocatorID   : 1
ProtocolType: ISIS       ProcessID    : 1
UpdateTime   : 2022-02-26 10:42:24.216
SID          : 2001:DB8:111:3::1:0/128  FuncType : End
Flavor       : PSP
LocatorName : locator_130              LocatorID : 1
ProtocolType: ISIS                     ProcessID : 1
UpdateTime   : 2022-02-26 10:42:24.217
Total SID(s): 3
```

The device also allocates dynamic End.X SIDs to IGP-enabled interfaces or sub-interfaces. Three locators are configured in this example, so each device dynamically generates three End.X SIDs for each channelized sub-interface. The following command can be run to check the End.X SIDs of links on the device:

```
[~HUAWEI] display segment-routing ipv6 local-sid end-x
forwarding
          My Local-SID End.X Forwarding Table
          ------------------------------------
SID : 2001:DB8:111:1::101:0/128 FuncType : End.X
Flavor : PSP
LocatorName : locator_128 LocatorID : 1
ProtocolType: ISIS ProcessID : 1
UpdateTime : 2022-02-26 10:42:24.217
NextHop : Interface : ExitIndex:
FE80::3AD5:E4FF:FE21:101 GE1/0/0.1 0x00000001
SID : 2001:DB8:111:1::102:0/128 FuncType : End.X
Flavor : PSP
LocatorName : locator_129 LocatorID : 2
ProtocolType: ISIS ProcessID : 1
UpdateTime : 2022-02-26 10:42:24.217
NextHop : Interface : ExitIndex:
FE80::3AD5:E4FF:FE21:102 GE1/0/0.1 0x00000001
SID : 2001:DB8:111:1::103:0/128 FuncType : End.X
```

```
Flavor : PSP
LocatorName : locator_130 LocatorID : 3
ProtocolType: ISIS ProcessID : 1
UpdateTime : 2022-02-26 10:42:24.217
NextHop : Interface : ExitIndex:
FE80::3AD5:E4FF:FE21:103 GE1/0/0.1 0x00000001
SID : 2001:DB8:111:2::101:0/128 FuncType : End.X
Flavor : PSP
LocatorName : locator_128 LocatorID : 1
ProtocolType: ISIS ProcessID : 1
UpdateTime : 2022-02-26 10:42:24.217
NextHop : Interface : ExitIndex:
FE80::3AD5:E4FF:FE21:111 GE1/0/0.2 0x00000002
SID : 2001:DB8:111:2::102:0/128 FuncType : End.X
Flavor : PSP
LocatorName : locator_129 LocatorID : 2
ProtocolType: ISIS ProcessID : 1
UpdateTime : 2022-02-26 10:42:24.217
NextHop : Interface : ExitIndex:
FE80::3AD5:E4FF:FE21:112 GE1/0/0.2 0x00000002
SID : 2001:DB8:111:2::103:0/128 FuncType : End.X
Flavor : PSP
LocatorName : locator_130 LocatorID : 3
ProtocolType: ISIS ProcessID : 1
UpdateTime : 2022-02-26 10:42:24.217
NextHop : Interface : ExitIndex:
FE80::3AD5:E4FF:FE21:113 GE1/0/0.2 0x00000002
SID : 2001:DB8:111:3::101:0/128 FuncType : End.X
Flavor : PSP
LocatorName : locator_128 LocatorID : 1
ProtocolType: ISIS ProcessID : 1
UpdateTime : 2022-02-26 10:42:24.217
NextHop : Interface : ExitIndex:
FE80::3AD5:E4FF:FE21:121 GE1/0/0.3 0x00000003
SID : 2001:DB8:111:3::102:0/128 FuncType : End.X
Flavor : PSP
LocatorName : locator_129 LocatorID : 2
ProtocolType: ISIS ProcessID : 1
UpdateTime : 2022-02-26 10:42:24.217
NextHop : Interface : ExitIndex:
```

```
FE80::3AD5:E4FF:FE21:122 GE1/0/0.3 0x00000003
SID : 2001:DB8:111:3::103:0/128 FuncType : End.X
Flavor : PSP
LocatorName : locator_130 LocatorID : 3
ProtocolType: ISIS ProcessID : 1
UpdateTime : 2022-02-26 10:42:24.217
NextHop : Interface : ExitIndex:
FE80::3AD5:E4FF:FE21:123 GE1/0/0.3 0x00000003
Total SID(s): 9
```

### 9.3.2.6 Network Slicing Solution Deployment — Network Slicing Path Computation and Establishment

In the SRv6 SID-based network slicing solution with IGP Flex-Algo used in the control plane, both SRv6 BE and SRv6 Policy modes are supported for path computation in network slices.

For SRv6 BE, network devices use IGP to collect SRv6 locators associated with the Flex-Algos advertised by other network devices on the network and compute paths to other network devices based on the metric type, algorithm type, and topology constraints in the FADs associated with network slices.

The following command can be run on a device to check IS-IS routing information of Flex-Algo 128:

```
[~HUAWEI] display isis route ipv6 flex-algo 128
            Route information for ISIS(1)
            -----------------------------

            ISIS(1) Level-1 Flex-Algo Forwarding Table
            ------------------------------------------
IPV6 Dest.       ExitInterface       NextHop
Cost     Flags
-----------------------------------------------------
---------------------------------
2001:DB8:111:1::/64 NULL0       -        0     A/-/-/-
2001:DB8:222:1::/64 GE1/0/0     FE80::3A5D:67FF:FE31:307
                                1000  A/-/-/-
2001:DB8:333:1::/64 GE1/0/0     FE80::3A5D:67FF:FE31:307
                                1100   A/-/-/-
2001:DB8:444:1::/64 GE2/0/0     FE80::3A5D:67FF:FE41:305
                                2000   A/-/-/-
```

```
2001:DB8:555:1::/64 GE1/0/0   FE80::3A5D:67FF:FE31:307
                              2000      A/-/-/-
2001:DB8:666:1::/64 GE1/0/0   FE80::3A5D:67FF:FE31:307
                              1200      A/-/-/-
2001:DB8:777:1::/64 GE2/0/0   FE80::3A5D:67FF:FE41:305
                              1000      A/-/-/-
     Flags: D-Direct,  A-Added to URT,  L-Advertised in
LSPs,  S-IGP Shortcut,
           U-Up/Down Bit Set,  LP-Local Prefix-Sid
     Protect Type: L-Link Protect,  N-Node Protect
```

For SRv6 Policy, an NSC is needed to compute explicit paths for an SRv6 Policy in a network slice. Network devices report the link administrative group (color) attribute information of the network slice's interfaces or sub-interfaces to the NSC through BGP-LS. Based on the network slice and Flex-Algo configurations on the NSC, the NSC generates the network slice's topology according to the FAD. And based on the links in the network slice's topology, the NSC can compute SRv6 Policy explicit paths — composed of the SRv6 End.X SID at each hop in the network slice topology — that meet service requirements. This enables service packets to be forwarded along the SRv6 Policy explicit paths in this network slice. For example, the primary path of the SRv6 Policy in network slice 1 is A-B-C-D, and the backup path is A-E-F-G-D. The following command can be run to check the status of the SRv6 Policies delivered by the NSC:

```
<HUAWEI> display srv6-te policy endpoint
2001:DB8:666:1::1 color 100
PolicyName : Policy1
Color : 100 Endpoint : 2001:DB8:666:1::1
TunnelId : 1 Binding SID : 2001:DB8:111:1::100:0
TunnelType : SRv6-TE Policy DelayTimerRemain : -
Policy State : Up State Change Time : 2022-02-21
09:39:52
Admin State : Up Traffic Statistics : Disable
Backup Hot-Standby : Disable BFD : Disable
Interface Index : 87 Interface Name : SRv6TE-Policy-1
Interface State : Up Encapsulation Mode : Encaps
Candidate-path Count : 2
Candidate-path Preference : 110
Path State : Active Path Type : Primary
```

Protocol-Origin : Configuration(30) Originator :
0, 0.0.0.0
Discriminator : 200 Binding SID : -
GroupId : 2 Policy Name : 1
Template ID : 0 Path Verification : Disable
DelayTimerRemain : - Network Slice ID : -
Segment-List Count : 1
Segment-List : 1
Segment-List ID : 2 XcIndex : 2
List State : Up DelayTimerRemain : -
Verification State : - SuppressTimeRemain : -
PMTU : 9600 Active PMTU : 9600
Weight : 1 BFD State : -
Network Slice ID : -
SID :
2001:DB8:111:1::11:0
2001:DB8:222:1::11:0
2001:DB8:333:1::11:0
2001:DB8:666:1::1:0
Candidate-path Preference : 100
Path State : Inactive (Valid) Path Type : -
Protocol-Origin : Configuration(30) Originator :
0, 0.0.0.0
Discriminator : 100 Binding SID : -
GroupId : 1 Policy Name : 1
Template ID : 0 Path Verification : Disable
DelayTimerRemain : - Network Slice ID : 1
Segment-List Count : 1
Segment-List : 1
Segment-List ID : 1 XcIndex : -
List State : Down (Valid) DelayTimerRemain : -
Verification State : - SuppressTimeRemain : -
PMTU : 9600 Active PMTU : 9600
Weight : 1 BFD State : -
Network Slice ID : 1
SID :
2001:DB8:111:1::21:0
2001:DB8:777:1::21:0
2001:DB8:444:1::21:0
2001:DB8:555:1::21:0
2001:DB8:666:1::1:0

### 9.3.2.7 Network Slicing Solution Deployment — Mapping Service Slices to Resource Slices

In the SRv6 SID-based network slicing solution with IGP Flex-Algo used in the control plane, to map service slices to resource slices, it is necessary to associate VPN services with SRv6 locators of network slices. The VPN services can then be associated with specific Flex-Algos. This enables the VPN traffic of the network service slices to be forwarded using the network resource slices associated with specific Flex-Algos. An example of the configuration is as follows:

```
<HUAWEI> system-view
[~HUAWEI] bgp 300
[*HUAWEI-bgp] ipv4-family vpn-instance flexalgo_128
[*HUAWEI-bgp-flexalgo_128] segment-routing
ipv6 locator locator_128 evpn   //Associate
locator_128 with the VPN instance named flexalgo_128.
[*HUAWEI-bgp-flexalgo_128] ipv4-family vpn-instance
flexalgo_129
[*HUAWEI-bgp-flexalgo_129] segment-routing
ipv6 locator locator_129 evpn   //Associate
locator_129 with the VPN instance named flexalgo_129.
[*HUAWEI-bgp-flexalgo_129] ipv4-family vpn-instance
flexalgo_130
[*HUAWEI-bgp-flexalgo_130] segment-routing
ipv6 locator locator_130 evpn   //Associate
locator_130 with the VPN instance named flexalgo_130.
[*HUAWEI-bgp-flexalgo_130] commit
[~HUAWEI-bgp-flexalgo_130] quit
[~HUAWEI-bgp] quit
```

In the SRv6 SID-based network slicing solution with IGP Flex-Algo used in the control plane, when SRv6 Policy explicit paths are used, it is necessary to configure the association between VPN services and the SRv6 locators of network slices, and to configure the tunnel policy of using SRv6 Policies and the color attribute for the VPN services. This enables service slices to be associated with SRv6 Policies in resource slices through the color attribute. For details, see the related description in Section 9.3.1 Deployment with the Affinity Attribute Used in the Control Plane.

## 9.4 DEPLOYMENT OF THE SLICE ID-BASED NETWORK SLICING SOLUTION

The slice ID-based network slicing solution supports both single-layer network slicing and hierarchical network slicing. This section discusses how to deploy the two types of slicing in such a solution.

### 9.4.1 Single-Layer Network Slicing Deployment

*9.4.1.1 Solution Description*

The slice ID-based single-layer network slicing solution provides higher flexibility and scalability than the SRv6 SID-based network slicing solution. In this solution, network slices with the same topology share distributed topology information and calculated routes, thereby reducing overhead incurred by repeatedly distributing control protocol messages and the workload involved in repeatedly calculating routes. For this reason, this solution offers high scalability. Currently, one typical way to realize this solution is to derive other network slices on the basis of the default network slice. The derived network slices and the default network slice have the same topology and can share the topology calculation result.

The slice ID-based single-layer network slicing solution has the following characteristics:

- Uses slice IDs as slice identifiers in the data plane. Each slice ID corresponds to one network slice.

- Allows slice IDs to identify different network slices' resource interfaces, sub-interfaces, or sub-channels. Slice ID 0 is used by the default network slice. Although IP addresses and Layer 3 protocols need to be configured for the interfaces of the default network slice, no IP addresses need to be configured for the resource interfaces, sub-interfaces, or sub-channels of the other network slices. This is because they directly reuse the IP addresses of the default network slice.

- Supports both SRv6 BE and SRv6 Policy modes for path computation and traffic forwarding in network slices.

  - When SRv6 BE is used, the mapping between the color attribute of a VPN instance and a slice ID must be configured on the ingress PE. Based on the color, the VPN service is then mapped to the network slice with the specified slice ID. During packet forwarding, an SRv6 BE path is determined based on the VPN route. An outer IPv6 header is added to the service packet, and this header contains an HBH Options header that carries the slice ID.

– When SRv6 Policies are used, an NSC uses protocols such as BGP-LS to collect topology and attribute information of each network slice, computes SRv6 Policy explicit paths in each network slice, and associates the SRv6 Policy candidate paths with the slice ID of each network slice when delivering these candidate paths to the headend PE. When forwarding packets of a service slice, the headend PE determines the desired SRv6 Policy based on the color attribute of the VPN instance bound to the service slice and encapsulates the service packets with an outer IPv6 header that contains an SRH and an HBH Options header. The corresponding slice ID is contained in the HBH Options header.

• Forwards packets according to the slice ID information encapsulated in the packets' HBH Options header in the data plane. Specifically, when forwarding the packets, a device looks up the destination IPv6 address to determine the corresponding Layer 3 outbound interface and then searches on the Layer 3 outbound interface for the FlexE interface or channelized sub-interface corresponding to the slice ID in the packets. After determining such information, the device sends the packets from the interface/sub-interface. This ensures that the data packets are forwarded using the reserved resource of the corresponding network slice, thereby providing an SLA guarantee for the slice service.

Figure 9.10 shows a typical scenario where the slice ID-based single-layer network slicing solution is deployed network-wide. In this deployment mode, resources need to be partitioned and reserved for network slices on all links across the entire network.

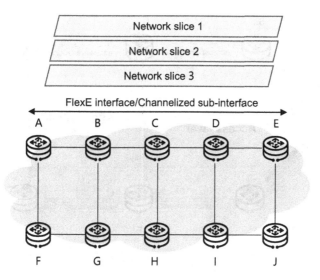

FIGURE 9.10   Network-wide slicing.

## 9.4.1.2 Single-Layer Network Slicing Solution Deployment Example

Figure 9.11 shows an example for deploying the slice ID-based single-layer network slicing solution.

In this example,

- FlexE interfaces are used for partitioning network slice resources. As shown in Figure 9.11, when network slices are created on a physical interface, FlexE 1/0/129 is used by the default network slice, FlexE 1/0/130 is used by network slice 1, and FlexE 1/0/131 is used by network slice 2. IP addresses are configured, and IGP is enabled for the interfaces in the default network slice. IP addresses do not need to be configured for the interfaces of other network slices because they reuse the interface IP addresses of the default network slice.

- Network slices 1 and 2 are created based on the network-wide topology, and corresponding slice IDs are configured for FlexE interfaces of the default network slice and other network slices.

- After SRv6 is enabled and an SRv6 locator is configured for each network device, a global End SID is dynamically assigned to these devices, and an End.X SID is automatically generated for each FlexE interface of the default network slice enabled with IS-IS IPv6.

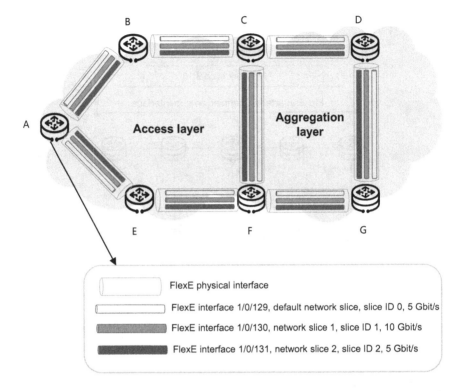

FIGURE 9.11 Example for deploying the slice ID-based single-layer network slicing solution.

### 9.4.1.3 Single-Layer Network Slicing Solution Deployment — Slice Instance Creation

In the slice ID-based single-layer network slicing solution, NSIs — including a default one and others — need to be created on each device. A default NSI needs to be created first. An example of the configuration is as follows:

```
<HUAWEI> system-view
[~HUAWEI]  network-slice instance 0 //Set the slice ID
of the default NSI to 0.
[*HUAWEI] commit
```

Then, a non-default NSI needs to be created. An example of the configuration is as follows:

```
<HUAWEI> system-view
[~HUAWEI]  network-slice instance 1 //Set the slice ID
of the non-default NSI to a non-zero value.
[*HUAWEI] commit
```

### 9.4.1.4 Single-Layer Network Slicing Solution
### Deployment — Topology Creation and Link Addition

Interfaces in the slice ID-based single-layer network slicing solution include those in both the default network slice and non-default network slices.

- Interface in the default network slice: a Layer 3 interface that needs to have an IP address configured and IGP enabled. Its slice ID is fixed at 0.

- Interface in a non-default network slice: a FlexE interface or channelized sub-interface created on a physical interface of the default network slice and used to reserve resources for the non-default network slice. No IP address or IGP needs to be configured for such interfaces because they reuse the interface IP addresses of the default network slice. A bandwidth value needs to be configured for these interfaces to reserve bandwidth for the related network slices. In addition, these interfaces require slice IDs to be configured.

**Deployment of an interface in the default network slice**

In this slice deployment example, FlexE 1/0/129 needs to be used in the default network slice, with the slice ID set to 0. An example of the configuration is as follows:

```
<HUAWEI> system-view
[~HUAWEI] interface FlexE1/0/129
[~HUAWEI-FlexE1/0/129]  network-slice 0 data-plane
//Configure the FlexE interface as the interface of
the default network slice.
[*HUAWEI-FlexE1/0/129] commit
[~HUAWEI-FlexE1/0/129] quit
```

An IP address and IGP need to be configured for the FlexE interface of the default slice. An example of the configuration is as follows:

```
[~HUAWEI] interface FlexE1/0/129
[~HUAWEI-FlexE1/0/129] ipv6 enable
[*HUAWEI-FlexE1/0/129] ipv6 address 2001:db8::1 127
[*HUAWEI-FlexE1/0/129] isis ipv6 enable 2
[*HUAWEI-FlexE1/0/129] isis ipv6 cost 1000
[*HUAWEI-FlexE1/0/129] commit
```

**Deployment of an interface in the non-default network slices**

A FlexE interface needs to be configured for network slice 1 and have its bandwidth configured. An example of the configuration is as follows:

```
<HUAWEI> system-view
[~HUAWEI]  flexe client-instance 130 flexe-group 1
flexe-type full-function port-id 130 //Create FlexE
1/0/130.
[*HUAWEI-flexe-client-130] flexe-clientid 130
[*HUAWEI-flexe-client-130] flexe-bandwidth 5   //Set
the bandwidth of the FlexE interface to 5 Gbit/s.
[*HUAWEI-flexe-client-130] commit
```

FlexE 1/0/130 needs to be bound to the slice ID of the default network slice (so that it can reuse the IPv6 address and IGP session of the default slice interface) and then configured with a slice ID. An example of the configuration is as follows:

```
<HUAWEI> system-view
[~HUAWEI] interface FlexE1/0/130
[~HUAWEI-FlexE1/0/130]  basic-slice 0   //Bind the
interface to the slice ID of the default network slice
so that it can reuse the IPv6 address and IGP session
of the default slice interface.
[*HUAWEI-FlexE1/0/130] network-slice 101 data-plane
//Configure a network slice ID.
[*HUAWEI-FlexE1/0/130] commit
```

*9.4.1.5 Single-Layer Network Slicing Solution*
    *Deployment — SRv6 Configuration*

SRv6 needs to be enabled on each device, and the source address (used for outer IPv6 header encapsulation) and an SRv6 locator need to be specified. The locator configuration includes specifying an IPv6 prefix, length reserved for the Function part of static SIDs, and length of the Args part. An example of the configuration is as follows:

```
[~HUAWEI] segment-routing ipv6
[*HUAWEI-segment-routing-ipv6] encapsulation
source-address 1::1
```

```
[*HUAWEI-segment-routing-ipv6] locator SRv6_locator
ipv6-prefix A1:: 64 static 8 args 16
[*HUAWEI-segment-routing-ipv6] commit
```

In this example, the encapsulated source address in the IPv6 header is
**1::1**, the locator name is **SRv6_locator**, the corresponding IPv6 prefix is
**A1::/64**, **static 8** indicates that 8 bits are reserved for the Function part of
static SIDs, and **args 16** indicates that 16 bits are reserved for the Args part.

After the configuration is complete, the following command can be run
to check the SRv6 locator information:

```
[~HUAWEI] display segment-routing ipv6 locator verbose
Locator Configuration Table
---------------------------
LocatorName   : SRv6_locator   LocatorID    : 1
IPv6Prefix    : A1::       PrefixLength: 64
StaticLength  : 8  Reference    : 4
Default       : N  ArgsLength   : 16
AutoSIDBegin  : A1::100:0
AutoSIDEnd    : A1::FFFF:FFFF:FFFF:0
Total Locator(s): 1
```

The command output shows the configured locator name, IPv6 prefix,
length reserved for the Function part of static SIDs, and start and end of
dynamic SIDs.

After an SRv6 locator is configured on a device, the device dynamically
allocates an End SID, which is shared by all network slices. The following
command can be run to check the End SID of the device:

```
<HUAWEI> display segment-routing ipv6 local-sid end
forwarding
        My Local-SID End Forwarding Table
        -----------------------------------
SID          : A1::1:0/128      FuncType     : End
Flavor       : PSP
LocatorName  : SRv6_locator     LocatorID    : 1
ProtocolType: ISIS        ProcessID    : 1
UpdateTime   : 2022-02-26 10:42:24.216
Total SID(s): 1
```

The device also allocates dynamic End.X SIDs to IGP-enabled interfaces or sub-interfaces. The following command can be run to check the End.X SIDs of links on the device:

```
[~HUAWEI] display segment-routing ipv6 local-sid end-x
forwarding
             My Local-SID End.X Forwarding Table
         -----------------------------------
SID          : A1::11:0/128    FuncType    : End.X
Flavor       : PSP
LocatorName : SRv6_locator     LocatorID   : 1
ProtocolType: ISIS       ProcessID   : 1
UpdateTime   : 2022-02-26 10:42:24.217
NextHop      :       Interface : ExitIndex
FE80::3AD5:E4FF:FE21:100        FlexE1/0/129
0x00000001
SID          : A1::12:0/128    FuncType    : End.X
Flavor       : PSP
LocatorName : SRv6_locator     LocatorID   : 1
ProtocolType: ISIS       ProcessID   : 1
UpdateTime   : 2022-02-26 10:42:24.217
NextHop      :       Interface : ExitIndex
FE80::3AD5:E4FF:FE21:200        FlexE2/0/130
0x00000002
Total SID(s): 2
```

### 9.4.1.6 Single-Layer Network Slicing Solution Deployment — Network Slicing Path Computation and Establishment

In SRv6 BE scenarios, devices calculate forwarding paths and generate corresponding forwarding entries based on the network slice topology information without needing special configuration. As such, the following focuses on the configurations required in SRv6 Policy scenarios.

In SRv6 Policy scenarios, an NSC can compute SRv6 Policy candidate paths based on the network slice topology and TE attributes. It can then advertise the SRv6 Policy candidate path information to the path headend by using BGP SRv6 Policy (or a similar method), with the slice ID information associated with the SRv6 Policy carried in protocol messages.

The following command can be run to check the SRv6 Policy status and slice ID information delivered by the NSC:

```
<HUAWEI> display srv6-te policy endpoint 1::6 color
100
PolicyName : Policy1
Color : 100 Endpoint : 1::6
TunnelId : 1 Binding SID : A1::1:0:101:0
TunnelType : SRv6-TE Policy DelayTimerRemain : -
Policy State : Up State Change Time : 2022-02-21
09:39:52
Admin State : Up Traffic Statistics : Disable
Backup Hot-Standby : Disable BFD : Disable
Interface Index : 87 Interface Name : SRv6TE-Policy-1
Interface State : Up Encapsulation Mode : Encaps
Candidate-path Count : 2
Candidate-path Preference : 110
Path State : Active Path Type : Primary
Protocol-Origin : Configuration(30) Originator : 0,
0.0.0.0
Discriminator : 200 Binding SID : -
GroupId : 2 Policy Name : 1
Template ID : 0 Path Verification : Disable
DelayTimerRemain : - Network Slice ID : -
Segment-List Count : 1
Segment-List : 1
Segment-List ID : 2 XcIndex : 2
List State : Up DelayTimerRemain : -
Verification State : - SuppressTimeRemain : -
PMTU : 9600 Active PMTU : 9600
Weight : 1 BFD State : -
Network Slice ID : 1 (data-plane) //Slice ID of the
network slice associated with the candidate path
SID :
A1::1:0:11:0
A2::1:0:21:0
A3::1:0:31:0
A6::1:0:1:0
Candidate-path Preference : 100
Path State : Inactive (Valid) Path Type : -
Protocol-Origin : Configuration(30) Originator : 0,
0.0.0.0
Discriminator : 100 Binding SID : -
```

```
GroupId : 1 Policy Name : 1
Template ID : 0 Path Verification : Disable
DelayTimerRemain : - Network Slice ID : -
Segment-List Count : 1
Segment-List : 1
Segment-List ID : 1 XcIndex : -
List State : Down (Valid) DelayTimerRemain : -
Verification State : - SuppressTimeRemain : -
PMTU : 9600 Active PMTU : 9600
Weight : 1 BFD State : -
Network Slice ID : 1 (data-plane) //Slice ID of the
network slice associated with the candidate path
SID :
A1::1:0:12:0
A4::1:0:42:0
A5::1:0:52:0
A6::1:0:1:0
```

## 9.4.2 Hierarchical Network Slicing Deployment

### 9.4.2.1 Solution Description

The slice ID-based network slicing solution also supports hierarchical network slicing deployment. In this case, different slice IDs are allocated to the level-1 slice (also referred to as the main slice) and level-2 slices (also referred to as sub-slices) to identify network slice resources of different levels. Specifically, in hierarchical network slicing, an SRv6 Policy is used for computing and establishing the explicit paths of sub-slices in the main slice topology. Resources are then allocated to the sub-slices along these explicit paths on the interfaces or sub-interfaces of the main slice. This makes it possible to forward the high-value services of the main slice in the sub-slices.[3] Services of the main slice and sub-slices can be planned according to service priority. The following provides a typical planning mode for hierarchical slicing:

- The common services of an industry or enterprise are deployed in the main slice. If these services have special SLA requirements, such as low delay, they need to be carried over SRv6 Policies. Otherwise, they can be carried over SRv6 BE paths. Service packets in the main slice need to be encapsulated with the slice ID of the main slice.

- High-value services of an industry or enterprise are deployed in sub-slices whose resources are allocated within the main slice. Such services are usually carried using SRv6 Policies. SRv6 Policy candidate paths that meet service requirements are computed by the NSC, and sub-slice resources are then allocated along the explicit paths represented by the candidate paths. Service packets in the sub-slices need to be encapsulated with the slice IDs of the corresponding sub-slices.

### 9.4.2.2 Hierarchical Slicing Solution Deployment Example

Figure 9.12 shows an example for deploying the slice ID-based hierarchical slicing solution.

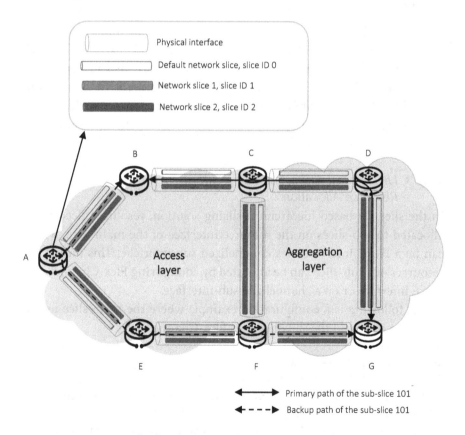

FIGURE 9.12 Example for deploying the slice ID-based hierarchical slicing solution.

In this example,

1. Hierarchical network slicing can be deployed on the basis of single-layer network slicing. Slice 1 (slice ID: 1) is used as the main slice, and a sub-slice with ID 101 is deployed within the main slice using Flex-Channel.

2. When calculating SRv6 Policy candidate paths for sub-slice 101, the NSC needs to associate the SRv6 Policy with the main slice to ensure that the sub-slice paths are calculated based on the topology of the main slice. In addition, to ensure consistent allocation of sub-slice resources, the SRv6 Policy of a sub-slice must use strict explicit paths.

3. The NSC delivers the computed sub-slice path information that contains sub-slice ID 101 to the path headend through the BGP SRv6 Policy (or a similar method). The NSC also needs to use NETCONF/YANG or another interface/protocol to deliver the Flex-Channel configurations of the sub-slice to network devices along the SRv6 Policy paths and allocate forwarding resources to the sub-slice.

### 9.4.2.3 Hierarchical Slicing Solution Deployment — Slice Resource Allocation

In the slice ID-based hierarchical slicing solution, resources need to be allocated to sub-slices on the resource interface of the main slice, which can be a FlexE interface or a channelized sub-interface. This means the resources of a sub-slice can be allocated by configuring Flex-Channel on a FlexE interface or on a channelized sub-interface.

The following is a configuration example where the main slice uses a FlexE interface and the sub-slice uses Flex-Channel:

```
<HUAWEI> system-view
[~HUAWEI] interface FlexE1/0/129
[~HUAWEI-FlexE1/0/129] network-slice 1 data-plane
//Add the interface to the main slice.
[*HUAWEI-FlexE1/0/129] network-slice 101 flex-channel 100
//Set the bandwidth to be allocated to sub-slice 101
to 100 Mbit/s.
[*HUAWEI-FlexE1/0/129] commit
```

### 9.4.2.4 Hierarchical Slicing Solution Deployment — Network Slicing Path Establishment

In the slice ID-based hierarchical slicing solution, an NSC is usually used to compute SRv6 Policy paths for sub-slices and then deploy sub-slice resources along the specified paths. Specifically, the NSC computes SRv6 Policy paths based on the topology and TE attribute of the main slice and delivers the computed explicit path information that contains the slice IDs of sub-slices to the path headends through BGP SRv6 Policy (or a similar method). In this example, an SRv6 Policy with 100 Mbit/s bandwidth is created in the main slice; the sub-slice ID is 101; the primary path computed by the NSC for the sub-slice is B-C-D-G; and the backup path is B-A-E-F-G.

The following command can be run to check the SRv6 Policy status and slice ID information delivered by the NSC:

```
<HUAWEI> display srv6-te policy endpoint 1::6 color
101
PolicyName : Policy1
Color : 101 Endpoint : 1::6
TunnelId : 1 Binding SID : A1::1:0:102:0
TunnelType : SRv6-TE Policy DelayTimerRemain : -
Policy State : Up State Change Time : 2022-02-21
09:39:52
Admin State : Up Traffic Statistics : Disable
Backup Hot-Standby : Disable BFD : Disable
Interface Index : 87 Interface Name : SRv6TE-Policy-1
Interface State : Up Encapsulation Mode : Encaps
Candidate-path Count : 2
Candidate-path Preference : 110
Path State : Active Path Type : Primary
Protocol-Origin : Configuration(30) Originator :
0, 0.0.0.0
Discriminator : 200 Binding SID : -
GroupId : 2 Policy Name : 1
Template ID : 0 Path Verification : Disable
DelayTimerRemain : - Network Slice ID : -
Segment-List Count : 1
Segment-List : 1
Segment-List ID : 2 XcIndex : 2
List State : Up DelayTimerRemain : -
```

```
Verification State : - SuppressTimeRemain : -
PMTU : 9600 Active PMTU : 9600
Weight : 1 BFD State : -
```
**Network Slice ID : 101 (data-plane)** //Associate the
SRv6 Policy with sub-slice 101.
```
SID :
A1::1:0:11:0
A2::1:0:21:0
A3::1:0:31:0
A6::1:0:1:0
Candidate-path Preference : 100
Path State : Inactive (Valid) Path Type : -
Protocol-Origin : Configuration(30) Originator :
0, 0.0.0.0
Discriminator : 100 Binding SID : -
GroupId : 1 Policy Name : 1
Template ID : 0 Path Verification : Disable
DelayTimerRemain : - Network Slice ID : -
Segment-List Count : 1
Segment-List : 1
Segment-List ID : 1 XcIndex : -
List State : Down (Valid) DelayTimerRemain : -
Verification State : - SuppressTimeRemain : -
PMTU : 9600 Active PMTU : 9600
Weight : 1 BFD State : -
```
**Network Slice ID : 101 (data-plane)** //Associate the
SRv6 Policy with sub-slice 101.
```
SID :
A1::1:0:12:0
A4::1:0:42:0
A5::1:0:52:0
A6::1:0:1:0
```

### 9.4.3 Deployment for Mapping Service Slices to Resource Slices

In the slice ID-based network slicing solution, service slices are mapped to resource slices by associating the color attribute of service routes with network resource slices. If SRv6 BE paths are used to carry services in a network slice, the mapping between the color attribute of service routes and slice IDs of network slices needs to be configured on devices. This is necessary so that network devices can determine the specified network slices based on the color attribute of service routes. Before a packet of a network service slice is forwarded according to the routing table in SRv6 BE scenarios, the packet is encapsulated with an HBH Options header that carries the corresponding slice ID. If an SRv6 Policy is used to carry services in a network slice, the color attribute of service routes can be directly associated with the SRv6 Policy. When a packet of a network service slice is forwarded using the SRv6 Policy, the packet is encapsulated with an SRH that carries SRv6 SID lists and also with an HBH Options header that carries the corresponding slice ID.

In SRv6 BE scenarios, the mapping between the color attribute of service routes and slice IDs needs to be configured on the ingress PE. This configuration usually applies to single-layer network slicing. An example of the configuration is as follows:

```
<HUAWEI> system-view
[~HUAWEI] network-slice color-mapping
[*HUAWEI-network-slice-color-mapping]  color 100
network-slice 1   //Configure the mapping between
network slice 1 and color 100.
[*HUAWEI-network-slice-color-mapping] color 200
network-slice 2   //Configure the mapping between
network slice 2 and color 200.
[*HUAWEI-network-slice-color-mapping] commit
```

In SRv6 Policy scenarios, the tunnel policy of using SRv6 Policies and the color attribute need to be configured for VPN instances. The color attribute is used to associate service slices with resource slices. This configuration applies to both single-layer and hierarchical network slicing. The user can configure a default color value for a VPN instance on the headend PE. An example of the configuration is as follows:

```
//Configure the tunnel policy of using SRv6 Policies.
<HUAWEI> system-view
[~HUAWEI] tunnel-policy SRv6-policy
[*HUAWEI-tunnel-policy-SRv6-policy] tunnel select-seq
ipv6 srv6-te-policy load-balance-number 1
[*HUAWEI-tunnel-policy-SRv6-policy] commit
//Set the default color value to 100 for EVPN VPWS
services in an EVPN instance in VPWS mode.
```

```
<HUAWEI> system-view
[~HUAWEI] evpn vpn-instance evrf1 vpws
[*HUAWEI-vpws-evpn-instance-evrf1] tnl-policy
SRv6-policy  //Associate the VPN instance with the
tunnel policy.
[*HUAWEI-vpws-evpn-instance-evrf1] default-color 100
//Set the default color value to 100 for instance
evrf1.
[*HUAWEI-vpws-evpn-instance-evrf1] commit
//Set the default color value to 101 for EVPN L3VPN
services in the IPv4 address family of the VPN
instance.
<HUAWEI> system-view
[~HUAWEI] ip vpn-instance vrf1
[*HUAWEI-vpn-instance-vrf1] ipv4-family
[*HUAWEI-vpn-instance-vrf1-ipv4] tnl-policy
SRv6-policy evpn    //Associate the VPN instance with
the tunnel policy.
[*HUAWEI-vpn-instance-vrf1-ipv4] default-color 101
evpn   //Set the default color value to 101 for
instance vrf1.
[*HUAWEI-vpn-instance-vrf1-ipv4] commit
```

## 9.5 NETWORK SLICING DEPLOYMENT USING CONTROLLERS

### 9.5.1 Introduction to IPv6 NSC UIs

This section introduces the homepage and network slice management page of Huawei's IPv6 NSC.[1]

#### 9.5.1.1 Homepage

As shown in Figure 9.13, the homepage mainly consists of two areas: slice statistics and slice management.

FIGURE 9.13   Homepage of Huawei's IPv6 NSC.

1. Slice statistics area: displays information of the created network slices on the current network.

2. Slice management area: displays detailed slice state information and allows you to create, modify, and delete a slice.

### 9.5.1.2 Network Slice Management Page

As shown in Figure 9.14, the network slice management page consists of four areas: network resources, slice detail management, slice topology and operations, and slice overview.

- Network resources: displays the list of devices on a slice network, making it easy to quickly select a specific device.

- Slice detail management: displays information about slice management, including predeployed link management, slice link management, activation management, and task management.

- Slice topology and operations: displays operations and network slice topology information, including connections between devices and links in network slices.

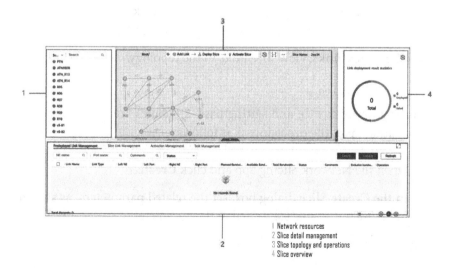

1 Network resources
2 Slice detail management
3 Slice topology and operations
4 Slice overview

FIGURE 9.14   Slice management page.

- Slice overview: displays statistics on the deployment results of network slice links, including the number of links that are successfully deployed and fail to be deployed.

### 9.5.2 Deployment of IPv6 Single-Layer Network Slicing Using Controllers

An NSC can be used to create numerous slices on a network. Compared with performing manual configuration on a per-NE basis, the NSC-based mode significantly improves the efficiency of creating network slices and reduces the chance of configuration errors. The key tasks involved in deploying a slice, as described in this section, are as follows:

- Create a slice: create a network slice and set basic attributes for the network slice. This task is fundamental for deploying a network slice.

- Add links: select the links that need to allocate resources to the network slice. This supports subsequent network slice instantiation.

- Deploy the slice: deliver network slice parameters, such as bandwidth, to devices in order to generate logical links of the network slice.

- Activate the slice: configure IP addresses for both ends of each logical link of the network slice and enable related protocols, including IGP, to achieve E2E connectivity for the network slice at the network layer.

- Check slice links: view slice links in the topology.

#### 9.5.2.1 Creating a Slice

Creating a network slice and setting basic attributes are the basis of the slice creation task. The procedure is as follows:

- Open the Network Slicing app and click **Create**.

- In the **Create Slice** dialog box, set the related parameters, as shown in Figure 9.15. Table 9.4 describes the parameters.

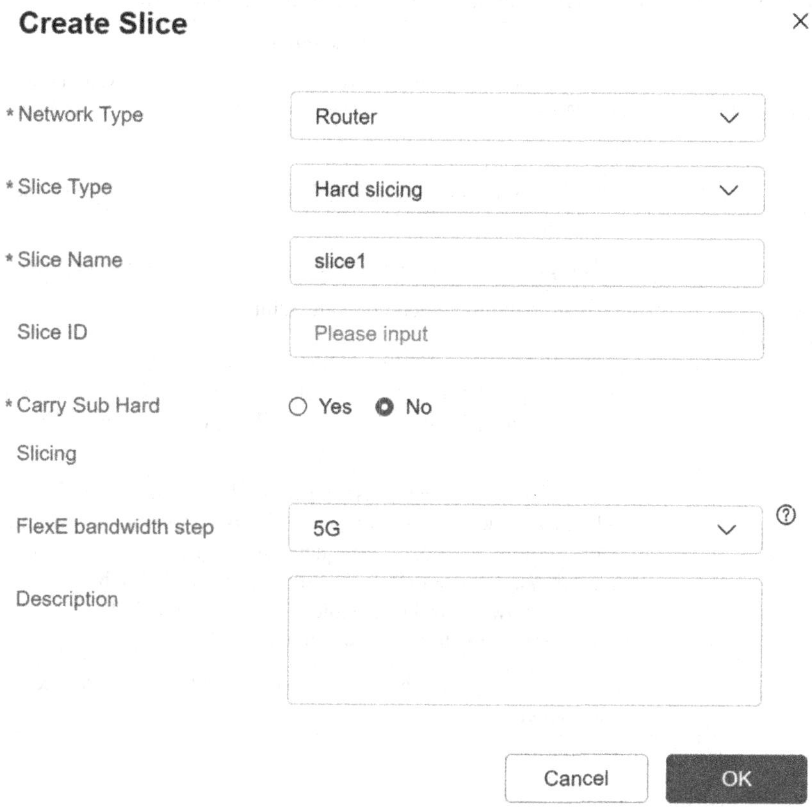

## Create Slice ✕

| | |
|---|---|
| * Network Type | Router ⌄ |
| * Slice Type | Hard slicing ⌄ |
| * Slice Name | slice1 |
| Slice ID | Please input |
| * Carry Sub Hard Slicing | ○ Yes ● No |
| FlexE bandwidth step | 5G ⌄ ⑦ |
| Description | |

Cancel    OK

FIGURE 9.15   Parameters for creating a slice.

TABLE 9.4   Description of the Parameters for Creating a Slice

| Parameter | Description |
|---|---|
| Network Type | Set Network Type to **PTN** or **Router**. |
| Slice Type | Select **Hard Slicing**. |
| Slice Name | Set a name for a network slice. |
| Slice ID | Enter an ID to identify the slice instance.<br>NOTE:<br>The slice ID range varies depending on the device type, as follows:<br><br>    − Router: 1–4294967294<br><br>    − PTN device: 1–16383  (Different devices support different ranges of slice IDs, which are finalized in the device specifications.) |

(*Continued*)

TABLE 9.4 (*Continued*)  Description of the Parameters for Creating a Slice

| Parameter | Description |
|---|---|
| Carry Sub Hard Slicing | If a sub-slice needs to be created on the slice, select **Yes**. Otherwise, select **No**. Note:<br><br>  – If this parameter is set to **Yes**, the hard slice does not need to be activated.<br><br>  – This parameter is available only when **Network Type** is **Router**. |
| FlexE bandwidth step | Set a bandwidth increment for a FlexE interface:<br><br>  – 5G: The final bandwidth of FlexE interfaces is a multiple of 5 Gbits/s. For example, if the planned bandwidth (manually set or automatically computed) is 6.5 Gbit/s, the final bandwidth will be 10 Gbit/s.<br><br>  – 1G: If the set bandwidth is not greater than 5 Gbit/s, the final bandwidth will be a multiple of 1 Gbit/s. If the set bandwidth is greater than 5 Gbit/s, the final bandwidth will be a multiple of 5 Gbit/s. For example, if the set bandwidth is 2.5 Gbit/s, the final bandwidth will be 3 Gbit/s; if the set bandwidth is 6.5 Gbit/s, the final bandwidth will be 10 Gbit/s. |
| Description | Describe the purpose of a network slice to facilitate network slice management. |

### 9.5.2.2 Adding Links

Selecting the links that need to allocate resources to the network slice supports network slice instantiation. The procedure is as follows:

- Open the Network Slicing app. In the network slice management area, click ⊞ in the **Operation** column.

- In the dialog box that is displayed, click **Add Link**. In the **Add Link** dialog box, set bandwidth and select links, as shown in Figure 9.16. Table 9.5 describes the related parameters.

- Click **OK**. You can check out detailed information about the links. After confirming that the information is correct, click **OK**. In the dialog box that is displayed, click **OK**.[2]

### 9.5.2.3 Deploying the Slice

This task involves delivering network slice parameters, such as bandwidth, to devices in order to generate new logical links for the network slice. The procedure is as follows:

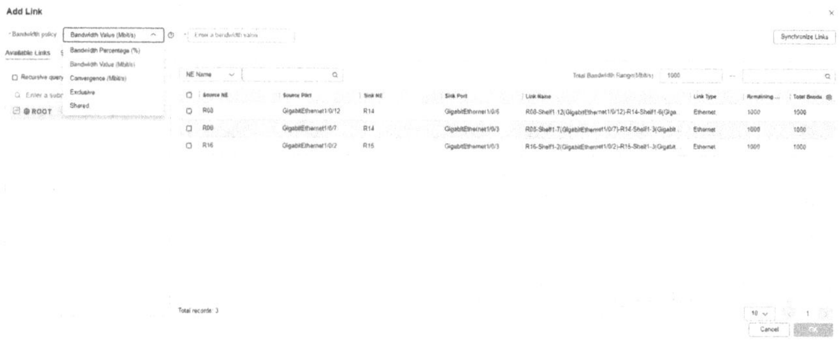

FIGURE 9.16    Parameters for adding links.

TABLE 9.5    Description of Parameters for Adding Links

| Parameter | Description |
|---|---|
| Bandwidth Percentage | Set the link bandwidth to a percentage of the total link bandwidth. |
| Bandwidth Value | Set the link bandwidth to an absolute value, which is usually a multiple of the bandwidth step. Select either **Bandwidth Value** or **Bandwidth Percentage (%)**. |
| Convergence | Set the bandwidth based on the link convergence ratio of network layers. When allocating bandwidth, the NSC determines whether the links belong to the access, aggregation, or core layer based on NE roles. The **Access Bandwidth**, **Aggregate Bandwidth**, and **Core Bandwidth** need to be set. |
| Exclusive | The current network slice will exclusively occupy the selected links if this parameter is set. As such, the selected links must not be occupied (wholly or partially) by other network slices. |
| Shared | The current network slice shares the selected links with other network slices. |

- Open the Network Slicing app. In the slice management area, click 品 in the **Operation** column.

- In the dialog box that is displayed, click **Deploy Slice** on top of the slice topology view. In the **Deploy** dialog box, review link information, as shown in Figure 9.17.

- Click **OK**. In the dialog box that is displayed, select **I have read the message and fully understood the operation impacts on services**, and click **OK**. In the **Information** dialog box, click **OK**.[3]

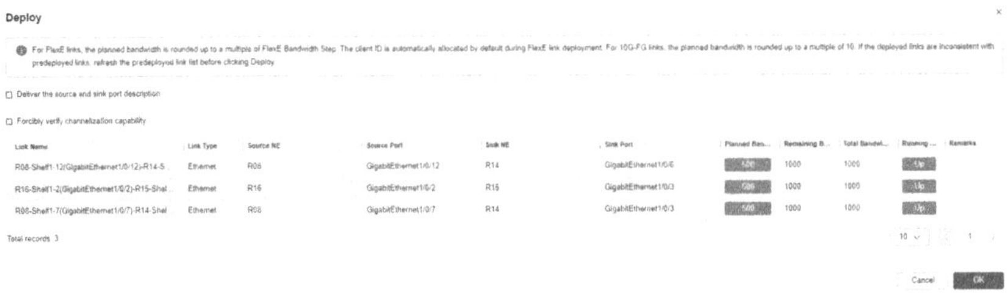

FIGURE 9.17   Slice deployment.

## 9.5.2.4 Activating the Slice

During slice activation, a network slicing solution type and related template need to be selected. Table 9.6 lists the available solution types and templates.

The following describes how to deploy a network slice using the NSC in the slice ID-based network slicing solution. Configure parameters, such as a slice ID for slice links, to implement E2E isolation at the network layer. The procedure is as follows:

- Open the Network Slicing app. In the slice management area, click 🖧 in the **Operation** column.

TABLE 9.6   Network Slicing Solution Types and Templates

| Network Slicing Solution Type | Template | Parameters Delivered to Devices |
|---|---|---|
| SRv6 SID-based network slicing solution | Template with the affinity attribute used in the control plane | Basic SRv6 configuration, creation information of slice links, IPv6 addresses of links, IGP IPv6 enabled for links, link administrative group (color) attribute, and multiplier of the link cost of the non-default slice to the link cost of the default slice |
| | Template with IGP Flex-Algo used in the control plane | Basic SRv6 Flex-Algo configuration, creation information of slice links, IP addresses of links, IGP IPv6 enabled for links, link administrative group (color) attribute corresponding to Flex-Algo, and multiplier of the link cost of the non-default slice to the link cost of the default slice |
| Slice ID-based network slicing solution | Single-layer network slicing template | Slice instance creation information, creation information of slice links, slice IDs of links, and basic slice of links |

## Settings        ✕

ⓘ Activation configuration has not been set for the current slice. Set it first.

Settings ⑦

\* Solution Baseline     Router-Slice ID     ⌄

\* Template:     Router-Slice ID-Template     ⌄

Cancel     Activate

FIGURE 9.18    Parameters for activating the slice.

- In the dialog box that is displayed, click **Activate Slice**. In the **Activate Slice** dialog box, configure activation parameters, as shown in Figure 9.18.

- Click **Activate,** and then **OK**. In the dialog box that is displayed, select **I have read the message and fully understood the operation impacts on services**, and click **OK**. In the dialog box that is displayed, click **OK**.

### 9.5.2.5 Checking Slice Links

The procedure for checking slice links is as follows:

- Open the Network Slicing app. On the network slice page, if the state of the network slice is activated and no slice link deployment failure occurs, the network slice is in the normal state.

- Click 🖧 in the **Operation** column to go to the slice management page.

- Open the subnet where the network slice is located and click [ Refresh ] on the right of the topology to display slice links of the network topology.

- Double-click a link to expand it and check detailed link information between devices.

### 9.5.3 Deployment of IPv6 Hierarchical Network Slicing Using Controllers

In the hierarchical network slicing solution, a level-1 network slice needs to be pre-deployed by a network administrator. A service-driven SRv6 Policy can then be created in the level-1 network slice, and level-2 slices can be created using Flex-Channel on network devices along the SRv6 Policy paths. Figure 9.19 shows the deployment process of slices in the healthcare industry. A level-1 network slice is deployed for the healthcare industry to isolate healthcare services from other services. To ensure the performance of the important remote ultrasound service and remote consultation service in the healthcare industry, two level-2 network slices are deployed in the healthcare industry slice: one for the remote ultrasound service and another for the remote consultation service. In terms of configuration, an EVPN service first needs to be created based on service requirements. An SRv6 Policy then needs to be created in the main slice for this service. Once this configuration is complete, the NSC instructs network devices along the SRv6 Policy paths to allocate resources to the sub-slices and deploy related parameters for the sub-slices.

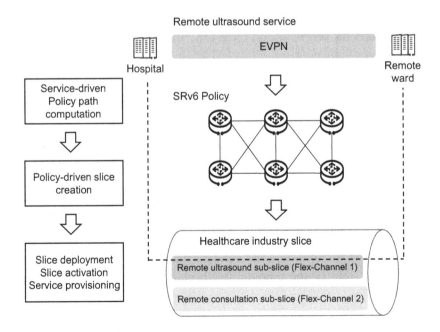

FIGURE 9.19 Service-driven network slice creation process.

To create service-driven network slices on demand, perform the following steps:

- Open the Network Management app and choose **Service** > **Create** > **L2 EVPN Service** from the main menu, as shown in Figure 9.20.

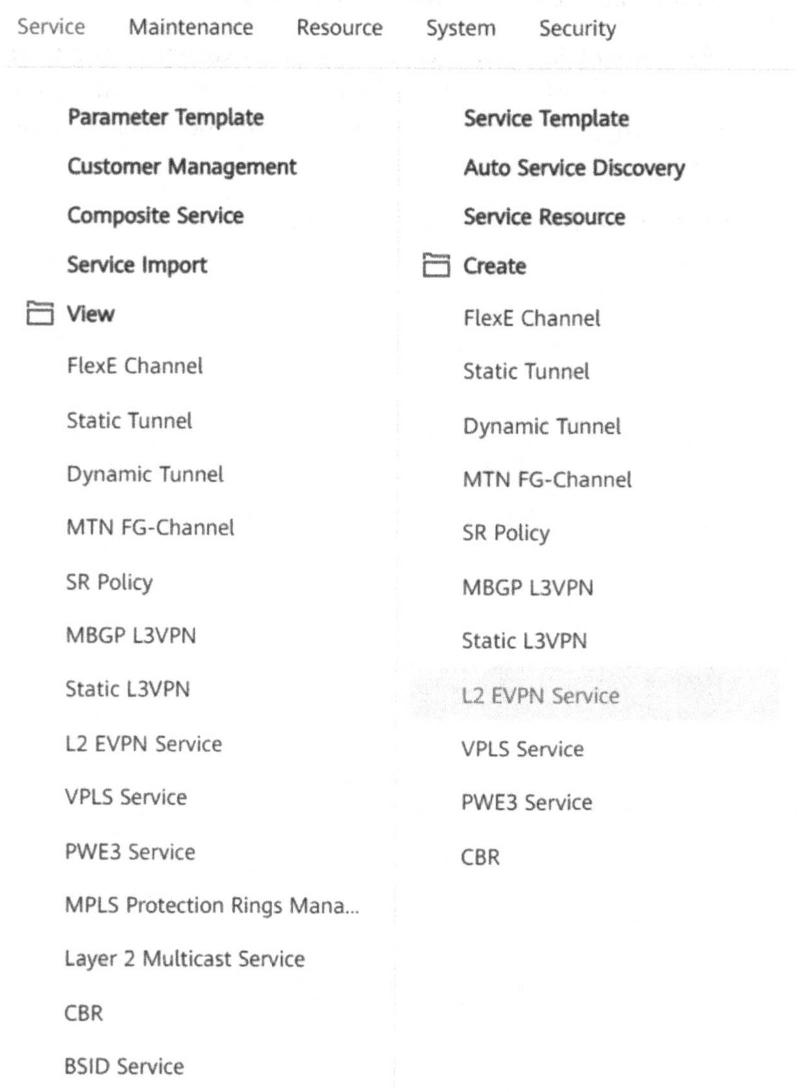

| Service | Maintenance | Resource | System | Security |
|---|---|---|---|---|

| | |
|---|---|
| Parameter Template | Service Template |
| Customer Management | Auto Service Discovery |
| Composite Service | Service Resource |
| Service Import | 🗁 Create |
| 🗁 View | FlexE Channel |
| FlexE Channel | Static Tunnel |
| Static Tunnel | Dynamic Tunnel |
| Dynamic Tunnel | MTN FG-Channel |
| MTN FG-Channel | SR Policy |
| SR Policy | MBGP L3VPN |
| MBGP L3VPN | Static L3VPN |
| Static L3VPN | L2 EVPN Service |
| L2 EVPN Service | VPLS Service |
| VPLS Service | PWE3 Service |
| PWE3 Service | CBR |
| MPLS Protection Rings Mana... | |
| Layer 2 Multicast Service | |
| CBR | |
| BSID Service | |

FIGURE 9.20  Creating services.

- Set sub-slice parameters.

  a. Set the sub-slice parameters listed in Figure 9.21. Specifically, set **Service name** to **Remote_B_ultrasonic**, **Service Type** and **Topology Type** to **P2P**, and **Slice Name** to **Medical_Slicing**.

  b. Enable **SLA Configuration**, set **Bandwidth (kbit/s)** to 100000, and set **Latency (µs)** to 100, as shown in Figure 9.22.

  c. As shown in Figure 9.23, enable **SLA Share Group Configuration** so that the NSC can deliver the Flex-Channel and other parameter settings to network devices along the SRv6 Policy paths of the sub-slices.

- Click **Apply** to deliver the sub-slice configurations.

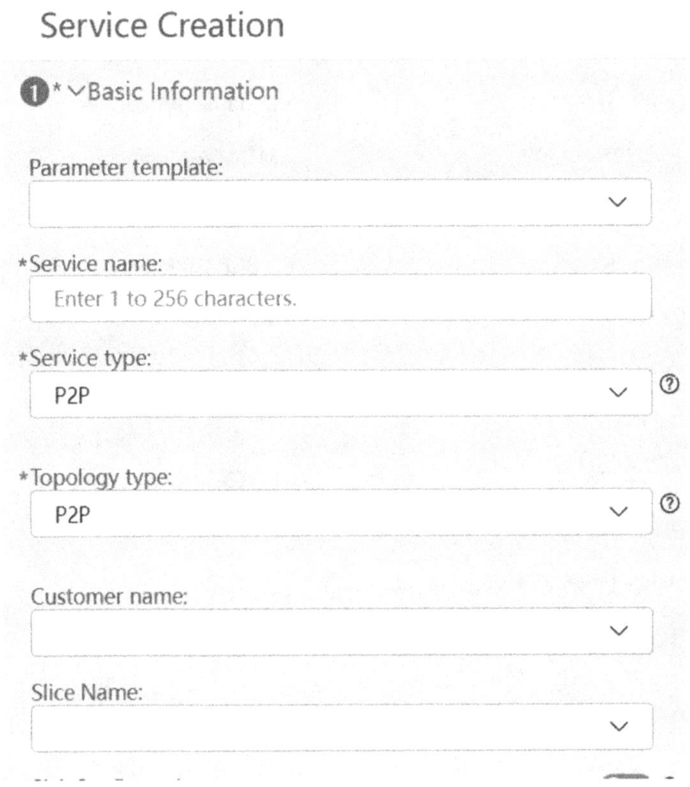

## Service Creation

**1** * ∨ Basic Information

Parameter template:

\[                                              ∨ \]

*Service name:

\[ Enter 1 to 256 characters.                       \]

*Service type:

\[ P2P                                           ∨ \] ⑦

*Topology type:

\[ P2P                                           ∨ \] ⑦

Customer name:

\[                                              ∨ \]

Slice Name:

\[                                              ∨ \]

FIGURE 9.21   Setting sub-slice parameters.

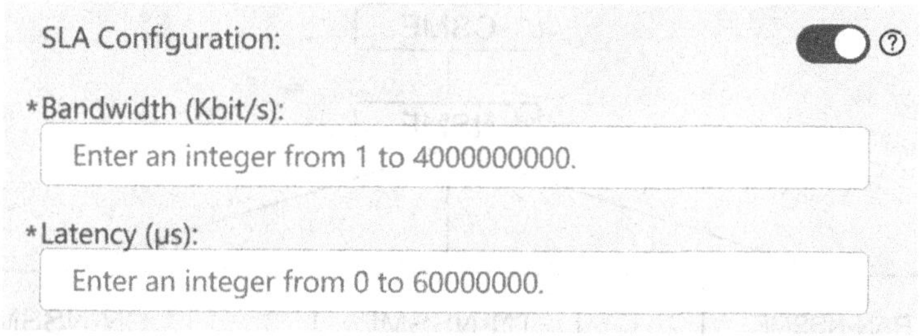

SLA Configuration:

*Bandwidth (Kbit/s):

Enter an integer from 1 to 4000000000.

*Latency (μs):

Enter an integer from 0 to 60000000.

FIGURE 9.22   Configuring SLA indicators.

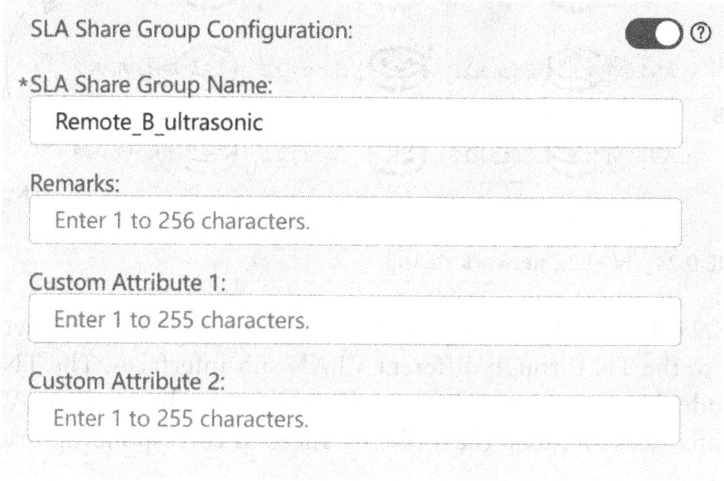

SLA Share Group Configuration:

*SLA Share Group Name:

Remote_B_ultrasonic

Remarks:

Enter 1 to 256 characters.

Custom Attribute 1:

Enter 1 to 255 characters.

Custom Attribute 2:

Enter 1 to 255 characters.

FIGURE 9.23   Configuring an SLA share group.

## 9.5.4  Deployment of Inter-domain IPv6 Network Slicing Using Controllers

Deploying inter-domain IPv6 network slicing using controllers mainly includes deploying network slicing within domains (as described in the previous section) and for inter-domain links (as described in this section).

### 9.5.4.1  5G E2E Network Slicing

In a 5G E2E network slicing scenario, network slice interworking and mapping are required among the RAN, TN, and CN. To differentiate the network slices in such a scenario, VLAN sub-interfaces are typically used on inter-domain links, as shown in Figure 9.24. The RAN

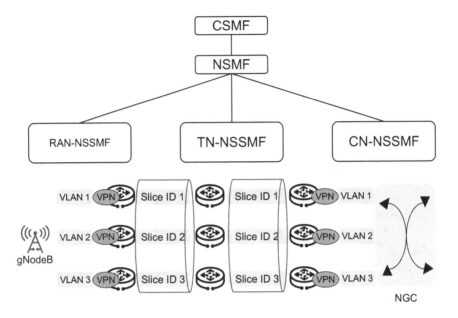

FIGURE 9.24   5G E2E network slicing.

and CN differentiate and transmit the services of different 5G network slices to the TN through different VLAN sub-interfaces. The TN border nodes bind services to different VPN instances based on the VLAN sub-interfaces and map the VPN instances to corresponding resource slices.

### 9.5.4.2 E2E Network Slicing with Hierarchical Controllers

On a large-scale network, E2E inter-domain network slicing can be deployed using hierarchical controllers, as shown in Figure 9.25. Domain controllers 1 and 2 manage network domains 1 and 2, respectively. At the upper layer, the super controller deploys E2E network slices by coordinating domain controllers 1 and 2. It does this by delivering E2E network slice parameters to the domain controllers through Southbound Interfaces. Each of the domain controllers is responsible for intra-domain network slicing deployment.

Currently, two inter-domain network slicing deployment solutions are available: the inter-AS Option A network slicing solution and the inter-AS E2E network slicing solution. In the inter-AS Option A network slicing solution, inter-AS links do not reserve resources for network slices — this

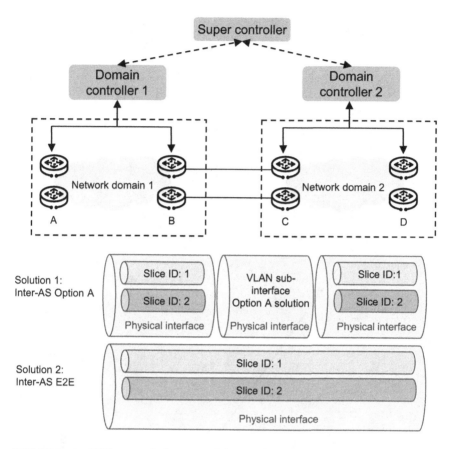

FIGURE 9.25   E2E network slicing with hierarchical controllers.

is similar to the common inter-AS Option A VPN solution. In the inter-AS E2E network slicing solution, inter-AS links need to reserve resources for different network slices and have slice IDs configured.

After deploying inter-domain network slicing using the super controller, you can check inter-domain slice link information on the controller's UI. Between different domains, solid lines indicate that slice links exist, whereas dotted lines indicate that physical links exist but slice links are not deployed, as shown in Figure 9.26.

### 9.5.4.3 E2E Network Slicing with a Single-Layer Controller

In an E2E network slicing deployment scenario with a single-layer controller, this controller is used to manage all the ASs, as shown in Figure 9.27.

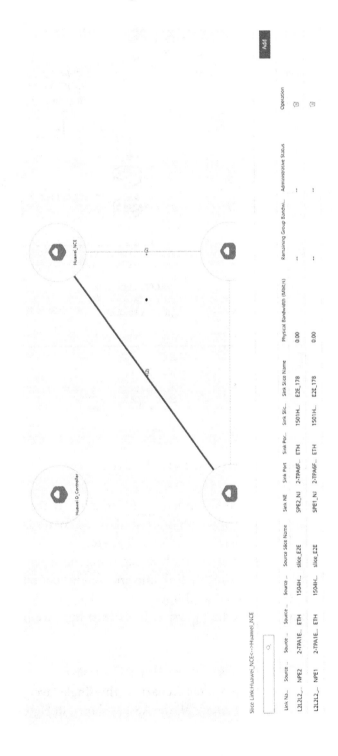

FIGURE 9.26  Inter.domain links with the super controller.

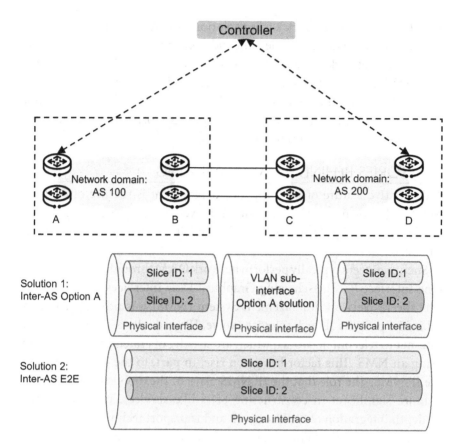

FIGURE 9.27   E2E network slicing with a single-layer controller.

Inter-domain network slicing with a single-layer controller can be deployed as follows:

- Inter-AS Option A network slicing solution: It is recommended that network slices with the same bandwidth granularity be created for different network domains and that the same slice ID be planned for different intra-domain network slices. If network conditions prevent such configuration, network slices with different bandwidth granularities and different slice IDs can be planned for different network domains. In this case, the NSC needs to deliver different network slice parameters to different network domains.

- Inter-AS E2E network slicing solution: It is recommended that network slices with the same bandwidth granularity be created for different network domains and that the same slice ID be planned for different intra-domain network slices and inter-domain links. The NSC delivers the same network slice parameters to different network domains and delivers the parameters of corresponding network slices to inter-domain links.

## 9.6 STORIES BEHIND NETWORK SLICING

A distinctive feature of network slice deployment is the use of controllers. While this makes deployment a relatively simple process and offers greater control, it goes against the O&M habits of traditional IP network engineers.

Such engineers typically perform network O&M through the Command Line Interface (CLI), eschewing Graphical User Interfaces. This is partly why the IP Network Management System (NMS) was not very successful in the past. As IP technologies evolve, IP gradually expands from the Internet to telecom networks, which are usually operated and maintained using an NMS. This factor has given rise, in part, to the development of the IP NMS. The role that the IP NMS plays in the mobile transport field is more significant in constructing SDH-like services. It promotes the in-depth integration of traditional IP and transport technical personnel.

Because network slicing is also a service developed by telecom carriers, it further deepens the integration of IP and telecom. Managing and controlling many network slices across an entire network involves both the deployment of numerous services and complex resource allocation and calculation. The IP NMS, as well as humans, lack the capabilities to complete these complex tasks. Consequently, using network controllers — which provide multiple functions, such as network control, management, and analysis — is necessary and will gradually become common practice for deploying IP services.

## NOTES

1  The NSC UIs vary according to the version. The specific NSC UIs are subject to the software in use.
2  The added links are displayed on the **Predeployed Link Management** tab page. You can view, modify, or delete them.

3 There may be some delay in obtaining link states. You can manually refresh the Slice Link Management tab page. If **Deployment Status** is **Successful**, the slice links have been successfully deployed.

## REFERENCES

[1] Dong J, Bryant S, Miyasaka T, et al. Segment Routing based Virtual Transport Network (VTN) for Enhanced VPN [EB/OL]. (2022-10-11) [2022-10-30]. draft-ietf-spring-sr-for-enhanced-vpn-04.

[2] Zhu Y, Dong J, Hu Z. Using Flex-Algo for Segment Routing (SR) based Virtual Transport Network (VTN) [EB/OL]. (2022-07-11)[2022-09-30]. draft-zhu-lsr-isis-sr-vtn-flexalgo-05.

[3] Dong J, Li Z. Considerations about Hierarchical IETF Network Slices [EB/OL]. (2022-09-07)[2022-09-30]. draft-dong-teas-hierarchical-ietf-network-slice-01.

# PART III

## Summary

# CHAPTER 10

# Industry Development and Future of IP Network Slicing

A s THE DEPLOYMENT OF 5G continues to grow and cloud-network services gain steam, IP network slicing is making significant progress
in standardization and industrialization. This chapter describes the standardization progress of IP network slicing. It also discusses the industrial
activities and commercial deployment of IP network slicing, and then
concludes by predicting what the future holds for IP network slicing.

## 10.1 INDUSTRY DEVELOPMENT OF IP NETWORK SLICING

### 10.1.1 Standardization Progress of IP Network Slicing

The Internet Engineering Task Force (IETF) carries out most of the standardization work related to IP network slicing. This work comprises
roughly two types of Internet-Drafts (hereinafter referred to as drafts):
those related to the IP network slicing architecture and those related to IP
network slicing realization.

The IETF Traffic Engineering Architecture and Signaling (TEAS)
Working Group (WG) is mainly responsible for formulating standards
related to the network slicing architecture and management models, while
the Source Packet Routing in Networking (SPRING) WG is mainly responsible for formulating standards related to the SR-based network slicing

solution. The IPv6 Maintenance (6MAN) WG and Multi-Protocol Label Switching (MPLS) WG are responsible for formulating standards related to the data plane encapsulation of IP network slicing based on IPv6 and MPLS, respectively. And the Link State Routing (LSR) WG, Inter-Domain Routing (IDR) WG, Path Computation Element (PCE) WG, and BGP Enabled Services (BESS) WG are responsible for formulating standards related to control protocol extensions used in network slicing, covering IGP, BGP, PCEP, and VPN, respectively.

### 10.1.1.1 Drafts Related to the IP Network Slicing Framework

The drafts related to the IP network slicing framework include the concepts and general framework of IP network slicing, a framework for realizing network slicing based on technologies such as VPN/Traffic Engineering (TE), and the application of IP network slices in 5G End-to-End (E2E) network slicing. Table 10.1 lists the corresponding drafts.

The VPN+ framework — defined in the IETF *draft draft-ietf-teas-enhanced-vpn*[2] — consists of the layered network architecture and layer-specific candidate technologies for realizing VPN+ services. To provide enhanced VPN services and thereby meet the strict Service-Level Agreement (SLA) requirements of various services in 5G and other scenarios, the draft proposed technical extensions that combine VPN and TE technologies. 5G network slicing is a typical application of VPN+. Figure 10.1 shows an overview of VPN+ standards.

### 10.1.1.2 Drafts Related to IP Network Slicing Realization

The drafts related to IP network slicing realization involve the following aspects: SR SID-based network slicing, slice ID-based network slicing,

TABLE 10.1    Drafts Related to the IP Network Slicing Framework

| Category | Topic | Document |
|---|---|---|
| Concept and general framework of IP network slicing | Terminology and general architecture of IETF network slices | draft-ietf-teas-ietf-network-slices[1] |
| Architecture for realizing IP network slicing | Enhanced VPN (VPN+) architecture | draft-ietf-teas-enhanced-vpn[2] |
| Application of IP network slices in 5G E2E network slicing | Mapping between 5G E2E network slices and IP network slices | draft-gcdrb-teas-5g-network-slice-application[3] |

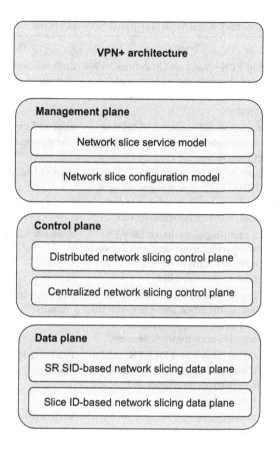

FIGURE 10.1 VPN+ standard overview.

hierarchical IP network slicing, inter-domain IP network slicing, user- and application-oriented IP network slicing, and IP network slice management models.

10.1.1.2.1 SR SID-based Network Slicing    Table 10.2 describes documents related to SR SID-based network slicing, classifying them as either data plane or control plane drafts. The data plane used in the SR-based network slicing solution adopts existing SR-based encapsulation. In this solution, the semantics of the SR SID and SRv6 locator are extended to indicate the topology, functions, and resources of the corresponding network slice of packets. The control plane of SR-based network slicing uses a protocol extension solution that requires minimal extension based on existing control-plane technology (such as multi-topology or Flex-Algo). Although

TABLE 10.2  Documents Related to SR SID-Based Network Slicing

| Category | Topic | Document |
|---|---|---|
| Data plane | Realizing VPN+ based on SR: defines VPN+ data-plane encapsulation and processing based on resource-aware SR SIDs and SRv6 locators. | draft-ietf-spring-sr-for-enhanced-vpn[4] |
| | Resource-aware SIDs: extend SR SIDs to identify the network resources reserved for packet processing. | draft-ietf-spring-resource-aware-segments[5] |
| Control plane | IS-IS multi-topology-based SR VTN: used to distribute information about network slice attributes (such as topologies and resources) between network devices. | draft-ietf-lsr-isis-sr-vtn-mt[6] |
| | BGP-LS multi-topology-based SR VTN: used to report information about network slice attributes (such as topologies and resources) to the controller. | draft-ietf-idr-bgpls-sr-vtn-mt[7] |
| | IS-IS Flex-Ago-based SR VTN: used to distribute information about network slice attributes (such as topologies and resources) between network devices. | draft-zhu-lsr-isis-sr-vtn-flexalgo[8] |
| | BGP-LS Flex-Algo-based SR VTN: used to report information about network slice attributes (such as topologies and resources) to the controller. | draft-zhu-idr-bgpls-sr-vtn-flexalgo[9] |
| | IGP Flex-Algo | draft-ietf-lsr-flex-algo[10] |
| | IS-IS multi-topology | RFC 5120[11] |
| | OSPF multi-topology | RFC 4915[12] |

this solution is relatively easy to implement, it has some limitations in terms of flexibility and extensibility.

10.1.1.2.2 Slice ID-based Network Slicing  In the slice ID-based network slicing solution, the IPv6 header is extended to carry a unified network slice ID, which indicates the network slice resources used for forwarding packets.

Based on the combination and extension of various control-plane technologies and attributes, the solution provides control-plane capabilities that support flexible customization of network slices and a massive number of slices. Table 10.3 describes drafts related to slice ID-based network slicing.

TABLE 10.3    Drafts Related to Slice ID-Based Network Slicing

| Category | Topic | Document |
|---|---|---|
| Network slice scalability analysis and optimization | Network slice scalability considerations and optimization suggestions | draft-ietf-teas-nrp-scalability[13] |
| Data plane | Network slice ID based on IPv6 extension headers | draft-ietf-6man-enhanced-vpn-vtn-id[14] |
| Control plane | IGP extensions for network slicing | draft-dong-lsr-sr-enhanced-vpn[15] |
| | BGP-LS protocol extensions for network slicing | draft-dong-idr-bgpls-sr-enhanced-vpn[16] |
| | BGP SPF protocol extensions for network slicing | draft-dong-lsvr-bgp-spf-nrp[17] |
| | BGP SR Policy extensions for network slicing | draft-dong-idr-sr-policy-nrp[18] |
| | PCEP extensions for network slicing | draft-dong-pce-pcep-nrp[19] |
| | BGP FlowSpec extensions for network slicing | draft-ietf-idr-flowspec-network-slice-ts[20] |

10.1.1.2.3 Hierarchical IP Network Slicing    The draft related to hierarchical IP network slicing (*draft-li-teas-composite-network-slices*) mainly describes the scenarios and requirements of hierarchical IP network slicing and analyzes the technologies for realizing hierarchical IP network slicing.[21]

10.1.1.2.4 Inter-Domain IP Network Slicing    The drafts related to inter-domain IP network slicing are classified as either architecture or data plane drafts. Table 10.4 lists the drafts.

10.1.1.2.5 User- and Application-Oriented IP Network Slicing    Table 10.5 lists the drafts related to user- and application-oriented IP network slicing, which involves APN-based network slicing and network slicing combined with intent-based routing.

10.1.1.2.6 Management Models    The management plane of IP network slicing can provide a network slice service model for the customer's higher-level operation system through the northbound interface of the Network Slice Controller (NSC). This enables the customer's system to

TABLE 10.4    Drafts Related to Inter-Domain IP Network Slicing

| Category | Topic | Document |
|---|---|---|
| Inter-domain IP network slicing architecture | Architecture for realizing inter-domain IP network slicing | draft-li-teas-composite-network-slices[22] |
| Inter-domain IP network slicing data plane | Data-plane encapsulation of IPv6-based inter-domain network slicing | draft-li-6man-e2e-ietf-network-slicing[23] |
| | Data-plane encapsulation of MPLS-based inter-domain network slicing | draft-li-mpls-e2e-ietf-network-slicing[24] |
| | SR-based inter-domain network slicing extension | draft-li-spring-sr-e2e-ietf-network-slicing[25] |

TABLE 10.5    Drafts Related to User- and Application-Oriented IP Network Slicing

| Category | Topic | Document |
|---|---|---|
| APN-based network slicing | Application-aware network architecture | draft-li-apn-framework[26] |
| Network slicing combined with intent-based routing | Intent-based routing | draft-li-teas-intent-based-routing[27] |

deliver the requirements of network slice services and collect attribute and state information about network slices. The management plane also provides a resource slice deployment model for the southbound interface of the controller to enable the creation and maintenance of network resource slices. There are two IETF drafts related to IP network slice management models:

- *draft-ietf-teas-transport-slice-yang*[28]: defines a service model for IETF network slices.

- *draft-wd-teas-nrp-yang*[29]: defines a deployment model for network resource slices.

In summary, multiple drafts, such as those related to the concept and general framework of IP network slicing, realization architecture based on technologies such as VPN/TE, and data plane and control plane of SRv6 SID-based network slicing, have been adopted by related IETF WGs. And SRv6 SID-based network slicing technologies and standards are relatively mature. At present, the standardization of IP network slicing is focusing on slice ID-based IP network slicing technologies. With the deployment and application of IP network slicing, the standardization of technologies such as hierarchical IP network slicing, inter-domain IP network slicing, and application- and user-oriented IP network slicing is being carried out step-by-step in the IETF.

## 10.1.2 Industrial Activities of IP Network Slicing

A series of activities have been carried out to further consolidate industry consensus and promote innovative applications of IP network slicing. Such activities include ensuring major device vendors' support for IP network slicing and carrying out IP network slicing interoperability tests, as well as holding WG discussions and industry forums.

So far, the European Advanced Networking Test Center has conducted two successful Flex-Algo interoperability tests, in 2019 and 2021, to verify the interoperability of Flex-Algo on network devices from multiple vendors. The tests covered advertising TE attributes required by Flex-Algos based on the IS-IS TE extension, measuring the network link delay based on TWAMP, and computing paths and forwarding packets based on metric types and link constraints defined by Flex-Algos. The results of the March 2021 test were presented at the MPLS+SDN+NFV World Congress in July 2021.

In November 2019, China's Expert Committee for Promoting Large-Scale IPv6 Deployment approved the establishment of the IPv6+ Technology Innovation WG. The working objectives are to (1) strengthen system innovation with next-generation IPv6 Internet technologies based on the achievements of China's large-scale IPv6 deployment; (2) integrate IPv6 technology industry chains (such as academia, device vendors, carriers, and enterprises) to proactively verify and demonstrate new IPv6 Enhanced network technologies (including SRv6, VPN+, IFIT, DetNet, BIERv6, SFC, and APN) and new applications in network routing protocols, management automation, intelligence, and security; and (3) take an active role in standardization activities and continuously improve IPv6 technology standards. IP network slicing — an important application of IPv6 Enhanced innovation — has gained widespread attention. At the IPv6 Enhanced industry salons held in June 2019, December 2019, June 2020, and September 2020, and at the China IPv6 Innovation and Development Conference held in October 2021, IP network slicing was widely presented as an important innovation topic.

At the end of 2020, the European Telecommunications Standards Institute (ETSI) established IPv6 Enhanced Innovation, a new Industry Specification Group (ISG), to promote IPv6 innovation and development. IP network slicing was again presented at the Webinar conferences held by ETSI in September 2020 and October 2021.

In 2019, 2021, and 2022, a dedicated session on network slicing was arranged at the MPLS SD & AI Net World Congress, where multiple network device vendors and network management service providers introduced the network slicing architecture and key technologies.

The preceding activities have played a crucial role in shining the spotlight on IP network slicing. As this innovative technology gains widespread adoption on carrier networks, the IP network slicing industry will become more mature and established.

### 10.1.3 Commercial Deployment of IP Network Slicing

IP network slicing has been deployed by multiple carriers around the world, including China Telecom, China Unicom, China Mobile, Algeria Telecom, and others on some of their networks. The experience of deploying IP network slicing is also shared in the industry through an IETF draft (*draft-ma-teas-ietf-network-slice-deployment*).[30]

In China, especially, the development of IP network slicing has been rapid — the demand for E2E network slices promotes the innovation and development of IP network slicing thanks to the large-scale deployment and use of 5G. By mid-2022, network carriers, including China Telecom, China Unicom, and China Mobile, had carried out more than 10 commercial deployments or pilot projects of IP network slicing. The ability to isolate services and guarantee performance with IP network slicing is becoming a major advantage that attracts a great deal of attention. As the number of IP network slices grows, IP network slicing has become an important value-added network service for carriers and has set a positive example for innovation throughout the industry.

The deployment of IP network slicing by China Telecom Ningxia is a benchmark project. This carrier deployed an SRv6-based slicing network to carry multiple industries' services, including healthcare, education, and enterprise Internet services. At the same time, Ningxia Telecom is planning to migrate some industry and public services from different private networks or Multi-Service Transport Platforms (MSTPs) to IP-based networks. By adopting IP network slicing, the carrier can isolate the services of different industries on its network and ensure that they do not affect each other. In this way, the carrier can guarantee the SLAs of each service while also significantly reducing the costs that would have been involved if an independent private network needed to be constructed, maintained, and expanded for each industry.

In this benchmark project, the carrier created three network slices, sharing one IGP instance, on its network in order to provide the resources and security isolation required by customers for healthcare, education, and enterprise Internet services. In the forwarding plane, channelized sub-interface technology is used to reserve independent bandwidth resources for each network slice. In the control plane, different affinity attributes are used to define the logical topology of each network slice. In each network slice, an independent SRv6 End.X SID is assigned to each link to represent the channelized sub-interface of the slice on the physical interface used for packet forwarding. As more industry and government services are migrated to this network, more network slices may need to be created. Accordingly, considerations need to be made for evolving to the slice ID-based network slicing solution in the future.

Multiple L3VPN services belonging to the same industry can be deployed on each network slice. For example, the network slice for the healthcare industry is used to carry VPNs connecting different hospitals and also carry VPNs connecting hospitals and insurance systems on the healthcare cloud. The traffic of these VPNs is mapped either to the explicit path of an SRv6 Policy or to an SRv6 BE path in the network slice according to the mechanism for mapping service slices to resource slices. Based on resource-aware SRv6 SIDs, traffic is steered to the channelized sub-interface corresponding to the resource slice for processing.

China Telecom Ningxia uses a centralized NSC to manage network slices and VPN services (Figure 10.2). Through this controller, the carrier can plan the topologies and reserved resources of network slices, deploy channelized sub-interfaces for network slices, map VPN services to corresponding network slices, and compute SRv6 TE paths based on service requirements as well as the topology and resource information of network slices. The centralized controller also enables the carrier to collect traffic statistics and performance monitoring information on network slices and VPN services in order to visualize network slice services and provide guaranteed SLAs.

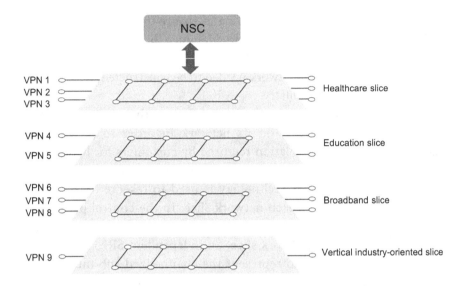

FIGURE 10.2 SRv6 SID-based network slicing deployment case of China Telecom Ningxia.

Another typical network slicing deployment case is Algeria Telecom's metro network, which supports IP network slicing. Algeria Telecom wants to isolate the video livestreaming services of sports events, the operation management services of stadiums, and the Internet access services of onsite audiences while also guaranteeing the SLAs of each service. The carrier also wants to isolate these services from other existing services on the metro network to ensure that they do not affect each other. To meet these requirements, four network slices are created on the network — one each to carry the video livestreaming services of sports events, stadium operation services, Internet access services of onsite audiences, and other services. All network slices share one IGP control protocol instance. For forwarding-plane resource partitioning, FlexE interface technology is used to reserve independent bandwidth resources for each network slice, and each slice is allocated an independent slice ID. This allows network devices to distinguish packets of different network slices based on slice IDs carried in data packets and forward the packets using the FlexE interface created for each network slice. Each network slice can carry one or more VPN services according to different service requirements. For example, the slice for sports

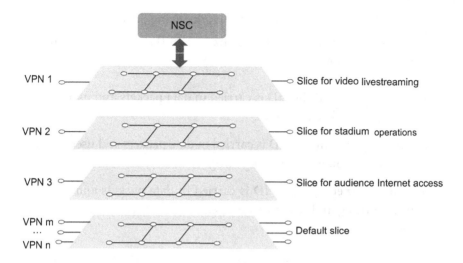

FIGURE 10.3    Slice ID-based network slice deployment case of Algeria Telecom.

event livestreaming is used to carry the VPN service that connects stadiums and video livestreaming centers.

Algeria Telecom uses an NSC to plan, create, maintain, and optimize network slices (Figure 10.3). For each network slice, the NSC computes paths based on the corresponding topology and resource constraints and distributes the SRv6 Policy associated with each network slice to the headend of the path. Based on the SRv6 Policy, the headend encapsulates the SID list (indicating the forwarding path) into service slice packets steered to the network resource slice and encapsulates the slice ID of the corresponding network slice into the packets.

## 10.2  TECHNICAL PROSPECTS OF IP NETWORK SLICING

IP network slicing is a comprehensive and relatively standalone technical system. A number of technical solutions have already been developed under the IP network slicing umbrella, including SRv6 SID-based network slicing, slice ID-based network slicing, hierarchical IP network slicing, and inter-domain IP network slicing. Looking ahead to the future, IP network slicing technologies will continue to develop, network slice-related services will be further atomized, network slicing will be finer-grained and more dynamic, and the performance of slice services will be more deterministic.

### 10.2.1 Further Atomization of IP Network Slicing Services

From the service perspective, the atomization of IP network slicing in the data plane is as follows:

1. An intra-domain slice ID is carried in data packets and used to isolate network slice resources.

2. An inter-domain slice ID is carried in data packets and used to realize inter-domain IP network slicing.

3. A 5G E2E network slice ID is carried in data packets and used for interworking and mapping between 5G E2E network slices and IP network slices.

In the future, IP network slices will be able to carry additional atomic services. This means carrying in the data plane more service identifiers, such as a topology ID and resource IDs of different service types.

#### 10.2.1.1 Carrying Topology ID in the Data Plane

An IP network slice can carry multi-topology or Flex-Algo information in the data plane to identify the topology or Flex-Algo associated with the network slice. In the current IPv6 network slicing solution, different SRv6 locators and SIDs need to be used to indicate the corresponding topologies, or Flex-Algos. If a dedicated topology or Flex-Algo ID is carried in the data packet, the SRv6 locator and SIDs are no longer used to identify the topology. This eliminates the need to configure a unique SRv6 locator and unique SIDs for each topology or Flex-Algo. Instead, the corresponding forwarding table is determined based on the topology or Flex-Algo ID in the packet, and the SRv6 locator and SIDs are used for table lookup and forwarding.

In Figure 10.4, network slices 1 and 2 have the same topology, as do network slices 3 and 4. Each network slice has independent resource attributes. According to the slice ID-based network slicing solution, Flex-Algo 128 can be used to define one of the topologies, and Flex-Algo 129 can be used to define the other one. Each network node needs to allocate different locators to Flex-Algo 128 and Flex-Algo 129 to distinguish between topologies. As more topologies need to be defined, the number of locators and corresponding SRv6 SIDs that need to be allocated increases significantly. This not only complicates network deployment but also causes scalability problems.

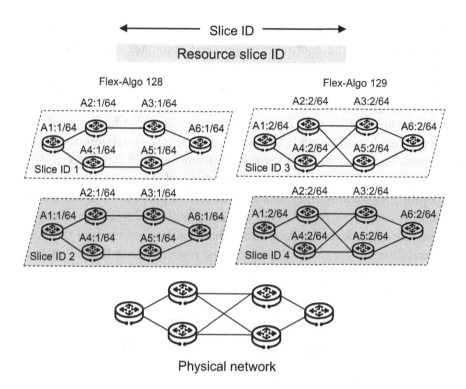

FIGURE 10.4 Allocating different SRv6 locators to different topologies or Flex-Algos in the slice ID-based network slicing solution.

To resolve the preceding problems, topology IDs can be introduced to the data plane. In this way, a network node does not need to configure different locators for different topologies. Rather, each network node requires only one locator, which can be used together with different topology IDs. SRv6 SIDs prefixed with the locator can be bound to different topologies or Flex-Algos. In this case, separate routing and forwarding tables need to be generated for different topologies or Flex-Algos. In the slice ID-based network slicing solution, however, because different locators are allocated to different topologies, forwarding entries of route prefixes corresponding to the locators can be stored in the same forwarding table.

During SPF-based route calculation, SPF calculation is performed according to topology attribute information corresponding to a specific multi-topology or Flex-Algo, and the calculated forwarding entries are stored in the corresponding forwarding table. The same locator can have different forwarding entries in forwarding tables corresponding to different topologies or Flex-Algos. In explicit path computation for an SRv6 Policy, the controller or headend computes constraint-based paths based on the topology and TE attributes of different topologies or Flex-Algos corresponding to slices and uses SRv6 End SIDs and End.X SIDs to program paths.

In Figure 10.5, during packet forwarding, the packet header needs to carry a topology ID in addition to the resource ID of a network slice. The network device can determine the forwarding table instance corresponding to the topology ID carried in the packet and then search for a corresponding forwarding entry based on the locator prefix in the Destination Address field of the packet. After obtaining outbound interface information, the network device determines the resources reserved on the outbound interface for the slice based on the resource ID in the packet and then forwards the packet.

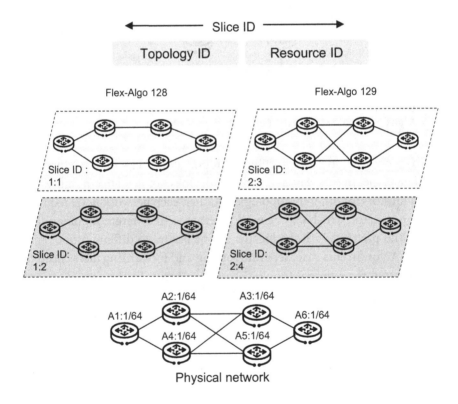

FIGURE 10.5  Topology ID in the slice ID-based network slicing solution.

The advantage of this solution lies in decoupling SRv6 locators and SR SIDs from topologies and Flex-Algos, thereby allowing different topologies and Flex-Algos to share SRv6 locators and SR SIDs. This eliminates the need for planning and configuring different SRv6 locators and SR SIDs for different topologies. In addition, this solution improves network scalability and reduces configuration complexity because it avoids introducing more network states to the control plane (and the corresponding advertisement of such states). Furthermore, SRv6 VPN SIDs do not need to be uniquely bound to a topology or Flex-Algo. Instead, they can be flexibly bound to different topologies or Flex-Algos based on service requirements or network status changes.

### 10.2.1.2 Carrying Resource IDs of More Service Types

In addition to providing a service SLA guarantee through resource isolation and topology constraints, IP network slicing can be further extended to provide services with other network functions — such as network security and user-specific policies — on a per-slice basis. To provide such services, the corresponding resources and identifiers of the services need to be provided on a per-slice basis. For example, a specific network slice needs to not only guarantee SLAs but also provide specific security services. In this case, when a network slice is generated, it is necessary to allocate forwarding resources (such as bandwidth) to ensure SLAs and allocate security service resources on corresponding network devices. Furthermore, binding relationships between the network slice and forwarding resources, as well as between the network slice and security service resources, need to be established. In this way, when a data packet carrying a slice ID arrives at a network device, related forwarding resources and security service resources can be obtained, allowing the packet to be processed and forwarded while also ensuring service SLAs and security.

As topology IDs and more resource IDs for other service types are introduced to the data plane of a network slice, these IDs can be carried in data packets using either of the following methods:

Method 1: Packets carry different IDs that correspond to different services and resources. As shown in Figure 10.6, a data packet can carry the topology ID, forwarding resource ID, and security service resource ID. The forwarding resource ID corresponds to the resource ID of a network slice.

| Topology ID | Forwarding resource ID | Security service resource ID |
| --- | --- | --- |

FIGURE 10.6   A data packet carrying different IDs.

Method 2: Each network device in a network slice maintains mapping relationships between the network slice ID and each of the topology ID, forwarding resource ID, and other service resource IDs. In this way, a data packet needs to carry only one network slice ID, as shown in Figure 10.7. After receiving a packet, the network device can obtain the topology ID, forwarding resource ID, and other service resource IDs corresponding to the network slice ID based on the local mapping relationship. This method expands the application scope of the network slice ID mentioned in this book, and the network slice ID not only corresponds to forwarding resources used to ensure SLAs in a network slice but also associates with a topology and resources of other types of services.

### 10.2.2  Finer-Grained and More Dynamic Network Slicing

As network slicing becomes more widely deployed, the granularity of network slices needs to be further refined to meet the increasing demand for dynamicity.

Currently, network slicing is mainly oriented toward industries and tenants. In the future, application-level network slicing may be supported, meaning that the slicing granularity will be further refined. This requires the forwarding plane to support finer-grained resource isolation and scheduling so that the control and management planes can maintain a larger number of application-level network slices.

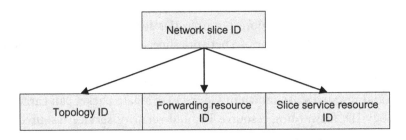

FIGURE 10.7   A data packet carrying a generalized network slice ID.

The dynamicity requirements of network slices are reflected in two aspects: (1) More dynamic topology changes. That is, the topologies and connections of IP network slices dynamically change as the locations of applications and users change. (2) More dynamic resource scaling. That is, the resources need to scale-in and scale-out dynamically as application and user traffic changes.

As the demand for dynamicity increases, network slices need to be dynamically created, and topologies and resources need to be dynamically adjusted. This is necessary so that IP network slices can be quickly provisioned and optimized in real time.

To meet these requirements for finer granularity and dynamicity, IP network slices must be able to be quickly provisioned in the future. The following methods can be used to quickly provision IP network slices:

- Pre-planning of IP network slices. That is, during IP network slice planning, only slice information is preset on devices rather than network slices being created. Slices can then be quickly instantiated, along with service access, and provisioned in seconds.

- APN-based IP network slices. That is, the APN attribute is carried in packets to indicate application group and user group information so that the network can provide fine-grained services more conveniently. APN can effectively support finer-grained and dynamic IP network slices. Specifically:

- *draft-li-apn-framework*[31] defines the APN framework. According to the application group and user group information carried in the APN attribute of packets, traffic can be mapped to corresponding IP network slices, thereby realizing application- and user-level network slices.

- The APN attribute carries information about network performance requirements, instructing a network device to reserve resources in the data plane and associate the resources with the corresponding IP network slice. In this way, IP slice resources can be dynamically reserved.

- In mobile scenarios, the locations of applications and users may change. However, because the application group and user group information in the APN attribute can remain unchanged, it is possible to map this information to a corresponding IP network slice, thereby ensuring that the mapped slice does not change in mobile scenarios.

### 10.2.3 More Deterministic Service Guarantee Through Network Slicing

Resource partitioning technologies such as FlexE interface, channelized sub-interface, and flexible sub-channel are currently used to implement IP network resource slices. These technologies can effectively ensure the isolation and SLAs of network slice services. As 5G Ultra-reliable Low-Latency Communication (URLLC) services develop, networks need to provide SLA guarantee for such services. For example, typical application scenarios such as smart grid, Internet of Vehicles, and Cloud VR place high requirements on SLAs.

To meet the SLA requirements in these scenarios, Deterministic Networking (DetNet) technologies emerge. DetNet integrates the technical advantages of statistical multiplexing and Time Division Multiplexing (TDM), providing a TDM-like SLA guarantee on an IP packet network. DetNet ensures low jitter and zero packet loss for high-value service traffic during transmission and provides an expected upper bound for E2E delay. For deterministic networks, the related standards are developed by the IETF DetNet WG.

According to *Deterministic Networking Architecture*,[32] published by the IETF, DetNet represents a series of technologies, including the following relatively independent ones:

- Resource allocation: Resources, such as buffer or outbound interface bandwidth, are allocated to a DetNet flow along its path to ensure QoS. DetNet resource allocation can reduce or even eliminate the delay or packet loss caused by packets competing for resources on the network. To ensure that the amount of data transmitted does not exceed the resources reserved for a DetNet flow, the network edge node or data originator needs to limit the transmission rate and maximum packet size of the flow. As such, DetNet flows are regarded as rate-controllable traffic, and sufficient resources can be reserved on the network for traffic forwarding. This means that congestion control is not required for DetNet flows. The queue management algorithm schedules potentially conflicting packets and allocates bandwidth based on resource reservation. The combined use of resource reservation technology and queue management algorithm helps to eliminate network congestion. Resource allocation addresses two QoS requirements of DetNet: bounded latency and an extremely low packet loss rate. Because resources are allocated to a DetNet flow on its path, in conjunction with the local queue scheduling and shaping methods (e.g., IEEE 802.1 Qbv, IEEE 802.1 Qch) of devices, it is possible to deduct the upper bound of the flow's delay at each hop and then deduct the upper bound of the E2E delay. Resource allocation can also solve the problem of packet loss due to packets competing for outbound interface bandwidth.

- Explicit path: To ensure that service performance remains stable and unaffected by topology changes, DetNet needs to use explicit path technology in order to constrain the routes of packets. In this way, it can prevent route flapping or other factors from directly affecting transmission quality. An IP network provides various protocols, including Resource Reservation Protocol-Traffic Engineering (RSVP-TE) and SR, which can provide explicit paths. In particular, SR does not need to maintain per-flow forwarding states on transit nodes, which only forward packets based on active segments. This is why SR is so scalable, which is a key factor in its wide-scale adoption.

- Redundancy protection: To ensure high reliability of service transmission, redundancy protection can be used. This technology enables a service packet to be replicated and transmitted along two or more disjoint paths, with the merging node retaining only the first copy of the packet that arrives. Also called multifed selective receiving, this technology enables services to be switched to another path without any loss if the original path fails.

These independent technologies can be combined to form a complete DetNet solution. By combining IP network slicing with DetNet and leveraging DetNet's new resource reservation and queue management algorithms, such a solution can better meet the deterministic latency requirements of emerging services such as 5G URLLC.

## 10.3 STORIES BEHIND NETWORK SLICING

The development of network slicing presents a generalization trend, which is mainly reflected in two aspects.

The first is the generalization of resources. In network slicing, the slice ID carried in a packet is used to indicate bandwidth resources allocated to a network slice. Network services have different SLA requirements; for example, some may place stricter requirements on latency. As discussed in this chapter's DetNet section, deterministic latency requires specific resources and mechanisms for latency guarantee. Accordingly, the slice ID in network slicing can be generalized as a universal resource ID, meaning that it can be used to indicate not only bandwidth resources but also resources that ensure deterministic latency. The draft on resource-aware segments describes possible resources in detail.[5] To provide SLA guarantees, resource-aware segments can be used to indicate many other types of resources in addition to bandwidth resources. This also applies to slice IDs. The generalization of resources is also manifested in the resource ID being used not only to indicate resources for ensuring SLAs but also to indicate resources for implementing other services (e.g., network security). This is another manifestation of resource generalization and means that network slicing can provide not only SLA-guaranteed services but also other types of network services through resource isolation.

The second is the generalization of network-slicing application scenarios. IP network slicing originates from 5G scenarios and is used to provide transport network slices in 5G E2E network slicing. The technologies involved in IP network slicing are also used on carriers' IP metro and backbone networks to carry not only mobile services but also fixed services, enterprise services, and more. Due to the wide application of IP technologies, network slicing technologies are also gradually introduced to enterprise networks in addition to being widely used on carrier IP networks. Enterprise campus networks, which are also carrying diversified services with different service requirements, currently use various overlay VPN technologies (such as VXLAN) to isolate services on the network edge. As network slicing technologies develop, resource isolation can be further realized on these networks to better meet the requirements of different services. And with enterprise cloudification undergoing continuous development, SD-WAN technologies are widely used. By combining these technologies with network slicing, better SLA and security experience guarantees can be provided for enterprise cloudification services.

The generalization of network slicing is closely related to the technical essence of IP network slicing. By adding resource identifiers to the forwarding plane, IP network slicing introduces a two-dimensional forwarding paradigm to IP networks. All services and scenarios that require "location- and resource-based" forwarding can be included in this system. In this sense, network slicing has gone far beyond the definition of its initial services and application scenarios.

# REFERENCES

[1] Farrel A, Gray E, Drake J, et al. A Framework for IETF Network Slices [EB/OL]. (2022-12-21)[2022-12-30]. draft-ietf-teas-ietf-network-slices-17.

[2] Dong J, Bryant S, Li Z, et al. A Framework for Enhanced Virtual Private Networks (VPN+) Services [EB/OL]. (2022-9-20)[2022-09-30] draft-ietf-teas-enhanced-vpn-11.

[3] Geng X, Contreras L, Dong J, et al. IETF Network Slice Application in 3GPP 5G End-to-End Network Slice [EB/OL]. (2022-10-24)[2022-10-30]. draft-gcdrb-teas-5g-network-slice-application-01.

[4] Dong J, Bryant S, Miyasaka T, et al. Segment Routing based Virtual Transport Network (VTN) for Enhanced VPN [EB/OL]. (2022-10-11)[2022-10-30]. draft-ietf-spring-sr-for-enhanced-vpn-04.

[5] Dong J, Bryant S, Miyasaka T, et al. Introducing Resource Awareness to SR Segments [EB/OL]. (2020-10-11)[2022-10-30]. draft-ietf-spring-resource-aware-segments-06.

[6] Xie C, Ma C, Dong J, et al. Using IS-IS Multi-Topology (MT) for Segment Routing based Virtual Transport Network [EB/OL]. (2022-07-29)[2022-09-30]. draft-ietf-lsr-isis-sr-vtn-mt-03.

[7] Xie C, Li C, Dong J, et al. BGP-LS with Multi-Topology for Segment Routing based Virtual Transport Networks [EB/OL]. (2022-09-12)[2022-09-30]. draft-ietf-idr-bgpls-sr-vtn-mt-01.

[8] Zhu Y, Dong J, Hu Z. Using Flex-Algo for Segment Routing Based VTN [EB/OL]. (2022-07-11)[2022-09-30]. draft-zhu-lsr-isis-sr-vtn-flexalgo-05.

[9] Zhu Y, Dong J, Hu Z. BGP-LS with Flex-Algo for Segment Routing based Virtual Transport Networks [EB/OL]. (2021-08-26)[2022-09-30]. draft-zhu-idr-bgpls-sr-vtn-flexalgo-01.

[10] Psenak P, Hegde S, Filsfils C, et al. IGP Flexible Algorithm [EB/OL]. (2022-10-17)[2022-10-30]. draft-ietf-lsr-flex-algo-26.

[11] Shen N, Sheth N, Przygienda T. M-ISIS: Multi Topology (MT) Routing in Intermediate System to Intermediate Systems (IS-ISs) [EB/OL]. (2015-10-14)[2022-09-30]. RFC 5120.

[12] Psenak P, Mirtorabi S, Roy A, et al. Multi-Topology (MT) Routing in OSPF [EB/OL]. (2007-06)[2022-09-30]. RFC 4915.

[13] Dong J, Li Z, Gong L, et al. Scalability Considerations for Network Resource Partition [EB/OL]. (2022-10-24)[2022-12-31]. draft-ietf-teas-nrp-scalability-01.

[14] Dong J, Li Z, Xie C, et al. Carrying Virtual Transport Network (VTN) Identifier in IPv6 Extension Header [EB/OL]. (2022-10-24)[2022-10-30]. draft-ietf-6man-enhanced-vpn-vtn-id-02.

[15] Dong J, Hu Z, Li Z, et al. IGP Extensions for Scalable Segment Routing based Enhanced VPN [EB/OL]. (2022-07-11)[2022-09-30]. draft-dong-lsr-sr-enhanced-vpn-08.

[16] Dong J, Hu Z. BGP-LS Extensions for Segment Routing based Enhanced VPN [EB/OL]. (2022-07-11)[2022-09-30]. draft-dong-idr-bgpls-sr-enhanced-vpn-08.

[17] Dong J, Li Z, Wang H. BGP SPF for Network Resource Partitions [EB/OL]. (2022-10-16)[2022-10-30]. draft-dong-lsvr-bgp-spf-nrp-01.

[18] Dong J, Hu Z, Pang R. BGP SR Policy Extensions for Network Resource Partition [EB/OL]. (2022-07-11)[2022-09-30]. draft-dong-idr-sr-policy-nrp-01.

[19] Dong J, Fang S, Xiong Q, et al. Path Computation Element Communication Protocol (PCEP) Extensions for Network Resource Partition (NRP) [EB/OL]. (2023-03-11)[2023-03-31]. draft-dong-pce-pcep-nrp-00.

[20] Dong J, Chen R, Wang S, et al. BGP Flowspec for IETF Network Slice Traffic Steering [EB/OL]. (2023-03-06)[2023-03-31]. draft-ietf-idr-flowspec-network-slice-ts-00.

[21] Dong J, Li Z. Considerations about Hierarchical IETF Network Slices [EB/OL]. (2022-09-07)[2022-09-30]. draft-dong-teas-hierarchical-ietf-network-slice-01.

[22] Li Z, Dong J, Pang R, et al. Realization of Composite IETF Network Slices [EB/OL]. (2023-03-13)[2023-03-31]. draft-li-teas-composite-network-slices-00.

[23] Li Z, Dong J. Encapsulation of End-to-End IETF Network Slice Information in IPv6 [EB/OL]. (2021-10-16)[2022-09-30]. draft-li-6man-e2e-ietf-network-slicing-00.

[24] Li Z, Dong J. Encapsulation of End-to-End IETF Network Slice Information in MPLS [EB/OL]. (2021-10-16)[2022-09-30]. draft-li-mpls-e2e-ietf-network-slicing-00.

[25] Li Z, Dong J. Segment Routing for End-to-End IETF Network Slicing [EB/OL]. (2022-10-24)[2022-10-30]. draft-li-spring-sr-e2e-ietf-network-slicing-05.

[26] Li Z, Peng S, Voyer D, et al. Application-aware Networking (APN) Framework [EB/OL]. (2020-09-30)[2022-10-30]. draft-li-apn-framework-06.

[27] Li Z, Hu Z, Dong J. Intent-based Routing [EB/OL]. (2022-04-28)[2022-09-30]. draft-li-teas-intent-based-routing-00.

[28] Wu B, Dhody D, Rokui R, et al. IETF Network Slice Service YANG Model [EB/OL]. (2022-11-07)[2022-11-30]. draft-ietf-teas-ietf-network-slice-nbi-yang-03.

[29] Wu B, Dhody D, Cheng Y. A YANG Data Model for Network Resource Partition (NRP) [EB/OL]. (2022-09-25)[2022-09-30]. draft-wd-teas-nrp-yang-02.

[30] Ma Y, Luo R, Chan A, et al. IETF Network Slice Deployment Status and Considerations [EB/OL]. (2022-07-11)[22-09-30]. draft-ma-teas-ietf-network-slice-deployment-01.

[31] Li Z, Peng S, Voyer D, et al. Application-aware Networking (APN) Framework [EB/OL]. (2022-10-09)[2022-10-30]. draft-li-apn-framework-03.

[32] Finn N, Thubert P. VARGA. Deterministic Networking Architecture [EB/OL]. (2019-10)[2022-09-30]. RFC 8655.

# Chapter 11

# Road of IPv6 Network Slicing

## 11.1 SEED SOWING

In 2013, SR and SDN began to gain wide attention in the industry. SR provoked a lot of debate in its early stages. In particular, many MPLS technical experts were very unhappy about SR's claim that it would completely replace LDP and RSVP-TE. I summarized five issues of SR in comparison with MPLS on the IETF mailing list (these issues were also described in *draft-li-spring-compare-sr-ldp-rsvpte*[1]). One of the issues was that the TE features supported by SR were incomplete. At that time, for example, SR did not support resource reservation for paths as RSVP-TE did. During my first visit to Huawei's US Research Center in California in 2013, I communicated with Richard Li about SDN innovation and was inspired by the idea of hierarchical controllers. This led me to think about combining them with bandwidth reservation-capable SR (which I called global MPLS labels at the time). In October 2013, I submitted the draft entitled "Framework of Network Virtualization Based on MPLS Global Label" (*draft-li-mpls-network-virtualization-framework*[2]) to the IETF. The draft contained two key ideas.

DOI: 10.1201/9781032699868-14

- Unlike RSVP-TE, SR was unable to reserve bandwidth in the data plane. SR segments, therefore, needed to be extended to represent not only nodes and links but also resources used to ensure SLAs.

- Carriers needed to provide customized networks for users. Besides the Virtual Private Network (VPN) services provided at the domain border, customized logical networks were required within a domain. In this case, carriers' networks and these customized logical networks needed to be hierarchically controlled by different controllers.

Back then, many people believed that SR provided highly scalable SR paths by flexibly combining segments such as node segments and link segments to meet specific customer requirements. However, they ignored the fact that SR facilitated the construction of virtual networks. In SR, a node segment is a virtual node, and a link segment is a virtual link. Combining them forms a virtual network (a set of virtual nodes and virtual links). In this sense, SR is also a technology well suited to providing virtual networks.

This draft was submitted many years ago, but at that time there were no customer requirements for bandwidth reservation-capable SR or virtual networks characterized by hierarchical control. As a result, the draft stalled until about 2017, when discussion on network slicing emerged in the IETF. Since then, the draft has found its way into public view.

## 11.2  INCUBATING

Huawei's success in the mobile transport field lays a solid foundation for 5G transport research, which we have been conducting since the emergence of 5G. The advantages of Huawei's End-to-End (E2E) network infrastructure products and solutions also facilitate this research. After in-depth insight analysis and research exploration, our 5G transport research settled on two key technologies: network slicing and deterministic latency.

In November 2016, we held the first side meeting on network slicing during the 97th IETF meeting period. Such meetings are informal and can only be held outside the period of formal meetings. The network slicing one was therefore scheduled to be held on a Tuesday night — the same night the IETF meeting's social event (usually a routine communication and dinner activity arranged by IETF organizers) was due to take place, but was cancelled. Although there were no other meetings or social events that night, we worried there would be a low turnout due to IETF partici-pants arranging private dinners or other social activities instead. Beyond our expectations, the side meeting attracted many participants, some of whom even said that it was more like a formal Birds of a Feather (BoF) — a formal meeting for the IETF to discuss the direction of new technologies and set up new working groups. It seems that learning new things is far more important than having a full stomach for IETF's "nerds" (IETF engi-neers' self-deprecating nickname).

The feedback we received from this side meeting showed that most participants were very interested in network slicing and that this was a topic the IETF needed to study. The participants also hoped that we could clarify the work to be done by the IETF for network slicing in technical fields. In response, we summarized the side meeting and divided the work into two parts: (1) network slicing O&M, and (2) technologies for realizing network slicing. Such division perfectly matches the current network slic-ing standards structure in the IETF.

This side meeting played a good role in popularizing concepts and warming up standards work as more and more IETF engineers began to learn about network slicing due to it. To follow up on this success, we held the second network slicing side meeting with partners at the 98th IETF meeting in March 2017. This meeting mainly focused on more detailed problem descriptions and application scenarios for network slicing. It sparked heated debates and attracted more than 120 participants (typi-cally, such side meetings attracted only 20–30 people at that time).

The success of the two consecutive side meetings gave us confidence in the prospect of network slicing and motivated us to prepare for the upcoming BoF meeting. Unlike a side meeting, a BoF meeting needs to clearly describe application scenarios, point out problems to be resolved, and provide feasible work plans and deliverables. To prepare for the BoF meeting, we did a lot of work with our industry partners. However, during the preparation, the focus of the participants began to diverge. Some peo-ple wanted to set up a new working group as soon as possible for greater innovations, while others wanted to realize network slicing by enhancing and extending the existing work of the IETF. In the network slicing BoF meeting during the 99th IETF meeting held in July 2017, to our surprise, the definition of network slicing triggered different opinions during the discussion of application scenarios. Many people still considered network slicing a concept of 3GPP and 5G, believing that the IETF did not need to provide a new definition for network slicing. Due to this opinion, the final conclusion of the BoF meeting was to extend existing technologies in the existing IETF working groups to support network slicing—the idea of setting up a network slicing working group in the IETF was not accepted.

From a technical perspective, it seemed that there were few new things to do for network slicing at that time. This was a time when MPLS was still dominant, RSVP-TE could provide resource reservation (isolation), and SR had not been widely recognized. Against the technical background and feedback at the side meetings and BoF meeting, we systematically organized the technical analysis and requirements related to network slicing and proposed the Enhanced VPN (VPN+) framework draft[3] in the IETF. VPN+, which is essentially network slicing, is a term we proposed based on the conclusion of the BoF meeting and the idea of enhancing the existing technologies in the IETF. Our intention was to use network slicing as an enhancement of VPN services, as VPNs provide service isolation only at the domain edge, whereas network slicing introduces intra-domain resource isolation. However, the name "VPN+" cannot show the direct relationship with network slicing and may mislead people to believe that the overlay VPN needs to be extended to support network slicing. In fact, most work related to network slicing technology extensions focuses on the underlay. However, because this VPN+ draft attracts a lot of attention, if we were to change the name after several updates, the version number in the draft name would start all over again from 00, making it difficult for readers to understand the structure and development history of the draft. Therefore, we have no choice but to carry on with the name VPN+.

## 11.3 SPROUTING

Research in 2017 and 2018 is critical for us. At the beginning of 2017, Wang Tao became president of Huawei Network Product Line and pointed out the shortcomings of IP innovation. In response, the Data Communication Product Line strengthened the operation of the IP Standards Strategy Committee (IPSSC) and set up innovation project teams for key standards, such as SRv6, 5G transport, and telemetry. Each project team consisted of key personnel from departments such as pre-research, standards, products/platforms, solutions, marketing, and sales, forming a joint task force for End-to-End (E2E) technological innovation. In terms of technology research, the "large-granularity" technology project mechanism was introduced to integrate research forces in different technical fields (including software, hardware, protocols, and algorithms) to set up large-granularity technology projects for technological innovation research. The Data Communication Product Line also developed the NetCity mechanism, carried out joint innovation with key customers, and built sustainable product and solution competitiveness through fast iteration. These mechanisms made our technological innovation work more organized, effective, and vital.

Network slicing is a key research direction of 5G transport. With the deepening of research and wider acceptance of SR in the industry, the combination of network slicing and SR entered our technology research scope, and the draft submitted in 2013 regained attention. Based on this, we conducted technology research on applying SR with guaranteed bandwidth to network slicing, carried out standards formulation, and developed a technical prototype based on the control plane of IS-IS Multi-Topology (MT). We also demonstrated the SR network slicing prototype and communicated with numerous customers, gradually deepening our understanding of what customers want in terms of network slicing.

Due to the streamlining of technology research and product/platform development, experienced experts in IP protocol development also took part in technology innovation. Driven by the IGP scalability issue brought by network slicing, Zhibo Hu first proposed the concept of separating network slices from topologies. Specifically, multiple network slices could share the same topology, meaning that the result of only one topology calculation could serve multiple slices, ultimately reducing the IGP load and improving IGP scalability for network slicing. This idea instantly wowed our research team and gained unanimous approval.

After SR-MPLS technology was relatively stable, the focus of SR technology innovation and standards formulation was shifted to SRv6. In March 2017, the SRv6 Network Programming draft was first released. Driven by commercial projects, we quickly devoted great effort to SRv6 technology research and development. While leading my team in SRv6 research and innovation, a question kept lingering in my mind: Since SR-MPLS already supported technologies such as VPN, TE, and FRR, was it worth realizing them again through SRv6, although SRv6 could simplify these functionalities? What was its value and significance?

During the technology research from 2017 to 2018, my thinking on this question went deeper and deeper thanks to the research work carried out by our teams in various emerging fields — including network slicing,

IOAM/IFIT, and BIER — as well as extensive technology exchanges with customers and technical experts in the industry. At the beginning of 2019, the answer finally came to me: We could use highly extensible IPv6 extension headers to easily support new network features (for example, IPv6 extension headers can be used to carry network slice ID information). In addition, we could use the native IPv6 attribute to conveniently simplify connection establishment and implement incremental network evolution. Those were difficult to implement through traditional IPv4 or MPLS. It was then that I realized the advent of a new network technology era. If it could be said that our previous research had been in the chaos of choosing MPLS or IPv6 in the data plane, everything had become clear since then — using IPv6 as the base shifted from a spontaneous selection to a conscious one. From then on, the focus of our research on network slicing technologies was shifted to IPv6 network slicing.

At the beginning of 2019, the VPN+ architecture draft was adopted as a working group draft by the IETF after being promoted for nearly 2 years. As the first working group draft related to network slicing in the IETF, it basically determines the technical architecture of IP network slicing.

## 11.4 GROWTH

Once we were clear about the direction in which network slicing technology was heading, we were overwhelmed by various relevant tasks that began to spring up. Looking back at this period, it was really a "barbaric growth" era.

At the beginning of 2019, planning and commercial delivery of IP network slicing officially kicked off. It was imperative to select an IP network slicing solution. How many slices did the customer network need to support? If the SR SID-based network slicing solution was adopted firstly to support a dozen network slices, but later the solution needs to be changed to the slice ID-based network slicing solution to support more network slices, would customers be willing to accept it? In the case that some customer networks had a mature MPLS deployment but a weak IPv6 foundation, how could these networks evolve smoothly to implement IPv6-based network slicing? Although the slice ID-based network slicing solution seemed like an attractive option, it required new IPv6 forwarding plane extensions and hardware upgrades for devices on the live network. In addition, interworking with devices from other vendors was involved. What if it was difficult to implement in a short time? With multiple options available, what was the right choice on the control plane protocol extension for slice ID-based network slicing? We were faced with numerous technical issues, but because many technical options were intertwined with customer requirements, it was very difficult to make decisions. Although most of my efforts were devoted to SRv6 work, I had to spare some time to deal with network slicing issues. At the beginning of April 2019, Rui Gu, Jie Dong, and I even had to hold a remote meeting with Zhibo Hu in the hotel corridor to discuss the solution selection despite the tight schedule at the MPLS World Congress in Paris. It wasn't until the end of April that we finally made the following decisions: (1) In the short term, the number of network slices required is limited, so the mature SR SID-based network slicing solution is used. And the SRv6 SID-based slicing solution is preferred, followed by the SR-MPLS slicing solution. (2) In the medium and long term, the slice ID-based network slicing solution is recommended. Flex-Algo can be used in the control plane. The IPv6 data plane is used in scenarios where many slices are required but the number of topologies is limited. (3) In the future, if many slices are required and many topologies exist, the MT can be introduced to support the slice ID-based network slicing solution.

Just as we were struggling to select technologies, one day I met Xinzong Zeng at breakfast and was shocked by his news: The commercial network slicing solution was to be delivered. He introduced the network slicing solution that uses affinity attributes. With this solution, SR Policies are exclusively used in slices, and the metric values of the links corresponding to slices are significantly increased so that all traffic forwarded through the shortest (BE) path is transmitted only in the default slice. With such a simplified solution to be delivered, I started to wonder if there was any point in us choosing how to extend Flex-Algo or MT to support network slicing. Before I got the answer, FlexE slicing was widely publicized in the market. The highlight of network slicing was emphasized to be the forwarding plane capability of FlexE-based resource hard isolation, but details about control and data plane functions were omitted. Later, we also learned of a solution that used the existing IGP multi-process to customize the topology to support two network slices: the 2B slice and the 2C slice. This solution was even simpler than the affinity attribute-based slice solution. With the commercial use of network slicing solutions, the situation became even more perplexing as concepts such as soft slicing, hard slicing, soft isolation, hard isolation, premium slice, express slice, exclusive slice, private line slice, private network slice, tenant slice, and industry slice emerged one after another.

The situation at the IETF was not much better. Network slicing, which was originally considered to be nothing but an enhancement of existing IETF technologies, gradually gained more and more popularity. Many vendors submitted drafts related to network slicing, and related terms sprung up like mushrooms. Although these terms were interrelated, they could not be unified, making it difficult to promote these drafts. Against this backdrop, the IETF TEAS working group sets up a network slicing design team to sort out network slicing-related work, define terms and frameworks, and strive to achieve convergence. This process was also very tortuous. The dispute over network slicing terms lasted for months until the new term "IETF network slicing" came into being, requiring compromises from all parties. Considering the fruitful work of VPN+, the design team held several discussions and decided to build its main output, "Framework for IETF Network Slices," based on the VPN+ architecture draft.

## 11.5 SYSTEM

With the expansion of the technological connotation related to network slicing and the continuous change of the technical solution, I came to the realization that the work on network slicing technologies was being done in a chaotic manner and might pose risks. At the start of 2020, I began leading the team to systematically organize network slicing technologies.

The systematic work of network slicing technologies began with laying out our standards work in the IETF. Standards must be well written to be an excellent carrier of technologies. In addition, a consensus should be reached both internally and industry-wide in terms of network slicing technologies. Standards are an important means for internal and external interaction and communication.

Due to the COVID-19 pandemic that broke out around the Spring Festival of 2020, I was isolated at home and remotely discussed with Jie Dong about the standards structure of the slice ID-based network slicing solution. We first agreed on the term Virtual Transport Network (VTN). Although we had been involved in promoting VPN+, we were unable to answer a basic question: What was the plus to VPN? Without an appropriate term, a series of protocol extension objects could also not be named. After determining the term VTN, Jie Dong and I took 5 days to complete and publish two basic drafts of the slice ID-based slicing solution. One of the drafts was about the VTN scalability framework, and the other was about data plane extensions for IPv6 carrying slice IDs. At that time, I felt anxious about the future, like many others, because of the COVID-19 pandemic. Thanks to the work we finished on network slicing, much of my anxiety caused by the COVID-19 pandemic was relieved, and the future of network slicing solutions became clearer to us.

Following the formulation of slice ID-based network slicing drafts, we improved the SR SID-based network slicing drafts and worked with China Telecom to launch four protocol extension drafts concerning IGP MT, IGP Flex-Algo, BGP-LS MT, and BGP-LS Flex-Algo. This work was to separate the protocol extensions for SR SID-based network slicing from those for slice ID-based network slicing and make these drafts' structure clearer. In addition, the standards draft of SR with guaranteed bandwidth was split into two drafts: the Resource-aware Segment draft and the SR for VPN+ draft. The two drafts were adopted by the IETF Source Packet Routing in Networking (SPRING) working group one after the other, making the standardization system of the SR SID-based network slicing solution more complete and mature.

In the first half of 2021, we held five technical meetings in succession to discuss network slicing technologies. The meetings covered alignment of basic concepts and terms, comparison and analysis of nine technical solution options for network slicing, hierarchical network slicing, inter-domain network slicing, mapping from service slices to resource slices, IP NSC's implementation, and the southbound and northbound interfaces of IP NSC. However, when various solutions were put on the table for discussion, the situation was more confusing than we thought due to the absence of many basic concepts, although network slicing had been deployed, and we were left scratching our heads during the discussions. After continuous research, special workshops, and brainstorming, we began to emerge from the fog with a greater sense of clarity. Based on the technical discussion, we launched four drafts related to inter-domain network slicing for the IETF 110 meeting in April 2021. Then we launched another two drafts for the IETF 111 meeting in July and a further four drafts — covering hierarchical slicing, intent-based routing, and network slicing deployment cases — for the IETF 112 meeting in November. In 2022, we have been formulating new network slicing drafts in the IETF. These drafts continuously improved the network slicing technology system, effectively consolidated the results of our technical discussions, and provided orderly guidance to the development of standards and industry.

During the systematic technology research and standards promotion, Zhibo Hu once told me, "We have taken network slicing too simply. Now I think it is a system, not a single feature at all." His words had a profound impact on me, and I realized that we had been considering network slicing merely as an enhancement and extension of SR without ever trying to decouple them. We still thought this way even after many unique technologies and protocol extensions emerged after slice IDs were introduced because the forwarding path establishment in the solution depended on SR. Thanks to the idea of establishing the "system," we continued our exploration more consciously in the following days. After discussing with experts of the campus network solution, we figured out that slice IDs could also be used together with VXLAN and GRE tunnels without the need to be coupled with SR. In addition, as the slice resource concept was generalized, slice resources were no longer limited to the bandwidth resources allocated to network slices and might refer to the resources used to ensure the delay, the resources used for security purposes, and the like.

The network architecture system consists of three important aspects: identification, forwarding, and control. However, for a long time in the past, IP network innovation focused only on the control aspect due to the lack of change in identification and forwarding. Network slicing introduced resource attributes, leading to a series of innovations regarding identification, forwarding, and control. These changes went beyond the original scope of network slicing and formed a more universal network architecture. Triggered by the network slicing work, I think that the IPv6 packets originated by Internet applications on the client or server side in the future may also carry such resource identifiers in the IPv6 extension headers. Furthermore, cross-multi-domain negotiation is required to guarantee resources in an E2E manner based on such resource identifiers. While there is still a long way to go, the extension of IPv6 to be able to carry resource IDs lays a solid foundation.

## 11.6 SUMMARY

The road to IP network slicing is a bittersweet process that can be simply attributed to a story of "resource identification." During this process, numerous colleagues participated in the research, development, and deployment of network slicing technologies and made significant contributions. This is a collective achievement. At Huawei, many colleagues involved in the network slicing work have changed their work or technical directions. Fortunately, colleagues such as Jie Dong and Zhibo Hu are still around me, devoted to this field, regardless of the ups and downs we experience. This ensures that our technology research and standards promotion on network slicing can continue unabated. We used to criticize ourselves for the lack of strategic patience, but I have since come to the realization from the network slicing work that, in order to achieve strategic patience, we must have an organization with strategic patience. The continuous dedication of the product line in the research and standards fields finally makes our network slicing solution polished and refined.

## REFERENCES

[1] Li Z. Comparison Between Segment Routing and LDP/RSVP-TE [EB/OL]. (2016-09-13)[2022-09-30]. draft-li-spring-compare-sr-ldp-rsvpte-01.
[2] Li Z, Li M. Framework of Network Virtualization Based on MPLS Global Label [EB/OL]. (2013-10-21)[2022-09-30]. draft-li-mpls-network-virtualization-framework-00.
[3] Dong J, Bryant S, Li Z, et al. A Framework for Enhanced Virtual Private Networks (VPN+) Services [EB/OL]. (2022-9-20)[2022-09-30] draft-ietf-teas-enhanced-vpn-11.

# Appendix

## Acronyms and Abbreviations

| Acronym and Abbreviation | Full Name |
| --- | --- |
| 3GPP | 3rd Generation Partnership Project |
| 5G | 5th Generation |
| AF | Assured Forwarding |
| AN | Access Network |
| APN6 | Application-aware IPv6 Networking |
| ARP | Allocation and Retention Priority |
| ASLA | Application-Specific Link Attribute |
| BBF | Broadband Forum |
| BE | Best-Effort |
| BGP-LS | Border Gateway Protocol-Link State |
| BGP-LU | BGP Labeled Unicast |
| BIERv6 | BIER IPv6 Encapsulation |
| CCSA | China Communications Standards Association |
| CIDR | Classless Inter-Domain Routing |
| CN | Core Network |
| CS | Class Selector |
| CSMF | Communication Service Management Function |
| CT | Core Network and Terminal |
| DA | Destination Address |
| DC | Data Center |
| DRR | Deficit Round Robin |
| DS | Differentiated Services |
| DSCP | Differentiated Services Code Point |
| EANTC | European Advanced Networking Test Center |

| ECMP | Equal-Cost Multiple Path |
|------|--------------------------|
| EF | Expedited Forwarding |
| eMBB | Enhanced Mobile Broadband |
| EPE | Egress Peer Engineering |
| ESI | Ethernet Segment Identifier |
| ETSI | European Telecommunications Standards Institute |
| FAD | Flex-Algo Definition |
| FRR | Fast Reroute |
| FL | Flow Label |
| FTP | File Transfer Protocol |
| GSMA | Global System for Mobile Communications Association |
| GTP-U | GPRS Tunneling Protocol for the User Plane |
| HIS | Hospital Information System |
| HQoS | Hierarchical Quality of Service |
| ICMPv6 | Internet Control Message Protocol version 6 |
| ID | Identifier |
| IEEE | Institute of Electrical and Electronics Engineers |
| IETF | Internet Engineering Task Force |
| IFIT | In-situ Flow Information Telemetry |
| IGP | Interior Gateway Protocol |
| IPE | IPv6 Enhanced Innovation |
| ISG | Industry Specification Group |
| IS-IS | Intermediate System to Intermediate System |
| ISP | Internet Service Provider |
| ITU | International Telecommunication Union |
| ITU-T | International Telecommunication Union-Telecommunication Standardization Sector |
| LDP | Label Distribution Protocol |
| LLA | Link-Local Address |
| LLDP | Link Layer Discovery Protocol |
| LP | Linear Programming |
| LSP | Link State PDU |
| MCF | Multi-Commodity Flow |
| MEC | Multi-Access Edge Computing |
| mMTC | Massive Machine-Type Communications |
| MP-BGP | Multiprotocol Border Gateway Protocol |
| MPLS | Multi-Protocol Label Switching |

| | |
|---|---|
| **MPLS TE** | Multi-Protocol Label Switching Traffic Engineering |
| **MRT** | Maximum Redundancy Tree |
| **MSDC** | Massively Scalable Data Center |
| **MSTP** | Multi-Service Transfer Platform |
| **MT** | Multi-Topology |
| **MT ID** | Multi-Topology ID |
| **NAT** | Network Address Translation |
| **NBI** | Northbound Interface |
| **NC** | Network Controller |
| **NLRI** | Network Layer Reachability Information |
| **NP** | Network Programming |
| **NRP** | Network Resource Partition |
| **NSC** | Network Slice Controller |
| **NSI** | Network Slice Instance |
| **NSMF** | Network Slice Management Function |
| **NSSI** | Network Slice Subnet Instance |
| **NSSMF** | Network Slice Subnet Management Function |
| **NTF** | Network Telemetry Framework |
| **O&M** | Operations and Maintenance |
| **OAM** | Operations, Administration and Maintenance |
| **OIF** | Optical Internetworking Forum |
| **OPEX** | Operating Expense |
| **OSPF** | Open Shortest Path First |
| **OSS** | Operation Support System |
| **PACS** | Picture Archiving and Communication System |
| **PCC** | Path Computation Client |
| **PCE** | Path Computation Element |
| **PCEP** | Path Computation Element Communication Protocol |
| **PCG** | Project Coordination Group |
| **PDN** | Packet Data Network |
| **PDU** | Protocol Data Unit |
| **PHB** | Per Hop Behaviors |
| **PHY** | Physical Layer |
| **PIR** | Peak Information Rate |
| **QoS** | Quality of Service |
| **RAN** | Radio Access Network |
| **RB** | Radio Bearer |
| **RPF** | Reverse Path Forwarding |

| | |
|---|---|
| **RSVP** | Resource Reservation Protocol |
| **RSVP-TE** | RSVP-Traffic Engineering |
| **SA** | Service and System Aspects |
| **SAFI** | Subsequent Address Family Identifier |
| **SD** | Slice Differentiator |
| **SDH** | Synchronous Digital Hierarchy |
| **SDN** | Software-Defined Networking |
| **SD-WAN** | Software-Defined Wide Area Network |
| **SFC** | Service Function Chaining |
| **SID** | Segment Identifier |
| **SLA** | Service-Level Agreement |
| **SLA** | Site-Local Address |
| **SLE** | Service Level Expectations |
| **SLO** | Service Level Objectives |
| **SNMP** | Simple Network Management Protocol |
| **S-NSSAI** | Single Network Slice Selection Assistance Information |
| **SP** | Strict Priority |
| **SPF** | Shortest Path First |
| **SR** | Segment Routing |
| **SR-MPLS** | Segment Routing-Multiprotocol Label Switching |
| **SR-MPLS TE** | Segment Routing-MPLS Traffic Engineering |
| **SRH** | Segment Routing Header |
| **SRLG** | Shared Risk Link Group |
| **SST** | Slice/Service Type |
| **TC** | Traffic Class |
| **TCO** | Total Cost of Operation |
| **TCP** | Transmission Control Protocol |
| **TDM** | Time Division Multiplexing |
| **TE** | Traffic Engineering |
| **TEDB** | Traffic Engineering Database |
| **TI-LFA** | Topology-Independent Loop-Free Alternate |
| **TLV** | Type Length Value |
| **TM** | Traffic Manager |
| **TN** | Transport Network |
| **ToS** | Type of Service |
| **TSG** | Technology Standards Group |
| **UCMP** | Unequal-Cost Multiple Path |

| | |
|---|---|
| **UDP** | User Datagram Protocol |
| **UE** | User Equipment |
| **UNI** | User-Network Interface |
| **UPF** | User Plane Function |
| **URLLC** | Ultra-Reliable Low-Latency Communication |
| **VLAN** | Virtual Local Area Network |
| **VPN** | Virtual Private Network |
| **VTN** | Virtual Transport Network |
| **VTN BSID** | Virtual Transport Network Binding Segment Identifier |
| **VTND** | VTN Definition |
| **WDRR** | Weighted Deficit Round Robin |
| **WFQ** | Weighted Fair Queuing |
| **WG** | Working Group |
| **WRED** | Weighted Random Early Detection |
| **WRR** | Weighted Round Robin |
| **ZSM** | Zero-touch Network & Service Management |

Printed in the United States
by Baker & Taylor Publisher Services